LIGHT ON A DARK HORSE

ROY CAMPBELL (1924)

LIGHT ON A DARK HORSE

An autobiography
(1901–1935)

by

ROY CAMPBELL

HENRY REGNERY COMPANY
CHICAGO · 1952

DEDICATED TO
My
Mother

TABLE OF CONTENTS

INTRODUCTION

THE last view I had of my native city of Durban, through an open port-hole of the Dutch hospital-ship *Oranje*, was what decided me, some day, to write some such book as this, as a grace or thanksgiving for the good times I have had, not only there, but in other parts of the world.

It was through an erroneous repatriation-order that I obtained this last panorama of my early home. That was in April 1944. I am, as a senior British N.C.O., a great believer in obeying orders unquestioningly and without expostulation, no matter how absurd they may be, simply because it saves time and ill-feeling; and here, for the first time in my experience, was an erroneous order which suited me right down to the ground. In spite of my Dominion nationality, as a South African, I was an Imperial British soldier, now permanently disabled, due for repatriation to England, where I had volunteered for military service on my return from Spain, and where I had left my wife and daughters. But when, in error, the order came for me to proceed to Durban, even had I not been in the habit of unquestioning obedience to orders, the prospect of eight thousand miles of luxury trip, with three or four weeks' leave in Durban sandwiched into the middle of it, with my mother, sister, and other relatives, would have been an overwhelming temptation to keep my mouth shut.

I had not been surprised when, on arrival in Durban, instead of being asked awkward questions, the Imperial Liaison Officer condoled with me for being sent the wrong way. That is typical of the decency and kindness of almost all British Officers; if they have any doubt, you get the benefit of it. As for getting away with anything, there was absolutely nothing to get away with. I had obeyed far more faulty orders to my own destruction and detriment; and could hardly be expected to hesitate when they redounded to my extreme convenience and pleasure. The number of British and colonial units to which I had been attached, including the R.W.F., the S.W.B., Intelligence Corps, the 12th East African Deception Unit, the King's African Rifles, and even Animal Transport, had apparently obscured my "medical nationality" (if I may coin such a phrase) in the eyes of the M.O.: and my broad South African accent had done the rest.

As a poor man, I have had to rely on World Wars and even on enemy action with consequent "survivor's leave" and other such windfalls to enable me to pay my family calls: though in this case it was a permanent disablement and complications of relapsing malaria which were my ticket for repatriation to the wrong country, where, on arrival, instead of being locked up, I had been granted my long delayed privilege leave.

I had already discarded my crutches and was able to get about with two sticks. Two of my brothers, whom I hadn't seen for eighteen years, were on leave from the South African Forces in Durban—one a Colonel in the South African Air Force, the other a Sergeant-Major in the Anti-Tanks. We drove about revisiting old scenes with my mother, sister and eldest brother, and recalling a thousand happy incidents which I had forgotten.

So it was that, after four weeks of sheer paradise, I lay looking out of the porthole, on a spotless white bunk in the *Oranje*, England-bound, returning to my wife and children. My sense of well-being was enhanced by the fact that I had often seen the same *Oranje* from the decks of troopships, from transit camps, from disembarkation ports, and lonely coast-watching stations, making her way in safety, like a fairy palace, with all her lights blazing, over the otherwise blacked-out seas. The last time I had seen her was from a coast-watching tower, where I was the only white man for very many miles around; this, however, hadn't worried me much, for my squad of Askaris, mostly Nyasas, were a fine lot from the K.A.R.'s. But there was something depressing, superstitiously so, about this camp where three of my white predecessors had died of malaria, and, the last one, whom I was relieving, had gone jungle-happy. Also, two Askaris had died of snake-bite and another had been knifed by the husband of a jungle-belle. My men, who were one thousand miles from their own tribe, were made to feel their unpopularity in the neighbourhood, not only with knives, but "Ju-Ju"; so they all really needed a bit of a change: and the camp had a melancholy atmosphere, though its beautiful surroundings were filled to overcrowding with all St. Francis' brigade of beasts, birds, trees and flowers, which can always keep me amused and happy. This brooding atmosphere heightened the glamour of the passing ship when seen from the jungle; and the memory of that rather sinister sojourn in no way detracted from it, now I was on board her.

As the *Oranje* began to sail out of Port Natal harbour, after re-fuelling on Salisbury Island, I saw the great town of Durban, which I had known when it was little more than a village, rising up so steeply, in tiers of skyscrapers, that nearly all the landmarks I had previously known were dwarfed or hidden by the new buildings. Yet everywhere I could see marks of what members of my family of ex-Irish bogtrotters have done to decorate, enliven, or deface the landscape; monuments of their energy, fantasy, or eccentricity, were visible in the shape of universities, colleges, hospitals, gardens, statues, and plantations.

Even their hallucinations and follies have always been on a grandiose scale, as when my cousin Ethelbert suddenly perceived his famous "iceberg" travelling, southward past his beach house, from the equator towards Durban at a terrific speed, and des-patched a native galloping post-haste to telegraph the news to the Durban Press, which unreflectingly blazed the news in headlines, so that thousands waited on the beach to welcome this unwonted arctic visitor. Then some scientific killjoy pointed out that ice-bergs don't usually travel so swiftly south from the equator dur-ing a tropical midsummer, in the teeth of a violent headwind. That iceberg is now a proverb—thirty years after. Someone suggested that he may have seen a four-masted barque in full sail, though none was reported in the vicinity: but for him it remains an ice-berg to this day. Nobody has ever found out what looked so much like an iceberg (in reverse gear) to my clever cousin.

As the ship turned round in the bay I could see the new Uni-versity College which my father founded, and, nearer the centre of the town, the vast Technical College, also his own creation, which grew from a night-school. Here, along with a few other volunteers, he used to teach youths unable to afford schooling, in his spare hours from his medical practise, in a dilapidated building, which he rented himself for the purpose. He had a fear of illiteracy, which I do not share, having met, among Spanish peasants who could not read, the most happy, cultured, brave, and dignified people on earth, far more intelligent than most profes-sors. Nevertheless these buildings are superb monuments to the pugnacity of a great and witty fighter in a single-handed battle against the money-grubbing, shop-keeping mentality of the successive Town Councils of Durban.

On the esplanade I could see the equestrian statue of Dick King, which was raised by my sister, Ethel, and executed by an Italian sculptor, to commemorate the hero of the immortal ride of six hundred miles in nine days through completely untraversed jungle, with a single horse, to seek relief for the British, besieged in the small fort-house at Durban, by the Boers in 1842. The photograph of this statue, which was erected after I first left Durban, was first shown me by that superb rider, in many ways the world's greatest horseman, my friend, Aimé Tschiffely, the hero of the ten thousand mile trek from Buenos Aires to Washington, through jungle, deserts, and cordilleras. Even more appropriately the postcard bearing the photograph had been sent to Tschiffely by that prince of writers and horsemen, the Scotch Hidalgo, R. B. Cunninghame Graham, who was then visiting his Natal relatives: and I was very proud to be able to tell Tschiffely that my sister was responsible for raising this fine piece of work—one of the few good statues in South Africa. My sister Ethel was known to the soldiers of World War I as the "Angel of Durban" and she performed much the same rôle in that War as her friend Perla Siedle-Gibson, known as the "Lady in White," did in World War II. Away up on the Berea, I could see my cousin Margaret's house which has the finest private library in Africa, containing all the rarest books pertaining to Africa, from Portuguese times onward, and eventually destined for the Nation.

Then, as we entered the channel to leave the port, the North Pier, that great breakwater, without which Durban's magnificent harbour would be an impossibility, began rushing past my porthole about forty yards away, recalling the thrills of fishing from it, for sharks, kingfish, barracuda, mussel-cracker, rock-cod, garrick and other big fish. This pier is also a piece of my family's handiwork. It was first built by my grandfather, William Campbell, in 1850, but, of course, on a much smaller scale, being for windjammers. With the help of natives, from the Bluff, on the opposite side of the channel, where you can still see the indent he made one hundred years ago with his blasting, he ferried the stone across on rafts. During rough weather the rafts so often capsized and spilled their cargoes to the bottom, that another embryo breakwater was formed along the bottom of the channel at right angles to the present one, stretching across the entry of what is now Durban Harbour. This was diagnosed as a solid "reef" by the first Administrator, or Premier, of Natal, Sir Harry Escombe, when planning the new harbour; and, waiving the advice of my grandfather and other *mere foremen*, he designed and had built, in England, at a cost of ten thousand pounds a monstrous apparatus, a cross between a super-dreadnought and a submarine bulldozer, to demolish the alleged "reef." This was eventually towed out to Durban at considerable extra expense to the newly-born community. Before the monster could arrive in Durban, the nature of the "reef" had been correctly diagnosed and dealt with, at the cost of a few shillingsworth of dynamite.

The mechanical leviathan was parked in the new harbour, where, for many years, it occupied far too much space and excited both the envenomed ridicule of the inhabitants, who had been bled white in taxes to pay for it, and the ribald hilarity of all seamen visiting the port. It became known as "Escombe's Folly"; and, finally, Sir Harry Escombe himself, unable to bear the reproach of it any longer, bought it for fifty pounds, from the Government, had it towed out to sea with explosive charges on board, and, when these failed to sink it, had it shelled by the guns from the fortifications on the Bluff, till the detested "white sea-elephant" finally sank forever into the Indian Ocean.

In spite of the nuisance occasioned by the accidental ghost-breakwater, or "reef," one of the leading harbour engineers once told me that my grandfather's workmanship was of such a high quality that the handcut stone of his first breakwater still serves, after a century, though invisibly enveloped in concrete today, as the basis and foundation of the present North Pier. Another was attempted by truly official engineers but you can still see the ruins of it. They were bureaucrats who did not love the great rollers or understand them.

Beyond the Breakwater, stretching away up the coast, I could see the miles and miles of sugar-cane plantations. This cane was also introduced by my grandfather—after building the breakwater and the first railway in Africa, one mile long, from this Breakwater round the curve of Durban Bay to Congella. When one can pick up just with a cursory glance so many signs of energy and industry it is enough to make a Prodigal interested in his family.

Now that we were out into the open sea, I began feeling once more that voluptuous swell of the long rollers: I could see a belated mollymauk (or was it an albatross?) flying on its side with its wings vertical, before it went out to sea for its siesta. All the lights of Durban and the Berea had begun to twinkle. There was no wartime black-out there. I could see the new "Marine Parade," receding like a more flashy super-Brighton, lined with glittering skyscrapers and luxury hotels. I can remember playing there when it was the old "Black Beach," a mass of dunes covered with pathla scrub and Hottentot-figs or mesembryanthemums, with only one tin shanty of a so-called "Hotel" made of wood and iron. I must confess I liked it better like that. Against the afterglow, as the lights receded, I saw the towering, double Table-Mountain of Inanda, and that of Maritzburg beyond, with the distant outline of peaks and bluffs far inland, which I had seen so many times from the decks of whalers and merchant ships; and over whose tops I had galloped with so many lovely amazons, on so many wonderful rides. The whole background of the adventures of my boyhood and youth suddenly came to life: and along the darkening shoreline I could still make out two white gaps in the darkness of the bush, made by the dunes at the mouths of the Umgeni and Umthlanga rivers.

At the north corner of the Umthlanga lagoon, just where my brother George's huts are in his forest sanctuary, a driftwood fire was burning on the beach, exactly where we had lit one the week before. Ten to one, it seemed that my brother, still on leave, was fishing there, had seen the *Oranje*, and had lit that fire in case I might be looking out, to say: "So long!"

Except for the fire on the beach, and one or two smaller lights, the whole shore had soon vanished in darkness.

I had been almost the only passenger, on the way down from Suez to Durban, on the *Monarch of Bermuda*, and even now, on the way back, there were hardly any more patients till we reached Tewfik, when they cleared us again for the more recently disabled cases from Sicily. This fact helped to neutralise any conscience-qualms I felt about my buckshee trip to Durban and back to the Suez Canal.

In the Sergeants' Mess, at the Convalescent Camp near Suez, they had laid odds against my "getting away" with it, so I surprised them all by being on the very ship that, eight weeks later, picked them up for repatriation on the return voyage. I collected my bets personally from my messmates, and we spent them on landing in England.

The leave to Durban and the other of my leaves which involved a transcontinental trip over almost the whole of Africa came to be spoken about as the exploits of a picaroon "getting away with murder," in the Sergeants' Messes from Edinburgh Castle to Knightsbridge, and even the Red-Caps' Mess at Kensington, where I have heard it recounted as the sort of thing a really clever "old soldier" can get away with in the army. It was even recounted to me as an exploit of one of my countrymen, by Regimental Sergeant Major Charles Mulvey of Princess Pat's Canadian Light Infantry, who heard it while he was a guest at the Guards' Sergeants' Mess in Whitehall. He was surprised when he learnt it was I, as he knew me well.

Nothing could be further from the truth than to think of this trip as risky or foolhardy. I would never gamble my hard-earned stripes for anything but the crown of promotion to C.S.M. It was a matter of obeying orders, presence of mind, accurate timing and placing, and knowing when and how to take one's opportunities.

I was discharged from the Army with "excellent" military conduct, and, even as a private, had never been on a charge. Also, as a Sergeant, or acting C.S.M., I never put a fellow soldier on a charge, since I got better results by taking off my stripes and offering to fight the culprit. I lost only one fight out of eight, but it was a good one: and it earned me one more life-long friend, Corporal Preece of the S.W.B. It is the best way of obviating ill-feeling, especially if you are giving away twenty years or so.

On reaching England, after such an interesting leave, I found that the recent renewal of old associations had given me a far more vivid feeling of the past than I ever experienced before; and that the impressions did not flash forth and vanish, as they used to when I lived an active life, but remained in a clear and steady glow of the memory. I think my memory was unconsciously reinforced by the knowledge that I am a cripple for life, have long ago passed middle age, and can never return to sailoring, soldiering, or to the gay horse-breaking racket of a life I led for so long in Spain. I have more exciting things to look back on than to look forward to, except in the one sphere of writing poetry—though this year, 1951, Domingo Ortega, the greatest matador in the world, has invited me to act as his picador in September and October. Although I cannot walk properly, I can still ride with my left stirrup shortened three inches. So it is still strictly *sedentary* work. It is partly out of gratitude for having been allowed to last so long, for I was by at least fifteen years the oldest Sergeant in an A.I. fighting Unit (the Twelfth East African Deception Unit) from which I was disabled, that I wish to record my previous adventures. I want to record, too, the happy times I have known; the beautiful countries in which I have worked, fought, and revelled: the fine ships I have sailed in; and the good comrades I have met on whalers and fishing boats, in the equestrian nation of cattlemen and toreros, and in the ranks of the Spanish and British Armies. I have served as a pedestrian and an infantryman, with Requetés, Welshmen, Cockneys and African Askaris; some of these were so primitive in appearance that they seemed to have been shaken off their trees, like fruits, by their chiefs, at the request of the recruiting authorities. Some filed their teeth to resemble those of sharks or tigers; and they stretched the lobes of their ears in loops like rifle-slings, so as to carry cigarette-tins and other ornaments: with the result that we had to wind the dangling lobes around the upper cartilages when they came on parade, lest, when sloping arms, they might push their rifles through their own ears! How I loved them all! There is nothing like life on active service for making men affectionate and loyal.

Ever since that first night out at sea and my last view of Durban, my memories have become clearer and clearer until I have at last been literally forced to write them out in this book so as to repay my debt both to Almighty God and to my parents, for letting me loose in such a world, to plunder its miraculous literatures, and languages, and wines: to savour its sights, forms, colours, perfumes, and sounds: to see so many superb cities, oceans, lakes, forests, rivers, sierras, pampas, and plains, with their beasts, birds, trees, crops, and flowers—and above all their men and women, who are by far the most interesting of all.

LIGHT ON A DARK HORSE

I

FOREBEARS

Y MOTHER's name was Dunnachie: she came of a family of
Highland Jacobites who left Scotland after 1745 but returned on the amnesty. My maternal grandmother was a
Gascon from Bayonne and though I never saw her, I inherit
through her my love of bulls, and of Provençal, French, and Spanish poetry. What little I have been able to rake up about my father's
family shows that he was descended from many generations of bog-
trotting Scotch-Irish peasants who were tenants of the Kilpatricks,
the squires of Carndonagh in North Donegal. They had, according
to family tradition, originally fled to Ireland from Scotland after
the defeat of the Earl of Argyll by Montrose: but for generations
they seemed to lie very low till one of them, a "crowder" or professional fiddler, in 1750 or so, was lucky enough to catch the eye
of one of the Kilpatrick girls, daughter of his landlord, while he
was fiddling at a ball given by the Squire. This was discovered by
her father who locked her in an upstairs room, but she escaped by
throwing out her mattress, and those of her sisters, and jumping
down on to them. There was a runaway marriage: but the squire
eventually forgave his favourite daughter, leaving her and her husband an equal share of his property with her sisters, though he had
pretended to disown the couple.

The ex-fiddler, who eventually became a magistrate, and a Colonel of the Volunteers, married a second time, a Miss Macaulay from Derry, and divided his property into four with his sons. So my great-great-grandfather inherited the farm of Strathsbridge, Parish of Donagh, two miles from Carndonagh. According to that valiant and fine writer, my friend, the late George Orwell, who had traced it out, I have the great honour to be related to his first wife, who was a Miss O'Shaughnessy from those parts—the heroic lady who saved his life during the massacres of International Brigadiers by their fellow-Reds in Catalunya: so apparently our family tradition relating to those parts of Ireland is quite valid.

By this marriage with the Kilpatricks my Campbell ancestors, after generations as labourers and N.C.O.'s, seemed to have temporarily risen in the world. One of them went to Scotland where, at the age of fourteen, he got a job making the first railway-line in Scotland, and after fifteen years hard work, became the manager of the Glasgow-Paisley railway at the age of twenty-nine. Seeing glowing accounts of Australia, New Zealand, and Natal, and being unable to rise higher in the ranks of railway supervision, he decided on going to Natal early in the last century. Having set sail on the *Conquering Hero* (Captain Cockburn), he arrived with his family after what was then a very short voyage of three months. A character named Byrne, the originator of the bogus emigration scheme on which he went, had banked the money of the one hundred and twenty-seven settlers who took part in it, "for safety in case of shipwreck." He told them plausibly that they would receive it back from his agent in Port Natal (now Durban)—but that was the last they saw of their money. He had no agent there at all.

So William Campbell arrived penniless in Natal, except for one hundred gold sovereigns which his wife had sewn into her skirt. In this he was luckier than some and he seems to have appreciated the fact. Except for the name, "Natal," given it by Vasco da Gama in 1498, and confirmed by the poet Luiz de Camões, hardly anything existed of a Colony except a trading settlement in the middle of thick bush populated by elephants, lions, and mambas.

There is a comic story called *Donogoo-Tonka* (by Jules Romains, I think). It describes how thousands of dupes are inveigled into a bogus emigration-scheme by fabulous descriptions of a non-existent city in the wilds of Brazil. They invest their money (which is promptly stolen) and set out for the position in which this fabulously rich city is supposed to be situated. They are expected by the floaters of the scheme to perish to a man, of hunger, blackwater, malaria, and yellow fever. On arriving, they find nothing there but jungle: but these very dupes and stooges are forced to create, drain, and build this El Dorado of their dreams on the spot by sheer hard work—or perish! The humorous tale of Donogoo-Tonka was told as a sheer fable by its author. But it is not in any way far-fetched. Durban was created in the same way as Donogoo-Tonka. How many more such towns may have been similarly created! The old émigré does not seem to have wasted any time in crying over his fate. When it was known that Byrne had absconded, he wrote in tolerable doggerel, a very convincing description of Byrne's methods of advertising his schemes about Natal.

"One day," said old Byrne, "when I'd journeyed out there,
I was taking a jaunt and enjoying the air:
My stick, as I wandered, got stuck in a sluit
And I found it next morning all covered with fruit:
Then I planted a tin-tack an inch in the ground
And it grew to a handspike, as next day I found:
Last letter I got from my friend Mr. Jones
Says, 'I'm using your handspike for quarrying stones'."
    etc., etc.

Like most of his descendants, especially my father, he was an extremely cheerful man, and that was owing to sheer hard work, which always keeps body and soul together on extremely pleasant terms. He wrote most of his letters in verse of this kind: they are all on the same easy-going level. Nearly all the notes which he wrote to his wife from the small sugar-mill he eventually started, were written in verse: so I must have inherited the malady from him as did my father, sister, and my two eldest brothers—unless the fiddler used to extemporise verses to his tunes, and was the prototype of us all.

Yet though it was the hard work and cheerfulness of such early settlers as those who came out on the *Conquering Hero* that made Durban into a great port, it cannot be denied that it was the old Byrne who was its catalytic *founder*. Without him, Port Elizabeth or East London, being nearer to civilisation, might have got

the start of Durban. Those one hundred and twenty-seven settlers
were all really tough workers.

Byrne continued to float emigration schemes to other parts of
the world. He had a habit of "dying" whenever he was badly
wanted by the police—after he had given up going bankrupt. But
after "dying," and producing bogus death-certificates even, he
would always crop up again under some new name, on the same
old racket. His victims, in exile in other parts of the earth, robbed
of the money to return and expose him, finally put a check on him
by writing to *The Times*, the *Morning Post*, and other papers, in
which they recognized the high-flown style of his advertisements
—and so succeeded in warning prospective emigrants. Things got
a bit too hot for Byrne. In the end he emigrated himself as he had
caused so many others to do; then he died, once too often; the last
authentic news reported of him came officially through J. B. Were,
the Chilean Consul in Australia, to say he had been killed at last
after successfully kidnapping two shiploads of South Sea Islanders
as slaves to the Coast of Callao.

Meanwhile Durban continued to grow. Here is a description of
it written by my grandfather much later on, in 1850, to a friend
in Scotland.

"First then I would have you know that Durban is a town of
shopkeepers. They flourished two years ago, but since then their
sun has been gradually setting, and some, myself included, now
call them the worst of the colony, too idle to dig, too proud to
beg—yet they must be fed. Well, a band of these conceived the
happy idea of petitioning the Home Government to let us have
out a few thousand convicts. They left no stone unturned for the
accomplishing of their object."

My grandfather, in opposing this scheme, caused such uproar
at the meeting of settlers to decide on the Question of the Convicts, that they were never mentioned again. This is how the local
newspaper reported it.

Wm. Campbell. "I read in a newspaper that in S. Australia
wages have been reduced by half since Convicts were introduced."
(Cries of "Lies. It's not true. Where's the paper?")

"Here it is." (Sensation. Roars of laughter.) "They tell us that there's a scarcity of labourers, but the *Sarah Bell*, now in port full of emigrants for the Australian diggings, gives the lie to that random assertion. The substance of the matter is that convict advocates want labour for nothing." (A voice, "Oh. But are we to go bankrupt?") "The working-man of Natal to go bankrupt!!" (Laughter) "Why, on my way home tonight I met two constables on the beach looking for bankrupts who were trying to escape on the *Sarah Bell*. I asked who they were and the answer was 'Shopkeepers of course'." (Voices, "Let's hear your remedy.") *"Go and work, sirs."* (Laughter and uproar) . . . etc. The hall was completely wrecked and the meeting did not continue.

There appears to have been no *work* my grandfather was afraid of, for besides building breakwaters accidentally or on purpose, as recounted in the Introduction, he was the foreman in charge of the building of the first railway in South Africa—it measured a mile and ran round one side of Durban Bay. He engaged in controversies with the famous Bishop Colenso, in the *Natal Mercury*—the latter, though a saintly man was deficient in wit and humour and his vast erudition, which daunted even Matthew Arnold, was no match for such light-hearted skirmishes. People today have forgotten the Colenso Controversy which nearly split the English Church in two from top to bottom. The Bishop and my grandfather became friendly later on; and my uncle, Sir Marshall Campbell, who was a boy at the time, recounted to me how he had waked at dawn to hear my grandfather and the Bishop still arguing about native polygamy as freshly as when he had left them to go to bed at nine p.m. the night before. Grandfather was against polygamy;[1] Colenso was for it. They seem to have been drawn together by that bond of sympathy for the natives which has distinguished the Colenso family and ours, though always in contradiction to each other, from most of the rest of our South African white compatriots: a sympathy which I can only ascribe to a very deeply ingrained Christianity which was as needful then as it is today, only then it was much commoner.

---

[1] So are many of the natives. "You are lucky," said Mungeni, a native boy, to me, "only to have one wife. When I go home, if I eat anything one wife prepares for me, I have to eat what all the others have prepared—it gives me indigestion all the time. And as for other functions—why that's even harder on a fellow."

I quote from my grandfather's letter and the extract from the *Natal Mercury* because it underlines the hereditary feud which always seems to have existed between our family and the shopkeepers of Durban. It continued in my father's life-long struggle for education for poor whites and natives, and is carried on by my brother Colonel George Campbell of the S.A.A.F., who holds my father's place as Chairman of the Technical College and the Howard University College. It was continued too in my stormy attempt to edit the review *Voorslaag* in Durban in 1926. My grandfather referred to himself as a "working man," which he was in the full sense of the word: and so are my father, my brothers, and myself. That is why, though I have twice been affiliated to a trade union, I could never be a "labourite"; the labourite is more preoccupied with loafing and striking than working.

My grandfather reared a family of nine through the direst poverty and hardship and they nearly all became prominent in the life of the colony, or abroad. The eldest son, William, relieved Shepstone as the Chief Magistrate on the Zulu border, when the latter came over with King Cetewayo after the Zulu War, to visit Queen Victoria. This uncle, who was highly esteemed by whites and natives alike, was placed in charge of the Zulu border. He was a most convivial gentleman, and he was thrown and killed, like Tam O'Shanter, on one of his wild gallops home on a dark night. The most beautiful of my aunts, Agnes, a saintly and radiant girl whose diaries reveal great intelligence, died at the age of seventeen. My Aunt Jessie took up Agnes's missionary vocation; had visions; and believed that she communicated with the Almighty. For want of Catholic instruction, she could not tell mystical experience from hallucination. She was a fascinating character, beloved by everybody, extremely plain, and always laughing. She was known to have smuggled whisky and brandy to dipsomaniacs in prison, and to have performed other quixotic actions, which put everybody in a good temper with her, and excused her obsessions, which included bursting into song at the most inopportune moments with *Onward Christian Soldiers* and *Fight the Good Fight*, etc. She refused to wear glasses for years because the Lord told her she would get her eyesight back by the exercise of Faith. Finally however the Lord told her she could have a pair of spectacles—and so everything was all right. I think, in spite of an obvious limitation, this lady had a real greatness about her. The natives adored her and so did all the jail-birds, invalids, and unfortunates who were brought in contact with her, and for whose sake she chiefly lived.

Few people enjoyed *living* so much as Aunt Jessie did, though her life was a truly tough one! I never heard her reproach any one, and although she never drank, she had a convivial expression, a wonderful smile, and a drooping eyelid in her old age, which made her look as if she was half-seas-over, which she was, but with love for everybody—half-seas-over to that Happy Land about which she was so fond of bursting into song.

My father's old Zulu nurse, Hannah Mgadi (the grandmother of my nurse, Catherine), was brought up with Aunt Jessie in my grandfather's family, and was a perfect replica in ebony. She died only the other day at the age of about a hundred and ten.

Aunt Jessie had a husband for whom my other uncles and my father were generally looking with shotguns. He used to turn up when he wanted money, disappear for years again and then suddenly turn up and escape again. Aunt Jessie adored him. One day he disappeared for good, but till her dying day, many years after, Aunt Jessie always felt sure he'd turn up once more.

The next brother was my uncle[1] Sir Marshall Campbell. It must be twenty-five years since he died, but so great is his fame still amongst the natives that when, on my way out in a convoy during the recent war, I spoke to one of the native porters, who came aboard the troopship, in Zulu, and when, unable to conceal his surprise, he asked me: "How did you, an English soldier, learn my language?" and I said: "Am I not the nephew of Machu and the son of Sam-Joj?"—he replied: "Like Hell you are—the nephew of Machu would be a colonel; so would the son of Sam-Joj[2]—not a sergeant, like you." This uncle was the only one of all my father's family to become rich though he was twice ruined; once through signing a promissory note for a friend so that he had to sell his whole farm, Aberfoyle, before his crops were ripe; and even his best riding-horse. He then became a manager of a sugar mill and estate at Umzinto, which he worked up into a big concern—and then the Scottish Bank failed in which all the money was invested.

[1] This was Senator Sir Marshall Campbell, whom the *Encyclopaedia Britannica*, in its reference to me, wrongly asserts is my father.

[2] Machu—Marshall. Sam-Joj—Samuel George.

Uncle Marshall married one of the most beautiful and aristocratic girls amongst the settlers—Ellen Blamey—a cousin of the O.C. of the Australian troops, Field-Marshal Sir Thomas Blamey.

This uncle owned a large house, called Mount Edgecombe, about fifteen miles out of Durban, and there we spent most of our Christmases. The dining-room contained about two hundred and fifty heads of different stuffed animals nailed by the scruff to wooden shields—including a two-nosed, four-eyed and four-eared calf which was born on the same day as I was, and according to the natives, augured that I should be a very great man—or a terrible criminal. They were very disappointed to see that, at the age of forty-four, I was only an acting-Sergeant-Major and had neither been hanged nor knighted! This great dining-room, which may have been a bit of an eyesore to some people, was for me a sort of Fairyland, especially when the Indian servants festooned it secretly on Christmas Eve as a surprise, with chains of flowers, pineapples, silver paper, and ribbons, criss-crossing each other from the horns of stuffed koodoos, on one side of the room, to the tusks of elephants on the other side and back to the horns of elands, and sables, and roans, all of whom peered (together with yawning lions and leopards) with glassy eyes, from festoons of flame-tree, flamboyant, bougainvillaea, golden shower, and syringa—as if to say: "What on earth have we got to do with all this?"

One Christmas dinner, when Dish and Corunna (the two waiters of whom I was very fond) had excelled themselves in flowery decorations, and were waiting at table, I cried out: "Dish's hand is shaking; he must have fever." Then, when Corunna served me with something, I noticed his hand was shaking even worse, and commented on it. Two mounted policemen were sitting as unexpected guests at the table. But it was natural that any passer-by on the main road should be asked to the Christmas feast.

After the dinner I saw Dish and Corunna, handcuffed to each other, being walked off to Verulam jail between the troopers: and two Zulu police with spears bringing up the rear. I ran after them in tears, crying to the troopers and begging the native police to let them go. The troopers had turned up in the middle of the Christmas dinner to arrest them for the murder of the cook who had disappeared the day before. The waiters had asked to be allowed to serve their last meal so as not to upset the family; the troopers had as kindly agreed. Of the family only my uncle knew the drama that was going on. Everybody thoroughly enjoyed the meal except those five who *knew*. The cook had been found that morning, with his throat cut, in the sugar-cane. He had disappeared the night before after excelling himself in his art for the next day. Dish and Corunna were hanged in the Verulam jail. This event cast a shadow over my childhood for some time—as I was fond of the cook, too.

My friend, Major Lewis Hastings, in *Dragons are Extra* (Penguin Series), has written exquisitely about Herr and Frau Pagel, of Pagel's Circus. They used to visit Mount Edgecombe regularly with their circus, and we loved them. Herr Pagel was the "Strongest Man in the World" who could pick up two elephants *and* his wife (that is to say three of them) on his back and walk around balancing them on an enormous sort of tray. His wife, a great character, was a Yorkshire woman, beautiful and intelligent in spite of her great size and strength. She must have been, when young, like Baudelaire's Giantess. When she was in the box office one had to take care of missiles in the form of live human bodies—drunks and other undesirables, whom she projected horizontally to a great distance without apparently breaking any bones. She was the "Strongest Woman in the World"—and stronger even than her husband!

The Herr was one of those meek German Giants who are never so happy as when carving miniature cuckoo clocks, or playing a flute. They combine the biceps of Hercules with the pale blue eyes (like forget-me-nots stewed in Nestle's sweetened milk) of a baby. Once the Herr got a little bit tipsy with my cousin, with whom he was arranging for a site for his tents. Although so strong he was affected by a couple of glasses. We offered him a lift home, but instead of being driven up to the front of the circus, he asked to be driven round the back, so that he could sneak into the lions' cage and sleep it off, because he was scared of Frau Pagel giving him a hiding.

"But if your wife is stronger than you and can give you a hiding, then she won't care a tuppenny damn about the lions, any more than you do," expostulated my cousin.

"Oh yes," Herr Pagel reassured us. "You see odder laties midd mice? They yump on a chair unt scream. Same like mein Frau midd lionces!"

The Pagels let me practise standing on their horses round the ring with a safety rope and I loved them both very much. They had a couple of big elephants which they used to take in a procession round Verulam to advertise their show. On opposite sides of the main street lived two retired functionaries who were deadly rivals in the annual flower shows at Durban. Sometimes one got the prize, sometimes the other. Their carnations were jointly the pride of Victoria County. They lived at daggers-drawn—or rather spades-drawn; for each spent the day with his spade in his hand gazing through his window and waiting for passing horses or mules to drop manure for their flowers. "A" had sharper eyesight but "B" was a better sprinter because "A" was huge and fat. It worked out pretty even till one of Pagel's elephants, exactly between their houses, dropped the answer to every gardener's dream. Even "B" used to watch for "A" to move before he swooped, since he couldn't see small bits of manure, but only beat "A" to it after he had accidentally indicated the position. But, on this occasion, he saw it at the same time because the piece of manure was bigger and fatter than even "A" himself, and nearer. So he beat "A" to it. There was a heraldic battle with spades over the mountain of manure—like the lion and the unicorn fighting for, but scattering, "the crown" all over the place. Like the Heralds separating Hector and Ajax, the kindly Pagels intervened, as the spades clanged together in mid-air; and it was typical of the Pagels' real humanity and goodness that, in order to restore peace, they saved up the next two instalments of manure and sent one each, in a donkey cart, to the quarrelsome gardeners. But the feud which blazed out over the elephant's manure ended in another spade-fight and a dreary lawsuit which impoverished "A," and ruined "B."

Talking about circuses reminds me of the time when my cousin Ethelbert bought the Durban Zoo, which had been condemned by the Town Council as an Economy Measure during World War I. He bought it lock, stock, and barrel, and the money went to the War Fund. If you go past Mount Edgecombe to this day you will probably see that half the donkeys have been crossed with zebras, and the cattle with anything from bison to wildebeest.

This cousin Ethelbert, the great hunter, who had the honour of showing the Princesses round the game reserves, and is the owner of a farm which beats any of the game reserves for interest and excitement, is nevertheless something of a Tartarin and a Quixote. When the Zulu Rebellion broke out, he was A.D.C. to the Governor of Natal. He had a sword, with all sorts of damascene twiddles and whirligigs on the blade, which apparently he had never had a good look at—for it was an ornamental, parade-ground sword, with a sharp enough point, but the edges were perfectly rounded, smooth, and blunt so that you couldn't cut a pat of margarine with it even if it were red hot. Nevertheless when he heard the news of war he wired home: "Have my sword sharpened on both sides!"

His début as a modern Noah, with a train for his Ark, was repeated more than once. When he bought the Zoo in Durban one of the pythons got loose and turned up in the Durban Library. Anyway it would have been coals to Newcastle to take it to Mount Edgecombe. No sooner had he got the bisons, buffaloes, nilgaus, tigers, etc., aboard a goods train, when the guard, heaving a sigh of relief, waved his green flag to the driver, and settled down eagerly in his van to read the news in the *Natal Advertiser*. He had breathlessly devoured "Temperance Notes" and was just turning to the even more thrilling "Wesleyan Items," when he looked up to see a bloody camel's head flying through the air at him, and fell back off his seat just in time to avoid being pulverised by it, though he and the *Advertiser* were spattered all over with blood, and I believe Ethelbert had to pay for a new uniform, with a gold braid cap and a red stripe down one leg of the pants. The camel who had popped up his head to admire the scenery had been guillotined by the tunnel, and his head thrown violently into the guard's van fifty yards behind.

When the animals were being detrained into cages at Mount Edgecombe the bull nilgau ran amok, treed the Scotch station-master and the native porters with all the spectators and assistants, and proceeded to release his fellow-prisoners by charging their cages, head-down, and smashing them to match-wood. The Indian clerk, besieged in the telegraph office, rapped off an S.O.S. In view of the immortality of the classical telegram sent off by the Indian station-master at Voi (Tanganyika) when the lion was trying to tear off the corrugated iron roof of the station to devour him, it is a pity that the text of this S.O.S. has been lost. The Voi station-master wired: "Lion fighting with Station. Please send suckers (succours) immediate." The "suckers" in this case arrived when most of the animals had taken to the bush and the sugar cane. They consisted of a mounted troop of the local militia with a Maxim-gun and a Pom-pom.

Meanwhile Mr. "X" of Blackburn, a village near by, who had been indulging in raw spirits, and was on his way to the station, was seen driving an extremely sheepish looking tiger before him with stones and telling it he didn't believe in its existence. It entered its cage again and went to sleep.

"Blackstockings," one of my girl friends, riding alone on her way home from school across Cornubia flat, was cornered between two water-buffaloes and the ferocious old nilgau, their compatriot, who became their comrade during the three weeks they terrorised the neighbourhood. She was forced to take advantage of a wattle branch on to which she leaped from the saddle while her horse galloped off pursued by the two water-buffaloes. This nilgau was so old that he had no hair except a couple of white bristles, and his horns were worn down to mere stumps—but he was extremely bad-tempered. I think he was shot by the police after devouring the wares, basket and all, of an Indian vegetable-pedlar.

I had some fun with the buffaloes out on Cornubia Flat, on one of my cousin Colin's polo ponies, getting them to chase me and swerving round and between them till I was reported by Mr. Paul, one of the Estate managers, and had to stop. The Society of Tauromachy of Laurenço Marques who have just elected me an honorary member on the occasion of the visit of Jao Nuncio, this year, have just introduced African buffaloes into the bull-ring. But I am probably safe in claiming that I was the first man to torry a buffalo on horseback on African soil.

The camel's mate was the only one of the Zoo beasts who made good; she was harnessed and used for scarifying cane-fields but she frightened many people, including our French Master, Mr. Snow, who was absentmindedly riding his motor-bike in from Verulam, and rounded the corner to meet this strange apparition. All the other beasts of the menagerie were either destroyed or recaptured by the end of a few weeks and quiet fell once more on Mount Edgecombe.

Still, this was by no means the only time cousin Ethelbert carted animals about in trains or lorries. He is for ever catching animals

in the wilds and bringing them home or presenting them to Zoos.
It runs in the family. Inhabitants of Dulwich, and those who went
to school at Dulwich College before World War I, will no doubt
remember seeing a boy riding to school there every day on a zebra.
That was my cousin Claud MacLaren from Lake Ngami, Aunt
Jessie's grandson.

There were two other aunts—Aunt Lily and Aunt Marie. The
former married Colonel Royston, after whom I was named. He
was in command of the Natal Volunteers, at the outbreak of the
Boer War, when they were outnumbered by about three to one,
by the Boers. These troops held their own very well before a
series of disasters, caused by the arrival of some Grand Opera
Generals, who took command and tried to use Aldershot-tattoo
tactics in the open veld. Colonel Royston died at about the time
of Ladysmith.

Aunt Marie married Sir Alfred Cowley of Brisbane, and lived
in Australia.

Another brother of my father's—Uncle Archie—had been one
of the first white men to enter Matabeleland.

The Matabeles are a branch of the Zulus. Their founder, Mzilikazi, was reared in the Communist régime of Tchaka, to whom
he acted, as a "Fascist Beast of a Trotskyite," in the rôle of a Tito.
Having suffered a military setback from the Swazis, this thug,
Mzilikazi, was due for liquidation with all his army as soon as he
presented himself and reported his ill-luck to the super-thug,
Tchaka. Both General and Army decided it was safer not to return home; so they deserted, emigrated, and set up their Soviet
elsewhere, exterminating and massacring thousands of other natives as they did so.

Hypocritical whites, who lament the injustice of Boer rule under Malan, should remember that from the native point of view
it is infinitely preferable to the Soviets of the Zulus and Matabeles
who gloried in blood and cruelty—"Mzilikazi" (the path of blood)
took his name just as Molotov and Stalin did theirs, to inspire fear
—the "grinder" and "the steel one." The Matabeles were driven
North to the present Matabeleland by a handful of mounted Boers,
in 1837, thanks to superb riding and marksmanship; and they
thoroughly deserved their punishment on account of the hundreds
of Boers, men, women and children, whom they had treacherously

set on and massacred. The Dutch were in what is now the Union long before the marauding Zulus or Matabeles who were first heard of round Mombasa in the seventeenth century.

My uncle became District Native Commissioner of a wild tract of country in Rhodesia (the Belingwe District) half as large as Wales. Lame from the age of six, when he permanently damaged his hip through being dragged in the stirrup by a bolting horse, he was nevertheless of a roving and adventurous temperament. When he first came there, the natives had nick-named him Umzike (reedbuck) but later, out of respect and love for him, they had changed the name of the reedbuck, throughout the country, to Uthlanga. On one occasion, when out hunting, I not knowing this, pointed to the spoor of a reedbuck and said, in Sintabele: "An Umzike has been here." The native hunters who were with me covered their mouths with their hands, as if I had uttered a blasphemy; and then they explained, as above.

During the Matabele War, in 1895, that tribe had listened to a sort of Delphic Oracle, who spoke out of the gorges of the Matopos. By means of ventriloquism, this so-called *Umlimo* obtained complete ascendancy over the tribe, and often gave advice and orders which were detrimental to the strategy and tactics of his people; as when the voice ordered the Matabele to allow all the white people, whom they had surrounded in Bulawayo, to pass out of the country unmolested.

My uncle, being a wonderful ventriloquist himself, and possessed of two hideous looking dolls, Bill and Jemima, which put any native fetish completely in the shade with their red noses, ginger hair and goggle-eyes, was able to eclipse all the witch doctors, from Bulawayo to the Portuguese border, including the *Umlimo* himself. He discovered the identity of the original "Oracle," then an old man of well over ninety, who proved to have been a disaffected headman, wreaking revenge on the Matabele Chief, Lobengula, by issuing orders and advice which had encompassed his downfall.

My uncle used his gift of ventriloquism to prevent trouble and bloodshed. His book, *The Mlimo*, about the old "Oracle," was published by P. Davies in Pietermaritzburg, under the pen-name of "Umzike." It contains extremely valuable historical material, but is vitiated by his literary ambition, for he tried to weave a "love-interest" (à la Haggard) into his otherwise fascinating book. This, the charming old gentleman informed me, would cause the book to "sell like hot-cakes." He was wrong. But for the interwoven romance the book would be of the greatest value to this day. No one knew the Matabele as well as he did.

My father, the youngest brother but one, became a doctor. Uncle Marshall lent him one hundred pounds a year, which enabled him to go to Edinburgh and qualify for his M.D. He played full-back for Edinburgh University.

It used to take my father three days to ride to school, when he was ten years old. He, and the native who rode with him, had to sleep out two nights running, before arriving at Hermannsberg, from Umhloti.

During the Zulu Rebellion, when my father was escorting a convoy of waggons with his company of mounted infantry, they were attacked by an impi of Zulus in a gorge, through which they were forced to pass. The "loyal" native division panicked and the oxen, eighteen to a waggon, tried to stampede. My father was in a far worse position then than the British at Isandhlwana but, after beating off several attacks and finally routing the enemy, he spent all night at the risk of his life (since shamming dead and leaping up again with an assegai is a favourite trick of the Zulu) seeking the wounded natives and giving them first-aid by the light of an old hurricane lamp. This they never forgot and, on the day of his funeral twenty years afterwards—the biggest funeral ever seen in Durban—the traffic was dislocated for hours by hordes of natives erupting into town without any trousers! A stupid law prevents them entering town in their native garb—though they allow Scotchmen to wear kilts—and it's quite common to see a raw native waiting by the boundary stone of Durban until he can borrow a pair of pants from one of the outcoming natives. The native women, too, are forced to cover their breasts. Considering that Scotchmen are allowed in without pants, in their native garb, it seems unfair that the poor natives should have to buy trousers. On the day of my father's funeral the law went completely to the winds as several thousand wild Zulus swarmed into the town to pay their homage to a chieftain of their hearts.

My grandfather and father both died fishing. The former was swept off a rock by a breaker and got concussion, and the latter, feeling that his time had come to die, went with my mother and sister to his favourite trout stream on the Mooi River. He instructed the native boy, every time he swooned, to pick him up and put the rod back in his hand, dashing water on his forehead, till he passed out in his final unconsciousness, fishing his favourite reach on his favourite river. He lived for a week or so after the last time he was pulled out of the water. Lying unconscious on his bed, he only once spoke to say how happy and peaceful it was.

It is no wonder that this extraordinary character proved so irresistible to Mark Twain, who corresponded with him for many years and stayed at our house when passing through Durban; the two families remain friendly to this day.

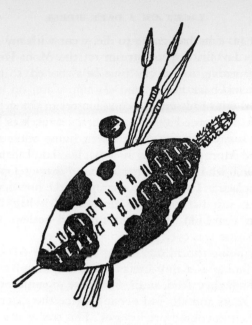

II

EARLY DAYS IN DURBAN

Though I had been to England as a baby I did not remember it. Yet the first thing I *remember* distinctly was seeing the sea. That first remembered glimpse of the sea was symbolical of my subsequent life, since I actually saw it first *through the legs of a horse!*

My Zulu nurse-girl, Catherine Mgadi, then aged eight or nine, had wheeled me further than usual on our morning outing in my strapped-in chair. We had been skirting hedges and railings along the sidewalk, which was still unpaved in those days, when a hedge suddenly stopped, and we came to an empty railed-in site, on a ridge of the Berea, overlooking the Indian Ocean. A horse had its head over the wire fence, and as we rounded the hedge and surprised it, it reared up and turned away: and I, looking down the grassy slope through its legs, saw a huge living expanse of glittering azure, like a peacock's tail, electrified with winds and solar fire. It took my breath away and when Catherine told me what it was, that Zulu word for the sea, "Lwandhla," which, in two syllables, Homerically expressed the pride and glory of the ocean and the plunge of its breakers, struck my mind with a force which no other word or line in prose or poetry has ever had for me since. I went on repeating the word "lwandhla" for days. It is the first word I remember *learning*.

My father, who had served as a volunteer in the siege of Lady-smith and had returned since on several leaves, was back at the front when I was born in a single-storey house at the very corner of Berea and Murgrave roads, in 1901. The late Lilian Bayliss, of the "Old Vic," who had been reading my *Flaming Terrapin*, went to my birthplace in Durban, photographed the house, and sent me a copy of it just before it was demolished, when I was about twenty-four years old. It was the first and perhaps the greatest compliment that was ever paid to me as a poet.

Over our house spread one of those enormous African fig-trees which, beginning as a tiny creeper, attach themselves to another tree, on which they feed, until, like some gigantic octopus, they strangle it, roots and all, and occupy twice the space, depth and height of their devoured predecessor. This tree was a super-giant, whose horizontal boughs shadowed hundreds of square yards. When it had reached its full girth and height, the mummified corpse of its strangled victim crumbled away, leaving a hollow crater twenty feet deep and five feet wide at the fork of its boughs, which filled up with water. As the trunk was far too wide, mossy, and slippery to climb, we never discovered this reservoir for mosquitoes which for twenty years were the plague of our little Eden. It was only found out when the tree was destroyed to build flats.

In this tree a large colony of gorgeous golden-weaver birds used to build, peeling off the long wicker strips, for their baskets, from the fifty palm trees in the next door garden, and flying back with green streamers trailing behind them, like long-tailed parrakeets. There was a large flat-crown acacia in our paddock, from one of whose horizontal branches we suspended an old motor tire after the manner of the safety ropes used in training for equestrian acts in the circus. Running and leaping against the pull of the rope one got up a tremendous elliptical momentum flying round in the air hanging by one's feet and picking up handkerchiefs from the ground. Large crowds of natives and Indians congregated on the main road at the foot of our paddock to watch this buckshee circus where we had our ponies also trotting round inside a wire circus. Thus we were able to settle on their backs with our feet or backsides as they rotated, and leap off again into the air without getting hurt. It was a perfect training for circus riding.

Herr Kruger's house next door, which finally became ours, was a beautiful, cubic, whitewashed, two-storey building, with a railed-in garden on the flat roof. This roof-garden overlooked our fig tree with its galaxies of weavers, redwings, and azure and green glossy-starlings, with brilliant scarlet and orange eyes, which came to feed on its figs, and rained down showers of song. This roof also commanded a magnificent view of the town, the sea, the coast, and the harbour. Herr Kruger had surrounded the house with the most exquisite jacarandas, flamboyants, flame-trees and palms, and I remember as a boy counting over thirty different kinds of rare fruit, exotic and indigenous, in that garden, apart from ordinary pineapples, mangoes, pawpaws, bananas, oranges and tangerines.

My father, Major Samuel George Campbell (Sam-Joj to the natives), C.M.G., F.R.C.S., besides qualifying for his M.D. second of his year in Scotland, about 1880, had other degrees from Vienna, the Pasteur Institute in Paris, and elsewhere. After the Boer War he returned to Edinburgh to take his F.R.C.S. While he was trout fishing on a Scotch loch, the boatman who rowed him, an am-bitious young highlander, who wished to emigrate, and later be-came a very distinguished citizen, offered to go out to Africa as his coachman. My father brought him back.

This Scotchman was a terror for the bag-pipes, the highland fling, the sword dance, etc., in which he himself had triumphed in all the Scotch competitions in the highlands. My elder brothers, Archie and George, were nine or ten years older than I was, and he taught them everything he knew about piping and dancing, with the result that they swept away as many juvenile medals at the Caledonian Society competitions, as their tutor won adult ones. From those times onwards, till recently, I always believed we were pure Scotch Highlanders by descent. I only discovered our Irish and French ancestry by accident.

To the compatriot of Wagner, Beethoven, and Bach, living on the other side of the corrugated iron fence which separated our two gardens, with his more exalted ideas of music, the braying of the bag-pipes (or "pack-vives" as he called them) was an insult and a nightmare. So whenever the "pack-vives" started up from our side of the fence, Herr Kruger, in sheer self-defence, would line up his entire staff of some dozen native servants, arm them with bricks, and get them to pound and hammer on the fence, and to yell with all their might, while two Indian waiters hammered on brass trays, as if they were trying to scare away a swarm of locusts. Then we would see Herr Kruger himself, rushing up the spiral companion-way which led to his roof-garden, where he would stand, like the Captain of a battleship, directing the salvos, volleys, and broadsides of cacophony which came from his side of the fence as a reprisal, waving his arms in paroxysms of fury, like the conductor of some infernal orchestra: and screeching and howling, as loud as the pipes themselves: "Harriple pack-vives! *Harr*iple pack-vives! *Ha-a-a-rr*iple pack-vives!"

Dooglie, the coachman, who then could scarcely speak anything but Gaelic, either mistook this for encouragement, rivalry, or applause: or else he was merely deafened by his proximity to his own instrument. I can only remember that he went on playing louder than ever—perhaps out of emulation, or maybe, contempt. All the dogs, donkeys, horses, and cattle in the neighbourhood would catch the excitement. Our horses and the cow, Nelly, would begin to gallop wildly about under the thirty mango trees in our immense paddock—which was bad for Nelly's milk.

The first two or three times this pandemonium began, Catherine (my nurse-maid) and I rushed from the scene in panic, and hid, sobbing, beneath my mother's bed, for the bag-pipes themselves were strange enough to a raw native girl, and since my mother was then nursing my younger brother Neil, I got a good many of my ideas from Catherine. After a bit, however, we began to feel a sort of awed, bewildered exhilaration on these occasions, and would run round in circles, leaping, jumping, pulling faces, waving our arms like Herr Kruger, and imitating the noises of the pipes, the natives, and the Herr, indiscriminately, by turns.

So deep an impression did these performances make on me that, even to this day, if, in Zanzibar, Lamu, Mombasa, Diego Suarez, Djibouti, or Tunis, I see the Muezzin or Imam going to his tower or balcony to call the Faithful to Prayer: or when I see the captain of a ship or one of his mates running up the ladder to go to the bridge of a ship—I feel a sudden depression the moment he walks out on to it, as if he has let me down. I feel sure that this can only be explained as a subconscious disappointment that he does not wave his arms and start screaming "Horrible bag-pipes!" I imagine that if one day I could prevail on an Imam or a Sea Captain to shout it just once on arriving at the top of the stair, I should recapture the exalted intoxication of the Kruger episodes.

As for the bag-pipes, owing to this association with Herr Kruger, I can't say that they kindle in me the same pugnacious patriotism that they do in other descendants of Scotchmen, but they certainly induce in me a wild hilarity, coupled with a desire to leap irresponsibly about, second only in intensity to that once induced by the voice and gestures of Herr Kruger. It is only when the pipes are played with drums that they really give me "ants" down my spine and stir my blood, as they should stir the blood of anyone bearing the name of Campbell, which has more V.C.s than any other name.

Alas for poor Herr Kruger, worse trials were in store for him than the bag-pipes! A pure "dolichocephalous Nordic type," of an almost albinoid blondness, with the palest of blue eyes, he had the shock of discovering that his pure blonde Nordic daughter had been put in the family way by one of the native servants, and they had to leave the country in record time, since in those days, few people, let alone Nordics, would have been able to face up to the scandal. My father bought the house and garden; we let our original house; and retained the paddock, which was necessary for my father's, mother's, and grown-up sister's horses.

There was only one motor-car near Durban in those days. It belonged to my uncle Marshall. It was a Panhard, an enormous thing, and could do a steady five or six miles an hour—for about a quarter of an hour. But I think he kept it chiefly to fiddle with the works as he and my aunt generally drove about in fast horse-traps. The chauffeur who came out from England with the car, later started the first garage in Rhodesia, and the first buses; ruined the old stage coaches; and became about the wealthiest man that country ever produced. His sister Louie, my aunt's maid, and the Swiss waiter Conrad, whom she married, and both of whom we all loved as children, all became rich, influential people.

My father always had two pairs of carriage horses for his medical practice. He loved speeding: and he always took advantage of urgent calls in order to stage "Ben Hur" chariot races, and

Jehu stampedoes, in his flying buggies, to the consternation of pedestrians and poultry alike. He stood on the board with the reins in his left hand, whirling a whip round and round with his right hand in the position of a Roman charioteer; and took the corners on one wheel, so that he was always in trouble with the police. The drawback in those days was that you could only drive fast on the sidewalk or pavement since the roads, when they were not roaring torrents, were strewn with boulders. But, one day, Father got an urgent call from Superintendent Alexander, whose wife suddenly becames dangerously ill. The Superintendent lived somewhere down the Umgeni Road, some miles away. Father arrived in record time by keeping strictly on the sidewalk. The patient recovered. From that moment he was never interfered with by the police again, but coursed his flying dustcloud freely, like a sand-devil, whirling all along the unmetalled pavements of our growing township.

He was reputed to be even faster at inspanning his horses in the middle of the night than the local fire-brigade, whose members slept sitting up beside the chariot in their uniforms. He made up for not sleeping in his clothes by rushing off in his dressing gown, when he looked more like a white-robed, classical Greek charioteer than ever, except for his face with its walrus moustache, which might have belonged to an ancient Gaul. The fire-brigade slept with the disselboom between the two horses, and the horse-collars immediately over their necks. But my father whistled through his two fingers, like a locomotive, as he rushed barefoot down the garden path towards the stable: the natives all shouted "Nkosi!" (Master!) in their sleep, and rolled over like the shadows under the boulders on the kopjes at noon, and went on sleeping; and the two night horses, Prince and Girlie, would be found already on each side of the disselboom trying to inspan themselves with their teeth—or so the natives said!

There was never any question, at the kindergarten I attended along with the children of the fire-brigade chief, as to who was the fastest driver, and raised the most dust. I, for my part, had to admit that the fire-brigade had the prettiest hats (brass helmets) and made most noise, because of the bells. But there were acrimonious discussions about inspanning and I remember feeling very indignant when the notion of the night horses inspanning themselves with their teeth, which I believed implicitly, was pooh-poohed.

And I was floored by the word "impossible"—"My dad says it's impossible." I've never liked the word since, thought I didn't know what it meant then, but it had such a final sound about it, and still has!

These poor children, with whom I had such acrimonious arguments about the respective merits of our parents as Road-Scorchers, were all involved a few months later in the most terrible tragedy. As an incident in the annual Military Tournament, their father proposed, in order to show off the prowess of his own fire-brigade, to rescue his own children from the simulacrum of a burning house, which was erected in the middle of "Lord's" cricket field. They spoke of their forthcoming performance in the Military Tournament, which they had rehearsed many times, and we all felt envious and wished we could be rescued too. My Ben Hur of a father was completely put in the shade for the time. One little friend actually got permission to go with the children of the fire-chief.

Catherine brought me and Neil away from the Military Tournament that evening, after the tent-pegging and wrestling on horseback, for our tea, though we cried out to stay on after sunset and watch the rescue. She said we could stay up till nine and watch it from the roof of our house, which overlooked "Lord's," now "Kingsmead," where the Test Matches are played, about a mile away; so that the blaze would be quite visible. Sure enough, we saw a sheet of fire go up, heard confused sounds which we took for applause, and went to bed full of envy for the children whose father could rescue them out of such danger.

Next day we heard the news that they, and the friend, had all been burned to death, before the eyes of their half-demented parents. Owing to some miscalculation, the canvas structure had gone up like gun-cotton in front of the helpless fire-chief and his brigade, before their hoses had had the slightest effect.

My father was the Major in Command of the Mounted Company of the Durban Light Infantry so he had to keep two chargers, Lance and Pompey, beside several polo ponies, since he was also Captain of the Durban Polo Team. My mother had two greys, carriage horses: and my sister, Ethel, a fine thoroughbred called Winston, after *the* Winston, who was already famous then.

Every morning Tom, an angelic old Zulu, who was with our family from the age of ten till he died recently, aged about seventy-five, would don a white suit and a scarlet tarboosh, inspan the greys, and ascending the box, drive my mother, Catherine, my two younger brothers, and myself down town. While my mother was shopping, the rest of us would drive down to the deserted "back beach," now the ornate Marine Parade, where amidst the ribs of an old, wrecked sailing-ship we could safely paddle, bathe, and play about without fear of sharks or backwash, for an hour or so before returning to pick my mother up at my father's consulting rooms.

We used to love passing the native eating-house where, behind enormous bars, a thousand Zulu Rickshaw-pullers tugged at tremendous whale and ox steaks, emptied quarts of heady "tchwala": and, in order to make their conversations heard above the din, roared like lions, louder and louder, till the thunder became deafening.

Gazing through the bars of this acre-wide cage into the smoky darkness, where oxen were roasting whole over flaring logs, one would see the hundreds of white or red plumes made of pampas-grass, horsetails, or ostrich feathers, which nodded between the white-washed crescents of cattle-horns fixed to the brows of the rickshaw boys. Flickering dimly in the reflection of the dancing fires of the infernal kitchens, these plumes and horns receded into the distance, along the ranks of tables, like the candles of a religious procession, or the tails and horns of a huge herd of cattle during a midnight lightning-storm—with the thunder laid on! It reminded me of the line of my old friend R. W. Service—"the cattlehorns were gleaming like the candles of the dead."

I once passed it in company with an Indian: and as we came within the full blast of this uproar, to which a football crowd seems quiet, my Indian companion, Samson, pointing through the bars into the diabolical pandemonium of black faces, feathers, and horns, and referring to the noise, bellowed into my ear, so that I could just catch what he was saying, the most perfect understatement I ever heard—"Just like bees, Mister," he roared, "just like bees, Mister!"

Near by there were the Indian and Native markets. The Native market still has a doctor who can cure anything from a broken heart to a nervous breakdown. But if you ask him for anything for a toothache, he floors you with some Zulu equivalent of the word "impossible," and laughs in your face at such ignorant credulity. In the Indian market there is always the juggler with his snakes and his astounding tricks. No birthday party amongst European children was ever complete without the jugglers. Both as a child and a grown-up I have never discovered a flaw or found an explanation for such tricks as "the Mango tree" or the placing of a child in a small basket and allowing any one to stab it clean through with an assegai. There are no trapdoors on the pavement where they practise, and they are always in the very middle of the crowd. The handling of venomous snakes, especially after they have been a long time in captivity and become tame and sluggish, is the part of their repertoire which is easiest, whether they extract the fangs or not.

As boys we used to catch snakes for the Zoo, for pocket money: and sometimes steal them from the Zoo and sell them back: and as for their response to sound, an overstrung ukelele will do wonders with them, though the Indians prefer a sort of calabash wind-instrument. Serpents hear, not with their rudimentary ears so much as with their tongues, which they are always thrusting forth like antennae. Ditmars says that snakes are insensitive to harmony or music and that Indian snake-charmers only use this to impress the human spectators. One dares not contradict such a great expert. All I know is that snakes are extremely sensitive to cacophony: and that the highest and most piercing note that one can play on a ukelele, using the metal claw, will excite the curiosity of all the reptiles within hearing distance and attract them to the sound—especially iguanas and tree-lizards. The overstrung ukelele is also an irresistible attractor of bats. (Collectors please note.)

During term time I always had a box of all kinds of venomous and other snakes hidden in the bush near my beehives. I always left the snakes pot-luck with each other, and each time when I came back at Michaelmas or Easter I would find that it was a non-poisonous snake, generally a mole-snake, which had survived, having eaten all the others. I would back the non-venomous mole-snake, who seems impervious to venomous bites, against any venomous snake in existence, since a mole-snake has not only an apparent immunity but also the power to strangle other snakes.

When my father gave up two-horse charioteering, he learned

a new kind of road-scorching in a Ford, and this nearly cost him his life. He was trying to avoid a dog, when he swerved in front of a tram, and his car was squashed between the tram and a lamp-post.

I remember that night when he was carried home on a stretcher, with five ribs broken and concussion, and it was touch and go whether he would come through. Huge crowds gathered outside the house, and I have never known the native grapevine-telegraph to work so fast. The accident happened at about half-past eight at night. At about three in the morning, some sand was thrown against my window pane, and I looked down to see two shadows at the foot of the palm tree outside my window. It was Tom and his cousin Malambula from their Kraal seventeen miles away. They were out of breath when I went down and had apparently jog-trotted all the way. A night-nurse had been engaged; and I told them on her instructions that my father was doing all right. But Tom insisted on staying the rest of the night at the foot of the stairs.

By ten o'clock next morning all our natives who were on leave at their kraals, were squatting around the stables, about nine of them, among them Neta and Umfundis', two boys of twelve or thirteen.

This is how the Zulu newspaper reported it:

"The Native People rejoice in the recovery of Dr. Campbell from the effects of his serious accident. The Doctor is the most popular gentleman in Natal. His kind nature is so well known that a misfortune to him is a misfortune to the whole country. Much as his professional ability is esteemed, yet he could be of still greater use to the Union of South Africa as the Administrator of the Province of Natal."—*Ilanga Lase Natal* (The Sun of Natal), January 4th, 1916.

This paper, in 1916, represented the Native opinion of the whole Province of Natal.

How popular he was even amongst the shady part of the white community, the crooks, and the criminals! There have always been crooks in the motor trade; after all, it took over from the horse-trade; and though I say it myself, who have been in that trade for

so long, there are more murderous villains in the horse-trade, as we shall see later in this book, than in any other trade.

To make a short story long, my father went one day to the Royal Hotel in Durban to attend Mr. Jack Hobbs, the famous English batsman, who was out there with J. W. H. T. Douglas's team of the M.C.C. I happened to be in the car. To be driven round in these new horse-less machines was a thrill of which we never tired in those days. Mr. Hobbs caught sight of me, waiting in the car, from the open-air lounge where he and my father were sitting; then, when the consultation was over, he asked my father to tea, came down the steps, and invited me to join them both. With that imaginative kindness that is common in most great men, he realised what a thrill it is in the life of any small schoolboy to meet such a semi-divinity as he then appeared to us all at school—second only to Herby Taylor in our eyes. I was transported into the seventh heaven when he started giving me signed photographs of himself which of course I displayed at school, and then basked in his reflected glory for weeks. The conversation grew very animated and we stayed there half an hour.

When we came out, one of the tires was flat. My father went to the tool-box to get the jack and the rest of the tools. They had been stolen. Just then a taxi-driver, whose family my father had attended free of charge, when the driver had been in jail, seeing my father scratching his head and looking perplexedly at the car, drew up and asked what was the matter, and whether he could help. My father thanked him, and they began work on the wheel. Meanwhile my father started grumbling in his comical way, and saying that with so many rich storeowners around with Cadillacs and Napiers, you wouldn't think they'd be so hard up as to rob the Ford of a hard-working quack like himself. The man said: "Don't you worry, Doctor, I'm going to tell the boys about this. They can't have known it was your car. I've taken the number: N.D.94."

About a week after, my father, whose car was always parked for three hours every morning outside his consulting rooms in West Street, went to put something in the tool-box and found all his tools returned with a note: "If we da known it was you, we da taken them off a someone else." That they were the identical set of tools taken was clear from the fact that they were returned in the same bag.

Father had some very curious cranky habits mostly concerned with the telephone upon which he depended partly for his practice—but he hated it like poison. Somebody always had to be left in the house to answer the 'phone. If it were answered wrongly, my father would come down on us like a Sergeant Major. This heathen instrument had the most comical effects on my father. If somebody rang him up and he went to answer it he felt deeply insulted if the speaker at the other end said: "Who's that speaking?" He liked them to say: "Is that Doctor Campbell?" or: "Is that you, Doctor?" If asked: "Who's that speaking?" he invariably replied: "Smith," which seemed to satisfy his *amour-propre:* for he would immediately recover his usual good spirits and say: "Oh, it's Doctor *Campbell* you want, is it? I'll go and fetch him." He would then walk away from the 'phone shouting in a shrill, affected tone: "Doctor! Doctor! Somebody wants you on the 'phone," so that he could be plainly heard: then return to the 'phone having set things right so that he couldn't be asked again: "Who's that speaking?" which he couldn't stand at any cost.

Once, by some fluke, when my mother was speaking to some other person, by a freak-crossing of lines she became disconnected with her caller, and connected with my father's consulting room; hearing a new voice breaking into her conversation she naturally asked: "And who's that?"—"Smith" came the immediate indignant reply. "Oh, I know *you*, Smith! Get along with you!" she replied.

He could never resist leg-pulling, particularly by telephone. Once he was asked, by someone who got the wrong number: "Have the sheep come?"

"Yes," he rejoined.

"Let me speak to the manager," said the voice.

"He's off today, sick," said my father.

"Where's the foreman?" asked the voice.

"Drunk."

"Tch! Tch! Tch! Well, I'd better come down myself. Where are the sheep?"

"All over the shop. . . ."

The poor fellow hastily hung up and dashed to find a tram. Then my father was sorry, but it was too late.

Everyone in our family has a complex about telephones. We all hate them. Apparently dislike of these instruments is not only a fad

of ordinary Campbells like us, for the late Duke of Argyll himself
refused to have one in Castle Campbell at Inverary.

This telephone complex was not lessened, in my case, after I had
been nearly killed by one. I was training as a private with the
R.W.F. at Brecon. I had volunteered and passed A1 though still
disabled from injuries in the Spanish War which took six months to
wear off. My N.C.O.s used to give me all the lightest jobs. I was
detailed to act as telephone orderly when the rest of the platoon
were at grenade practise, which was unnecessary for me on account of my experience, with the Spanish and Portuguese, when I
had handled every sort of grenade from home-made ones to British
Mills, Skoda, Mexican, Russian, German, and Spanish ones. We had
been priming the grenades in the marquee adjoining the Camp
Commandant's tent—Sergeant H. Davies, of the 1st Battalion
R.W.F., and Corporal Hughes, and myself. When told I needn't go
to grenade practice, I took off my wet denims, and put on a dry
battle-dress, which saved my life. I settled down to read *Don
Roberto*, a wonderful biography of Cunninghame Graham, the
hidalgo-gaucho and descendant of the great Montrose, by Aimé
Tschiffely; he had just given me a copy, and I was soon galloping
away over the pampas in my imagination. There was a tremendous
thunderstorm going on at the moment and this chiming in with the
detonations of the grenades up at the "bay" about one hundred and
fifty yards away, provided an appropriate accompaniment to the
rip-roaring episodes in the early life of the great hidalgo and his
fellow-pistoleros.

This camp (with the rifle-range and grenade bays) was near the
top of two big koppies called the Brecon Beacons, in a canyon
called Cwm Gwdi, which means, in Welsh, "the valley of the
owl." The camp was shared by Borderers and Fusiliers jointly.
Suddenly I found myself sprawling on the ground; my left leg
was completely numb and my right one was tingling as if it had
been pumped full of soda water or lemonade, or as if a million
cocktail-ants were marching on it. I had seen something hot shoot
down the tent-pole against which I had one boot, and two long
tongues of blue fire either went into, or shot out of, the fusebox
under the telephone, but I did not reason it out. Naturally, I
thought that I had put my boot on a detonator that had been care-
lessly dropped when we were priming the grenades. Yet the smell

in the air was not that of an exploded detonator, but of N_2O_4 (nitric acid gas) which I was too dazed to sort out as the smell of lightning.

I rushed out of the tent swearing: "What swine of an unsoldierly lout drops detonators on the ground when he is priming grenades? etc., etc." When I got outside my boot hissed and steamed as it went into a puddle, and the heat suddenly started blistering my foot so that I almost yelled, and had to unlace it as quickly as I could. Colour-Sergeant Campbell of the S.W.B. was on his way to the tent which was sending up a cloud of steam. "Aren't you dead, Baldy?" he said. "Indeed to goodness, man, that was no detonator! You were struck by lightning, man. Yes, indeed! What does it feel like, man?" He laughed.

A big crowd had gathered by then, all laughing. We went inside the tent. The telephone was completely useless. The tent pole which had been wet was now completely dry with a thin black line running down one side of it. I went and put on my plimsolls. The sole of my boot was like burnt blotting-paper.

A Don R. was sent to Brecon to fetch a R.E.M.E. to repair the telephone and the telephone-wire which had melted in one place where a pole wasn't properly earthed. I thanked God that the telephone was now out of order, and put my chair in the furthest corner of the marquee and went on reading about the exploits of that very different kind of Don R. *(Don Roberto)*.

Then the R.E.M.E. Corporal turned up. After questioning me, he asked: "What's all this?" pointing to some silver beads on the floor, which had been scattered for about a yard about the base of the tent-pole. Silver beads! They came out on my forehead all right, too, as it suddenly began to dawn on me how nearly I had been cooked alive . . . "Could it," I gulped, "could it . . . ?" and I picked up the boot and showed him the sole.

"What! ! ! Were you wearing that boot when it happened? Whew! Yes, those are the hobnails all right, melted as fine as pin-heads some of them!" He got out a match-box and began collecting them. He then asked if he could take them away, and show them to his electrical mates: he said he had never seen anything like it in his life.

"Man, indeed to goodness, you can have them. I never want to see them more," I said.

"Man indeed, I reckon it was a chance of one in a thousand, whatever," he said, "and if you didn't have changed your wet clothes, as you said, you would have been roasted like a mutton."

From then on, my instinctive phobia for the telephone became no longer instinctive, but completely conscious and intellectual.

I wrote recently to a friend in Toledo where there is only one public 'phone-box, to boast that I had four telephones in my office in the B.B.C., which was perfectly true. My secretary, Miss Chasmar, and I had a couple each, one "external," and one "internal," though I could never get used to them. The friend in Toledo, an abattoir worker, did not believe me; he was as polite as he could be, but he reminded me of my Gascon blood. Finally I got a signed statement from Captain Spicer, R.N., the administrative chief of the B.B.C. Talks Department, to confirm that I really had four telephones. The cattlemen of Toledo have framed this affidavit, and I have become an almost legendary figure in consequence!

My father's tendency to leg-pulling often had serious effects, which he bitterly regretted. It was almost impossible for him ever to get a proper holiday, when we went up country, for in the country sick natives would come to besiege him from miles away, and even those who weren't sick but merely idly curious to have their fortunes told, or those who wanted rain made. No distinction is made between these functions in native medicine. They are expected of any doctor. In the end, in order to keep down the numbers, he stipulated that they must bring a fowl apiece, as they do to their own witch-doctors, as a consulting fee.

The result was that the whole place was crawling with chickens, which in their turn attracted pythons, and every kind of wild cat from the ordinary "mbodhla" or wild cat to the "umhlangalis," "nsimbas" and other super-weasels and mongooses: from the nocturnal "bush-baby" to the ferocious red lynx, which will attack and kill a man by leaping on his back and tearing him till he bleeds to death, for no motive at all.

It was when one of these was hiding in some buck-weed near the chicken run that a native called "Nkomozoniwe" ("the cattle have fallen down") saw its back, thought it was a red-druiker or "nkumbi," and came running to tell me to get the gun. The two big shot-guns were out with my brothers. As a rifle would be dangerous so near the sheds, I came noiselessly with him upwind along the damp path with a single ball cartridge in my small .410 bore: we waited about two minutes and then I saw the buck-weed moving slightly. I gradually eased round till I could see a reddish back: I let the supposed "buck" have it, saw it fall, and was walking up to it unconcernedly when there was a ferocious hissing snarl, something sprang through the air at me, and as I dodged, a beautiful red lynx, vomiting blood, rolled in its last agonies at my feet. On another occasion with a ball cartridge in this same tiny specimen gun I killed a stembuck in Rhodesia at over a hundred and fifty yards.

The chickens brought by the natives had to be accommodated wherever possible in different out-houses, barns, and sheds. A python sixteen feet long went into one of the sheds, by means of a drain about six inches in diameter, to have a snack. It was a close fit but after it had swallowed seven chickens it couldn't get out except for its head. A native boy saw its head and neck sticking helplessly about six feet out of the pipe, and brained it with his knobkerrie.

These knobkerries are the favourite weapons of the Zulus for fighting each other, for hunting, or for self-defence. Zulus are legally subject to various restrictions; not only are they forbidden to enter a township without putting on trousers, but no Zulu may carry a stick into Durban with a knob larger than he can insert in his mouth. One often sees the native policemen testing them in the streets. This precaution saves a great many broken heads in the street-fights in Durban. But the knob-swallowing test gives an unfair advantage to a man who's had his teeth knocked out. The police themselves carry sticks with knobs the size of grapefruit; and they need them!

One day on the side of the Inthlosan Mountain, during a terrible drought, my father was flying an enormous kite which had been sent out to us for Christmas from my grandfather. It was a brilliant yellow colour, three feet broad, and six feet high. We were on the side of that magnificent mountain facing towards the Drakensberg Range, which ridged the western skyline some hundred miles away, soaring high above the clouds, and the scenery between was a riot of jagged cobalt and heliotrope rock-ridges, with yellow grass-lands dyed, here and there, with purple cloud-shadows, and chequered with shaggy black tracts of forest and wattle. It was a sight such as eagles must see every day, but I have seldom seen anything to equal it, except some views I have had from the sides of Kilimanjaro, Kenya, and the Sierra Nevada. Above us in the huge vertical Krantzes, baboons were barking. Far down beneath us on a winding kaffir path was a procession of natives, dwarfed by our height to the size of ants, making for a distant kraal of bee-hive huts.

We had already tied six balls of strong twine to the kite and had only one left but the kite was still climbing. It was a mere speck in the sky, but so different in colour from any of our eagles, that the natives saw it glinting and flashing yellow in the sun as we played it like some gigantic kingfish in the wind. They all halted. Apparently the twine glistened, too, like a spider's thread, and this enabled them to trace it to our tiny group on the mountain-side. I was about six years old at this time, which was just after the 1908 Rebellion. The natives despatched three of their number in our direction and meanwhile the rest of them all squatted down to wait; any excuse to sit down and "bema gwai" (take snuff), which they place between the lower gum and the under lip.

After a time, the three envoys arrived where we were. Saluting very ceremoniously, they all squatted down. Soon one of them enquired: "You wouldn't be after making a bit of rain, would you, with that thing up there, Dokotela (doctor)?"

"Yes, of course," said my father, "that's *precisely* what I am doing."

"When may we expect it, Dokotela? and will you be expecting chickens from everybody in the land when it comes?"

"I think it should come about midday the day after tomorrow," said my father, putting his finger in his mouth and holding it up to see which way the wind was blowing: putting on his reading-glasses and screwing his eyes up at the kite: "Yes, the day after tomorrow, without fail, shortly after midday. As for chickens, I don't know. It's very hard work—I may have to ask for some cows."

Now, natives are very sensitive about cattle. The name of the boy "Nkomozoniwe" (the equivalent of Dolores in Spanish) which I mentioned a page or so back, meaning "the cattle have fallen down," was given because that boy was born during the huge rinderpest epidemic which decimated the cattle, the buffalo, and the wildebeest throughout Africa. It is the saddest name, next to Dolores, that I know. Cattle to Zulus are far more important, and infinitely more useful, than dogs to Kensingtonians: the Zulus only part with them in exchange for wives. At the mention of charging a fee in cattle the boys looked as uneasy as the average Englishman would look if the Government were to suggest nationalising dogs. After a little while they descended to their friends. One could distinguish certain microscopic gesticulations in the group which the news seemed to excite.

Had no rain come, everything would have been all right. By next day we had completely forgotten my father's blarney, and so had he. The "day after tomorrow" dawned cloudless. But at lunch-time when we were sitting at table, a kind of twilight seemed to fall. We all went out and saw blue-black clouds, like the smoke of some burning petroleum-mine, rushing up from behind the Inthlosan! They twisted in terrific spirals and moved at a great speed, as if *falling upwards*, like an inverted Niagara. There wasn't a breath of air. Then suddenly, beside the main peak of the Inthlosan, which is a steep cone with a rounded top, an inverted cone formed, about the same size as the peak, pitch-black, with a sharp point hanging about two-thirds of the way down the peak, from which it began to separate and travel rapidly away. Suddenly a terrific wind started. I did not see what happened to the inverted cone, whatever it was, because at that moment Catherine dragged me indoors, and our room was on the wrong side of the house. However all that afternoon it hailed, thundered, and poured in spouts: the rivers rose to such a height that no post came for a week: we were completely isolated.

Some days after it started, some half-drowned natives came to tell my father that they had had quite enough rain, thank you: and then he suddenly remembered his irresponsible blarney. More natives came the next day to say things had gone far enough, and that the floods were doing more damage than the drought had done. The situation was uncomfortable: it was not long since the Rebellion and we were isolated amongst a considerable population of natives who held us to blame for the floods.

In order to set things right my father convoked some of the headmen; it would have been useless to deny that he had made the rain: he pointed out that he had only undertaken to make the rain with the greatest reluctance after being pestered for months and months to do so, both in town, and here in the country. Was it not true that he had refused to make rain for weeks and weeks? His reluctance was due to the fact that though he had excellent medicine to make rain, he had no medicine to call it off. The rain would therefore have to wear itself out. As it would have been a physical impossibility for the rain to go on forever, it did stop very soon after, to everyone's relief.

After this storm had intermittently deluged the country for a fortnight, the sun came out shimmering over a landscape that was all awash like the background of the *Surrender of Breda* by Velazquez in the Prado; and if we looked towards the mountains, the rocks were all sinewed with tiny glistening rivulets and mini ature cascades. It was then that I saw, for the only time in my life, the most beautiful aloe in all the world, in flower. This aloe only lives in the shadow of overhanging precipices, and only feeds by inhaling the substance of the rainbow and the morning mist. The Nubigens (or cloud-born aloe), on this occasion, burst its buds, and was in full flower high overhead, in several places in the Krantzes that lost themselves in the white mist, even when the moon was blue over the plains.

The myriad streamlets rushed down towards the Umgeni and Lion's rivers, that merged on the horizon into a single mirrored sheet, with wattles, willows, and gum-trees standing knee-deep in their own reflections. There was a tinkling and gurgling sound of water for two days after the rain had ceased.

In all that stormy fortnight, such is the force of the English language, the thing that struck me most was the image of a downy yellow duckling lying drowned in a drain. I must often have heard the phrase, "a dying duck in a thunderstorm," in adult conversation: and this helped to imprint the picture so clearly in my mind at the age of six that, whenever I hear that simile used in conversation, the image of this little yellow duck returns to me far more vividly than the whole blurred majesty of the mountain storm with that terrible black inverted cone (waterspout, trombe, cyclone, or whatever it was) which had formed at the side of the mountain, and then rushed away into the darkness beyond.

Some years later when riding on one of the hills in this neighbourhood to fetch in a bull from its pastures, I saw another strange

sight: a meteor came flying from over the south-eastern horizon
and fell, as we thought, over the hill on which we were herding.
My companion was one of those Gaelic-speaking Scotchmen who
come from round the Dargle. We two children could only con-
verse in kitchen Kaffir as he knew no English, and I little Gaelic.
We were both frightened, but afraid to show it. We had no conception of what this thing could be that looked like a sixpence
rushing across the sky and leaving a white line of smoke, like aero-
planes do now in the stratosphere. Nevertheless, we galloped over
the rise and down into the next valley to see what had fallen, but
could see nothing where we judged it must have come down. A
few days later I read that a meteor had fallen in Basutoland—*about
a hundred and fifty miles farther away than we thought!*

My father was a prodigious swimmer, and steamers used to
heave to off the coast of Scotland thinking that he had been capsized from a boat. Swimming very far out to sea in South Africa
is impossible because of the sharks, and risky even in the bays
and harbours: only in lagoons and river mouths from which the
crocodiles have been exterminated can you find a long stretch of
water suitable for ordinary swimming.

Once my father was on a holiday—when he was sent for by
someone who had got dangerously sick many miles away. On the
way there the Umgeni river was in full flood, but he told me to
saddle two horses and go with him. When we got to the river, he
gave me his watch and cigarette case, and, telling me to take the
horses home, stripped and went into the swirling and boiling
rapids. I thought I'd seen the last of him and rode at least half a
mile down the bank looking for him when suddenly I saw him
just opposite getting out on the bank unhurt and trotting off on
a twenty mile trek almost in a state of nature.

He was always in a hurry both on entering and leaving the
houses of his patients. This caused dogs to fly at him and bite him
on several occasions, till he developed the aim of a Bisley champion
with bricks and half-bricks. On one occasion, having brained in
this way a dog that rushed at him with its jaws open, the owner
told him it wouldn't have bitten him; but my father replied: "Did
you expect me to offer the dog my calf first to test whether he
would bite it or not?"

He was altogether queer about animals. On one occasion a
starved stray mangy cat had about six kittens in our stable. He

decided to chloroform them as the place was overrun with wild cats which preyed on the birds he loved so much. He sent me all over the place to get milk, fish, cream, etc., etc., and gave the cats such a meal that they could eat no more. Having given them the one and only spree of their lives, he proceeded to chloroform them; and so safeguarded the lives of his favourites, the birds, for whom he made our garden into a veritable sanctuary.

Upon wild animals my father had sometimes an almost hypnotic effect. Once he was walking with my mother and a friend, Mrs. Kimber of Maritzdaal, along the side of the forest near our beach-cottage, when he saw a bushbuck ram watching them from some distance away. "I wonder if I could stroke it," he said. Then telling the others to remain perfectly still, he actually did so—walking slowly up to it, stroking it, and walking quietly back to them while the buck remained absolutely still. This was not the Kruger National Park, where the animals have ceased to be shy; but north of the Umthlanga Lagoon where they were habitually hunted by us for food and leather—and the bushbuck most of all, not only for its excellent meat, but the toughness of its leather which provides the finest "voorslag," or end-lash, for the great twenty-foot ox-waggon whips. On hearing what my father had done with the buck, my elder brother and I went out after it with a lasso and a shot-gun, thinking it must be either mad or wounded. But it no sooner saw us in the distance than it bounded off barking in full alarm, with the white flash of its tail fully erected, showing that it was as sensible, wary, and active a buck as could be found for a league around.

On account of his kind-heartedness my father, who was very abstemious himself, though he liked seeing people merry, was always besieged by "drunks." A sure way of getting the price of a drink off him was to claim to have been in the siege of Ladysmith with him. On one occasion a "drunk" reeking of Cape Brandy, which is like rusty barbed-wire to drink, with all the barbs turned backwards, accosted him for five bob (which was the cost of two whole bottles then). "There you are, my lad," said my father. "Now go and get properly drunk."

"Oh no! I wouldn't think of getting drunk on your kindness—this is just for a night's lodging," said the drunk.

"What!" said my father, who hated humbug. "Give it back at once! The very idea of it! I thought you needed it for drink."

"Well, sir, all right," replied the man, "I might drink your health with some of it."

"Carry on then! And don't be such a damned humbug another time!"

My father never charged actors, artists, authors, schoolmasters, rabbis, priests of any denomination or creed, or professional soldiers, or any of their families, for medical attendance—the result was that he was in considerable demand, always overworked and underpaid. But it repaid him a thousandfold in the universal affection he inspired, and in his friendship with such people as Mark Twain and Lilian Bayliss. He attended the latter, when she and her family were in a travelling company of actors; she was fifteen at the time. Ever since then our family always received the greatest kindness and hospitality from the Clemenses in America and from Miss Bayliss in England.

It was through my father's sharing and cherishing my literary ambitions that I was able to get a start as a writer, and make a name at Oxford before I set off on my wanderings. I inherited his unselfconsciousness in dealing with my fellow men, so that whatever country I have visited, it has not been as a millionaire tourist staying at hotels, but working with and sharing the lives of the people, even the most exclusive people, such as the fishermen and cattlemen of non-Riviera Provence, and the vaqueros of Castile and Andalusia. Thanks to him I am able to address the barrack-square as a Sergeant-Major, and explain the parts of a machine gun, speaking as one ranker to another, in English, Swahili, or Chinyanja; I can address the English Society at Oxford or Cambridge from the same platform as T. S. Eliot, or Sir Osbert Sitwell: confer ceremoniously in flowery Zulu or Sintabele with delegations of headmen: I can join a knot of stokers in a pub in Glasgow or Liverpool as one of them: I can lecture in French or Castilian to the Universities of France or to the *Atenéos* of Madrid and Barcelona: I can give a talk to the Portuguese people, from the B.B.C., in Portuguese, on street-warfare, Civil Defence, and fire-fighting, as I did in 1941, when there was a scare that the Germans might try to push through the Peninsula: and feel equally at home in the Sergeants' Mess or at the high table at Magdalen College. Above all, from a utilitarian point of view, I owe to my father my mastery of horses which has been my passport through every frontier.

The place where one really learns best to ride horses is, paradoxically enough, in the cattle-kraals. I cannot remember when I
first tried to sit on a bucking calf. The cattle-kraals, built as stock-
ades on the coast, are made of stones further up country; the
walls resemble those one sees in Derbyshire. The trampled muck
and mire soften the falls and save one from broken bones. The
movable hide of a bare-backed and bucking steer or ox is far
harder to grip with one's legs than the bare-back of a horse. We
used to go into the kraals clothed only in a pair of shorts, emerging covered in mire from head to foot, and black as the ace of
spades.

To become good riders children should always be started on
bare-backed calves. The mire of the kraal acts as a cushion and
there is little risk of injury though one may be thrown several
yards at every fall. Cow-dung is a perfectly clean and disinfectant
element. Even our Governor-Generals sleep, in the hot weather, in
thatched rondavels walled with a mixture of cow-dung and mud,
which hardens into a firm heat-resisting cement. The perfect hut
is one walled in this manner and floored with a mixture of cow-
dung and cow's blood which hardens and takes a polish like
ebony so that one can see one's own reflection in its black depths.
That is how the Zulu Kings and Chieftains pave their floors. The
cattle-kraal is also an excellent place for breaking-in difficult
broncos, since it not only provides a soft cushion to fall on, but
it limits the height and violence of the bucking.

III

A HUMAN RHINOCEROS

W HEN the Almighty issued the various species of animals with their uniforms or hides (so runs the Bantu fable) he also issued them with a needle apiece with which to sew them on. The rhino, always a bundle of nerves, carried the needle in his mouth while looking for a convenient place in which to sit down and sew on his skin. On the way he got a fright and accidentally swallowed the needle. This explains why he is so uncomfortable and bad-tempered and why there are creases and folds in his ill-fitting skin. It explains also why rhinos (which will walk miles to relieve themselves on the same midden) will always paw and scatter their manure about, scrutinising it and studying it as they do so. They are said to be still looking for that needle (—in a veritable haystack!).

"Mbetchan" (or "No-Needles" as we white boys called him) was a white store-keeper up the north coast of Natal. By the natives, whom he thrashed unmercifully, he had been beautifully nicknamed "Rhino" on account of his long snout, which resembled a rhino-horn, and the fact that he always carried a nasty rhino-hide sjambok on a sling around his wrist. He also had huge pouches under his eyes and ears and chin, as if his hide, like a rhino's, had been badly "sewn on," and he had as vicious a temper as a black rhino.

He had once shouted something opprobrious to my cousin Colin, when he was passing in his car. Colin, who was a hot-tempered man, quick with his fists and the last of our family who was said to be trigger-happy in the old style, had got out of his car and arranged No-Needles so that he had to be carried into his store and laid out in his own bar.

I used to ride or train past No-Needles' store out to Dunolly, my cousin Colin's house, twelve miles up that road, every week-end at the beginning of the First World War, when I was twelve. Sometimes I would go there during the week and be back in Durban next morning in time for school, with a bushbuck or a duiker swinging over the pommel of my saddle. The reason for my going out there so often was because my cousin had left Nat-alie, his newly-wedded wife, there all by herself, while he went to German West Africa with the Natal Mounted Rifles. I was very fond of Colin and Natalie, and as she was expecting her first child, I set myself up as a sort of mixture of a watch-dog, armed guard, and a page-boy all rolled in one. I looked after her comfort; per-formed her messages in town; gave orders about the maintenance of Colin's horses, and his prize Jersey bull, and, in co-operation with the induna, Nyali (a native we all loved very much, who had been through the siege of Ladysmith with my father), saw that Natalie, who was a very capable manager, was not let down in the running of the farm.

Their lazy boy, Mnugeni, who was a favourite with me, be-cause of his wit and also because he was a comical buffoon and a good hunting-boy, was about two years my senior. I had known him since I was four or five; he often came hunting with me, when I was old enough to handle a rifle properly and the care of an older man, like Nyali, was no longer necessary.

After I was eleven I could bring down a charging buck and knew most of the answers in the Bush, far better than I do now. In those days, all I needed, to take a wild bee-hive, was a hoe or an axe, according to whether it was in the ground or in a tree. I never dreamt of getting stung—except for an *accidental* sting or two. Yet, when I had been in Europe for six years, I had so completely lost the bee-man's art and confidence in hive-taking, that the bees smelt the acid of nervousness (they get upset by it, as a horse or bull does) and went for me as soon as I approached. It was on an occasion when I had intended to show off and impress my wife with my skill, by taking a hive between the planks of our verandah. But I had to stop and swathe myself in the mosquito-net from my bed, in order to avoid being stung. Every time I stooped to pick up a piece of comb, this net draped itself so closely to the seat of my thin pants that I received a dozen stings. I had to stoop about twenty times. The result was that, for a week afterwards, I had a posterior like a desert-bush-woman, after she has just camel-shipped a three-weeks' water-supply in the camel-glands of her hips and buttocks. Instead of impressing my wife, I looked ridiculous, but we enjoyed the honey and the bee-grubs (bush-man's rice) none the less. I have never taken a hive since then without gloves, hat, face-net and the thickest pair of pants I can find.

Schillings mentions a conversation between a Masai and a Kik-uyu: "If I tried to take a hive as you have just done," said the Kikuyu, "the bees would have stung me to death." "Very true," replied the Masai. "You carry burdens on your head for the white men, and so the bees hate and despise you. As for me, I wander free over the plains with my herds, and so the bees love me." In some such terms might my boyhood have addressed my manhood on the subject of hive-taking.

Sometimes I went hunting bushbuck with Simon, a boy who had been Colin's personal servant in German West Africa. On one oc-casion two dogs misled me by baying after the unwounded female, instead of the wounded Inkonka, as we call the bushbuck rams. I was carrying a shotgun at the trail and running between the rows of sugar cane towards the place where the dogs were barking, and I ran straight on to the horns of the wounded buck. There was neither time nor room to shoulder the gun, but a fluke shot from the hip saved me. Both horns and a triangular bit of skull lay in one piece, four yards away. On that same day I had shot a valuable domestic pig in mistake for a bush-pig, which made me the laughing stock of Mount Edgecombe for weeks—though, thank God, the story never reached Durban where I was some-what timidly paying court to the most beautiful pair of pigtails I have ever seen before or since.

I had been told that, owing to a bush-pig in a certain patch of cane, the Indians had downed tools, and would not cut any more. The mill manager had offered me five pounds if I would kill it, since they can be fierce and dangerous. The patch the Indians had left was circular, about thirty yards in diameter. I stood on the hillside with Simon holding the horses a little above this patch so that I could cover the opposite hillside if the pig broke cover in that direction. The dogs were in that patch for at least an hour yelping excitedly and going round and round, when suddenly a pig broke cover and rushed off, choosing for his breakaway the very point which would give him the most cover for the longest time, till he reached the exposed spot which he would have to cross to make the rise and vanish.

I first saw him when he was two hundred and seventy yards away, going all out against the sun, across a scarified field and with only thirty yards more to make in order to crest the rise. He had thought out his getaway beautifully, with great skill. Had he kept his head he would have saved his life and my reputation as a hunter. But my second miss, raising the dust in front of his nose, turned him at right-angles, presenting a better target, since he had hitherto zigzagged like a duiker as he ran. All pigs are extremely intelligent—as George Orwell shows in *Animal Farm*. With the third shot he took the count. I sent in another bullet to make sure: then, as it was so far off, I sent Simon to pick up the animal, which I thought was the bush-pig, put it over his saddle, take it to the mill, and collect the five pounds, of which I promised him a share, while I went on in search of meat better suited for the table than the supposed bush-pig, which we in South Africa don't eat for fear of swine-fever.

Simon, a location native and a soldier's servant, had never seen a bush-pig nor a prize Hampshire hog. He turned up at the mill to ask for the fiver and make a laughing stock of me . . . with one of Colin's prize pigs, which had escaped some weeks before! That it was the pig that had caused the panic of the Indians there was no doubt—but we did not get our five pounds, and when I came riding back later past the mill showing off, with that de-horned bushbuck across my saddle, my shot-gun on my thigh, and my horse dancing as prettily as a circus horse, I was greeted with the most hilarious hooting and jeering. Even the two engine-

drivers of our miniature railway, Jock and Sandy Smith, hooted
on their bantam engines; and the only reason the hooter of the
mill itself was not played on that occasion was because it might
have spread the alarm of a cane-fire. It was no use trying to explain that I had only seen the pig at two hundred and seventy
yards against the sun, and ridden on in search of venison. It
would have made it look as if one were afraid of ridicule. So I had
to grin and bear it. I had the compensation, however, of being the
envy of the whole of my school, who never heard of this humiliation.

The trade I did in horns and hides was colossal. The other boys
used to take them home to the Transvaal and pretend to their
parents that they had shot them while in Natal. In return for
giving a skin to the Trappist Monks at New Hanover I could get
no end of beautiful girths, veld-shoes, and yards of Voorslag for
my stock-whip, made out of other skins, free of charge. They
also made python-skin belts for me, and shoes for a girl I will call
"Pigtails!"

Mnugeni sometimes used to ride part of the way with me when
I was riding back to school. We used to make a bit of a detour,
having got up long before sunrise, so as to pass by various patches
of forest which had been left in the sugar cane, in case we could
pick up some venison for my mother or my cousin. If I had already left some at Dunolly during the week-end, I would disem-
bowel the buck, give the insides to Mnugeni, lift the lightened
buck with Mnugeni's help, and by means of a thong passed
through the incision in its houghs, and another round its horns,
make it fast to the saddle before me. Sometimes we would skin and
split the buck longitudinally with a machete, and each carry off
half, and sometimes Mnugeni would ride back with the whole
buck. There was a spruit at the end of our territory, adjoining
the main road. Beside the spruit was a hollow tree where I hid my
soap and a towel. There I used to wash off the blood and change
into a clean shirt so that, after dropping the buck and leaving the
horse at home, I could get to school by nine.

On one occasion a bushbuck had given trouble and I looked
like being late for school. I had wounded it at about one hundred
and fifty yards away with a rifle-shot from the saddle as it stood on
the side of a cane-break in the valley beneath. As we were strictly
forbidden to leave a buck wounded, I had to risk my life for this

one, and also my headmaster Langley's wrath, which was almost as serious to me.

I took the shot-gun from Mnugeni, giving him the rifle. The buck had doubled up a cane-furrow through the trash which resounds and crackles like a machine-gun when brushed by the body of a man or animal. This trash is the dead growth of previous years and remains attached to the cane stems, cluttering up the narrow alley-way between the stiff rows of planted cane. It is dangerous to the eyes so that when pushing along a cane-row, we always held our arms before our eyes, since the edges cut like a knife, and more than one of our overseers has lost an eye like this.

I had identified, from the bloodspoor, which alley the buck had chosen, and knew it was unlikely to change from one alley to another till it broke cover at the other end. By standing still every few seconds I could hear it crashing ahead. Then suddenly I realised that the crashing was coming my way, only just in time to raise my shot-gun with the muzzle at about the height of the buck, which would be invisible till it reached me. I backed a couple of yards which faintly increased the visibility between the now thrice-separated trash. As soon as I saw the trash stir, I fired with the barrel apparently almost touching the skull of the buck, which knocked me flying, thought it must have been already dead when it hit me and fell on top of me. I immediately tried to grab its horns before I realised that it was inert, and that there were no horns there to grab—only brains. The horns had been blown off at the base, just as before when I was with Simon.

By that time I was in real danger of being late for school, so I did not take the precaution of tying on the head, since it had no horns, but simply looped a thong through a cut in the hind-leg tendons, and kept the buck balanced across my horse with my hands. I took the rifle from Mnugeni, gave him the shot-gun, pushed the rifle into the gun-bucket at my hip, and tightened the girth rather more than usual. I hitched one point of the pair of shot-off horns into the gun-bucket, beside the gun, to take back to school and barter for cricket bats, etc., since they had not been spoilt but had come off in a single chunk of bone. (Even if they had come off separately, the native cake-pedlars would have given me a hat full of cakes for either horn, as they prize hollow horns, keeping "medicine" in them.)

Besides being afraid of being late for school, I dreaded having

to ride past No-Needles' place, for he would often come out and
start cursing and jeering at me, and saying all sorts of things about
my ancestry, which I pretended not to hear. All his cronies would
join him, too.

Attached to his store was a bar, nicknamed "The Snake Park"
(after Dr. Fitzsimmons' famous snake park—then in Port Elizabeth) because its habitués were always supposed to be seeing
snakes. In these bars, South African brandy is the most effective
drink procurable at the lowest price. To drink it, in its crude,
cheap state, is only comparable to swallowing red-hot porcupine
quills.

That morning I was coming along at a fast trippel and praying
that No-Needles wouldn't have opened the store yet. He had not
only opened it but, because it was Monday and he knew I should
pass, he was waiting outside with a Great Dane he had just bought!
He knew that Colin was away at the front, so he thought he would
revenge himself on me. (He regretted it three years later, when I
gave him the same treatment as Colin had given him—the minute
I was big enough to stand up for myself—it was my sixteenth
birthday present to myself. But he regretted it before that, too!)

As I went past he didn't address me, but only said "Saa!" quietly
to the Great Dane, which means "attaboy" in South Africa. The
Dane came snarling at the horse and the blood dripping from the
dead buck seemed to excite the brute all the more. It snapped at
the horse so that it started leaping and rearing, and, in spite of
my efforts, threw the buck trailing down on the ground though
it was still attached to the girth by the thong. The dog then for a
moment left the front of the horse, which was waltzing sideways
away from the buck along the main road, and began snapping at
the trailing head of the buck. So it went on for a hundred yards or
so. Then I threw the horns into the devil-thorns at the side of
the road and pulled out the rifle with my left hand, but the little
bay horse was bouncing and bucking so hard that I couldn't get
a shot in at the dog which didn't threaten to ricochet right into
No-Needles' store (and perhaps kill one or two jail-birds as
well). No-Needles saw the red light and tried to call his dog off,
but it was growling too loudly to hear. Waiting till the horse was
at a favourable angle I lifted my left leg over the pommel, slipped
to the ground and gave it to the dog point blank as he turned to

face me. I had filed the tops of all my bullets so that they were dum-dums. And that was the end of the Great Dane. No-Needles who had run in for his rifle was now being frantically restrained by his cronies who had come in for the "hair of the dog" and who had no doubt been promised an amusing spectacle—to be left not only with the hair, but the hide and the bones of another dog.

Afterwards No-Needles swore that he was only going to shoot my horse in return for my shooting his dog. But I was between him and the horse, so I couldn't have known that and, as I was sober and he wasn't, I should probably have got him first, though I have never yet pointed a gun (even an unloaded one) towards a man except in war. He was screaming in paroxysms, but when I saw they had got his rifle away from him, I turned my back and walked after my horse as calmly as I could, in despair now about getting back to school in time, as it would take fully half an hour to quieten the horse, and hoist and lash the buck on again. In imagination I saw the headmaster Langley's whiskers rising over his desk, and resigned myself. I hated No-Needles, but I both hated and feared Langley, like the Devil. As there was nothing I could do about him, or to him, even in self-defence, in the end I took it all out of No-Needles, who was more fun. I still get terrible nightmares about Langley, but I never dream about No-Needles.

While I was quietening down my horse and trying to lift the buck over the saddle, in full view of the infuriated mob on the verandah of The Snake Park, who, though restraining No-Needles, were jeering all the louder as my efforts became more breathless and desperate, the late Doctor Hill, of Verulam, came along in a Ford on his way to town with a native. Having ignored the drunken crowd on the verandah, many of whom he had treated for D.T.'s, and seeing the dead dog, he thought it had been run over, and ordered his boy to jump down and drag it to the ditch at the roadside. Then he saw and recognised me in my difficulties, and I told him what had happened. He cut the thong and ordered the boy to place the buck between the hood and the exposed petrol-tank of his old 1914 model Ford, saying he would drop it in at our house on his way down town. He warned me against looking back or going back, but I suddenly remembered the horns, and as soon as I was completely hidden from him by the dust of his car, I turned my

horse and galloped back to where I'd thrown them. The Snake-fans
who had been discomfited by the appearance of such a redoubtable
witness as Dr. Hill (who was their snake-charmer too) had retired
again to the bar-side, but one of them, through the door, saw me
pick up the horns and remount; and I cantered off followed by another salvo of curses. Freed from the burden of the buck I was able
to make up for lost time by galloping, and got to school with one
minute to spare. Having done all my homework on the Friday before leaving, I had nothing to worry about, thanks to Dr. Hill.

Miss Pigtails, whom I had neglected for hunting and looking after
my cousin Natalie, now broke my heart by transferring her affec-
tions to an older boy who had more sense, time, and chivalry. (She
was anyway about three years older than I was and must have
laughed at my calf-love.) It became more than I could bear when I
saw her new beau using for his wristwatch a python-skin strap I had
given her, an iguana skin belt, and a beautiful python-skin writing-
case, which I had had made for her by the German Trappists at
New Hanover. It did not occur to me that owing to my neglect I
thoroughly deserved to be superseded. If had only learned the lesson there and then that love is a full-time job and must come first!
But Pigtails wasn't the last to serve me out that excellent lesson, by
any means.

My humiliation was more acute when, with my usual foolhardi-
ness, I challenged my rival with his borrowed plumes, and was
hammered solidly for as long as I could stand up, and long after I
could see, or remember. This fight strained my heart so that for a
couple of years I was not allowed to play rugby or tennis or take
any exercise except riding and shooting. I used to lose my breath
and gasp like a fish for hours at a time. But it made me take to reading, which was good.

Hitherto Bruce, my brother, four years younger than I am, had
been a complete prodigy in reading as well as in sport. Up to the
age of ten, neither my father nor my sister could stump him with
any name out of Greek mythology. Then, because of the overstain
of playing both in the first fifteen and first eleven of his preparatory school with boys of fourteen and thirteen, he got St. Vitus
dance which laid him out for two years. On his recovery he showed
less and less inclination for intellectual and classical things and
more and more for practical things. Moreover he became one of

the greatest athletes in the country and, before he went over to American football, was the only South African schoolboy to be selected for the Inter-Provincial Currie-Cup rugby team (that is the equivalent of being selected to play for England, Scotland or Wales—perhaps even better, since few all-British teams have ever beaten Natal, Transvaal, Orange Free State or Western Province).

Pigtails left me very sorry for myself for at least four weeks, but I don't believe in crying over spilt milk. Laughing over it is far better.

The other girl, whom I called Blackstockings, because they were compulsory at her school, used to go out every day to a station near ours: sometimes we would go by train together and hold hands. We were forced to use the train because one day when I rode her home on the crupper of my horse, her father and mother showed me a shot-gun and told me to lay off her altogether. He had had a bang at one of her sister's suitors and left a couple of loopers in his back. Hearing of this a week after, I respected him as a man of his word.

The train used to stop at a station near No-Needles' store. You could just see the roof and the back premises which was a bar for coolies. It was a tin roof about a hundred and twenty yards away in the valley. Rushing along the platform, as if taken short, to the "Gents" place, which was at the extremity of the platform, I would extract my sling from my pocket as soon as I was out of sight round the bend of the corrugated iron screen. Inserting a six-ounce stone I would whirl it and drive it with terrific velocity at the resounding drum of the roof. As there was a forge down there in the valley no one on the platform worried much about the thundering clang of the corrugated iron. But No-Needles and his snake-charmed pals, being situated only a yard from the point of impact, would almost leap out of their skins.

No one ever saw the stone (quartz) till it had already struck and bounced so high that it was impossible to trace its original trajectory. I would get back into the compartment to find Blackstockings convulsed with laughter, having heard the thunderous report. Then, as the train moved out into the open, we would see the dozen or so Indians who had been squatting around the back-yard waiting for a pal to stand them some of No-Needles' rot-gut, capering round in circles and expostulating, while No-Needles and his ser-

pentine friends chased them around with sjamboks, cursing them
for destroying his roof. No-Needles wouldn't have dared to lay
about his prospective customers even if they had been the culprits,
since the Indians have *esprit de corps* and were quite capable of
boycotting his dramshop, let alone picking up half bricks and letting fly. (It was upon natives he used his rhino-hide and had once
scourged a cousin of Mnugeni's into unconsciousness, for a petty
negligence.) But it made a wonderful picture.

No-Needles got a dozen six-ouncers during five weeks, almost
on the same rusty sheet of corrugated iron, which buckled it badly.
Then I got a seven-ounce lead sinker, completely round, and gave
him the last one which went right through and smashed bottles and
glasses to the unspeakable fury of the serpent-brigade. It was only
then that the roof-bouncing became connected with the passing
of the train. The police searched all natives and schoolboys next
day for any sort of missiles; and Blackstockings warned me. The
next time we went without any sling. We saw builders mending the
roof. I told Mnugeni, Mnugeni told his cousin who rejoiced, and
by and by it got back to No-Needles, but by then Colin was back
from the war, so No-Needles was afraid to try anything on and
decided to bide his time. In the end I caught him poaching bushbuck does, which are royal game. I waited till he had parked his
gun against a tree and was bending down to start skinning the doe,
then I stalked him, caught his gun and pushed it over an embank-
ment, and went for him all out. I kept his gun and the doe.

When my cousin Colin came back from German West Africa,
he was so pleased with the way I had looked after Natalie that he
gave me a wonderful sporting Mauser, looted from the best gun-
smith in Windhoek, with a pistol-grip and a hair-trigger, a stock of
expensive cream-white wood, exquisitely carved, and a sling of fine
leather—the whole thing worth, I should think, about one hundred
pounds. He also gave me two service Mausers, and the bay horse I
had been riding in and out of town. This horse was a beautiful cross
between an Arab and a Basuto, and I had taught him to trippel so
smoothly that I could stand upright on the saddle. I started doing
this in order to amuse Natalie's son, Murray, who was born while
Colin was still away. I developed this faculty of standing on the
saddle after seeing a film of desert Arabs, till I could stand barefoot
going at a full gallop and firing my rifle over my head to show off

to girls. Later this faculty made an impression in Italy on the Campagna and in France on the Camargue—but I eventually spoilt my sense of balance through deep-sea diving which injured an eardrum, causing myasthenia, so that sometimes, even on terra firma, the whole street appears to me to be tilted sideways.

Colin showered these gifts on me for what had been a great pleasure and an honour in guarding the household. It would have been a duty, anyway, on the part of a kinsman. My uncle, Marshall, gave me a fine push-bike with which to scorch to school—for he, too, said he was grateful for the way I had looked after his daughter-in-law and Natalie herself gave me ten pounds, a fortune for a boy in those days—which I spent on books. I went to the bookshop in Durban and, putting the ten-pound note on the counter, said: "Please, sir, give me ten pounds' worth of poetry books." The bookseller remained open-mouthed for several moments, surprised that such a tough-looking urchin, with a Natal accent, should be asking for ten pounds' worth of poetry books, but he gave me a large parcel. When I opened it in front of Natalie she was very tickled to see Laurence Hope and Ella Wheeler Wilcox jumbled up with Dryden, Milton, Pope's *Iliad*, Wilhelmina Stitch, *a complete Shakespeare*, *The Golden Treasury*, R. W. Service, Omar Khayyam, Baudelaire and Ronsard. However, I had read the whole lot through from end to end in six months, lowbrow and highbrow, good and bad alike. And I still have several levels of enjoyment (highbrow and lowbrow) which are not in any way connected with each other. Because of this mixed reading I am intellectually at home in the Sergeants' Mess or the Athenaeum Club.

The same bookseller, years afterwards, looked down his nose and sniffed when I asked him for a copy of *Flaming Terrapin*. "Why, is it no good?" I asked humbly. "I only wanted to get it because I saw such good reviews in *The Times*, *The Nation* and *The Athenaeum*, etc."

"Oh," he replied, "the English papers know Roy Campbell is Dr. Campbell's son, and they all praise him fulsomely in order to keep on the right side of the Doctor."

It was my turn to remain open-mouthed! But it gave me a measure of the esteem in which my father was held in Natal.

When I returned to Africa, in 1924, I hunted again with Mnugeni, and then an episode took place which is still talked about

among the natives. They referred to it in the nicknames and titles
by which they saluted me when I was recognised on my re-arrival
on leave in 1944.

In 1924 it had leaked through to Mnugeni, by the grapevine telegraph, that I was expected; and there he was on the breakwater to
meet me, with a couple of tough old fighting cocks as a present,
when the *Umtali* (one thousand tons) sailed in, terribly battered
after a stormy voyage of seven and a half weeks (instead of the
usual three) during which she had nearly foundered. In twenty-
four hours she had only made eight miles, when rounding the Cape.

Mnugeni recognised me, after six years absence, and started
shouting all sorts of greetings: "Mathlathlela! Mathlathlela! My
Soldier!"—etc. "Mathlathlela" was the name given to me to express,
onomatopœically, the shuffle of my outsize flat-feet when I was a
child. I am now six foot two, and I take size ten, which is small for
my height, but I always have difficulty in getting fitted because of
the *height* of my instep. But the name stuck for good. It was merely
regular exercise that rectified this deformity of flat-feet, from
which I suffered till I was thirteen or so.

"All right, Mnugeni," I shouted back, "I am with you. We shall
hunt once more together."

On the second day of my arrival, however, I ran into my old
school-friend, Leif Egeland (recently the South African High
Commissioner in London), and he asked me to go with him on a
whaling expedition, before he went over as a Rhodes Scholar to
Oxford. Leif's father owned or directed one of the two big whaling
companies in Durban, where mostly humpback, blue whale and finner are hunted. Durban is also the last port in the world from which
the sperm whale is regularly hunted; it has now almost completely
withdrawn to the Indian Ocean and breeds round the Seychelles.
But this was in June during the season of the great hundred-foot
blue whales, or sulphur-bottoms, which are thrice as exciting to
chase and harpoon as the sperm whale because of their vastly superior size, strength, and speed.

On this occasion we were forced to return to port by mountain-
ous seas such as I have seldom encountered before or since. The two
breakwaters formed one cloud of spray which nearly covered the
front of the bluff and it was almost by guesswork that we steered
the tiny craft back between them to the harbour.

Before setting out again, I got into touch with Mnugeni. A drive was arranged of those big Javan deer, about the size of water-buck, and very like them, which, in the same way as the rabbits in Australia, have multiplied and spread through the cane country through the indiscretion of some of my zoo-buying relatives; now they were becoming a scourge to the sugar-farmers.

At the beginning of this drive I saw a large stag running along in a shallow stream towards me. I discovered then that Mnugeni, who had been celebrating, had forgotten to load my shot-gun, so I leaped down into the stream and intercepted the stag, while it was tossing a dog which it killed. I was knocked over with a flesh wound on the hip, recovered, and throwing myself on the animal, went for it with my bare hands. After much tossing and tussling, I got a leverage on its horns, wrestled it down, and gradually drowned it, in less than eighteen inches of water.

The present estate-manager, Mr. Whitfield, the native-beaters and Mnugeni all stood round in a circle and watched this. Then the natives composed a song about it on the spot which is still sung to-day, and danced round and round me singing while the culprit, Mnugeni, wearing my old cattleman's corduroys, three times too big for him (I had worn them when Augustus John had painted my portrait three months before), tottered drunkenly around, boasting of my prowess and of the part he had played in educating me. In fact it was due to the carelessness of the drunken old scoundrel in not loading the gun, that I bear to this day a scar on my hip, and an ugly hole on each side of my Achilles tendon.

However, I had been anxious to impress the boys that I had not degenerated, and I think that was one of the happiest days of my life, marred only by the fact that my wife was not there to see.

I saw little of Mnugeni after the stag episode, for I lost interest in hunting with guns as being too dull, having experienced the hand to hand stuff. I have often before and since then gone in to a wounded bushbuck and fought it out with a knobkerrie.

Two days after the stag hunt the weather improved and I was back in the whalers, off and on, till the end of the whaling season. Then I engaged in the stormier venture of editing *Voorslag*. This is all described in the *Waygoose*, so it would be redundant to retell it here.

Many of the people mentioned in this chapter are dead, but my cousin, Natalie, is well with a grown-up family, and her son, Murray, for whose amusement, when he was four years old, I used to play so many equestrian tricks, visited me in Spain just before the Civil War. Mnugeni, when I last enquired for him on my army leave in Natal, was (alas!) doing a ten-year sentence for manslaughter; he had killed a man in a knobkerrie fight, after an illegal brewing of cane-spirit. I shared digs at Oxford with my fellow-Romeo; he showed me the marks of the loopers he caught from Blackstockings' father's shot-gun. He had meant about as little mischief to Blackstockings' sister as I had to Blackstockings. He had just left a bunch of flowers for her and had not ridden a hundred yards when the angry old man let fly and peppered both him and his horse. Blackstockings and her sister inspired what Dylan Thomas once said he thought was my best poem, *The Sisters*. I wrote it years afterwards, when I remembered having seen the two girls just before sunrise, ride out their horses into a cove at low tide. It was a beautiful sight indeed and one for which I am very grateful, though I am no peeping Tom and had been engaged in the prosaic task of sitting up all night in a milkwood bough in the hope of getting a shot at some bush-pigs. The sling, by means of which I bombarded No-Needles' roof and which made Blackstockings laugh so much, has earned me the respect of the shepherds of the Gredos, the Alps and the Pyrenees, and it too is the subject of another of my poems. Simon, the co-hero of my tame-pig episode, is now an educated native who follows my career in the press and reads my books so I "konzela" (or commend) myself to him here.

IV

THE SURLY TUTOR OF MY YOUTH

IN 1910 I was sent to the Durban High School (Preparatory) along with quite a bunch of boys who were to become well-known later on: Leif Egeland, the High Commissioner; various Olympic Champions, such as Clarence Oldfield, Sid Atkinson, and "Springbok" cricketers and rugby-players like the Siedles, whose sister, the famous Perla, is well known as the "Lady in White" to every British soldier who ever called in at Durban with the convoys during the war. They remember her for her magnificent voice, and all she did to heighten morale by welcoming the overcrowded and battered troopships in to Durban. Noel Langley, the brilliant playwright, and the son of our headmaster A. S. Langley, was born when this preparatory school was started, and he joined it just before I left. But he was around all the time I was there.

The Durban High School, till A. S. Langley took it up, had been an extremely scruffy school, despised for playing soccer (stigmatised at home as a "coolie game"). Langley, the son of a dour Calvinist missionary, was a tremendous personality. He started the school playing rugger and ran it as a super-English-public school. He was the queerest mixture of a sensitive artist and a stern disciplinarian. More than half the school would have died for him: and even I (who abominated him) was always elated for days if I could accidentally earn a word of praise from him. He hated me with a deadly hatred from the beginning, not for anything I had done, but for the fact that my father had founded the Technical College, a "soccerite" school, for poor children, where they could get educated free: thus cheating Langley of a mass of human material which might have been welded by his MASTER-HAND.

Langley impressed upon the whole school that the "Tech" was something contemptible: I got the idea that there was something shameful about it. In expelling boys for theft, sodomy, laziness, scruffiness, or imbecility, he would always say in his harangues in front of the whole school of five hundred: "The Tech is the place for swine like you." If ever I made a mistake in Latin grammar, I was never allowed to forget the fact that I was associated in the mind of the whole school with the Tech. At close range in class he could see from my expression that he drove a knife right through me every time he mentioned the Tech ("Get along with you to the Tech! What are you doing at my school?") and raised the scornful sniggers of the whole class. He revelled and gloated in the misery he inflicted on me. That was his roundabout way of getting at my father whom he feared and respected.

It is a very curious thing that though he was a fine artist, a really good painter in his spare time, it was the two best-known artists who have issued from his school, his son, Noel, and myself, who suffered most from him. I was thrashed frequently, as I thoroughly deserved, but I am none the worse for that, and quite as hefty and lively as any of those he spared. A healthy child does not worry two hoots about a hiding as soon as the smarting stops: it is preferable any day to sitting indoors on a sunny afternoon or being ridiculed, held up to the school as a freak, and nagged at without being allowed to reply. That was sheer hell to me.

I was made the vehicle of the old man's envy of my father, who knew nothing about it, and thought he was paying the rival school a friendly compliment by sending his sons there. He always thought Langley a staunch friend of his. My younger brother Neil suffered the same persecution, though he was only there three years, and he was the best full-back the school ever had.

This is the way in which Langley would try to break my spirit: I won my stripes as the youngest Sergeant in the Natal Cadets. He had me stripped by secret order without even telling anyone why. I was never promoted after making the requisite scores and retiring, to a higher game in cricket: but kept for years among children up to my waist so that in the end I took to clowning and being completely subversive. Eventually, to make up for the loss of my stripes, I was promoted by incontrovertible tests to Sergeant Major of the new Reconnaissance squad, much to Langley's annoyance.

During drill afternoons this Recce squad of mine was allowed to go off on practical "exercises" out-of-town, which was just over the ridge from our school. From the point of view of military training the time was excellently spent. The chief thing, and the most flagrantly neglected in all soldiering, and above all in Recce work, is *Taking Cover*. The Spanish army is absolutely hopeless at it and, but for this grave fault, it would be the finest army in the world, for its size, to-day.

There is no better way of learning this priceless art, apart from hunting buck, than by going when one is young into such peerless fruit-growing country as rolls out for some miles behind Durban. There were ferocious native and Indian sentries, armed with sticks and accompanied by dogs, on every hilltop. The district is perhaps equalled elsewhere in the world, but scarcely excelled for the size and succulence of its pineapples, pampelmooses, oranges, grape-fruits, guavas, pomegranates, persimmons, lychees, loquats, sweet-lemons, plantains, ladies-fingers, butter-bananas, spanspec, water-melons, strawberries, avocado-pears, umtundulugas, umdonis, amantingulus, breadfruit, custard-apples, grenadillas, tangerines, mandarines, clementines, figs, Brazilian cherries, roseapples, gula-gulas, sugarcane, etc., etc.

Seldom, for the training of youth, was such an incentive to achievement more perfectly balanced by such a grim, frowning and snarling discouragement from failure. In such surroundings the general principles of Reconnaissance imposed themselves instinc-tively and automatically.

We had a depot in the garage of a friend's house, up Windmill Road quite nearby; and these fruits and vegetables were a godsend to some of the mothers of the boys who came from gardenless, slummy parts of the town, where there were no large gardens. My lads became truly proficient in practical recce-work. Perhaps map-reading, star-guidance, and compass-training were a bit neglected. But as for my squad—

> "Like phantoms they had learnt to glide their spoors,
> To leak through key-holes, and to fade through doors."

Our excellent Natal Cadet training concentrated chiefly on drill and marksmanship. In that respect we were the best school in the

British Empire at that time. We took the Schools of Empire Shield off the Edinburgh Academy, and held it for years. If there had been a Schools of Empire Shield given for practical recce-work, for rustling away huge bunches of bananas, making pineapples vanish from under the noses of their proprietors, and evaporating vast watermelons into the air, our squad would probably have won the Shield—or, if not, merely spirited it away, as it were.

Most of this was done scientifically by a development of the diversionary tactics used in baboon hunting and explained later in this book. Few of my squad were caught and beaten up. Coming back in couples to our depot from our recce-exercises always reminded me of a charming picture in our old family Bible, of the scouts returning to Moses from the promised land with samples of fruit.

In the end, Langley's training had some very great compensations, for it made me completely insensible to literary boycotts, or unfair criticism, either from bull-fighting critics, South African political writers, or literary reviewers: things that would break the hearts of other writers only made me laugh! And I can defy public opinion, even at its most frantic, as in the case of the Spanish War or the Colour Bar in South Africa, without turning a hair. I am still afraid of Langley, however, though he died long ago. If ever I have a nightmare it is generally about Langley—though I owe him the best half of my character, and a sound knowledge of Latin.

What I blame him for chiefly is for causing me to kill my second-best friend, Sid Wright. As soon as I could get permission I came back to box, though Dr. Mackenzie saw my heart was too strained after my bout with Pigtails' boy-friend to stand more than a round or two at a time. This was written on the Doctor's chitty that I gave to the boxing-pro, Mr. Baker, who on his retirement became the famous witty "Barber of Durban." Every day he exposed to the passing trams, on a blackboard outside his shop, his comment on the affairs of the day—whether it was my cousin "seeing icebergs," or the abdication of the Kaiser.

I had hastened my return to boxing because I was now grown to the same size as Pigtails' boy-friend, now a prefect, and I wanted to even things up. He was now eighteen and I was fifteen. Langley came into the gym, saw me there, and said to the Pro: "What's that lout doing there? Have they sent him from the Tech? Where's he been all this time?" The Pro said I had had a strained heart, but was good for two rounds and then he showed him the chitty. "Make him put on the gloves then," said Langley, "and that other rabbit with him." This was my best friend, Ian Henderson, a beautiful boxer. After the second round, quite automatically, having seen the Doctor's chitty, I began to undo one of my gloves with my teeth holding the other hand out to my friend, Sid Wright. "Oh, no, you don't!" shouted Langley in a rage. "We want no 'Tech' malingerers in this school. You'll go on boxing till I tell you to stop." Baker expostulated with Langley and said he would take no further responsibility. I fought the next round and began to get slightly the worst of it, as Ian was a good fighter, and however hard he tried to pull his punches, both our bloods were up, though I was gasping and wheezing.

It was a rule in the gym that one never fought the same person for more than three rounds. So Langley, seeing I was thick with Sid Wright, let Henderson go, and made me keep on fighting—this time against Sid. Sid was a gentle and mild boy who, in spite of being big and strong, pulled his punches out of sheer good nature, though his defence was excellent. He simply *could not* punch hard, by temperament.

Langley got furious when he saw no blood, and, coming up quietly from behind, cut me across the back with his cane. "Fight, you swine! Fight, you Technical socrerite! I won't have any ma-lingering in my school!" Exasperated, I went all out to finish it off at once, if I could. I was swinging blindly and viciously when one of my wrists connected with Sid's jaw and neck just under the ear. Sid dropped like a stone, stark unconscious, and white as a sheet. It was the first and only time any boy had been knocked out stark cold and unconscious in the history of the school. It made a terrific impression. There was a dead hush. I could not help that nasty little quarter of Gascon blood from peeping out and flashing Langley a look of triumph mingled with reproach—as much as to say: "There now, look what you made me do. Yes: and look what I *can* do!" I was quite surprised, as Sid would have been, had he been conscious.

Langley was now in a state of icy fury. He racked his brains and remembered that a year or two before it was Pigtails' boy-friend who had given me such a terrible knocking about: Langley knew all the gossip of what went on, unofficially. He ordered Pigtails'

boy-friend to put on the gloves with me. I saw
again. But this time I was beyond myself. The pr
together enjoyed my tenacity during his first vic
been much smaller than he. He was taken aback
given poor Sid.

How I went the three rounds, I don't know
getting the same hammering as before, but foun
second wind. The next thing I remember was
tears in his eyes, taking off my gloves, and saying
done!" Langley had walked out half-way throu
friend was shaking hands with me and grinning
closed. He left boxing that night "in order to
study for the matric." Everybody told me that
tails' boy-friend far worse than he had me, tho
oftener: but I had rocked him properly the only
I contacted him.

I began thoroughly and conscientiously to
persecutions. The two brothers, Pat and Ia
Ridgeway, now, I think, a K.C. in Durban, Sid
had formed into a sort of gang called the Fezela
was subversive. Langley's prefects all fell out
if by magic—following Pigtails' boy-friend's
Ken Ridgeway, Pat and Ian Henderson, and n
finals, which Ken won from Pat. Langley had
for something two weeks before. But he had t
about us all, when he handed out the prizes
hands with all of us in front of the school!

Sid was the only one of the Fezelas who di
in the three remaining weeks of the last term
twice with his neck, fainted, and often becar
around with his hand on his ear. He never r
ways joked about it. Some time after he rea
he went out with his girl to the bioscope, an
gallery from cerebral haemorrhage.

To make up for Langley there were some
first and foremost, that King of Men, Bill Pa
Rugby player, who, enlisting in the ranks
fifty-three in the Second World War, was t
the V.C. I shall never forget when after m

been all this time?" The Pro said I had had a strained heart, but was good for two rounds and then he showed him the chitty. "Make him put on the gloves then," said Langley, "and that other rabbit with him." This was my best friend, Ian Henderson, a beautiful boxer. After the second round, quite automatically, having seen the Doctor's chitty, I began to undo one of my gloves with my teeth holding the other hand out to my friend, Sid Wright. "Oh, no, you don't!" shouted Langley in a rage. "We want no 'Tech' malingerers in this school. You'll go on boxing till I tell you to stop." Baker expostulated with Langley and said he would take no further responsibility. I fought the next round and began to get slightly the worst of it, as Ian was a good fighter, and however hard he tried to pull his punches, both our bloods were up, though I was gasping and wheezing.

It was a rule in the gym that one never fought the same person for more than three rounds. So Langley, seeing I was thick with Sid Wright, let Henderson go, and made me keep on fighting—this time against Sid. Sid was a gentle and mild boy who, in spite of being big and strong, pulled his punches out of sheer good nature, though his defence was excellent. He simply *could not* punch hard, by temperament.

Langley got furious when he saw no blood, and, coming up quietly from behind, cut me across the back with his cane. "Fight, you swine! Fight, you Technical soccerite! I won't have any malingering in my school!" Exasperated, I went all out to finish it off at once, if I could. I was swinging blindly and viciously when one of my wrists connected with Sid's jaw and neck just under the ear. Sid dropped like a stone, stark unconscious, and white as a sheet. It was the first and only time any boy had been knocked out stark cold and unconscious in the history of the school. It made a terrific impression. There was a dead hush. I could not help that nasty little quarter of Gascon blood from peeping out and flashing Langley a look of triumph mingled with reproach—as much as to say: "There now, look what you made me do. Yes: and look what I *can* do!" I was quite surprised, as Sid would have been, had he been conscious.

Langley was now in a state of icy fury. He racked his brains and remembered that a year or two before it was Pigtails' boy-friend who had given me such a terrible knocking about: Langley knew all the gossip of what went on, unofficially. He ordered Pigtails' boy-friend to put on the gloves with me. I saw Baker expostulate again. But this time I was beyond myself. The prefect had not altogether enjoyed my tenacity during his first victory, when I had been much smaller than he. He was taken aback by the dunt I had given poor Sid.

How I went the three rounds, I don't know: I imagined I was getting the same hammering as before, but found I was getting a second wind. The next thing I remember was Baker there, with tears in his eyes, taking off my gloves, and saying, "Well done, well done!" Langley had walked out half-way through. Pigtails' boy-friend was shaking hands with me and grinning, with one eye half closed. He left boxing that night "in order to have more time to study for the matric." Everybody told me that I had bruised Pigtails' boy-friend far worse than he had me, though he had hit me oftener: but I had rocked him properly the only two or three times I contacted him.

I began thoroughly and conscientiously to deserve Langley's persecutions. The two brothers, Pat and Ian Henderson, Ken Ridgeway, now, I think, a K.C. in Durban, Sid Wright, and myself had formed into a sort of gang called the Fezelas (Scorpions) which was subversive. Langley's prefects all fell out of the boxing class as if by magic—following Pigtails' boy-friend's lead. The Fezelas—Ken Ridgeway, Pat and Ian Henderson, and myself all reached the finals, which Ken won from Pat. Langley had nearly expelled Ken for something two weeks before. But he had to make a long speech about us all, when he handed out the prizes: and he had to shake hands with all of us in front of the school!

Sid was the only one of the Fezelas who did not reach the finals; in the three remaining weeks of the last term at school he went sick twice with his neck, fainted, and often became giddy. He walked around with his hand on his ear. He never reproached me but always joked about it. Some time after he reached home in Jo'burg, he went out with his girl to the bioscope, and died suddenly in the gallery from cerebral haemorrhage.

To make up for Langley there were some superb masters there—first and foremost, that King of Men, Bill Payn, the great Springbok Rugby player, who, enlisting in the ranks at the age of at least fifty-three in the Second World War, was twice recommended for the V.C. I shall never forget when after my first enlistment I was brought back to school he came up (just after his first return from the front in the First War) and found me washing off Langley's hiding in the change-room with all the admiring Fezelas and sub-Fezelas looking on; he came up in front of them all and shook hands with me and said: "Hard lines, Digger! Better luck next time you try to get away." As he was Langley's favourite master, it took some doing.

Then we had the finest history master in the world, Captain Blackmore, M.A. Oxon. He had a really colossal historical insight. I remember his saying in 1916: "They say there's going to be a League of Nations, and Peace after this war. The League of Nations will bring about the next war. It will be a place for the intrigues of International Masonry and it will probably centre round Geneva or Amsterdam. The only good thing that ever came out of Geneva is the Rhône! War is only a sort of subsidiary sideline of this main industry, which will continue again after the next war it provokes, under some other name, and so on ad infinitum, till you get World-Federation and that will end in the biggest explosion of all! Ha! Ha! Ha!" Then his old pot-guts would shake like a jelly and he would beam benignly. This devout Protestant was kind-hearted as an old Carmelite Friar, and looked just like one. He had acute historical vision, like an X-ray, of all the base sham, and hypocritical self-seeking which underlies all modern Egalitarian Utopianism, Fabianism, Communism and Socialism.

Since I predicted in 1936 that in the end the mutual abomination of Red factions would preponderate so heavily over any antagonism towards their common enemy that the Spanish War would end on a mutual massacre of Spanish Republicans by Republicans, with the Nationalists acting as a referee—people have said, "But how did you guess?" Trevor Blewitt, the political Producer of the B.B.C., was flabbergasted with my "guess-work." None of it was guessed. It was only "Potty" Blackmore's training in historical range-finding and reconnaissance.

The other excellent masters I can remember with gratitude are: Major Townley (killed in the First World War), Messrs. Black (the present headmaster), Gorst, Pape, Hodges, Fraser, and Snow—all brilliant, cultured, and charming men. Not to mention "Betsy" Martin, one of the finest Rugby coaches that ever lived. Langley himself was a great man, though he did happen to take a dislike to me (I was almost unique in that respect). But my father's ghost had the last laugh, for in the end his school of "scruffy soccerites" defeated Langley's ruggerites at their own rugger—and both Langley and I were there to see it in 1924 or 25! Not only that: Langley lived to see the hated "Tech," my father's creation, have offspring—a University, an Art School, an Observatory, and laboratories and workshops—which entirely outgrew his own excellent school.

V

HOLIDAYS IN RHODESIA

UNCLE Archie's two sons, Nigel and Marshall, came from Rhodesia to school in Natal, where they spent most of their holidays with us. Nigel, the elder of the two, was my senior by two years and, in spite of the fact that he used to tease and ridicule me, sometimes beyond endurance (which was very good for me), I hero-worshipped him. I imitated his Rhodesian accent and all his mannerisms with such effect that, twenty-three years after I had last seen him, when I was a Sergeant attached to the King's African Rifles in this last war, I was everywhere mistaken for him, especially once when I was posted to replace him. On another occasion, passing through Broken Hill, where I slept in the bed that he had just left, on his way home from South Africa after being disabled, I was roughly awakened with: "Wake up, Nigel!" by another Sergeant whom I had difficulty in persuading that I was not Nigel but his cousin.

Several times I was within an hour or two of meeting Nigel during the war, and previously in different ports when we were working as sailors in the inter-war period; but so far we have been doomed to miss each other, though sometimes only by minutes. The last time I met him was in England in 1920 when he had just returned as a lieutenant in King Edward's Horse from the

Archangel Expedition. On the *Oranje*, on my trip back to England, in 1944, I was pointed out to some officials as "the Sergeant who used to swim across Kiliadini harbour from an anchored Intelligence craft, all among the sharks—just to get a bottle of whisky." I had difficulty in denying this, but it was obvious I had been mistaken for Nigel and that this was one of his escapades.

A legend everywhere, completely fearless, and the most popular N.C.O. in any of the African Commands, Nigel was disabled in the first days of the Abyssinian Campaign but went on serving with the Intelligence as a coast-watcher in the jungle. Without knowing about Nigel, immediately I was disabled from Wingate's 12th East African Deception Unit, I volunteered for this unpopular but extremely interesting task, and I was posted to Lamu, the very spot where Nigel had been serving previously.

I reaped the greatest *kudos* everywhere for being his cousin, in every Sergeants' Mess in Kenya, Abyssinia, Madagascar and North Africa. My great regret is that I missed meeting him. Far more than any of my literary friends, he had a formative influence on my life and character. It is a great pity that his powerful and original intellect, his adventurous spirit, and his great gifts of humour have never found expression in literature; for his life has been far more adventurous and interesting than mine.

Since Nigel and Marshall spent so much time with us, I used to go sometimes with them up to Belingwe, Rhodesia, to stay with their parents, Uncle Archie and Aunt Poppy, for long holidays. We used to travel four days by train, and another five or six days by ox-waggon.

The train journeys up to Rhodesia were always a treat not only because of the strange company we met but also because of the changing scenery, so different from that round Durban. We used to wake up, on the morning after we had entrained, somewhere near Majuba Mountain or Mount Prospect where there was a pass through the Berg into the Transvaal. The train had to shunt several times on to different lines in order to zigzag its way up the face of the mountains. This Western part of Natal, between Pietermaritzburg and the Transvaal border, contains some of the most beautiful country imaginable. Unlike the tropical coast, it is temperate, and even cold. All the fruits of Northern Europe grow there as well as they grow in England, and the altitude ranges from three to five thousand feet. There are great precipitous forest-crowned ranges such as the Kaarkloof where delicious clear springs cascade down through rocks covered with moss, maiden-hair, and other ferns. Tree-ferns, orchids, and bush lilies grow under the huge lichen-covered stems of yellow-woods, umkuthlas, and other giants of the forest. The stream-beds are moraines of mossy boulders populated with thousands of hyraxes, or "rock-rabbits" as we call them. Where the streams emerge from the forest highlands into the open, they go winding through groves of European weeping-willows and are often full of trout imported from England and America, which flourish in our mountain rivers and streams.

After Mafeking the train went through the fascinating semi-desert game-country of Bechuanaland where we spent our pocket money on carved dolls representing all sorts of wild animals, and carved by the natives of these parts, who sold them on the plat-forms of the stations. They also sold beautiful skins and karosses.

The funniest experience I had was buying an "ivory" bracelet from one of them. I imagined it to have come from an elephant which they had hunted along with the other animals whose skins they sold. Inside it was the legend: "Made in Birmingham." It was celluloid. Woolworth had got there before me.

There is a great charm about this country although the pep-pery red dust gets into one's eyes, mouth, and ears through every chink in the train; it is terribly hot; and the country is flatter than a billiard table. I used to stay for hours on the observation balcony watching the endless horizons reeling past.

> "Where each horizon by a vaster swallowed
> Repeated but the bareness of the last."

We often saw ostriches, eland, sable, and other wild life. Though it is waterless, this part of the country is well wooded and full of tall red ant-heaps sometimes rising to a height of twenty feet. As one approaches Rhodesia the scenery becomes more and more park-like; granite hills become more frequent and more fantastic in their shapes. Although the Matopos are not high, they look far wilder than any other hills or mountains in Africa. Kenya, Meru, Ruwenzori, and Kilimanjaro are all magnificent, but somehow the

Matopos are more haunting because of their weird shapes. Just as in Spain, the low, rugged lonely Sierras Morenas seem more impressive and awe-inspiring, with their wildness, than all the snowclad majesty of the Sierra Nevada, the Pyrenees, the Gredos, and the Cantabrians.

The Matopos are mostly low jumbled masses of huge round boulders heaped in piles and forming the most unusual caverns and chasms. Sometimes you get a solitary boulder two hundred feet high perched like a rugby-ball for a place-kick. Sometimes you get mushroom-shaped rocks standing in lines, and as high as houses. Sometimes, as if the children of giants had been building castles with spherical bricks, you get an amazing design, wherein chance, the laws of nature, and the erosion of water have resulted in far more astounding combinations than the imagination of a Dali or a Heath-Robinson could produce. They sometimes reminded me of those harmonographs in which the mere swinging of a pencil outdoes all the efforts of conscious art. The "hill" I remember most clearly was a small one and stood all by itself in an open space. It was called Finger Kop and consisted of three huge fingers of rock, the central one vertical, with a boulder balanced on top of it, and the others leaning outwards from the same point where their bases disappeared into a jumble of round boulders and trees, each boulder as big as a house.

Whether we detrained either at Balla Balla (which means Koodoo) on the West Nicholson branch-line, or at Insiza on the Main line, we were equally distant from our destination, Belingwe, about one hundred miles away. The Shabani line had not yet been built. We could see the huge pointed peak of the Belingwe Range, four or five days' journey away by ox-waggon. Along this road to Belingwe my Uncle Archie once killed six lions within twenty-four hours of their taking one of his oxen. The story, with a photograph, appeared in the *Wide World* magazine and excited a great deal of comment at the time, about July 1909.

The road traversed the line of ancient ruins and gold-workings of which the most famous is Zimbabwe. The Dhlodhlo ruins where we often camped are smaller than the Zimbabwe, but more perfectly conserved and more elaborate in their design. In these ruins we used to grub about for arrowheads, ancient beads, and other things, which we gave to our school museums. In the neighbourhood, for hundreds of square miles around, we were always coming upon traces of fortifications and gold-workings, and we also found lead musket balls, oxidised snow-white, which, we pretended, may have belonged to the ill-fated expedition of the Portuguese under Baretto in the sixteenth century.

When we arrived at Belingwe, after celebrating our reunion with my uncle and aunt, my two cousins and I were allowed to clear off into the wild country with the ox-waggon. This leisurely method of travel is surely the best in the world. It leaves the traveller free to make expeditions into the adjoining country, to follow honey-guides and take hives, or to make a hunting detour, yet never get left behind by his bed and kitchen. He treks during the cool of the morning and afternoon, outspanning during the heat of the day to let the oxen graze and drink, and to pass a pleasant siesta under some great shady fig, mahogany, or marula tree. About twenty miles a day is the average trek. The ox-waggon is the traveller's house, or his ship, with bunks and table complete.

I found it a delight when the lions began to roar and to shake the darkness with their voices: I felt then that pleasant and awe-stricken sensation that I was able to experience in the pre-Disney days, when I could still get up a thrill about the "King of Beasts." The cattle were all enclosed in their corral of newly-lopped golden mimosa boughs with their terrible two-sworded lion-proof thorns. We stacked the fires higher and lay on our backs under the stars singing with the natives for the sheer joy of being alive, singing all through the night, falling asleep and then waking to pick up the song again, while others dozed off, who, in their turn, automatically re-awakened to pick up the rhythm.

Sometimes we went to the foot of the great peak, which was full of leopards and baboons. At other times we would follow the course of the Umchingwe and the Ingesi rivers, which were full of hippos and crocodiles. Sable antelope, koodoo, waterbuck, wildebeest, and zebra abounded in these parts, also smaller buck such as impala, reedbuck, klipspringer, duiker, stembok.

When we arrived in some remote place, the local natives would collect around our camp bringing huge calabashes full of beer, and install shelters round our camp. At night, we would hear the snorting, the bellowing, and the fighting of hippos: the roaring of lions: or the barking of baboons in the crags above us. The hippos during the day were quite tame. Shaking their little pink ears with their eyes and nostrils only just above the water, they would come and inspect us from quite near. Once we had to destroy one because he was attacking the natives' gardens and even eating their huts. Our camp looked like a Chicago meat-yard with miles of strips of hippo-meat hanging (as if from washing-lines) to be smoked and preserved according to the native custom. Hippos fight very savagely between themselves, nearly always on land, gashing each other laterally with their terrible tusks, sometimes mortally.

The silver sands of the rivers, powdered quartz, served us daily as news sheets where we could read whatever had happened in the dark and where we could actually reconstruct the story of what we had heard in the night. Sand is a wonderful news sheet. For instance, once near the Sabi river, I saw the spoor of three lions and a small hippo, with some blood. The hippo's spoor disappeared into the water and that of two lions emerged from the water a few yards further downstream, telling of an unsuccessful attempt on their part to get the hippo before it reached its native element. In our camp by the Sabi we had heard all the splashing, the grunts, and the general uproar, as two of the lions had ridden their intended victim into the crocodile-haunted water from which they were lucky to escape.

There seems nothing a crocodile will not eat except an elephant, a hippo, and a sitatunga. In spite of the huge size of a rhino, the crocodiles will sometimes get one: for a rhino's chief instinct is to go after and attack whatever molests him, and in his fury, when seized by the nose or lip, instead of using his huge strength to back out to safety, and fight his adversary on land, he plays its own game by going further into the water after the reptiles, and getting drowned by them. I don't know what sort of a protection the sitatunga, the most aquatic of antelopes, uses against crocodiles, unless it is his own natural wariness. As for the waterbuck, the queer creosote-tarry taste of its meat may render it unpalatable to crocodiles.

There are many things harmless enough to us which are deadly to reptiles. For instance the drop of nicotine that collects in the stem of a pipe will kill a big python instantly, as if it were prussic acid.

Up from these two streams which alternated between still, acacia-shaded pools and rapids, going downwards as if in steps, steep mountain sides sheered up on each side covered with rocks and trees. Our camp in 1917 was at the mouth of a small tributary of the Umchingwe before it passed into the Ingesi. This tributary, the Dobi, opened a level space which was shaded with golden mimosas. Along the banks of the pools where the waterlilies and weeds were thick at the side of the rushes, ran those strange little birds, the lily-trotters, with their outsize toes which keep the waterlily leaves from sinking beneath them. They measure nearly as long from toe to heel as from head to foot; with their claws outspread they span as much space as the open fingers of a big man, yet they are not much bigger than corncrakes. Sometimes one would see further down the river small groups of flamingos too beautiful to shoot, although they are a great delicacy. There was also a great variety of other birds, from the handsome golden-crowned cranes and several varieties of herons and ibises, down to the ubiquitous weavers which nested in the reeds or, being infallible weather-prophets, in the surrounding trees, if heavy floods were due that year. There were a great many teal, too, and wild duck; and the surrounding country was full of francolins and guineafowls. The great bustard or paaw, weighing up to forty pounds, was the finest table-delicacy amongst the birds of those parts. It seemed specially created to satisfy the gargantuan appetites with which we returned from our all-day explorations, spooring sable, koodoo, and wildebeest through leagues of broken country.

High above our camp, on the topmost crags, where the baboons barked all day long, the magnificent dark-chestnut fish-eagles with their snowy heads, necks, and shoulders, soared with their laughing cry, from their nests in the forks of the highest trees. Klipspringers perched against the sky on pinnacles and pin-headed footholds: or leaped from rock to rock with an amazing sense of balance. Baboons are the most mischievous and wantonly destructive animals on the bushveld. They will always insist on harming more of a maize or millet crop than they can ever eat, though they do a certain negative good by eating scorpions and insects which they find by overturning the loose rocks and boulders with which that part of the bushveld is always covered. The bushveld is littered in many places with recently-upturned stones. The baboons snatch off the scorpion's sting with considerable skill and pop the scorpions straight into their mouths. I recommend this diet to Mr. Grigson, the hedge-happy English author, "croquer d'araignées," expert on comestible spiders, and gnat-snapper in chief of the insectivorous brigade.

As children, we used to amuse ourselves with scorpions much in the same way as English boys do with chestnuts or "conkers," testing their strength against each other. We used to go round with large biscuit tins covered with panes of glass and, turning up stones, collect whatever we could find in the way of scorpions, centipedes, and tarantulas. We would shake them up together with the scorpions found by other boys, until they fought and devoured one another. I had a big black flat scorpion, about eight inches long, which lasted out for months against all comers until I finally presented it to a baboon chained up outside Mr. Payley's store, Belingwe. The gift was much appreciated.

We were the bane of the baboons' existence, since they live at war with mankind. Seven or eight of us, including some of our natives, would show ourselves half a mile away and approach openly to within danger-notice of the baboons' sentries, which they always post on the summit of the nearest hill while marauding. As our group passed behind a rock or a bank, we would shed two or three of our number (the armed ones) and the sentries of the baboons would remain unsuspicious, though always on their guard, thinking, when the group appeared again, that it consisted of the same number of humans as they had originally sighted. The main group would then sit down in full view of the baboons. The sentries could only count up to four or five, and had we gone with a smaller group, they would immediately have noticed that some members had not shown up again from where the group had momentarily disappeared. This would have so alarmed them that they would have called off the rest of the troop in the knowledge that they were probably being encircled or stalked by the humans who had not shown up.

Those of us who had stopped out of sight would make a wide detour until we came within range. Then would begin a race on the part of the baboons to reach the krantzes at the top of the range. With their Old Man bringing up the rear they would race up the hillsides scampering on all fours, but standing up to help their youngsters over the difficult places, even spanking them, in human fashion, if in curiosity they looked back or lingered. The nearest we generally managed to get to them would be about four hundred yards, and we fired across the echoing valleys and canyons, making more noise than inflicting casualties. The baboons would slow down with weariness every now and again, till the next bullet put another spurt into them and they scampered furiously once more for a few yards. Eventually they would all have disappeared, except for casualties, into the rocks that crowned the hill.

One day, having left the other natives to skin and cut up a sable bull, when I had run out of ammunition, with one Matabele messenger, who was armed only with an assegai, I blundered into the middle of a huge troop of baboons whose sentry must have been day-dreaming. I spent a very unpleasant twenty seconds in the midst of them while they rushed to and fro collecting their youngsters: and a huge male baboon, with razor-sharp fangs and hair bristling upright, stood up fifteen yards from me roaring and barking in a frenzy of hatred, and only backing off after the others had made their get-away. The baboons would have had us at their mercy if they had known that my rifle was useless.

That same morning, partly owing to the fright we got from these baboons, the messenger and I lost our way—a most unpleasant experience in a rainless country. It was only late in the afternoon, eight hours after, that I noticed we were standing on our own waggon-tracks and only half a mile from camp. I had been all day without water in the blinding heat, and was never so thankful in my life as to see the smoke of our camp rising over the trees.

On that day, too, I had another narrow escape. Things like this never happen singly. I have always found that frights, like cheques, come in bunches several at a time, and then leave you alone for months.

Before the dew had even started to dry on the grass and when one least expects such a thing, in the chill of the early morning, a big mamba had shot out of an ant-bear hole a yard to my right and crossed in front of me at a great speed, raising its head for one terrible moment and then lowering it to continue at the same speed. As I only had a rifle, not a shotgun, I was helpless and merely "froze" where I stood, which probably saved me. Although about ninety per cent. of snakebite deaths in the Union are due to puffadders, which are much more common, the mamba is by far the most terrifying of our snakes since his bite, like that of the cobra, is lethal owing to the fact that it injects poison into the nerves rather than into the veins, as does the adder. Only one snake in Africa seems to have a venom which poisons both veins and nerves. That is the hideous Picasso-blue, cubist-patterned Gaboon viper.

Immediately after this scare, completely out in the open, I saw four majestic koodoo bulls on the edge of a wood of brilliant golden mimosa trees. Their beautiful shaggy silver beards, manes, and tails flashed electrically in the pure morning sunlight; and so did the dazzling white stripes that harnessed their red-golden bodies. They were pretending to fence and foil with their huge horns that rolled over their backs in magnificent spirals to a length of four or five feet. I have seldom seen an Arab or English horse, or a Spanish bull, that could equal them in their graceful and aristocratic carriage. They played and bounded in the sunlight as if they had just sprung forth from the hand of the Maker on the fifth day of Creation. When they caught sight of us, with their noble heads flung back, their horns undulating level with their backs, their great white bushy tails erected, their manes and beards streaming out, and their bodies bounding and scattering dew and pollen, they galloped off barking loudly into the labyrinths of flowers that closed behind them, firing off clouds of golden smoke in their wake.

A giant eland bull, if it is full grown and in good condition, can challenge comparison in sheer magnificence, though not in elegance and grace, with a koodoo bull. The giant elands of East and Central Africa that weigh two thousand pounds, and have a majesty in common with Michelangelo's *Day*, are the largest of all African antelopes. They have bovine dewlaps and curly foreheads like bulls with tremendous necks and shoulders, and broad backs. In their best condition they are almost orange-coloured, with brilliant white stripes. A fine eland bull grazing peacefully among the flowers is the finest expression of tranquil majesty and harmless strength that it is possible to find in Nature. It recalls Jupiter, when he carried off Europa, as the daffodil-coloured bull, in Moschus. Though surprisingly agile, for such massive beasts, and wonderful jumpers and mountain-climbers, they can be ridden down on horseback if forced out into the flat open country. The same applies to all the bushbuck family, including koodoo, nyala, and of course the aquatic sitatunga. A sitatunga can be run down on foot by natives, if they can get between it and the water, for its long swimming-toes prevent it from being able to move freely on land. It relies not so much on its speed as on the ease and strength with which it can negotiate or force its way through thick undergrowth, bush and reeds.

Bull elands are liable to get very fat. They are fairly easily domesticated, not being fierce like their bushbuck cousins. Some friends of ours, the Sclanders, who lived under the Berg, used bull elands for transport in their ox-waggons in Natal. The meat, I have been told, is the best of all the big game venison, but I have never been able to bring myself to shoot one.

I am often haunted by the beautiful forms that symbolised those free happy times camping in the veld. Whenever I doodle absent-mindedly, I find the koodoo, eland, sable, waterbuck, impala and bushbuck nostalgically bounding on to the paper from the old index-finger, whose trigger has now become a pen. The hardest to draw of all these beautiful animals, and the hardest to shoot, both on account of its ineffable grace and its agility, is the impala. It is known as the "springbok of the low-veld," not so much because of any physical resemblance, but on account of its prodigious powers of jumping; these excel even those of the springbok. One of the loveliest sights imaginable is the reddish-golden arc formed by the bodies of a herd of impala as they leap clean over a stream or (so as not to leave any tell-tale spoor) over a wide waggon road. They seem not so much to leap as to fly: and their aerial acrobatics compare with those of other smaller antelopes as the flight of swallows, swifts, or bee-eaters compare with the flight of other birds.

The most beautiful of the larger antelopes, not including the waterbuck (which is more like a stag), seem to belong to what I may roughly call the bovine and the equine categories. I have dealt with the bovine, the eland-bushbuck family of tragelaphidae which includes such superb beasts as the kudu, the bongo, and the inyala—all outsize bushbucks in full-dress fancy uniforms. If anything can equal the other tragelaphs in majesty, it is the great fighting sable antelope, which, except for his horns and cloven hoofs, is to all other intents and purposes a fiery, pitch-black race-horse with a snow-white belly, and the tail and stiff fanlike mane of a mule. His neck is magnificently arched; he snorts like a horse, trots, canters, and gallops more like a horse than other antelopes, which tend to a see-saw movement, lifting the withers and the rump alternately. The generic name of the sable, "hippotragus," describes it perfectly. The sable, his brother the roan, and their cousin the oryx, have terrible annulated horns crescent-shaped in the two former cases, and between them they have accounted for more lions, men, and dogs than the whole of the eland-bushbuck family, of which only the smallest, the bushbuck itself, is a truly great fighter.[1]

On the eventful day when I got so many scares—from getting lost, meeting a mamba, and gate-crashing accidentally on a scorpion-party of baboons—I came on a herd of sable antelopes in a valley beneath me only about seventy yards away. I was looking down on them through the tops of two acacia trees. There was a magnificent bull amongst them but he was almost entirely screened by cows and calves and I only had permission to shoot a bull. The herd, thoroughly alarmed by some chance eddy of scent, had not yet located us nor made up its mind in which direction to move. It was a magnificent sight to see twenty glittering, silken, black bodies poised for flight, with their necks arched, their manes erect, their eyes flashing, and their nostrils quivering. Then suddenly they broke and stampeded, giving me a chance at the bull as he disappeared under the tree-tops. I wounded him and followed the bloodspoor but all I could get from then on were snap-shots at him through the scrub and undergrowth, so that when he was finally brought to bay I only had one bullet left, having foolishly in the early morning dusk pocketed two clips of .303 bullets in mistake for Mauser bullets.

All African antelopes are extraordinarily tough and will carry away with them and survive wounds which would kill ordinary domestic oxen almost on the spot. After an attempt to charge when I stopped him with my last bullet, he finally sank to his knees, covering himself with his horns with which, like a great batsman, he scornfully deflected the spears and knobkerries of the natives who were with me—I felt a lump rise in my throat, though I was then a more-or-less heartless and trigger-happy urchin of fourteen. Finally the spears drove home and he sprawled out dead after a chase of about five miles since the first shot.

---

[1] For its size certainly it is the greatest fighter of them all.

Those queer cattle-like creatures the wildebeest and the harte-beest cannot be compared with such animals as the kudu and sable for beauty yet they are, with the zebras, perhaps the most typi-cally African of all the bigger animals. The peculiar affinity or al-liance which seems to exist between zebras and wildebeest, who always graze together, is paralleled by the wild-horses and cattle on the Camargue. It is amusing to speculate whether it is that they pool their instincts of warning. It may be that the wildebeest, being more intelligent, though less suspiciously alert than the zebras, en-courage the latter to seek the shelter of their horns so as to lessen the numerical odds of being taken by lions—just as one prefers any company to none when bathing in the surf, because then there is less danger of being caught by a shark. (Even one companion halves the risk.)

That all the cattle family are more intelligent than the horse family can easily be seen in the fact that with a horse "out of sight is out of danger"; horses which are being pursued or rounded up will fall to grazing as soon as they out-distance their pursuers and are lost to view. Cattle will continue evasion manœuvres long after they are out of sight, calculating on the likely moves of their pur-suers. Nowhere is this more obvious than in the tactics of wounded buffaloes, which are a diabolical mixture of patience, cunning, treachery and ferocity. The donkey is the only member of the horse family that shows any nous or powers of calculation, and his cleverness is generally perverse. The zebra is nearer to a donkey than a horse.

Both wildebeest and zebra love wheeling round in circus-like formations. A mixed herd of these was stampeded through our camp once, near the Athi river, by a pride of lions who had sent their killers round to the other side of the camp to intercept the fugitives. All except one of both species managed to thunder through the camp without even pulling out or tripping over a single tent-rope. The exception was a zebra that collided fully with a small tent, fortunately empty, and having rolled itself into a sort of animated sausage by the fury of its struggles, it lay like a mummy swathed in canvas with only its head protruding. When we plucked up courage to come out of our tents after the hurricane of snorts and hoofbeats had passed, we flashed our torches around and found the trussed-up zebra. By pulling at the tent ropes, we gradually unrolled the beast which got up and seemed to be either dazzled or stunned, for it remained standing and trembling in the camp all night until just before dawn when it suddenly made off at a gallop.

The colouring of zebras is always said to be a natural camouflage. In my experience a zebra is the most conspicuous of all veld animals, except the many types of light-coloured gazelles, whose pallor is conspicuous and who attract additional notice by their restless movements and the quivering of their tails.

On the veld, especially in the brilliant sunlight, which reduces all colours to undertones and half-shades, or in the bush where the shade does much the same thing, immobility, *not* colouring or design, is the essential of invisibility. The greatest wizards of invisibility are not the animals which carry the most vivid, elaborate, and sensational camouflages (though a leopard is hard to beat) but those entirely drab-coloured and low-statured animals such as the bush-pig and the tiny blue duiker. Nothing else in four-footed Nature can equal the silence and suddenness with which a bush-pig can vanish even when you have almost got your sights on him. In photographs, as to the ordinary eye, the zebra always stands out more clearly than any other animal: the most that can be said in favour of its camouflage is that it is a wonder that a design so bold and glaring does not advertise itself even more conspicuously since the "blurring" essential to all camouflage only becomes effective at several hundred yards.

We can only judge the effectiveness of animal camouflage in relation to our own eyesight, not to that of the lions and leopards, that prey on them. None the less we *can* compute certain facts about the sight of the animals themselves. Most of the hoofed and horned animals seem to be colour-blind and only sensitive to light and darkness, white being the hue that arrests their attention most. They do not recognise shape unless it is in motion. This can be proved easily by approaching animals in the open and "freezing" each time they raise their heads to stare: the game of "statues" or "Don Tancredo" as played in the French and Spanish bullrings is another proof of this. A bull is interested in all rags as long as they move, but he is not interested in a rag because it is red, since he can't see red. It is octopuses that are excited and caught by red rags. The sight of red infuriates them. They are extremely sensitive to colour in every sense and change colour like chameleons.

Another animal that shows up both to the camera and the eye is the hartebeest which, though reddish, occasionally glistens with a silky sheen that catches the eye at a great distance and comes out white in a photograph. There are several distinct species of these extraordinary beasts, all withers and no croup. They are tireless gallopers and can hold their own with a horse. Their close relation, the tsessebe, which is the swiftest of all buck, is something between a hartebeest and an impala, both in size and appearance.

With the new technique of rough-riding, standing in the foot-rests, as taught in the modern British Army, on Matchless motor-bicycles, which are specially adapted to cross-country racing and can go almost anywhere that a horse can go—through bush, up mountains, through mud and over rough ground; anywhere, in fact, save through water, up rock cliffs, or through dry loose sand—we were able to test the relative speeds of various animals during this last war while training in East Africa. On low gear the bikes could get up to forty miles an hour on short grass, and we managed to pass everything after a few hundred yards except hartebeests and gazelles. But the giraffes gave us a surprise. My friend Captain Bruce Penman, who suffered independently the same temptation to chase animals in the same way but at another place and time, was the only one of us who paced the "swift-footed ostrich," and he was very disappointed, he tells me, to find it couldn't do more than thirty miles an hour in open smooth country.

The giraffes, with their ponderous gait, appear to be moving on a slow-motion film, oaring the air, as if it were water, and moving their left legs simultaneously in the same direction, forward or back, and their right legs simultaneously in the opposite direction. They rock from side to side and give the illusion of a clumsy slow gait. Yet they are covering the ground at a very great speed indeed; furthermore, one daren't follow too closely. They commanded the absolute awe and respect, which I expressed in my poem *Dreaming Spires;* for when we came up with a herd of giraffes we generally closed our throttles and waited for them to get out of the way; that is to say we did so after we received our first warning from a giraffe cow that turned round and scattered us like chaff before the wind.

I received two confirmations of this warning—once when I went to ask for a supply of water for my Unit from the Commandant of a P.o.W. camp with my comrade Sergeant O'Dwyer of the Innis-killing Dragoons. The prisoners were making a road through to Central Africa. We noticed a lion's head, freshly severed, lying on the ground, with the skin pegged out nearby, and thought it was a shooting-trophy. When we had done our business I asked the Camp Commandant: "You've been doing a bit of shooting, sir?"

"No, sergeant," he replied, "this is the most extraordinary thing I've ever seen. In broad daylight today down there in the valley this lion was trying to get at the calf of a cow-giraffe in full view of this camp. He was skirmishing in and out when suddenly the cow managed to get in a kick with her forefoot in the neck. We heard the crash from here. She nearly kicked his head clean off; it only required a knife to sever it. We went down and skinned it and brought back the head which one of my Italian P.o.W.'s is go-ing to stuff as a memento of such a strange occurrence. You see there is no other mark or wound on the skin of the lion." I thought he might be pulling my leg but an Italian P.o.W. later told us the same story.

The other confirmation of the warning can be seen inside the giraffes' cage in the London Zoo, where the bull, having got angry, left the dunt of his hoof without apparently hurting his hoof in the least. They say that the kick of a giraffe next to a whack from the tail of a blue whale, a finner, or a sperm whale, is the fourth most powerful blow that can be dealt by any animal in the whole world. I heartily believe it and advise all bike-chasers of big game to lay off from chasing giraffes: that is, in case I have given them any ideas of doing so in this book.

One of the thrills of our holiday in Rhodesia was a trip to the paintings of the Bushmen in a cave in one of the spurs of the main Belingwe Range, from which the view over the Matopos was truly superb. The scrub country between the ranges was full of rollers, or bluejays as we call them, including the European kind, which I have seen occasionally in Cornwall, and which abound in Provence, Spain and Portugal. But the most beautiful of these very beautiful and pugnacious birds were the lilac-breasted and racquet-tailed rollers; the former a blend of azure, pale blue, lilac and violet, with long swallow-tails, and the latter a similar bird with spatulated tips to the swallow-tails which give an extra grace to its gyrating flight and make it look like a gigantic butterfly. I have seen a marvellous battle in the air between one of the enormous white-necked ravens that roost on the crags of Kilimanjaro and two of the lilac-breasted rollers, like spitfires attacking a heavy bomber and making bits of it fly all over the sky. These rollers always perch on the topmast twig of the tree and insist on driving most of the other birds away from their vicinity.

The ground-scrub and undergrowth was always full of many kinds of birds. Wax-bills (relation of the goldfinches) that ranged in colour from red to blue varieties. Then there was always the "Go 'way Bird" or grey lory, of which I have spoken already, long-tailed strikes like magpies, and the beautiful, long-tailed, tiny doves which are about the commonest birds northwards from Mafeking to the Zambezi river.

The rivers in Southern Rhodesia were always full of fish which the natives trapped either by wedging cone-shaped wicker traps between the stones in the rapids, or else by pounding the beans of the mimosa thorn-tree and throwing the powder into the pools. The fish were drugged by this and came to the surface so that they could be raked in with reeds; the fisherman always of course keeping an eye open for crocodiles which can flick a man into the water with a blow from their tails.

We learned some amusing games as children, up in Rhodesia, from the Matabele and Mashona boys of our own age—one was a sort of cricket, in which the bats were toy assegais. The two sides, armed with pointed throwing sticks, formed up on each side of a mark, standing in open order, and facing at right angles to the line they formed. The bowler, from the dividing mark, bowled a huge potato-like root (whose native name I forget) the size of a melon, in a direction parallel to the line of the rival team and about three yards in front of it. The root was of an irregular shape and bounced unpredictably while the "batting side" tried to transfix it by throwing their small assegais at it. Then the "ball" would be returned by the other side. If the "ball" was speared by a throw before passing the last of the file it counted to the batting "side," if not, it counted to the "bowling side." Thus one was spared the monotony of cricket, for each team had a collective innings at every second ball!

The Mashonas held several dances and festivals while we were on our holidays in Matabeleland, and I could not help being struck by the superiority and sprightliness of their music over the monotonous droning of the Zulus and Matabeles, though a war-dance by the latter when in full costume, with ostrich feathers, shields, and spears, is an unforgettable sight. One feels the ground tremble beneath one's feet and gets caught up and exalted in the savage rhythm of it. D. H. Lawrence would have loved it; and it seems the one thing that has survived their communisation by Tchaka, Dingaan, and Mzilikasi.

VI

OCTOPUSES

As a child I never had any difficulty in raising money. Besides selling the horns and hides of the animals I shot, I could always find buyers, among the natives, for the lories' feathers and other "medicines," and there were various other ways in which I could make money so that, with hardly any pocket-money from my parents, I was usually richer at school than the sons of Johannesburg Jews and Kimberley diamond merchants. I always wondered where the point came, between my boyhood and majority, at which I lost this amazing faculty of money-getting, so that, between the ages of twenty and forty-five, I was completely poor.

When the mailboats came in from England, some of my school friends and I heard how the Canary Islanders dived for money; so we tried to set up a rival industry, as we were expert divers, by hiring a boat in Durban Harbour and asking the passengers to throw coins from the decks of the liners. All flat silver coins are easy to catch under water because they proceed very slowly, remaining almost horizontal, and zigzagging obliquely, a foot from side to side, for every inch they sink downwards. If you are on a level with them you can see their shadows pencilled beneath them, and if you are underneath them they show black discs against the daylight above. A silver coin is easy to catch up from above, if the sun is shining, because it glints rhythmically, and by letting the breath out of your lungs you can be down on it, like a hawk, to a depth of fifteen or twenty feet, put it between your teeth, and then pull for the surface with open palms, arms, and legs before your lungs give out.

The Durban water-police came along with a launch to our display, and stopped us on account of sharks, just when we were beginning to do famously. The twin brothers Archie and Roy Meickle, Hamish Charteris, a kaffir-boy Umcutchuluza (working for the Meickles), who somehow or other had learned to swim almost as well as a white child, and I, all felt that our talents were being wasted, and so we decided to shift our diving-pitch, to where there were less water-police. Thus it was that we used to make excursions to Isipingo and other places outside Durban, seaside resorts where there were Jews and other seaside visitors from Johannesburg. In many of these places swimming baths had been blasted out of the rocks. The baths were filled and cleaned out by the high tide, but remained clear and still at low-tide. Apparently they were municipally owned, for no private owner ever came to drive us off, even though the baths often got flooded with ink from octopuses during our shows; for we started staging octopus-fights. These shows became so popular, however, that the majority of people were always on our side. We almost cut out the Indian jugglers since, to an inland person, catfish (as we call octopuses in Durban) are far more spectacular than any snake. Though we never had one weighing more than about ten pounds, that was quite enough to shake us about under water.

The system we employed was to explore the shelves under the rocks with gaffs and the minute one felt something yield to yank it out at once before it could even get a hold on its own refuge; thus we would catch two or three octopuses and hide them in a basket. Then we would go bathing in the swimming bath along with the Johannesburgers. Next, an octopus would be surreptitiously introduced into the bath and one of us would shout to the bathers: "Hey, people, look out, there's a big kind of animal in the water there, which sucks all the blood out of your veins." Those of us who were in the water would simulate panic *(pour encourager les autres)* and soon the pool would be empty, with an ideal circus of spectators, ready set all round for the show to begin. If it looked as if there were non-visitors-from-up-country in the pool, we would pretend there was a sea-snake. That would fix them for the time being, and they would join the Johannesburgers on the rim of the pool. The rare black and yellow sea-snake is almost as deadly as a mamba. It *is* a sea-serpent, and those fat-heads who don't believe in such things should go and see it at the South Kensington Museum, all complete with its rudder-like tail, fangs, and all.

When we had cleared the pool we would begin a show that put all the snake-charming acts of the Indian jugglers in the shade: because, to an amateur, an octopus is a far more horrible, slimy, hideous, venomous-looking, and altogether creepy monster than the most dangerous reptile, though in a shallow pool it is innocuous. In character, however, it is the nastiest piece of work in Nature. It is completely cold-blooded, can feel no pain, and will even crawl through a fire on the beach, instead of going round it, in order to return to the water, yet it will crawl around any obstacle with the greatest cunning in order to prey on a fellow-octopus. It does not mate, even, being a self-fertilising hermaphrodite and a cannibal.

When we had got the spectators agog we would dive in, all four of us, leaving the native lad on the edge to indicate where the octopus was if he shot away, with his jet-propulsion apparatus, out of range of our under-water vision. Sometimes he would squirt a cloud of ink at the start but the four of us would dive through it together, and he would soon be driven out of his cloud, retreating and trying to manufacture more ink as quickly as possible. In the end by means of splashing and diving after him we would corner him at the shallow end of the bath.

Whoever caught the octopus first would let it get a grip all over him with its feelers; then rising up from the waist-deep shallow water, he would pretend to struggle, scream, and howl: "Help, help, it is strangling me and sucking all my blood!" We would pretend to be trying to help our comrade but to be terrified and unable to save him. Then we would tug at the tentacles, trying to detach the suckers, which gave kiss-like smacking reports as they were detached, in a manner guaranteed to turn the stomachs and send a quiver up the spines of the toughest Johannesburgers. They would see the skin blistered with red sucker-marks, which were quite painless, but looked nasty enough.

After that one of us would unscrew the bottle of red ink which each one of us carried in our slips, and we would roll about, milling and yelling in the shallow water, as if in a welter of "blood" and foam: till the boy who had the octopus would turn it inside out by catching in one hand the flap of the aperture at the root of the feelers, and pushing the head of the beast with his other fist so that it went through, as one does when unrolling a pair of socks. Though this operation requires practise and skill, and it gives a sickening "plop," it paralysed the beast at once. Otherwise one bit it deeply between the eyes which killed it instantaneously: but the former system was far juicier as it produced some extraordinarily hair-raising gurgling and sucking noises, which nearly made the audience jump out of their skins. We would then offer to repeat the show if, when the native boy had taken round the hat, the results were satisfactory.

We had such a success with this act that it made no difference when the visitors knew it was staged from the beginning. They would clamour for the show as soon as they saw us coming with our baskets; and then for one encore after another, till our octopuses were finished. Some days we had three pounds or so in the kitty. The pierrots and jugglers came to hate us at all the resorts.

Our shows were put an end to by the fathers of my three companions, when they discovered about our shameless and mercenary behaviour. My father, thank heaven, never found out.

The native boy, Umcutchuluza, and I are the only ones of this troupe left alive. Charteris was killed by a shark while bathing near Beira. When I last came across Umcutchuluza, in 1926, his job was to push his arm through miles and miles of sperm-whale intestine, searching for lumps of ambergris—a well-paid, soft job, but a smelly one.

The small octopuses which we used for our shows are not to be confused with the deep sea squid of which I once saw a huge piece stranded at Park Rynie, Natal. These squids are said to be the biggest inhabitants of the globe, when they reach their full size. Unlike octopuses they have ten tentacles, two longer and thinner than the others; their bodies are in two sections, whereas the octopus is single; they are self-fertilising hermaphrodites, like octopuses, and give birth by growing an extra feeler which detaches itself, drifts away, and then turns into another squid. Unlike the boneless octopuses, they have a big oval bone in their bodies.

I have seen sperm whales vomit big pieces of squid when harpooned; and when they are being cut up one finds fairly big ones inside them, about twelve or thirteen feet long. The claws which squids have in their mouths are almost exactly like lions' claws. They are the reason for the ambergris which solidifies softly around them, in the stomach of the whale, to protect the intestines from being scratched by them on their way through. Claws are always found embedded in lumps of ambergris. At the whaling station you see natives pushing their arms through endless sleeves of whale-intestine in search of these pellets which are extremely precious.

Both the squid and the small octopus are excellent to eat, and even their ink is a great delicacy. In Natal we eat them as curry, but in Spain they either fry them in flour after battering them with rolling-pins, or between stones, to make them tender. Sometimes they stew them in their own ink.

In the Mediterranean the small octopus grows dangerously bigger that it does on our coast, and it can give one a bad time under water since it is sometimes just too big and tough to be turned inside out; and that is the only way to kill them properly, except by biting or cutting them so as to sever the vital nerve between their eyes. That one fatal spot, in the pre-goggle days of diving, was difficult to locate through a mass of weaving feelers, especially in the thick super-salty water of the Mediterranean, which tires and itches the naked eye under the surface far more than the almost fresh water of the Indian and the Atlantic Oceans. An octopus is almost invulnerable except in the eye-nerve, or when he is pushed inside out. No amount of hacking and cutting until he is literally in ribbons is effective elsewhere.

Thanks to Mr. Gilpatrick, the pioneer "Goggler," who put submarine vision on a level with ordinary aerial vision and paved the way for the frog-men, the risk of not locating the eyes of the beast has been obviated for ever. I hear, with gratitude, that he names me as one of the pioneers of the frog-men in one of his famous books. This revolutionising of underwater sight means that the danger of being drowned by an octopus is considerably lessened, though, if one is without a knife and the octopus hidden in a cleft, it might possibly exhaust and drown one, even with goggles on.

I had a slight refresher course in octopus fighting during my stay by the Mediterranean and again, in 1924, when I was on the rocks at Umdoni fishing with Judge de Waal, the son-in-law of General

Botha and, like his father-in-law, a tough Boer of the old school.

We were fishing on a ridge of rock above a clear, transparent pool about ten feet deep, when I saw a big catfish at the bottom. It was barely visible on the yellowish carpet of seaweed for these creatures change colour like chameleons; it was a mottled colour, like a small leopard-skin rug, and its lidless blue eyes, the nastiest thing about it, were scrutinising us both. I jumped in fully clothed, went for it with my hands and kicking with both feet as hard as I could on the bottom broke its hold on the seaweed and brought it to the surface wrapped round my shoulders and neck. It was a big one, weighing eleven pounds. Judge de Waal, who had hunted every kind of wild beast, told me afterwards that he had to sit down when he saw it, for the strange perfume, and the sucking sound of the octopus had really made him feel faint and sick. Hearing that from such a tough old campaigner, I was able to understand the gruesome pleasure derived from our youthful antics along the populous South Coast seaside resorts.

VII

PEACE COTTAGE

ONE of the places I loved best as a child was the Umthlanga lagoon. It was then full of fish which have since been decimated by the irresponsible discharge of chemicals, etc., into the river upstream. We had an old ramshackle cottage in the middle of the forest about half a mile to the north of it. My uncle called it Peace Cottage and it was situated about thirty yards from the beach. It was connected to the lagoon by two buck-paths and an unmetalled road. At night it was lit up by a sort of Morse code of electric blue thunderflashes from the inrolling breakers which shook the house and made the candles tremble with every crash, as they cascaded into phosphorescence, illuminating the twisted boughs of a giant milkwood tree which over-arched the house. The branches of this tree descended to sweep the ground on one side, fifteen yards from the main trunk, and formed a triumphal arch for the carriages and horses of our visitors.

In a glade nearby, under two other milkwood trees, was a stable with the huts of Mali, a nonagenarian Zulu, and of Papatom, a French-speaking Mauritian (of an even darker hue than the Zulu) from whom I first learned French . . . of a kind. These two delightful old men were pensioners of my uncle; the former a devout and trouserless pagan, and the latter a devout Roman Catholic, and both the despair of my mission-happy Aunt Jessie. Papatom was employed as a volunteer fisherman.

In front of the house were rocks which at low tide rose out

of the water, and swarmed, in the pools they retained, with cray-fish, octopus, and other delicacies. The pools were carpeted and festooned with green, purple, orange, white, and scarlet seaweed and anemones, and in them, too, scintillated thousands of delicious rockfish, like so many sunbirds and butterflies amongst the brilliant gardens and flowers of the sea. The rocks themselves were covered, one could almost say they were *formed*, in part, by the most lus-cious oysters and mussels—not to mention useful rock-bait.

When General and Mrs. Botha and their family came down to stay at the Cottage, I was detailed to keep them in venison and to show their sons how to shoot buck; though they were almost grown up. The Boers have more or less exterminated their game. That's one reason why the 1914 Rebellion was so easily repressed, for want of good marksmen. I think that, not excepting Kruger himself, General Botha was one of the greatest, kindest and wisest South Africans who ever lived, whether white, black or yellow: and Mrs. Botha was a sheer delight, unaffected by fame and celeb-rity, and always full of kindness and good-nature.

Among other people to whom my uncle occasionally lent the Cottage were the nuns of the French orphanage at Verulam. I was also told off to see to their needs and to hunt buck for them. Papa-tom fished for them and, being a very devout man, it delighted him to be of some use to co-religionists who spoke the same, or almost the same, language as himself. My uncle also sent a private police-man with assegais and kerries to guard the house, and to chop fire-wood.

The Mother Superior, I believe, was a Countess; a tall and beauti-ful woman with a truly radiant face who could hardly keep from laughing to hear a little white boy rattling off Mauritian patois. I took myself in those days even more seriously than I do now; and I remember how all the younger nuns and the orphans used to laugh when I came in with a buck, made them long and ceremoni-ous speeches, in patois, advising them as to how it should be cooked. Then, having skinned and cut it up for them myself, I fetched panniers full of ice from the mill five miles off, where it frosted into huge blocks, as a sort of by-product of the industry, I believe: for bits off these blocks were always to be had for nothing.

There were lots of pigtails among the orphans: and every day, having ceremoniously taken off my hat with a sweeping gesture to the crowd of nuns and orphans who assembled on the verandah to watch the departure of "le petit monsieur"—I would deliberately rear up my horse five or six times on its hind legs to show off my importance, exactly as I had seen Tom Mix and W. S. Hart do in the Bioscope in Durban. I loved working for them and used to nail up solemn and pompous notices on the milkwood tree, officiously advising them how to go about their daily affairs, in French patois: "Ma Mère et mes Soeurs, quand on se baigne dans la mer, il faut faire attention au backwash et aux requins; il ne faut pas se mélanger avec l'eau trop profonde parce qu'il y a les poulpes et les courants qui sont très forts. Il faut que les orphelins restent dans les eaux calmes et pas profondes. Oui, ma mère et mes soeurs, c'est vraiment comme ça. Signé. Votre serviteur, Roy Campbell." It was Papatom, who could neither read nor write, who told me to address them as "Ma Mère et mes Soeurs" and to put at the end "Signé. Votre serviteur." I cannot reproduce the original mis-spellings or the patois.

It was about this time I got my first write-up in the English and Dutch Press.

About 1914, just before the war, a Dutch professor (whose name I forget) and his wife came from Leyden University to Natal with introductions to my father and uncle. He was on a scientific mission to procure the foetus of an aard-vark, which apparently has some unique characteristics in its development, and also a live female for the Zoo in Amsterdam. This elderly professor and his wife were a charming and cheerful couple, and I was told off, as the naturalist of the family, to entertain them.

I was getting quite well known in this line; even the London papers had devoted several paragraphs to my precocity as a naturalist, when, in the absence of my father, I represented him in entertaining Sir Evelyn Wrench, the President of the Overseas League, and his sister, on their voyage round the world. I was only twelve at the time, but I was able to show them the animals, and explain to them some of the lore of the forest. Sir Evelyn made me the chief subject of one of his weekly letters to the Press in England, and the gist of it was that he thought he had discovered a prodigious pocket-Munchausen, but that he found from game-wardens and scientists that all the marvels I had recounted were scientifically correct and true.

As a night-hunter, I had very good night-sight and although we never shot aard-varks I had seen them when I was sitting up for porcupines and bush-pigs. Though common and ubiquitous and useful, because they kill so many white ants, aard-varks are hardly ever seen. But their holes are everywhere—a constant danger to horses, especially to imported horses, and a refuge for pythons and mambas.

My father and uncle asked me how I would catch an aard-vark, because the females required had to be caught alive. I abandoned the idea of trying to catch them at night but asked for a gang of natives with spades. We dug a trench, sixty yards away from a fresh hole, about thirty yards long and eight feet deep, roughly bisected by the line of direction in which the hole seemed to be pointing. Then we put a Scotch Terrier down the hole. The result was that the aard-vark tunnelled like mad to get away from the terrier which was nipping its tail. It couldn't turn round in its own hole, and only has one instinct (to burrow) when in danger. It soon came out into the trench but, before we had realised it was there, it had half disappeared through the opposite wall of the trench. We had a terrific struggle to hold it. As good luck would have it, it turned out to be a male; so, although the holidays were ended, I got an extension to go on hunting for the females.

It was not till the third and fifth captures that we secured the required females and this earned me another week's holiday from school. I was written up as an infant prodigy in the Dutch papers of that time: and it was more or less taken for granted that I was heading for a career like that of Selous or Pretorius: or at least that I was going to become a distinguished Naturalist.

Our nearest neighbour at Peace Cottage was a venerable Arab storekeeper. He supplied most of our requirements in the way of fish-hooks, lines and wire traces. His house and store were overhung by the most glorious kaffirboom tree which was in flower throughout the whole winter; for then it shed its leaves, and its silver-white twigs and branches exploded into a conflagration of scarlet blossoms, whose honey attracted swarms of spangled sunbirds, which flitted like moths on viewless wings from blossom to blossom, sucking the nectar. These trees are so brilliant that they seem to glow in the twilight even after the sun has gone down. The sunbirds, of which there are a score of common varieties, are our

African equivalent of humming-birds; their feathers overlap like fish-scales of emerald, ruby, turquoise, and gold.

I can think of no more pleasant manner of idling the time away than to lie, as this old fez-crowned Arab did, in his nightgown-like white robes, in a hammock in the crimson-purple crepuscule which served this dense mass of bloom for a shadow, with the twin forks of his snowy beard lying over his chest and stomach, and reaching almost to his thighs, like the newly-combed and washed tails of two circus-horses. His hammock was of emerald silk with trailing fringes. On his chest was a small pink book which I vaguely imagined to be the Koran, or the works of Hafiz or Firdusi, which always lay between the forks of his beard. From time to time he would pick the book up and scan it, while the sunbirds snowed down thousands of sweet bean-scented flakes over his white robes and whiskers.

The Suluman, for so we and the natives called him, had one end of his hammock attached to the trunk of the tree, and the other to the iron railings of his verandah. With a foot touching the corner of the verandah he would set the hammock rocking like a dream-boat in the ripples of his reveries. His shop was full of native bracelets, beads, catapult rubber, sweets, fishing lines, and hooks; it was always associated in our minds, from our earliest childhood, with Santa Claus, whom he resembled exactly with his brick-red face and red fez, except that he wore a white instead of a red woman's "nightie." In later days he was still a mystery and I shall never forget the disappointment, when, after hoping to engage him in a conversation on Arab or Persian poetry, I found that the little pink book he carried and studied so often was neither the original of Omar Khayyam nor Firdusi nor Hafiz, but Gamage's Catalogue translated into Arabic!

His countless offspring howled, tumbled about, and wrestled amongst the chickens and dogs by the wayside, while his grown-up sons, perfectly groomed and dressed in the European style, with watch-chains and button-holes, served at the counter inside, always with exquisite courtesy. In fact the courtesy of one of them, Ali, nearly cost him his life twice in two hours.

This excellent young man had a passion for a kind of sweet known as Moor Balls, flavoured with anis, and hard as billiard balls, of which they are about half the size. They take about two hours to suck, and are too hard to bite. The shop was full of them. Their virtue is that they last so long, and the natives and Indians are very fond of them. Young Ali became a chain-sucker of Moor Balls, on account of their proximity and abundance in his Dad's shop. Whenever a customer entered, Ali, knowing it was bad manners to speak to anyone with his mouth full, used scrupulously to spit out his Moor Ball into a handkerchief which he kept in his pocket till the customer was gone, when he would resume his chain-sucking.

One day a surprisingly important-looking individual (a European commercial traveller) suddenly turned up in a car. Ali had forgotten his handkerchief. Being so polite, he hated to speak with his mouth full. He hated equally to frighten the newcomer by the sight of a cheek looking like an outsize in gumboils, or the full cheek-pouch of a monkey: so with quixotic courtesy he decided that the Moor Ball, though too big to fit elegantly into his cheek, was just small enough to swallow. Raising his neck in the manner of a hen after drinking, he gave a terrific gulp (later, he showed me how, with his mouth empty); but alas! the Moor Ball rolled into the wrong billiard-pocket—Ali's windpipe, instead of down his gullet. Ali wheezed and choked out an apology to the stranger, meanwhile pointing to the glass jar of Moor Balls and to his windpipe. The stranger held Ali up by his ankles and shook him, but he simply went bluer in the face.

The only thing to do was to call the Suluman, bundle Ali and his Dad into the car, and drive off hell for leather to the mill in search of the Resident Doctor, who happened to be approaching from the opposite direction at about sixty miles an hour, on an urgent call to the Indian barracks on the same road. The two cars narrowly missed colliding. The one Ali was in rushed up a bank and turned a complete somersault, but the occupants miraculously escaped alive. Up had come the Moor Ball from Ali's windpipe; and Ali and his two companions seemed none the worse except for bruises. It was only after the doctor had kindly dropped them at the store and departed again that Ali discovered he had broken his leg; he had not noticed this in the excitement and relief of bringing up the Moor Ball. So after all the doctor had to come back once more.

A similar thing happened to me when I was twelve years old. I had some lead shot in my mouth and a catapult in my hand, and was peering up, like a drinking hen, into a treetop, in search of some fruit-bats. One of the lead shot rolled straight down into my lung; it was too small to stop the breathing passage, but I knew exactly what had happened. I had seen where the lungs were while skinning and cutting up buck. I walked slowly to the chemists at the mill (it was before they had X-rays laid on) and told them. A slight froth came up as I walked and I had a queer cough. They told me not to worry, as I had surely swallowed it. I stood on my head for a long time with no result, then I went to bed. A small girl-cousin, seeing me early next morning lying asleep on my chest with my head over the side of the bed, took a flying leap on to my shoulders to frighten me. This saved my life, for the next thing I knew was that the pellet jumped into my mouth. My relief was unspeakable, and when I told my father about it, I could see by his shocked expression that I had had a narrow escape.

VIII

THE LAGOON

A HUNDRED yards down the slope from the Suluman's shop, the road to Peace Cottage crossed the drift of the Umthlanga river, which, a little lower down, became a lagoon. The road loosely skirted the lagoon, till it turned off near our boathouse at right angles through the bush and came to an end under the great milkwood tree at Peace Cottage. Seaward for two miles, almost from the drift itself, the lagoon zigzagged through reedbeds, touching alternately, with the elbows of its wide bends, the bush-covered hills and precipices at whose base the road wound, and the steep banks of the thickly forested hills across the valley. One of these precipices is still the haunt of a terrible old mamba. There is a ruined pump-house originally intended for irrigation, but finally abandoned because of this snake, which nobody seems ever to see, unless they are unarmed. It is said to have difficulty in sloughing the skin round its neck; the old skin clings to its head in tatters and waves in the wind like a bunch of ostrich plumes, so that the natives think it is one of their dead chiefs "ranging for revenge" in full regalia.

The poor Indian, who was the first to man the pump-house, was killed by the mamba, and buried near our boat-house; his grave was supposed by the natives to be haunted, not only because a pot or a pitcher of food acted as a sort of tombstone to his grave, and was often replenished by his friends, and depleted by birds: but also, probably because the Indians had staged some of their tricks in the vicinity in order to scare the natives and protect the grave from desecration.

The natives are very superstitious about Indians. As children we were infected by native superstition. We were not scared of riding through any of the ruins and obsolete European graveyards in the neighbourhood: yet none of us liked passing this Indian's grave except in company, during the day, and armed to the teeth. We would then quicken our paces, and pass, talking loudly or singing, to keep up appearances. Even in broad daylight I would make a detour, if alone, and go home by way of the shore, which was much longer, rather than pass by the grave with its pot of curry and rice. The exact nature of the spook I never elicited, because the natives were loth to talk of it. But the few items I did gather concerning it were very contradictory. Mnugeni said he had seen it. It was a little fellow about two feet high, just like an ordinary Indian in every respect, but, instead of a head, it had a "candle like those they screw in the roof at the Big House" (electric light bulb) and it was extremely foul-mouthed and abusive. Other accounts of it were even more hair-raising. Some confused it with the river-god or watersprite known as the "Tokolotcha." This gentleman is a kind of super-Priapus, who carries his insignium of office over his shoulder, at the slope, like a Grenadier guard carries his rifle. His head is more in the shape of an ordinary hurricane lamp than a bulb.

Once I disgraced myself by an extraordinarily cowardly loss of nerve, when I had been frightened by some other boys into thinking I had been mortally poisoned, and shrieked for help, rolling on the ground. They had given me some madumbi leaves in a lettuce sandwich; this produces a most excruciating, unbearable sensation, which shrinks one's throat and convulses it, but it is a sensation which calls, none the less, for dignity. I was ashamed of my outburst and determined to recover my honour and self-respect by passing the Indian's grave unarmed and at night, putting some rice on it to prove I'd been there.

I was about eleven or twelve at the time and had ceased, theoretically, to believe in ghosts. I went out three times on three different nights but was overcome by fear each time and returned before I reached the grave. Then I hit on a compromise, and decided I would go armed. When I was sure that my mother and brothers were fast asleep, I got up about midnight and went out under the milkwood. There was no wind: the skanchals, crickets, and night-jars had the whole forest creaking and chirping; I could hear, too, the distant roar of the frogs and bullfrogs from the lagoon, and the sigh of the surf at low tide. The night was cloudy but the moon was nearly full.

I got on famously until I was only twenty-five yards from the grave, when I became aware of two luminous eyes staring at me with a blinking yet devilish malignancy. The roar of the frogs, now that I was near the lagoon, was all but deafening, but it was heart-ening like the roll of drums, and I could hear each hooting-frog separately as its shriek went off like an engine whistle amid the general uproar. I was terrified, but the noise of the frogs gave me courage: and I was still sane enough not to shoot, in case it might be some Indian practical joker trying to scare me away from the grave. I pressed up the safety-catch of my shotgun and in a very shaky voice, which must have been drowned in the din, asked who-ever it was to come out of the shadow, or I would fire. The eyes continued their terrible gaze. They were far more terrible than the eyes of lions or hyenas. They seemed supernatural. There was no glint for them to reflect since the moon was veiled, yet they were distinctly and brilliantly luminous. What is more, they seemed to be eating, like nitric acid, into my very heart and soul with their terrible, gloating, and loathsome glare. I could bear it no more. My scalp bristled with terror. Uttering a fervent prayer, I aimed and fired a charge of buckshot.

To my amazement the two eyes separated about a yard apart, and went out. Then after a second or two, like fiery stitches tack-ing up into the air, flew two harmless fireflies, unhurt, though dis-turbed by the hot wind from the whistling buckshot as it passed. They had been sitting about ten inches apart on two slightly wav-ing straws stripped from some sugar canes, which the monkeys had left in a tree as they dragged some cut canes after them into the forest. The two straws, moving almost imperceptibly to and fro, had given an air of frowning concentration and intense animation to the two sparks of the flies. Had they not been the only two flies abroad that night, I could never have made such a foolish mistake. But such are the powers of the imagination, when heightened by fear, that these flies had become really the most terrifying experience I had ever had. But frights never come singly.

As soon as my heart had started beating again I went gingerly forward and scattered my pocketful of rice on the Indian's grave; then I decided to dash home via the beach as it was less ghostly, deceitful and incalculable than the bush. To reach the beach I had to negotiate about a hundred yards of bush, but the moon had come out, so I made a dash for it. Although I was relieved to be still alive after my fright, I had by no means regained my equanimity and was still trembling.

No sooner had I got on to the buck-path leading to the shore than there was a clatter as of twenty wood-pigeons in the tree overhead, and the most dismal outcry in what seemed a human voice. Then a great white shadowy form rose into the faint moonlight and vanished in the sky. To me it looked like a white-shrouded man, with a black face, and it seemed about six feet tall. I raced for the beach, tripping over monkey ropes, falling, and recovering myself and my gun several times in my panic, before I reached the shore.

No one was ever able to tell me, until years afterwards, what I had seen, and everybody thought I was a liar, even if they did not say so. I put it down to hallucination or some Indian's jugglery. It was only in 1943, when camping out near the mouth of the Juba river in North-East Africa, that I heard this terrible and unmistakable voice again—"like the shriek of a lost soul being hurled into the bottomless pit"—as Finney describes it in Roberts' superb edition of *South African Birds*. It was the voice of one of the very rarest and largest of all South African birds of prey—the Great White Fishing-Owl, which at the date of my adventure was as yet unclassified. That was the only time I ever heard it in our lagoon; and I doubt if any white person ever heard it there before or since. In all my years in the African wilds I have only heard it twice. It is unforgettable. The funny thing was that when I saw it I could see no wings at all, only a white cylindrical figure rising in the air, with a black face.

I have experienced an hallucination produced by fear in broad daylight, similar to that which was produced by the fireflies. One

very hot day I was negligent of the path in front of me, and I got
a very big fright from a yellow cobra (the only one I ever saw in
thick bush country). It rose with its head two feet from my groin,
was too close for me to fire, and I had actually to knock it sideways, as it struck, with the barrel of my shotgun, before stepping
away and killing it. For an hour or so afterwards I was "snake-
happy"; afraid of putting my foot even on roots, or bits of decayed monkey-rope which had fallen to the ground. About twenty-five yards away in a dark patch of shadow the coiling root of
a tree lay across the path, bare on top but growing into the ground
underneath. There was a bush-shrike sitting on it. I caught the
movement of the bird at one end of the root; then I saw the dark
coil of the root, about nine feet long, lying across the path. The
bird immediately became (for me) the head of a mamba and the
root the body of a mamba. I let fly at the head; the "body" lay still.
So I thought I had missed and fired again. I went up and to my
astonishment found a root and a dead bird instead of a snake! Mnugeni, the native, who was behind me, thought I had gone mad but
of course he had not been near enough to death to get the stimulus
of the first fright which had upset me. He did not let me forget
about it for a long time. If ever he wanted to annoy me he would
make the sound of a bush-shrike, or hop about on two feet together
as it does on the ground.

On some nights when the fireflies really came out in all their
glory, the lagoon, the reed-beds and the steep slopes of the forest
were a magnificent sight. Myriads of cross-stitches of fire reflected
in the still black water, with the reflection of the stars, made a
faint green fictitious Aurora Australis. The reeds seemed to be
furred and frosted with green light, and I can believe the story of
Dr. Gorgas, who during the Cuban War performed a serious operation by the light of a glass jar full of fireflies. As we rowed singing over the water, we used to put them in the hair of whatever girls
we had with us in the boat till they shone like the Virgins of the
Macarena, the Sagragio, and Our Lady of the Star, in the shrines of
Seville and Toledo. The girls looked so fine that they didn't seem
to mind having to comb the flies out of their hair afterwards; in
fact, we generally did this for them.

These lagoons are a feature of the African coast which is extremely poor in estuaries. Few of them run out into the sea except

at intervals when they are flooded and force the sandbanks which dam them. Their release is often a superb spectacle, especially when the mouth of the lagoon has to be opened artificially, because the breakers in their incessant crash and thunder have piled up the sandbanks so high that the flooded river is unable to force them out, but goes on accumulating water. This floods and damages the inland plantations, and threatens the vast and valuable nesting places of the myriads of white egrets, which destroy our locusts for us, and constitute, with the migratory European storks, one of the greatest blessings and ornaments that the Almighty has vouchsafed both to our country and to my foster-country, Spain.

In cases when the river refuses to burst its dam and deliver itself to the sea, a general holiday is declared in the neighbourhood. Indians turn up with spades and hoes and start digging a trench to connect the lagoon with the sea. No more than a trickle is required to initiate this colossal spectacle of power and beauty. I have effected the junction, on one occasion, when the lagoon was so near the top of the dam that it sufficed to draw a line through the sand with my bare toe to start the seaward trickle on its way. In ten minutes that tiny ribbon of water was a thing of irresistible power, like a gigantic fireman's hose, collecting momentum from the pressure of the thousands of tons of water behind it. If you struck it with an oar, the oar would rebound as from a solid surface of steel or marble; but soon you had to retire, for it began to hollow its banks and might easily bury you, or sweep you out to sea.

As it ate down to the subterranean rocks which underlay the sandbank, it would take on the switchback formation of a series of steep arcs. But it was generally cylindrical in shape and of the same diameter as the London Underground railway tunnels. It was at first black in colour from the mud it had churned up from the bottom; then gradually reddening as the inland alluvium came down in its wake. This horizontal waterspout, striking against the seven ranks of the advancing combers, would crush them down beneath its weight. They tried to swerve in, vengefully, and attack it from the side, sending up huge fans of spray and recoiling on themselves in frenzied whirlpools, as they finally collapsed, only to be ridden over by the next cavalry-charge of foam that swerved in once more to try and attack that droning cylindrical torrent from the side. The frontal percussion of this torrent was so strong that only the faintest undulation showed each time where it cut through the breakers; and they made no headway in their sidelong attack. In half an hour millions of tons of water and mud would have rushed through the outlet, finally to burst the whole dam, and redden the sea for miles around.

As the lagoon emptied itself, it shallowed down to sea-level, leaving sandbanks dry or ankle-deep, where one could pick up stranded fish in sackfuls, or else chase and cudgel them in the shallow water. This was what the Indians loved. The natives, most of whom had not learned to eat fish in those days, would look on and laugh with a sort of polite complacent superiority, like Englishmen when they see Frenchmen eating snails or frogs.

Once at low spring tide, when the mouth was being opened, the lagoon seemed to overdrain itself. We had been allowed to take the boat out into the channels separating the sandbanks. Before we knew what we were in for, we heard a great roar as of a hundred machine guns opening fire. Through the mouth appeared a steep tidal wave or bore, rushing towards us at a greater speed than that of an ordinary breaker in the surf. At its entry into the lagoon it appeared to be several feet higher than the water over which it was advancing towards us. Unlike an ordinary breaker it was terraced above the lagoon and the water was level behind the crest of its advancing wall of foam. I was anxious on account of my two little brothers, a native who couldn't swim, and my new Mauser rifle which Colin had brought me from Windhoek. Our boat was not a surf-boat but an ordinary rowing-boat made for ferrying men and meat across the lagoon. I told the native and my brothers to lie down in the stern, and from long experience of instructive calculations about surfing (though I had long ago discarded the effeminate surf-board and used my own body for surfing) I decided, as the wave was fanning itself out over a wider area and losing height and power, to try to surf it with the boat, which I adjusted at right angles to the wall of the advancing wave.

When the wave struck the stern I was rowing as hard as I could: the boat tilted to a steep angle and shuddered all through: the native and the boys held fast, but the Mauser came crashing down into the bows and hit me a blow on the knee, which I can still feel in damp weather. Somehow the bows kept in the right direction and for the next three minutes we were treated to a glorious surf-ride up our own lagoon, more exhilarating than anything I can think of that ever happened to me before. Spray was fanning out from the bows as from the front of a speed-boat and when finally the wave died out into a ripple we had been carried about three-quarters of a mile up the lagoon.

One other adventure of a less pleasant kind happened to us when my brother George was rowing and my cousin Nigel, Guy Kimber (a friend, who now owns the most beautiful farm in Natal, "Maritzdaal"), Mnugeni, and I were all out in the boat together. Only George was able to handle a gun, being then about twelve: of the rest of us not one was over six.

An enormous python began swimming after the boat. George started rowing away from it but every now and then took the shotgun to the stern and fired at it; then it would disappear, swim under water and reappear again. Heavy buckshot at forty yards scattered too wide to tell on the slender periscope of the snake. At this, I started howling, and my dear brother, who always rather spoilt and fancied me, wanting to cheer me up, and thinking Mnugeni wouldn't understand English, consoled me thus: "Don't howl, you bloody fool, Roy. It won't eat you. They always eat black kids first."

How on earth Mnugeni understood this when he'd only been with us a month or so, was only aged six, and even today can hardly speak a word of English, I don't know. But on hearing it, or instinctively understanding it, and seeing me drying my eyes, he set up an even worse hullabaloo than I had.

In my previous potted autobiography *Broken Record*, I discounted the idea that this snake could have been concerned with attacking us and thought it might have followed us out of curiosity—since I don't see how it could have got into the boat straight out of the water. (Dr. Fitzsimmons pooh-poohed the idea that one of his escaped pythons could have accounted for the disappearance of a certain "Mr. X"—and I believe in *most* of his opinions.)

Later on, about ten years after, we were followed, at the same bend in the lagoon, by the same or a similar python, at night. It swam right up to the gunwale of the boat, and, not being armed, I gave it a crack with the oar in the glare of an acetylene lamp which I was using to catch mullet. Thereupon we rowed away as hard as we could. All of us, George who was on leave from the Royal Flying Corps, Mnugeni, and I, recalled the previous experience and imagined that it was a python with a screw loose.

In 1943 Dr. Gray was attacked by a python a hundred yards away from this spot, on the bank, which makes me think that somehow this snake knew very well what it was about; and that it must have been the same snake—over the thirty-five or forty odd years separating the original adventure from Dr. Gray's. Dr. Gray only escaped with his life, after a twenty minutes' struggle, because he had a couple of brave and strong friends with him who wrestled with the snake and forced it to release him by jabbing at its eyes with a pen-knife whenever it got a new grip.

That snake is still there inhabiting that part of the reeds and, on my last day's leave in 1944, we shot one of its offspring or relations. This family seems to have left the trees of the forest to dwell in the more inaccessible reed-beds. Pythons are almost as aquatic as crocodiles and easily swim for hours at a time under water.

On some evenings the grey mullet would rise in thousands in the lagoon, and on others there would not be a ripple on the face of the water. The conditions that caused them to rise were unpredictable and seemed not to depend on wind or weather, or moon. When they were rising we used to light our lamps and wait for the fish to jump into the boat. The chief pre-occupation of the fisherman, when the mullet are rising, is to avoid getting knocked out by the big ones striking him on the jaw or behind the ear.

On these nights, every shoal of fish we passed discharged flights of silver arrows, most of which either went clean over or struck the sides of the boat, but the rest fell flapping and slithering into it. Sometimes we had to extinguish the lamps for fear of overloading and sinking the boat.

I have had considerable experience of grey mullet both in South and East Africa and in the Mediterranean when I fished them commercially in the *étangs* of the Rhone Mouth for the sake of their roes which, from Cannes to Montpellier, and especially in Marseilles, fetch a higher price, weight for weight, than caviare: that is to say when they are treated in the right way, pressed between boards with rocks on top of them, and dried and salted to the required hardness. In Provence this dried mullet roe is known as *poutargue*, in Spain as *botargo:* Cervantes speaks of it with relish in *Don Quixote de la Mancha*. The mullet we fished in the Mediterranean were of the same species and sub-species as ours but their behaviour was different. Whereas in Natal one merely lights a lamp and waits for them to jump into the boat, in the Mediterranean, when spearing with an acetylene flare on the bows of the boat, one has to use the greatest dexterity and skill. The mullet are attracted by the flare but only as comets are attracted by the sun just to whizz round it once and away. It is highly skilled work to stop these spin-bowled quick-silvery googlies, yorkers, leg-breaks and off-breaks of greased lightning with a heavy fishspear; the knack comes just as one is despairing of it, for one has not only to be quick but to compute by the depth the number of inches to allow for refraction. I have made from five to seven pounds' worth of francs, during fine nights in September or October, by spearing the thick-lipped grey mullet, or *nègres*, for their roes.

IX

MORE ABOUT PEACE COTTAGE

Quite as memorable as any of our jaunts on the lagoon or into the forests were the long winter evenings at Peace Cottage when my mother would play the piano for us and we would sing the old Gaelic, Highland, or Border songs she had learnt from her grandparents in Scotland.

My mother knew a thousand ways of amusing us on these long evenings, by making all sorts of toys, mostly out of paper. She was a magician with her hands. The great Spanish writer Unamuno, who also had a passion for folding paper into toys, said he was dumbfounded by my mother's toys, which included a paper kettle in which water could be boiled, without burning the paper, over the flame of a candle. When Messrs. Pitman persuaded my mother to show them her designs and she gave them some thousand or so, that famous firm made a big book of them which has sold far more editions than all the books I have ever published—and has been in use for years in all sorts of children's schools and hospitals and institutions for the blind where they have amused hundreds of thousands of people.

These pastimes were invaluable to us when on the occasion I am about to describe we were stranded and isolated at Peace Cottage for many weeks by a flood. In practical things, too, my mother was more expert with her hands than anyone else I have ever known, from sewing to making fishing nets, from invisible mending to mechanics.

A year or two before World War I there was a terrible deluge, during which twenty-nine inches of rain were registered in three days at Mount Edgecombe. Not only was the drift impassable for weeks, but the road was swept away entirely from beneath the mamba's precipice. It happened just at the end of the school holidays. To our huge delight, we were stranded for several weeks at Peace Cottage, and had to live entirely after the manner of Swiss Family Robinson, without any contact with the outside world. All the lagoons along the coast not only broke their banks, but came roaring down with such loads of uptorn trees, driftwood, reeds, sugar-cane, and bits of kraals and houses, that when the fury of the accompanying sea-tempest had subsided and the waves had re-vomited along the shore the total weight of what the river had washed down into them, there remained a record high-watermark in the shape of a barrier of reeds and driftwood, chest-high in places, seldom less than waist-high, a couple of yards in width, and fifty or sixty miles long. It formed the foundation, in some areas, for a new and permanent series of sand-dunes. Most of the other permanent sand-dunes in this area have been formed over the middens of mussel-shells left by the prehistoric beach-walkers (strand-loopers), who are said to have resembled bushmen. On the top of these sand-dunes grow the hottentot-fig, a ground creeper (common all over the French Riviera), with thistle-like flowers and bunches of finger-like prismatic leaves, pointing upwards. The juice of its leaves is a sovereign cure for sunburn. Also there is a plant with fibrous roots and green fleshy leaves in the shape of smooth discs or thinly worn pebbles. These two wild plants grip the sand and save the dunes from wind-erosion, so that they do not shift as in the desert.

The ridge of river-debris, after the flood, ran along the base of these strandlooper-dunes. As soon as the sun came out and we were able to go down on the beach, we walked along this new barrier. Dead buck, cane-rats, bush-pigs, every kind of snake from pythons to mambas, wreckage from ships, life-belts, cases of tinned salmon, oars, planks from lifeboats, hawsers, dead fish and porpoises, smashed crates, baskets, dead cattle, masses of seaweed, and a million different fragments of whatever can run awash or be carried off by wind or water in their most frenzied moods, lay heaped up in this rampart of wreckage. We walked along it choosing different objects which had come from ships, or houses inland; and giving the quietus to half-drowned snakes and iguanas. It took us three days to collect what we wanted along the two miles of shore that separated our lagoon from the next tiny lagoon which made a breach in this rampart and a fire-break also. The stench of drowned animals became very strong; so as soon as the sun had dried it sufficiently and the wind was in the right direction, we set fire to this barrier of rubbish, after sunset.

It was a magnificent sight to see a fire two miles long winding serpent-like along the beach in the high wind. It was clearly seen from Durban, twenty miles away, by Commander Lindsay and all the naval people who were in charge of the battery on the Bluff; and when he put the telescope to his eye he saw the shadows of our diminutive bodies flung up on to the low clouds of smoke by the terrific glare. We looked like the giant spectres in the Brocken, as we danced on the dunes and sang with the elation of the tremendous spectacle of glory, like an inverted Niagara of fire, which we had created out of so much drab and useless rubbish.

Later on there was a hurricane in which Papatom's and Mali's houses collapsed on them. Papatom died from his injuries; Mali survived a brief period but lost a leg. During his delirium, the dear old pagan, Mali, dreamed this dream which shows that Aunt Jessie's descriptions of heaven and her illustrated Bible had in the end made a vague impression upon him. He did not recount it as a dream, but as a fact.

"I died, Inkosan, and my spirit came to a beautiful big house such as white men live in, even bigger than the big house at Mount Edgecombe. Outside this house was a man just like the Suluman, only much nicer. He said, 'Mali, you have died; and you are going to come and live in this big house. But this place is like Durban. You can't come here without pants. A "Bechu" (buckskin figleaf) is no good here. So I'm going to make you come alive again, so that you can go back and ask the white people that belong to you' " (a fine touch!) " 'to give you a pair of pants.' "

He passed away with a smart pair of pants over his arm, which were buried with him—just in case he was refused admittance again by the Suluman-like individual, whom I take to have been Saint Peter. He had probably heard of the latter, too, from the "creole" Papatom, the fisherman.

Papatom, unlike Mali, wore pants. In his room, which was coated with smoky cobwebs, was a burnished crucifix which shone like a star amidst the coils of fishing lines, the éperviers and palangres, the crayfish catchers, the sea-lice catchers, the rods and the reels. Within a suitcase beneath Papatom's bed was an immaculate tailor-made silver-grey suit with a silver-grey bowler hat, which, every fourteenth of July, he would put on in order to walk up to the mill and celebrate this heathen anniversary with his compatriots, all of whom, paradoxically enough, were good Christians.

For a whole week Papatom would disappear and then, late one night, you would hear the strains of the "Marseillaise," in a high cracked voice, piping through the roar of the winter winds in the forest, the thunder of the surf, and the far-off orchestration of the frogs. It would be Papatom coming home and walking from side to side of the road "en faisant le berger," as they would say in Provence with their superb Homeric imagery—as if he were a shepherd urging on its way a dense flock of invisible and extremely refractory sheep.

Whenever reading that dismal poet of Shropshire, I come across the beautiful line about

"Shepherding the moonlit sheep,"

by which was meant hanging from the gallows against the sky with the moonlit fleeces of the clouds around one's knees, the dismal heathen image becomes for me a thing of joy. It is Christianised and jollified by the indomitable little figure of Papatom as he braved the huge night, the Tokolotchas and ghosts, valiantly teetering homewards, like a wire-walker, along the brinks of precipices; crashing through brakes and jungles, and splashing through quagmires in the rear of that imaginary flock of strays and stampeders; and singing that magnificent Royalist song, which by some irony has been selected as the national anthem of a second-rate, corrupt, Levantine-masonic Republic.

Papatom was buried by the saintly old Breton priest, Father Kanqui, in the little Catholic cemetery near the mill. The honey-suckers and sunbirds scatter the jacaranda blossoms over his grave from the silver-stemmed tree which we planted there, and which now, after thirty years, has reached its full height. It looks, when in flower, as if a whole acre of thickly-clustered blue-bells had suddenly been showered up into the sky against the sun.

In talking about our different squires at Peace Cottage, I must not forget Mapupa, a relation of Tom's—my mother's coachman. He was killed in a Faction-fight in 1928 and found lying dead with twenty-five assegai wounds in his body, which shows that he must have put up a good fight. Mapupa worked chiefly for my brother George, but when George went abroad, he often came hunting with me.

Mapupa, though a fine-looking six-footer of a light reddish colour (there were some albinos amongst his relatives), was very much in love with a girl of his tribe who did not requite his love. Nevertheless he was generous enough to wish her no ill. In spite of composing songs in her praise which were in Fourth-Programmese Zulu and of a "modernism" which baffled any attempt to elucidate their meaning, he was a true poet at heart. Every morning, just at dawn, he went down to the seaside, filled his mouth with the bitter froth of the sea, and, spraying it forth with all the strength of his lungs against the level rays of the sun so as to make rainbows, shouted the name of his beloved, "Nongazi," through the flying rainbows that he thus created to her glory. It was an impressive sight to see this great naked warrior roaring forth the name of his Dulcinea against the roar of the breakers. When he had done this about twenty times, he would have cheered himself up no end and be ready to face the day's work.

Poor Mapupa! I felt for him about that time, as I fell in love properly and hopelessly with a grown up lady of the most amazing beauty, for which she and her elder sister were already famous in English society. This lady was not only dazzlingly beautiful but extremely intelligent and fairly fizzing, like champagne, with vi-tality, good nature, wit, and humour. I had to disguise my feelings in order to be able to take her out hunting on the same horse as myself, sometimes riding pillion and sometimes sitting in front. She was a veritable Artemis and learned to shoot like a veteran hunter. She was five foot ten in height, with a figure like a goddess's, and when her golden hair was blown back into my face, I would almost swoon with ecstasy. Moreover, at this time, I was crazily intoxicated with Keats's *Endymion;* this added fuel to my flame and I worshipped this girl secretly as though she was divine. I affected the utmost outward indifference to her, in case she should give me the bird or laugh at me, and it was better to bask in her smile than be given the sack for trying to take liberties. Though reared in England, she came of an old colonial family, and people of her class and mine were imbued in those days with an almost peasant-like sense of honour and chivalry: I was terrified that being too young to marry her (sixteen) I would incur her wrath or ridicule if I declared my passion. I think now that she knew, or guessed, and was probably amused by me, since she had had half the officers of the Natal regiments at her feet and was used to everyone being crazy about her.

These days passed for me in a mood of ineffable bliss mingled with despair. She became a wonderful riflewoman and horsewoman and I taught her not only to jump beautifully on horseback but plenty of other stunts besides. The one I liked the best, because it brought me momentarily in contact with her, was to gallop our horse at full speed, bareback, with her hanging on behind me, straight over the bank of the dune into the deep water of the lagoon, falling with a terrific splash, in which the horse and we two riders would be completely submerged. The horse seemed to love being turned into a water-chute and would charge the bank again and again without any urging.

When the time drew near for this young lady to leave us, for she had to go back to the school at which she was acting as gym-mistress, I decided on the last night to tell her how I loved her—and let her laugh if she must! We were out on the lagoon in the darkness sitting in the back of the boat with a blanket over our knees. My hands in those days were completely calloused from rein, rope, and oar, and I had about as much sensitive feeling in them as a horse has in the outer shell of its hoof. I determined I would take hold of the beautiful Amazon's hand under the blanket and hold it while I told her of my adoration.

I edged my hand slowly to where, squinting terribly, I thought

I saw her wrist disappear, to my right, under the blanket: now I felt the side of my hand was touching the side of hers. It did not flinch away. I said a silent prayer, and with all that breathless excitement with which I launched myself out of the trapdoor for my first parachute jump, I made a convulsive grab for what I had taken to be the side of her hand. It gave easily and tenderly; I could almost imagine I felt it throbbing; for a moment I was in ecstasy; then it coldly dawned on me through the horny callouses of my palm that I had only got hold of a fold in the blanket!

Utterly oblivious, "in maiden meditation fancy free," the goddess sat there humming a tune, with her hands in her lap. She had not even noticed my desperate manœuvre. Sweat poured from my forehead: the bottom had fallen out of my whole universe. All my strength of will and courage had gone into that first effort: my heart nearly stopped beating: I gave up hope.

She left next day. We corresponded for two years after that, without meeting. I was still in love with her months after I came to England. When I passed through Africa during this last war as a mere Sergeant I heard that she was Colonel and Commander-in-Chief of all the African women's services, and still (said my informant) the most beautiful woman in the Services.

Before I end my memories of Peace Cottage, I must recount what happened to a great friend of mine and his wife, whom I like equally well, when they stayed with us there.

This couple have been married twenty-five years and they are inseparable, yet they have never stopped quarrelling since they were engaged. The wife came out from a rather exclusive British girls' school and, though she had been born on the High Veld, she had become over-pommified—for one who has to live in South Africa. They were driving into Durban, by car, from Peace Cottage, and were just skirting the lagoon under a bush-crowned hill, when some natives rushed out of the cane and stopped the car. "Please, boss," asked their spokesman, "have you got your shotgun with you, because we have trapped a python in an antbear hole; we are trying to dig it out but it is very big and dangerous."

We always carried a shotgun in the car, not only in the hope of sniping a guineafowl by the roadside, but for protection against the old mamba by the precipice.

My friend, on being accosted by the natives about this python in the antbear hole, consulted his watch and decided that he just had time to deal with the snake before going on into Durban, where he was due to preside at a court martial that morning. His wife agreed to wait and he left her in the car. He got to the top of the hill just in time to see one of the natives drop right through the roof of the antbear hole (which had suddenly caved in) and sink armpit-deep into the coils of an enormous python which was so taken aback that it pushed its head clean out of the hole in front of the shotgun and was promptly bumped off. The native was fished out of its coils none the worse.

My friend then asked the natives if they would sell him their share of the python for the skin. Upon their acquiescence, he paid them, and hacking off a length of monkey-rope from the bush with his knife, he tied this round the snake's neck, so as not to spoil his uniform with the blood and slaver, and began to drag it down the hill towards his car. Of course, it was still writhing, as all snakes do for hours after death.

When he came in sight of the car, he appeared to his wife to be racing downhill with the twenty-two foot snake after him—according to her pommified interpretation. She immediately started the car in a panic, and drove off to report that he had been eaten, leaving the infuriated husband stranded by the roadside with about three hundred pounds weight of useless python, miles from anywhere, and hours late for the court martial.

On the same hill where the natives unearthed this python, which caused such a domestic tiff, Saunders, the Manager of the Blackburn Estate, on which Peace Cottage is situated, while riding along a narrow buck-path in the long grass, suddenly saw, lying across the path between the long grass, part of a python, at least a foot in diameter and three feet in circumference. A python such as has never been seen before or since! It was in 1924 when I had just come to take over Peace Cottage with my wife and baby daughter Tess, who had both arrived the day before from England. From where he had halted, watching the python, Saunders could see us unloading the waggon. He did not want to shout so he semaphored with his arms, and I understood at once it must be a python or a mamba. While he was signalling, the python slipped over the path and Saunders was just in time to see its tail disappearing in the grass towards a mass of dense scrub about four feet high and twelve

feet wide. It was the sort of scrub which reminds one of an enormous roll of vegetable barbed wire, composed chiefly of num-num
and *wait-a-bit* thorn. The latter is so-called because each barb is
composed of three thorns like fish-hooks bent in different direc-
tions, and when you disengage one hook from your clothing or
skin, you immediately engage the other two. So you have to *wait* a
considerable time in order to get free unless you are prepared to
pull out your knife and sacrifice a few square inches of your shirt
or pants.

While I was cantering up the hill with the gun, Saunders dismounted, and when I reached him he was peering into the invisibility of the dense thicket of *wait-a-bit*. "He's in here all right. You
can hear him shuffling about. A python as thick as you are round
the waist—thirty feet if he's an inch! Twice as thick as any I ever
saw before," he told me.

Dimly I made out the bulge of what seemed a truly tremendous
fold of python but it took us nearly three-quarters of an hour to
find the outline of the python's head since we didn't want to spoil
the skin by shooting at the coils. I must confess I was surprised and
disappointed at the smallness of the head, which I blew to bits. I
reached in my arm to the shoulder and began to pull the dead snake
out by the neck; there had been no mistake about the thickness.
The part of it which Saunders had seen in the middle of the path
was the bulge formed by a bushbuck which it had just swallowed
whole! Digestion had not started so I cut out the buck and gave it
to the natives who by this time, hearing the shot, had assembled;
I did not want my wife to see, on her first day in Africa with a baby
of her own, what had happened to the buck. It must have been quite
enough of a shock for her to be greeted by a snake alarm within
five minutes of arriving at her new home, before she had even un-
packed.

This was not by any means the last of her snake adventures. One
windy day we were both standing in a ravine on the South Coast
and looking up at a great lammergeyer hurtling along on the gale
far above the great moss-draped yellow-wood trees, hundreds of
feet above us. As they crashed their antlers together in the hurricane, I noticed a movement a foot away from my wife's knee; it
just caught the corner of my eye. It was one of the most beautifully
coloured green mambas I have ever seen, having just shed its old

skin. It was swaying and seemed about to strike. Fortunately I had
a stick in my hand, and whisking my wife out of the way, got my
stroke in first. It was a small snake, five feet long. The reason why it
had not cleared off at our approach, as mambas generally do, was
that it was already severely injured. The great boughs, grinding together over head, had apparently pinched it and kinked its spine, so
that it had fallen from a height on to the rocks beneath and this had
partially paralysed it; otherwise it would have struck, and then
there would have been no remedy on earth.

The only man I ever knew who survived a mamba's bite was
Senator Maurice Evans, my cousin Natalie's father. He received a
slight peck, on the tip of his finger, from a green mamba which he
had gashed with his spade and which died as a result. He was very
ill for months, and then became blind for the rest of his life. I have
never heard of anyone surviving the bite of a black mamba.

X

BIRDS

Along the coast was a little ravine called Mpampanyoni, which we loved very much. One of the glories of this ravine was that beautiful birds continually flew across it, as its name suggests, for it was crested on each side by tropical forests. Looking up you would see the lories (which are generally almost invisible in the treetops) suddenly burst into the clear blue air like a salvo of green-and-crimson rockets on a dark night, fairly crackling and sizzling with electric fire. The streamlet which ran through the ravine was often stained crimson, as if a wounded buffalo had bled to death in it, by the copper scales which form the crimson pigment of the lories' wings; when they bathe themselves, it literally "comes off in the wash," as no other birds' pigment has ever been known to do. This pigment is replaced a few hours later by an even more dazzling layer of microscopic scales, which fairly blaze each time they open the quills of their wings.

There are two general main species of lory—green and blue. The splendour of the crimson wing is enhanced by green or blue wing-coverts and black tips to the quills. Only one species of lory, the grey, almost identical in shape with the green, is entirely drab—but it is full of character: a truly satirical and striking bird: Nature's practical joker. Unlike his relatives who frequent the thick lush jungles, he is one of the most conspicuous features of the thorny, sun-dried bushveld. Here, in comparatively open country, he is the bane of hunters. He is known as the "Go 'way" bird from his habit of following humans at a safe distance and squawking again and again, in a piercing voice, the two syllables "go 'way," "go 'way," "go 'way." Like the various types of rhino-birds and tick-birds who give warning to the game on whose parasites they feed, the "Go 'way" bird is a congenital alarmist. Being a vegetarian he is quite disinterested, but he has probably been cursed by natives and Europeans alike more than any other species of bird or animal on the bushveld. He remains, however, the one conspicuous ex-ample of the Good Samaritan as far as other wild creatures are concerned.

In the reed-beds by the lagoon was a sanctuary of snow-white egrets, which assembled there nightly, after flying back in small flocks from all over the country. When disturbed they would rise up in thousands, in the crimson twilight, and fly over their own rose and white reflections in the still, black water. In Africa, as in Spain, they follow herds of game and cattle, which they use as beaters to flush the grasshoppers and locusts: and you can see them sitting on the backs of buffaloes or cattle waiting to hawk the in-sects as they rise. Beloved alike by man and beast everywhere, they are fairly tame and I have several times had one of these beauti-ful creatures rest on my shoulder while riding with cattle. Further up the river on the side of the forested hill was also a colony of laughing ibises. As we rowed past in the night they would take flight and cause the most deafening and devilish uproar of clanging laughter.

In the summer the golden weaver birds stripped the reeds for wicker for their nests; and each leafless reed, tipped with the flam-ing wings of the weavers as they fluttered and sang round their nests, looked like a taper with a flame at the top. During one Holy Week at Seville, I was with a South African friend who knows our lagoon, and when he saw the vast processions of candles and tapers and heard the singing of the thousands of happy Christian people —he asked me: "What does that remind you of?" "Why," I said, "it reminds me of the chooks nesting on the lagoon at home!" "Ex-actly," he replied, "just what I thought myself!"

On the banks of the lagoon wherever they were vertical, kingfishers and bee-eaters tunnelled their nests horizontally into the hard, red soil which overhung the water. You could always distinguish their nests from the holes of rats or snakes, because on each side of the base of the semi-circular opening you could see the grooves made by their folded wings; on a miniature scale these looked something like the ruts worn by chariot wheels on each side of the old Roman roads.

There were at least fifteen kinds of kingfishers on the lagoon, from the huge spotted kingfishers to the two tiny lazuline gems, a little larger than wrens, one wearing a fantastic crest, and the other even more beautiful in its classical simplicity.

To the Zulus most kingfishers are "medicine," with sinister magical qualities, yet somehow I have always loved the kingfisher more than any other bird.

When a day-sighted bird, which is more or less night-blind and which should be back in its nest soon after sunset, takes to flying in the dark, the result is often fatal. Kingfishers seem to be the only birds who do not observe regular hours. Two tiny and beautiful crested malachite kingfishers flew right into the verandah wall of Peace Cottage and broke their necks one dark night. Woodward mentions a similar case in his excellent book *Natal Birds:* and I have heard of many others.

I remember once, when I was doing the last bit of homework I ever did in my life, before running away to join the army, I was sitting under the light on our veranda in Durban, and what appeared to be a dazzling violet and rufous moth suddenly fluttered round the lamp and down on to my trigonometry book. It was one of those exquisite Natal kingfishers, more beautiful than any flower or butterfly in the world, with intelligent, shining eyes, and a pale scarlet beak, a little larger than a wren. It was only dazzled by the light, and it was quite unhurt.

A day or two before, the beauty of a girl had dazzled me in just the same way. She was, and is still, remarkably like my wife (though of course I didn't know that then. So, oddly enough, was my best friend Ian Henderson—he might have been my wife's twin brother). I had fallen desperately in love at first sight with this girl, Gwen, and when I met my wife four years after, it seemed that Gwen's face had been a sort of prophetic pointer to this new polestar of my existence. Gwen had black curly hair, dark eyes and a slightly Jewish profile, with a beautiful slim figure and a high fore-head.

Actually she was one of those dark Welsh girls of the same breed as my wife, a dark-haired Celtic type, with a very white skin, rosy cheeks and fiery black eyes, and a dusky slight fimbriation of the upper lip, almost Spanish. I did not know Gwen's surname but I heard her friend call her "Gwen": and I found out where she lived by following them both in a daze, at a very respectful distance. As she passed me, she had looked straight into my face, but as if she didn't see me, for she was still animated with whatever she was talking about. A shiver of joy and fear went right through me (though I tried not to stare at her) and volted right through my marrow down my spine, into my very boots.

This thing has only happened to me at first sight three times in my life. I know that it was no romantic sentimentality, as I have seen the grown-up lady since; she is a very fine character, liked by everybody, and loved by her husband, with a big family of chil-dren; and she is still exquisitely beautiful at fifty. She was in every way worth the devotion she aroused.

Long after that first shock of meeting, I continued to feel wave upon wave of "ants," as the French call that sort of needles-and-pins that you get down your back after reading a superb line of poetry, or making a good pass in front of a bull, or seeing a picture like the *Assumption* of El Greco or the *Surrender of Breda* by Velazquez. I experienced the same sort of thrill when I first saw, unfurled and hoisted to the roof in the Cathedral of Toledo, the hundred-foot blue pennon which Don Juan of Austria flew from his mainmast at the Battle of Lepanto: and when in the harbour of Gibraltar, during this last war, I heard everybody cheering and ran up on deck of the tanker to see the *Ark Royal*, battered, but still afloat, returning to port. I felt it again when I escaped across the veld in a stolen corpse-lorry from Toledo, under fire from my own friends in the Alcazar. I could see the tremendous silhouette of the fortress burning against the sunset and a huge red and yellow flame streaming from the north-eastern tower, thundering out level in the gale for about fifty yards, and flapping symbolically as if to re-place the red and golden banner that had just been shot down from the same tower by the Red artillery. I took this heraldic flame as a certain augury of victory—which it was!

The face of a girl or a woman can be terrible in its beauty, "Terrible as an army with banners." And I must have been absolutely crazed by the beauty of Gwen's face; for when I saw that this kingfisher was far more beautiful than any flower on this earth, I wanted to give it to her, though I didn't know her to speak to. I had been sworn in by a Recruiting-Sergeant Shell, and was due to leave for Potchefstroom next evening. I might never see her again. Hanging around in the neighbourhood of her house, with a lover's eye, I had subconsciously checked up only the day before that there was a dog on the premises and a father too—but town fathers didn't often possess shotguns. I went to the ice-chest and got out a couple of cutlets for the dog and a piece of liver, which I put in my cadet's mess-tin.

Carrying the little kingfisher with the utmost tenderness I made my way towards Gwen's house in the brilliant moonlight. The wind suddenly started blowing noisily and clattering in the palms and wild bananas; it was blowing from the kennel towards me, which made my offering superfluous. Also it was blowing from the direction of the whaling station and suddenly brought with it such a stench of whales that the whole town was almost asphyxiated that night, as angry protests in the Press revealed next day. Even a dog could hardly have smelt an intruder in that awful stench of whale. Nevertheless I was so grateful for getting past the dog that I left the meat (mess-tin and all) as a present for it next day.

All the Cerberus-episodes, in the descents to the underworld, in Dante, Homer, and Virgil's *Æneid*, Book VI, have always had an intensely intimate meaning for me, owing to my anxiety about dogs when I was engaged in such urgent nocturnal missions as this.

The windows of the house had been shut to keep out the stench, so I started figuring out which would be Gwen's room, examining the curtains of each one in turn, and going right round the house to do so. Eventually I plumped for the one that had the frilliest curtains. I pushed the window up almost imperceptibly with a knife which I opened with my teeth, as I was hanging on to the kingfisher with the other hand. My heart was in my mouth. Though it was in town I was still shotgun conscious, remembering Blackstockings' Dad. Nobody stirred, I popped the kingfisher into the room, and gradually shut the window, and sprinted off home.

Next day I was up at seven and patrolling up and down outside the garden hedge to spy out if Gwen had got the kingfisher. After about half an hour up went the window with the frilly curtains: but instead of my beautiful Gwen appearing at the casement like a suburban Rima, with the kingfisher perched on her finger like an enormous sapphire, as I had imagined, there was her Old Man with a walrus moustache, lathering his chin and singing, in a rather raucous voice, "Waiting for the Robert E. Lee."

I was far too shy and proud to make a successful Romeo and when I did eventually get introduced to this young lady I was so awed by her beauty as to be tongue-tied, so she found me uninteresting. So much for kingfishers! I never found out what happened to the one I released in that bathroom. But I very soon learned a different manner of approach: and I was on the spot all right when, four years afterwards, I eventually met my wife.

Nesting among the kingfishers by the lagoon were two or three varieties of bee-eaters which are simply streamlined kingfishers who live on bees instead of fish—or beetles, as some kingfishers do. The commonest was the brilliant green bee-eater (called the Little Bee-Eater), the size of a swallow, with its neat yellow quills veined and tipped with black. Bee-eaters, with swifts and swallows, are the finest flyers amongst the small birds. I have found the European variety all over Africa, Spain, Italy, and Southern France. South African varieties are found as far north as Lamu on the African coast; and once while sailing a small dhow by myself from Mombasa to Zanzibar, eight bee-eaters alighted on the antenna of the lateen sail, far out at sea. The antenna was almost horizontal and lying at right angles to the course of the dhow, since I was using the sail spinnaker-fashion to make the most of a very faint following wind. These bee-eaters were of a variety I had only seen in Madagascar and the Comoro Islands, a very beautiful species, with a red chest and an emerald green back. They stayed with me two hours, heraldically perched along the antenna, in perfect symmetry, four on each side of the mast, and thoroughly enjoying the movement of the dhow. They were neither exhausted nor thirsty but merely companionable. At about three in the afternoon they all made off in a direction where there was no land, right down towards the middle of the Mozambique Channel between Madagascar and the African coast. This is the only time I have ever seen these beautiful birds over the sea.

I shall never forget the joy with which I first hailed the unmistakable cry "kweru, kweru, kweru," common to almost every
variety of bee-eater (except the little one), when I was in France
working on the pylons which take the electricity from Arles to
Marseilles. "Kweru, kweru" (their native name in Swahili), I
heard their thrilling and joyful cries as they shot like emerald
rockets over the pinewoods between Port de Bouc and Saint Mitre.
I had not known they were European birds: although I knew that
Virgil didn't like a certain bird called Merops Apiaster which fed
on his bees in the *Third Georgic*, I didn't realise it was the bee-eater.
Although they did not build their nests in our lagoon banks, we
once had a visit from a large flock of carmine bee-eaters, the rarest,
largest, and most beautiful variety; and as they rose from the reeds
it looked like a part of the battle of flowers at Nice or Barcelona,
with red and blue flowers pelting to left and right.

Again I saw a wonderful sight when clearing jungle in a fever-
stricken camp somewhere south of Mombasa, with an extremely
smart young soldier, the Free-French Corporal, Paul de la Haye
Duponsel of Tamatave, who had been working on the crocodile-
factory near there when we took over. He had volunteered with
our unit during the reduction of Madagascar.

Duponsel and I had finished clearing a proper barrack square
leaving nothing except the two baobabs beneath which our hut
stood. Then we dismissed the Askaris. This banda or hut was made
entirely of coconut palms but under the previous occupier it had
collected a vast number of tarantulas, scorpions, centipedes and a
pair of cobras under the floor. We chased these out by burning
sulphur and killed most of them as they crawled out. We felt much
cleaner and less creepy. Our only water supply consisted of a pile
of green coconuts, each full of ice-cold milk even on the hottest
day. The local water was brackish and purgative so we sat enjoying
our well-earned rest, each with a green coconut in his hands three-
quarters full of milk, and brimmed to the top from our gin ration.
We had set fire to the long grass, the scrub, and the palmetto surrounding our smart new square of red sand. As the flames began to
roar and crackle through the dry scrub, clouds of smoke-drunken
and half scorched insects rose up: and we were watching the black
fork-tailed drongo shrikes as they dived through the smoke, hawking at beetles and bumble bees.

Then suddenly I heard the high-pitched stirring cry of the bee-eaters, and, looking up, I was more than delighted to find that there was a great swarm of two or three hundred carmine bee-eaters, like a shower of roses falling out of the heavens. They were about to do us the honour of visiting our grass fire, and of giving us the most wonderful display of aerial fireworks that I've seen since Peace Night in Hyde Park in 1919. We sat back against the baobab sipping our cool drinks and revelled for nearly an hour in their beauty, skill, and courage.

The roses that fell from the sky on the day of the canonisation of Saint Thérèse of Lisieux can scarcely have excelled these birds in colour, because, with the almost level rays striking them at a great altitude, they seemed to outshine the most wonderful flowers, as much as most flowers outshine their leaves. The flames were now crackling on the long grass and palmettos, and sending up an inverted cataract of sparks and black smoke, filled with scorched and stupefied insects. Then, from the height of about a hundred and fifty feet, the birds all simultaneously inclined their flight and swooped like dive-bombers, hurling their seraphic streaks of ruby and sapphire at the curtain of smoke and flame, striking through which, they seemed to ricochet at a steep angle to the same height on the other side, where they revolved, without pausing, in their own length, and repeated the process. They could have hawked an equal number of escaping insects outside the zone of fire: but they obviously took a real delight in the danger, and in matching their own solar flames against the plumes of the conflagration, which they outshone in brilliance as they outglanced it in nimble flight. They emerged from the smoke unsullied—quite unlike us when we attempt similar feats. Whenever during mechanical acrobatics, at military displays or trick-riding competitions, I have jumped the motor-bike off from a sloping platform through the "Wall of Fire," four or five times, my clothes and face have become grimy and my hair caked with soot: but the bee-eaters' feathers, all streamlined so smoothly backward, and insulated by their speed, afforded no more purchase for the tiniest spark, or grain of smut, than a hard-nosed bullet spinning forward from the clean grooves of a rifle-barrel.

After a hundred baptisms of smoke, sparks, and fire they remained unsinged, and spotless as before. Some came to rest in the baobabs above us and we were able to admire their burnished shapes, over a foot in length, with long forked swallow-tails, blue tail-coverts, red breasts, and rosy scythe-like wings whose tips almost crossed as they folded over their backs and tapered, along the tail, to twice the length of their bodies, as with some swifts.

These red bee-eaters excel the swifts, as flyers, in everything but speed, for they can poise for longer motionless, move backwards, and have a sort of helicopter technique in rising and falling. When they had sated their appetites it was late afternoon; and Paul Duponsel and I sat spellbound at the spectacle while they marshalled themselves for their departure, after their display of celestial fireworks. They now started certain measuredly rhythmic evolutions as they began, gradually, to turn in one direction, towards the setting sun.

Some of them moved slowly and smoothly in their now horizontal flight, at the rate of billiard balls just before they come to rest; then as soon as their movement had slowed down to imperceptibility, with a single easy stroke of their wings they would shoot forth in advance of the others; alternately gliding, feigning a suspended immobility, and then accelerating into a streak of crimson lightning once more. It was plain that they consciously enjoyed this aerial choreography, and that they have a mathematical sense of movement and design far beyond that evinced by other birds, for example, in the lovely chevron-formations, which aviators have learned from wild geese, but which are primarily utilitarian rather than aesthetic, since they enable each flyer to profit by the wind that rushes in the wake of his predecessor. I had already noticed a mathematical sense of precision about the Madagascar variety of bee-eaters when they settled on the cross-spar of the dhow.

It is certain that birds which have attained such a super-normal beauty both of form and of colour must be visually sensitive to an uncommon degree (even for birds)—unless their colours are merely designed to attract or disarm the bees on which they feed, by simulating flowers. But this idea is discounted by the fact that most bee-eaters are green, like leaves, and this is the only variety, among a dozen, in which the colours of flowers preponderate over those of foliage. They seem impervious to the stings of bees and wasps and this is all the more remarkable because the honey-guides, far tougher-looking birds, who also have a great deal to do with bees, are furnished, as snakes are, with hard sting-proof, transparent membranes, like glass shields, which can be brought down between their eyelids and their eyes.

Honey-guides lead honey-badgers or men to hives, because they themselves are unable to break into the hollow tree or dig up the earth in which the hive is hidden. There are many varieties of honey-guides; they resemble cuckoos, and their alliance both with men and badgers is one of the most fantastic things in nature. The natives firmly believe that, if its own share of the plunder is not left to the bird, it will revenge itself on the culprit on the next occasion by guiding him to a mamba, a rhinoceros, a lion, or a slippery precipice. They attract notice, when touting as guides, by flapping their wings and twittering in an unmistakable manner.

Writing of the skill of birds in flight reminds me of the great albatrosses and their smaller brothers, the mollymauks, which haunt our shores, and the way in which, when escorting ships along our coasts, they weave to and fro, with or against the fiercest wind, with almost equal ease. Their most remarkable characteristic is their love of flying sideways with one wing tip often feathering the waves and the other vertically pointing to the sky. They were always to be seen from our beach.

We have yet a great deal to develop in our knowledge of streamlining. It is the shape of birds and fish, rather than their muscular power, that enables them to move with such momentum and velocity up through cascades, and against strong head-winds. You can see this if you release a dead trout which has been accurately balanced, with its head upstream, in shallow rapids. Without even the aid of its fins, it will move forward for an inch, or even several, until it loses its balance, rolls over on its side and is whisked away again downstream. This means that, with its shape alone, the trout almost neutralises the speed of the river. Similarly the mere shape of a sail, especially the lateen cut, almost neutralises the speed of the wind, against which it can make headway at a very oblique angle. All the great birds of prey (and where are they more magnificent than in Africa?) are superb flyers; but as they excel all other big birds of the land, so they are all excelled by the Bateleur Eagle, which in beauty is equal to any of the others—the martial, the black, the crested, or the white-headed sea eagle—and the most frequent visitor to our lagoon. It is far finer to look at than the ubiquitous Golden Eagle.

The Bateleur Eagle, or the Berg-hen as we call it locally, is pitch black with beautiful white patterns on its wings, which are shaped like the knives of Albacete. Its head is large and makes it look, from far off, like a gigantic bumble-bee. Its beak, legs and eye-balls are a brilliant scarlet. Its neck is a glittering black, with feathers folded like fish-scales, but erected on the head to form a handsome, semicircular crest. The back, between the wings, is sometimes brown, sometimes cream-coloured. These Berg-hens take a delight in freak-flying. Sometimes with one wing upright and the other horizontal they hurtle along at a furious speed and begin rocking rapidly from side to side. They also perform this rocking motion when the tips of their wings are raised to the angle of an acute V. Then the "rocking" can become even more furiously pronounced and will be continued over a distance of half a mile at a time. They can kill snakes, though (not having witnessed the act) I don't know how, since they are not furnished like that long-legged eagle, the Secretary Bird, the greatest of all snake-eaters, with snake-proof yellow leggings. They probably use their wing-quills to strike the snake down before fastening their talons on its head. One seldom *sees* them alight even on trees or rocks. A couple used to visit me every day at my coast-watching banda and sail past about thirty times at a prodigious speed only about twenty feet above my head, scrutinising every object and especially the cookhouse shack with its reek of roasting camel, zebu, goat, or donkey. They are carrion-feeders sometimes, but are generally predatory, and I have often seen them sailing past with snakes dangling from their scarlet claws, so that Shelley's pet image is not so far-fetched as it might seem. I once saw one with a brilliant long green mamba or boomslang trailing behind it, as the green streamer of a stripped palm-leaf trails behind a weaver bird.

Of other birds that haunted our lagoon I remember in particular one albino night-heron which I almost mistook at first sight for one of the egrets. This friendly bird used to fly silently around our boat when my wife and I rowed up the lagoon in the evening and we became very fond of it.

Then there were the storks from Europe, which only once visited our coast, and for a good reason. Although these birds preferred our uplands, yet, during the last World War, they were dismayed by the thunder of the battles raging across the line of their return to nest in the church-steeples, castles, and Roman aqueducts of Spain, where they are so beloved by the whole population. They therefore turned back to hibernate in Natal, but had to seek the coast for warmth, and honoured our strip of forest exclusively with their presence. The whole enormous forest-clad hill of the Hawaan on the Durban side of the lagoon was white with myriads of storks for weeks, till it became warm enough for them to disperse once more to the grassy uplands, which they know so well.

There are several other birds among those which haunted the lagoon and its forest-environs which it would be ungrateful of me to forget. (So much of the character of African places derives from their birds, that half the place-names in Zulu—Majuba (doves), Impangeni (guineafowl), Tegwine, etc., etc., derive from birds also.) First comes the Tegwan (or hammerkop), the patron saint (ornithologically speaking) of my hometown of Durban, known still to natives as "Tegwini," the place of Tegwans. This weird wading bird builds enormous outsize nests in the forks of trees overhanging rivers. Their nests are five times the size of storks' nests, though they themselves are smaller than ducks. They are the "Malvolios" of the birds, and the dances of the males when wooing the females are a side-splitting spectacle of flat-footed ineptitude mixed with romantic enthusiasm. They are revered for certain magic qualities by the natives, and their death at human hands is punishable by devastating floods, according to the superstition.

The commonest bird in Africa, the Toppie as we call him (and to hell with pompous names like "Black-Capped Bulbul"), is a great character, cheerful, laughable, friendly, courageous, and a terrible drunkard, passing out blotto when the Inkberries and Syringa berries get over-ripe and fermented. He is always the first bird to spot, and to begin scolding, a dangerous snake. When you hear the Toppies scolding you can grab your shot-gun for you will be led infallibly to where some boomslang or mamba has been discovered by the Toppies, who seem disinterestedly to enjoy warning other birds and human beings, and act to snakes in the same sabotaging manner as "Go 'way" birds do to hunters, except that only too often they come within the hypno-magnetic radius of the snake, and fall victims themselves.

The hornbills and monkey-birds (Wood-hoopoes) give a pleasantly satirical mockery to the life of the bush. The tree-hornbills are Groucho Marx—in a feathered incarnation; and the monkey-birds, called by the natives "chattering old women," are an amazing mixture of physical beauty and cacophonous ribaldry.

Then there is the Narina Trogon, a beautiful retiring bird similar to the lory, and the South American Resplendent Quetzal, called by the eighteenth-century traveller, the Chevalier Le Vaillant, after his steatopygous Hottentot mistress, Narina. Don Quixote seems quite normal when one has read the Memoirs of this great ornithologist, the friend of Buffon, who insisted on hunting the lion and the leopard in his best Court suit of "Blue-boy" silk, with white gloves, ostrich-plumed hat, and lace ruffles in order to show his respect for the royalty and nobility of these beasts. His scorn for the "ill-bred" Boers who hunted them far more efficiently, in their old clothes, is delightful. He rewarded Narina for her favours, and Klaas, her brother, for his services as guide, by calling after them the beautiful trogon, and the bird known to this day as Klaas's Cuckoo. This is the ruby cuckoo, which, if not quite so beautiful as its emerald twin-brother, is none the less, with the golden cuckoo, a close runner-up.

Le Vaillant's chivalry and scientific enthusiasm came to grips very amusingly in his Memoirs, for though he was passionately fond of Narina, he couldn't forbear recording the anatomical differences (far more pronounced than between us and the Japanese) which disconcerted him during his first attempts at intimacy with this strange inamorata, who, owing to the astounding development of her posterior, was almost as tall when sitting down, as when standing up. The English translator (though he was writing in the middle of the eighteenth century) was entirely nonplussed. Asterisks were left and an apology was made to the Noble Lord to whom the translation was dedicated: "My Lord, Modesty forbids that I should continue, etc., etc." Le Vaillant, the rival in eccentricity of the delightful Waterton, as good a writer, and as charming a man, deserves to have his Memoirs reprinted and edited by somebody like Aldington, who has enriched us almost as much with that sort of research as with his own creative work.

Everywhere in the reed-beds were to be found those beautiful cousins of the weaver birds, the widow-birds and the bishop-birds. The widow-bird is scarcely bigger than a bull-finch, but his long black tail sometimes reaches to a length of twenty inches; these birds are a great feature of our uplands where the finest variety, the "Sakabula," is quite a common sight. On the coast we had to be content with three or four smaller varieties.

One of the bishop-birds, whom the natives call "Umlilo" (fire) and we call the "blood-fink," is a truly extraordinary creature. In the mating season, the cock, a dull grey in winter, puts on a uniform of scarlet and black. Contrasted with the pitchy blackness of the rest of him, the scarlet half of his feathers, fluffed up on his back like a powder-puff, radiates an almost dazzling brilliance so that even in the blaze of the African noon, which reduces the colours of everything else to a neutral grey, your eyes will be arrested and drawn at a great distance by this tiny bead of blood. The pugnacious little bird whirrs audibly along, like a tiny machine-gun, showing off to his drab coloured hens, and challenging fights from the other cocks, or from any other bird he sees. Both widow-birds and bishop-birds shed all their fine colours, long tails, and extra plumage in the winter and become almost indistinguishable from their females.

XI

DOCTORS AND WITCH-DOCTORS

As soon as my two elder brothers were ten and twelve they were sent up country to boarding school, and we saw little of them, except during the holidays. I was, as I have said before, nine years younger than my elder brother, and two years older than my younger brother, Neil, who died on active service in North Africa in the last war.

In a family like ours we are always separated, when young, by wars and by going to different countries overseas, in search of education and adventure. My eldest brother, Archie, went in 1909 to Ontario Agricultural College; George went to Edinburgh, in 1911; both volunteered in August 1914, served in the R.F.C. and never saw home for ten or twelve years, except during brief leaves, when they were passing from one front to another.

I volunteered first in 1916 but was brought back again at once; I volunteered again, with better success, in 1917, but eventually, while on active service, I had my age betrayed by a family connection who was only a staff-wallah, and jealous of my being a soldier. My father then let me sign on for a cadetship in the R.F.C. at the age of sixteen. After six months on the waiting list I was rejected for blood-pressure, and because I could not produce a birth certificate of the right age. When I came over to go to Sandhurst the war had ended, and I was directed to Oxford. From Oxford I soon drifted away to the Merchant Service, and then to the Mediterranean and the cattle-countries.

I only saw Neil once again, after I was seventeen. He went to Edinburgh after George had left. Bruce, the youngest, went to

Baton Rouge, Louisiana, and then to Honolulu. If I cross my brothers' tracks once in ten or twenty years it is not abnormal, though we
are all bound by a very strong clannishness and by a similarity of
tastes—we are all mad about fishing for one thing.

My brother George's adventures as a doctor among the Zulus
are quite as remarkable as my father's. He was away up in the thorn-
veld, lion-hunting near a kraal where the late King Solomon (son
of Dinizulu and grandson of Cetewayo) was visiting with his full
retinue of wives and indunas. King Solomon suffered some kind of
seizure, which is mortal if not attended to, but can be dispelled quite
easily by European methods. Some local natives, hearing my
brother was a doctor, implored him to go and help, so he immediately offered his services. The native witch-doctors and many of
the royal queens objected, being sticklers for tribal etiquette. But
seeing that things had become desperate, the counsellors sent for
my brother, after having rejected his offer and given him a long
journey for nothing. As a human life was at stake, my brother returned and cured the King, having given him a shot of morphia,
which, of course, relieving his pain, produced a wonderful and
magical impression on him.

Upon recovery he promoted my brother to the "best doctor in
the Province of Natal" by means of a long hyperbolical article, in
my brother's praise, which he had inserted in the Zulu newspaper.
It appeared that even witch-doctors weren't in the running, where
George was concerned. By Royal Command all loyal subjects were
told that they should consult my poor brother for anything that
ailed them. The result was that he nearly had to flee abroad from
the multitudes that besieged him. The King had praised him
amongst other things for not charging any fee—and that of course
attracted thousands more.

Shortly after his recovery and before the publication of the article, the King and his people had sent counsellors to ask my
brother in what way the Zulu nation could reward him for having
saved their sovereign. Intending to have a leg-pull in revenge for
having been snubbed and kept hanging around by the witch-doctors and wives, George asked them: "How much do you love
your King?"

"So much that we would give our lives for him," said one.

"And all our possessions," said another.

"Oh, there's no need to go to such lengths," said George. "Just let every Zulu who owns more than two cows give me one of them."

The dumbfounded consternation on the faces of the headmen was a picture. Then my brother explained that he was only joking, in revenge for having been kept waiting and sent away. He wanted no fee at all, he said, and sent them on their way rejoicing, in spite of having teased them unmercifully by saying: "In spite of all your blarney, I can see that not one of you values his King or his life as much as a single cow."

The funny thing was that two years later during a drought the same counsellors came back and offered George in dead earnest the very same fee he had asked in jest for curing the King—if he would go up to Zululand and make them some rain. He explained that if he could make rain he would be only too glad to do it free, since his own garden needed it as badly as theirs: but that it was a sheer impossibility for any doctor, black, white, or yellow, to make rain. This last statement they certainly did not believe, since rain-making is the first item in the repertoire of anyone claiming to be even a mediocre doctor, to their way of thinking. They went off feeling slightly puzzled and hurt: but that my brother retains a tremendous prestige among them even now is clear from the fact that he is one of the few white men alive whom they have ever honoured by inviting to initiation ceremonies, and other sacred mysteries and rites.

It must be remembered that the Zulus, during the most important period of their history, were subjected to an extreme form of to-talitarianism which disoriented them as violently as their shock with white civilisation. The Zulus were subjected to Communism, which is supposed to be a modern phenomenon, one hundred and forty years ago. Although their subsequent history has caused them to be generally regarded as a military race, they are really a pastoral race. Under Tchaka and Dingaan, almost all who could safely escape without reprisals to their families sought bondage under the whites, in preference to their own Tzars, since they were bolshe-vised, collectivised, and militarised to a degree beyond anything that has happened in Europe under the National-Socialisms of Lenin, Stalin or Hitler. Our servants for four generations were descended from émigré Zulus, lucky enough to penetrate the iron curtain of the Tugela. We notice that these Demagogues always attack and destroy the traditional Faith or tribal beliefs of their fellow-countrymen, before being able to enslave them. Faith can move mountains: but Credulity (its inevitable substitute) can move whole continents: and it requires the most blatant credulity to believe in the Utopian futurism of "classless societies," "thousand-year Reichs," "five-year plans" and other demagogic blarney current in Europe during the last two hundred years, amongst people who have had their faith destroyed.

Far more people have been imprisoned for Liberty, degraded and humiliated for the sake of Equality, and tortured and murdered in the name of Fraternity during the last thirty years than in the previous thousand under less hypocritical forms of despotism. Nothing is more blatantly obvious than that ever since that volcano of blood and pus, the French Revolution, France has steadily declined from being the first power in Europe to a third-rate masonic republic, divided against itself to such a degree that one half of the inhabitants can generally be relied upon to side with an invader against the other half, which it will persecute remorselessly at the behest of its latest invader, whether German, American, English, or Russian. All political activity which has been attempted outside of tradition during the last one hundred and fifty years has worked out in the inverse sense from its original intention. We owe to the egalitarian and libertarian frenzy of the French Revolution, which was one of the greatest disasters of all time, nearly all the restrictions which are the curse of modern life—passports, identity cards, concierges, registry in hotels, the internment of innocent aliens during hostilities with their countries, and a thousand other barbarous plagues. The direct result of the Revolution in France was the wholesale conscription of citizens, bourgeois and artisans, and the lowering of the military profession from a voluntary and highly poetical *vocation* to a sort of punitive drudgery.

Inexperienced bookworms, like Marx and Nietzsche, imagined that by such simple expedients as the elimination of the top-dog or the under-dog, a desirable state of affairs could be attained. As put into practice by Lenin and Stalin, the theories of Marx have filled the world with more pitiless top-dogs, and the theories of Nietzsche, as put into practice by Hitler, produced a far greater number of piteous and miserable under-dogs—than they were originally intended to eliminate.

That Socialism is a phenomenon that can crop up among the

people of any culture at any state in their development can be seen not only in the case of the Zulus, but in that of the Tierra del Fuegians, whom Darwin and, later, their superb historian, Don Lucas Bridges, showed to be completely communised even to the point of atheism which is the final and inevitable concomitant of complete communisation.

The Zulus are therefore savages, as distinct from primitive peoples, in the sense that they are not in a state of innocence, but have descended from a higher status of culture. If they did not have a definite faith to lose, they at least had tribal traditions and superstitions which had sufficed them through centuries of pastoral and agricultural life. These were all disjointed by their militarisation. With the coming of Tchaka they lost the art of song and of dancing in which they are inferior to most other native tribes, though their conversation is always highly stylised—and can be classified as their national art. Their poets, under Communism, were confronted with the same choice as faced Myakowsky, Yesenin, and the Russian poets—the choice between complete servility, like Tuwim the Jewish panegyrist of Red Poland, suicide, execution, imprisonment, and utter incomprehensibility. Incomprehensibility and servility won. The present Zulu name for a poet, Isibongo, the "Thank-you Man," or, as we should say, the "Yes-Man," prefigured the rôle of the artist under Stalin and Hitler to-day.

In the last one hundred and fifty years a great many natives escaped across the iron curtain of the Tugela boundary, and settled in Natal, preferring servitude under the whites to complete slavery under their own dictators. White rule at its worst is actually preferable to what the Zulus and Matabele suffered and inflicted on other tribes. But that is no excuse for its being as bad as it is. What is really laughable, though, is that our Afrikaaners should be hauled up before U.N.O., which includes members of states like Israel, reeking with the massacres of defenceless Arabs, and Russia, whose slaves are treated infinitely worse than the Dutch have ever treated the natives.

It is necessary to remember that the military tradition of the Zulus is an overlay on an older and deeper pastoral tradition, and that is why they can hero-worship men like my father for their bravery as soldiers even when enemies, and at the same time love them for their kindness and consideration. Nevertheless they retain some of the worst decayed relics of their previous civilisation in the form of witchcraft and black magic. The evil accruing from the belief that all illness is due to some secret malevolence on the part of another person is responsible for a life full of uneasy suspicion of their neighbours, and perpetual anxiety.

Dilettante tourists like the witty and intelligent Geoffrey Gorer, the author of *Africa Dances*, deplore (as if there was nothing better to do than to jitterbug and dance highland flings, or the African equivalents of them) the influence of missionaries in giving the natives a new and less miserable outlook, because they are then liable to forget their tribal dances. I have always noticed, as an N.C.O. and a fellow-ranker with thousands of Bantu, and also as a South African, that the Christianised or Mohammedanised native was a better and happier man than the "Noble Savage" with his terrible, haunting fear that makes him suspicious of his friends and a far more abject prey to his witch-doctors than any European "intellectual" is to his psycho-analysts; than any Fabian food-crank is to vitamins or proteins; or than the most backward European peasant could be to the most unscrupulous of priests. Recent history has proved that wherever you get rid of your priest, you have to have a policeman, an S.S., or a Commissar, armed with a knout, to replace him.

The *order* which is necessary to human life has either got to be voluntarily kept, from religious or moral motives, or else compulsorily enforced. The answer to all idealistic anarchism was comically and paradoxically given by the Spanish Anarchists themselves when they were under persecution by their Communist allies. A G.R.O. was published saying: "What Spanish Anarchism requires most is organisation." Religion is therefore the only alternative to the police State and slavery in the long run, even for us. That this is so was recognised by Stalin, Tito, Hitler, Trotsky, Rakosy, Beirut, Dimitrov, and others who have seen, in the Catholic Church, the chief source of resistance. As Hitler said himself, it was from the Catholic Church he met with the hardest resistance. The Bolsheviks appear to think the same as the Nazis about the relative resistance-power of Catholics and Protestants.

Gorer's idea that the Christianised native is inferior to the kraal native is repeated everywhere in literature written by Kiplingised Englishmen about South Africa, in books like *Jock of the Bushveld* and in Cullen Gouldsbury's poems. In *Jock of the Bushveld* Jim Makokel, the Zulu, had a violent race-hatred for Shangaans and all other natives who weren't Zulus. With the obvious approval of the author of this degrading piece of Kensingtonian Cynolatry, of which a dog is the real hero, Jim Makokel beats up and persecutes all other natives except Zulus, sets the dog on them, and reserves special contempt for a mission-boy who reads the Bible. This attitude is typical of the Englishman in Africa, and it is obviously his intention to keep the native as ignorant as possible in order to exploit him more easily: but every reason is given for this, except the true one.

It is the same with their arguments against the Spanish War: they suppress the fact that they are jealous of a race which has twice managed to retain its traditional faith in spite of far worse punishment than the English "rebels" received from the foreign mercenaries of Henry VIII in the "Pilgrimage of Grace."

The average Englishman, at home, bewails the brutal conduct of his compatriot abroad towards the natives. This has always been an insoluble mystery to me—for they are exactly the same type. That is a hypocritical way of washing one's hands of oneself. In a similar way the Anglo-Saxon of the Northern U.S.A. deplores the attitude of the Southerner towards the blacks when, if he were a Southerner, he would obviously behave like one. And all four unanimously and hypocritically get cold shivers down their spines when they read their own accounts of the work of the Spanish Inquisition, which forbade slavery, and tried to stop it as early as the sixteenth century; for which reason Drake staged his Pearl Harbour act on Cadiz.

Spanish rule conserved millions of the aboriginal Indians in South and Central America, while they were systematically destroyed in North America (all but a few Museum Specimens on Reserves) by Anglo-Saxons of the same race as Charles Kingsley and Prescott who hypocritically indicted the Spaniards of cruelty. Spaniards are only cruel to animals, not to people or children. The destruction of the entire native population in Tasmania, at the hands of Britons, by "driving" them like pheasants from end to end of the island, has no counterpart in Spanish colonisation.

One thing is certain: Latin and Celtic peoples are not generally attacked by colour-feeling and prejudice in the same way as English, Germans, Dutch, and Norwegians; who appear to be allergic to negroes.

The Scotchman, Dunn, and the Irish sailor, Finn, who founded Durban, seem to have left several thousand coloured descendants each. I think it was silly to interbreed, though I have no colour prejudice. Hybrids are rarely any good, except in the case of a donkey stallion and the mare of a horse. When superannuated English society-tarts take up negro lovers, it is generally a sort of perversion like the exaggerated feeling for dogs and cats. I knew one who went negro in order, as she said, to "study conditions amongst the negroes." Having selected the negro with the largest "condition" she could find, she brought him to Europe. I knew this couple and they happened to call on me in a Levantine port where all the inhabitants are partly coloured, being descendants of the galley-slaves of Louis XIV. I was working in this town in partnership with three very deeply-coloured Saracen-like gentlemen and they were highly indignant when they saw me sitting at the same table with a negro. I explained it away by saying it was an aunt from South Africa with a dear old faithful servant. It did not help matters when she started wiping his nose for him in front of everybody, and then putting his tie straight.

It is extremely interesting to see how colour-feeling attacks coloured people themselves—but it is generally a reflection of that felt by their white overlords. I have seen a betrousered Zulu refer to an untrousered one as a Kaffir ("Kaffula"), and while I was in Ceylon, in 1943, our lads, Nyasas, Kikuyus, Kavirondos, Bagandas, Nandis, Dohluos, Njemps, of the King's African Rifles, were boycotted, as jungle-wallahs, by the shops and cinemas, although the Singhalese are quite as black as they are. There was a foretaste of the recent Durban riots in this discrimination.

One sinister result of white resistance to the spreading of Christianity amongst natives is that Communism is spreading in its place. From its very nature, Communism is defenceless against the same form of infiltration as it practises on other communities and, as will shortly be seen, it will prove just as vulnerable to masonic or racial cliques, and secret societies. Rajk, the last gentile to be in power in Bolshevik Central Europe, fell to Semitic infiltration—as a non-Jew. Yet high up in the Russian Party non-Jews are starting to oust the Jews. In Africa secret societies flourish on a more fantastic scale

than anywhere else: and if Communism were ever to get a foothold in Africa the results would be highly spectacular, and very
different from what the bookish inventors of Communism had
envisaged. Anyway, totalitarian state-capitalism is all that they
have produced.

There is no doubt that the average native is socially inferior to
the white man, but he should not and cannot be prevented artificially from eventually becoming his equal, for the good of all
concerned. The present disqualification of the native from so many
aids to his own betterment is exactly on a par with the natives'
treatment of each other. We are behaving about a quarter as badly
as the Zulus and Matabeles did to their fellow Bantu, and it will do
us little more good than it did them, since, out of the opposition
they set up, and out of the refugees that escaped their toils, the
happy Basuto nation arose which proved far more powerful than
either of them. But the opposition we are setting up is subsidised
from abroad, and we may end by ranking the majority of the population in violent opposition to the white minority, which happened
in the mad revolution of Haiti, when the black Emperor, Jean

Christophe, out-Caesared Nero and Caligula in the name of Liberty and Equality.

We must never forget that theoretical Bolshevism is the most attractive dream-bait that was ever invented. Though practical Bolshevism may be the most diabolical and cruel hook that was ever inserted into bait, and stuck through the nostrils, you cannot expect a rustic Zulu to be proof against the seductive blarney which completely seduced the "knowing and sophisticated" intellectuals of England and Western Europe for so many years.

XII

THE DURBAN BREAKWATER

IN THE more secret-looking pubs round the Dockside near the
Breakwater or North Pier, in Durban, one can see groups of
unkempt conspirators conversing in hushed voices as if they
were plotting the overthrow of human society. Each has an ancient-
mariner-like expression which could be guaranteed to hypnotise
and detain the thirstiest wedding-guest for hours. Fortunately for
the community, these strange human amphibians are not interested
in weddings, funerals, feasts, and other functions which concern
our own common-or-garden existences. They seem entirely pre-
occupied with hearing out each other's yarns. But for the unblus-
tering quietness of their voices, you would take them for Bolsheviks
or Nihilists: and besides, instead of encouraging each other with
the convulsive Southpaw ataxia of the lifted fist, they are distinguished by a more pleasing and persuasive semaphore. They appear
to be accompanying the low musical hum of their voices on invisible accordions, by extending and contracting their palms in con-
tinuous rhythm; and occasionally extending their arms so wide
that they appear to be trying to stretch outsize imaginary concer-
tinas beyond the limits of their capacity. In this position they remind you of becalmed albatrosses and mollymauks, when they fling

their wings wide in the hope of catching a breeze that will enable them to "take off" from the sea.

It comes upon one as quite a surprise, on overhearing a snatch of their conversation, that this weird semaphore is merely a vast exaggeration of the sign by which the harmless but fanatical freemasonry of *anglers* (when describing the size of their catches) can be recognised all over the world, from China to Peru. These are none other than the redoubtable Breakwater-fishers of Durban to whom Brian Vesey-Fitzgerald devotes the climax and grand finale of his monumental classic on the "Big Game Fishes of the World!"

As for overthrowing Society, these sunbroiled human crustaceans have long ago thrown it over, as it has thrown them over, completely. In Durban I have seen more respectable doctors, bank managers, clergymen and lawyers turned into hobos by this passion for fishing than by the combined vices of drink, drug-taking, gambling, or hemp-smoking, though a neighbour of ours, named Joe Barnett, did provide the most extreme case of hoboism that I ever heard of, through hemp-smoking: only returning home late at night, at first, to take food which had been placed for him at the edge of the bush: then, finally, throwing away even his breeches, and living on whatever Grigson-tucker of scorpions, comestible spiders, bugs, beetles, and lizards he could find by turning over stones, as he learned to do from the baboons of the Inthlosana. We came on his tracks where he had been digging with his hands for roots, a trick which no baboon or monkey could teach him. That was his last human trait. He was very elusive and I never saw him, but those who *did* described him as having a huge red beard, and long shaggy hair down his back like a woman's. They said that he learned to run on all fours as easily as he could run on two legs, and he used this method for jungle-crashing horizontally through the undergrowth. He would rush off through the thick bush, barking like a bushbuck or a baboon.

A young second-cousin of mine was escorting an elderly spinster, Miss Mary MacArthur of the Dargle district, on her way home, when, at the Drift of the Dargle spruit, their horses shied, and they were suddenly confronted by Joe, stark-naked, on all fours, drinking like a buck on the bank at the side of the bush. He leaped upright: then gave a series of ferocious snorts and barks, and launched himself, like a diver, into the undergrowth, on all fours, galloping off with terrific jerks of his posterior, and disappearing in a crash of foliage just as a startled bushbuck might do. His mortal remains were eventually found in the mountains some time after a blizzard. I have seen his spoor so fresh in the mud of the Dargle spruit that the water had not yet filtered into it: meaning that I had only missed seeing this strange sight by a minute or so.

The passion for fishing amounts to insanity in Durban. Where else in the world are "fish describers" given as birthday presents? These consist of two arms with extended palms, roughly fretsawn out of plywood, and each measuring about five feet long; they are meant to save reminiscent anglers from unnecessary arm-strain when recounting their experiences. Such were the pair presented to my famous Cousin Ethelbert by my brother Archibald. When held out horizontally, for accordion-practice, they give Ethelbert the wing-span of a wandering Albatross, or a Spitfire Plane, and come in handy for describing some of my cousin's catches when he is in a confidential mood—which is frequent enough. They are feather-light and easy to handle.

These Durban rod-fishers, in spite of their common eccentricity, are sticklers for their own conventions. All records are void if shoulder-straps or harness are used to ease the strain. Only a belt with a leather socket for the butt of the rod is allowed. If anyone relieves an exhausted fisherman, even momentarily, in his five-to-six hour tussles, except by pouring sea-water from one's hat on to his reel, to keep it from catching fire and singeing the line, it amounts to disqualification. On his right hand, the fisherman is allowed to wear a "palm" of doubled ox-hide to keep his flesh from being charred by the red-hot friction of the reel when braking its speed. No gears or brakes are allowed on the reel. If an ounce too much pressure is applied, the strong silk line will break like a rotten cobweb. I know of no game which requires at the same time such physical stamina and such delicacy of touch as that exacted from our breakwater fishermen in their herculean struggles with the huge ton-weight Rolls-Royces and Cadillacs of the Boulevards, Ramblas, and Cannebières of our flowering ocean-floor.

After reading the *Compleat Angler* I once had a nightmare that Isaak Walton turned up on the breakwater at Durban and was broken up in a tussle with our "Bernard Shaw." Now this "Bernard" was an angler-proof shark, who used to frequent our breakwater year in and year out. He could easily be identified, though only by his tactics, for he was only seen alive once. He knew of some submerged wreck, rock, or other obstacle, about a hundred yards due N. East of the light at the end of the North Breakwater. Around this, taking a couple of turns, whenever he was hooked, he obtained the purchase necessary to break the newest line like mildewed pack-thread. He took a delight in playing the anglers, as if they, not he, had been the fish, and then he would suddenly strand their lines high, if not dry, round the submerged obstacle about which he invariably knotted them.

That he preferred whalebait on the hook to whalemeat by itself could easily be deduced from his submarine strategy, which never varied. For when he and his fellow sharks were following the dead whales into port and plugging round white holes in the blubber of the huge, blue pumped-up carcases that the whalers were towing into Durban Bay, "Bernard" would leave his companions directly they came abreast with the end of the breakwater. While his fellow-sharks followed the dead whales up the narrow channel between the breakwaters, right up to the very slip, where they were hauled ashore with winches, "Bernard" would break away and cruise along, on the *outside* of the North Breakwater, creating such havoc amongst the fishing tackle, and running off with so many lines, that the old stagers would simply reel in their tackle and smoke till he had gone. Nobody ever had the slightest doubt but that "Bernard" liked his "iron rations" literally, not metaphorically. It was impossible to mistake his presence since the minute he ran out with the line he always broke it at the same spot in the same way. One got used even to the feel of him, for he chugged like a brand-new motorbike, and felt more like an outsize kingfish than a shark, since he was very swift, though at the same time he made his weight to be felt inexorably.

They say that the fish derived his name from the venerable sage of English literature, and was called after him on the only occasion when he was properly seen, cruising along in a dead calm with his dorsal fin high above the surface, and his back only a foot beneath, in the crystal-clear water. He appeared thus in person to three witnesses of unimpeachable reliability—three famous fishers of the breakwater, namely "Bluepointer" Wilson, "Rocksalmon" Johnstone, and "Musselcracker" Finlayson. From the descriptions I obtained from each of them independently, yet agreeing with each other in every detail, and also from the view I subsequently had of his dead jaws and headpiece, with all the hooks and traces sticking in them, I gather that the long festoons of myriads of silvery wire traces, with rotten old lines attached, trailing from the hooks in his jaws and gullet, and with coppery swivels glinting on the ends of the traces, glimmering and twining, shimmering and shining, looping over his forehead, drooping under his chin, and fimbriating with so many hirsute radiations his only visible feature, which was a portion of a sheepish grin in the shape of a circular-saw—all these factors combined to give him a peculiarly shaggy, woolly, left-wingish appearance such as we have come to associate with modern British intellectuals in general, and Fabians in particular.

It was as if the second-hand wig of some old bluestocking (which had previously belonged to one of the earliest leaders of the suffragette movement) had been stuffed into an old, damp bed-sock and allowed to tousle and be-Joadify itself there for twenty years: then pulled out and stuffed into a frowsy old sofa on which H. G. Wells had made love to a bluestocking: then pulled out and stuffed into a mattress which had belonged to the Sidney Webbs: then set upon by an army of fishmoths and shredded into a trillion fibres: then left out in the rain to mildew till each infinitesimal fibril was itself furred with fifty kinds of sub-penicillin:—and then take the square root of the result, suddenly multiply it 2,000 times and turn it into a tiger-shark weighing well over 20 hundred-weight.

Only by trying to follow these complicated operations in your mind's eye can you hope to obtain the haziest idea of the superhirsute appearance, the frowsiness, and the size, of the apparition as it travelled along in the crystalline element, so near the surface, at a speed of about 29 knots. The effect produced was of an outsize ichthyological Struwwelpeter with eyebrows like birds' nests, bristling upright shocks of hair, whiskers, and moustachios revolving and twirling in a thousand quiffs and whigmaleeries, and even peeping coyly and fluffily from his gills (or "ear-holes" as we call them) like the beard of the lady at the Circus.

The sight of such a hairy looking shark was too much even for Bluepointer Wilson though he had once been a barber's assistant up in the Marico district, on the Mafeking Road, in proper Taakhaar country, where people only wash, shave, or have a haircut once or twice in a life-time, except when they are put in gaol, or when Boer patriarchs begin to trip up on their own beards. In fact, he had been employed chiefly by the mounted police at the gaol. Although no man on God's earth was more used to the sight of hairiness, Wilson was completely nonplussed. With his two companions he just gasped and gazed in silence, not being able to believe his eyes.

As the awesome apparition vanished, the three fishermen all reached simultaneously for the two-and-sixpenny bottle of raw Cape Brandy in their joint tucker-bag. As Bluepointer was unrolling the bottle from a copy of the *Natal Advertiser*, he suddenly stiffened, for there, on the very front page, was a portrait of Bernard Shaw, on the occasion of his sixtieth birthday, which was being celebrated that very week.

"Well, I be ——," cried Bluepointer, "if that isn't magic! I'm —— if that isn't the photo of the —— old —— of a —— himself! The spit of him!" Handing the newspaper to Musselcracker, who could read, he bade him decipher the words under the photo. The hitherto invisible shark became known as "Bernard Shaw." It wasn't possible to convince Wilson that it was an accidental resemblance; that the portrait was that of a man who resembled the shark by the bristling appearance of his hair, beard, ears, eyebrows, and nostrils, not the identical shark itself. He always swore it was the photo of the fish and that both the photo and the name of the fish had been obtained "by machinery, wireless, Marconi, or one of those new things."

Though it may seem a far cry from Fish to Fabians and from Sharks to Shavians, yet the Bait-swallowing principle underlies all egalitarian Utopianism, which is the ultimate refinement and metaphysical expansion of Deceit—very often self-Deceit. Huge capitalistic fortunes have been made, by hypocritically preaching against them, by Fabians and other socialistic types, merely by this old-fashioned method of exploiting human Credulity: which is only another word for Bait-Happiness. This lucrative form of preaching has netted more absolute power and wealth (as in the cases of Stalin, Lenin, and Hitler) than any less hypocritical form of robbery, plunder, swindling, theft, or piracy.

The idea underlying all practical or theoretical Utopianisms is to get you to accept a shilling's worth of Bait—buckshee: then, when you have entirely swallowed it down, hook and all, to sting you for the price of the angler's hook and line: his fare to the sea-side (first-class): his hotel expenses: his wine bill: his expensive fishing rod, four-geared reel, and brand-new silk line: then the gaff and the landing net: then his fare home: then for the stove, fuel, frying-pan, fennel, parsley, and frying-fat, in which the Bait-Happy victim is to sizzle—without forgetting the roll of sanitary torche-cul with which his captor will take leave of all that remains of his protégé when the processes of mastication and digestion are over.

So Bernard, the expensive shark, who did so many thousands of pounds' damage to fishing tackle, and in general treated anglers as anglers treat little fishes, was not so strangely named after all: and the Utopian inferences pertaining to his baptism, though accidental, were very apt indeed.

As soon as the whaling season ended, Bernard would swivel from a diet of whalemeat to one of mullet, caranteen, and pilchards. He seemed indifferent to the nature of the bait as long as the hook, trace, and sinker were there; he was even known to take a baitless hook, with which "Sardine" Saunders was trying to jigger some big black mullet at the side of the jetty, take it for a promenade round the submerged object, snap his part of the line and make off with the bare hook sticking into his jaws. The Indians never felt any mystery about Bernard. Govindar Sammy, who eventually caught him, was very proud of having landed a "holy guru" or "fakir shark" who pierced his cheeks, tongue, and lips with hooks.

I don't think sharks are sensible of pain since I have seen sharks cut open by flensing spades when trying to steal blubber off a moored whale. Though dying, they devoured their own entrails as they sank out of sight, without any loss of gusto or enjoyment.

Bernard went on doing a great deal of damage, till about twenty years ago. His career came to an end when the Navy were carrying out improvements on the North Pier. (During World War Two they ruined it completely, from a shark-fisher's point of view, by shortening it.) On this occasion however they merely closed the pier to shark fishers. Missing his snacks of steel, copper, and lead; noticing perhaps that the gannets, in thousands, were all flying south in endless chains only a yard above the water where even a sub-merged shark could see their shadows against the sky: noticing also that his fellow-sharks had all gone cruising southward and that there was hardly a fish bigger than a blacktail or a mullet that had not gone with them to meet the great annual migration of pilchards coming North from the Polar Seas, in May, at the beginning of the cold weather—Bernard fatally decided on a jaunt down the coast in the direction of Umzinto, where his skull and jawbones can still be seen hanging from a mango tree in the vegetable garden of Govindar Naidu Sammy, the pedlar of fruit and vegetables. The hooks and traces have now almost rusted away with the weather of the last twenty years, but from what can still be seen anyone can judge what a formidable sight it was when whiskered all over with lines and traces. I paid it a visit while on army leave in 1944.

At the time of Bernard's death, I was living at Umdoni nearby, in a cottage on the shore, engaged in editing *Voorslag*, with William Plomer and Laurens van de Post, who took no interest in fishing. The latter became a very fine soldier in World War II.

Samson Pillay, my Indian servant, was the most pleasant and intelligent fishing companion. He was then about fourteen, and was a ragged urchin I got from Mrs. General Botha, for whose family he was previously the bait-catcher, at Botha House, half a mile or so away. All British ex-Servicemen who were in military hospital either at Howick, Oribi Flats, Springfield, or any other big South African hospitals, will remember Samson as the owner of the "Fast-Quick-Ready Laundry Services," which smartened up their battle dresses for jaunts into Durban or Pietermaritzburg. He now owns three cars, and is a highly prosperous man, I am glad to say.

Samson and I were very excited waiting for the migration of "sardines" to come. I had never seen the phenomenon before, since I had lived only on the Zululand side, North of Durban; and the shoals peter out under the terrific massacre by sea-birds, fishes, and porpoises, long before they reach the North Coast. They generally swerve out to sea and disperse twenty miles south of Durban.

It was about half an hour before sunrise when Samson woke me to say the "sardines" had come. Going on to our verandah, I was astonished at what I took to be the faint foreglow of sunrise on masses of banked white clouds: but when I rubbed the sleep out of my eyes I realised that the clouds were made of birds.

Along the coast they formed a galaxy about forty miles long. According to the Press, that one swarm reached from Port Shep-

stone to Kelso junction, though in an hour or two it had almost
entirely dispersed. Far out to sea were other swarms like clouds of
smoke against the faintly-lit horizon. Nearer, they looked like
swarms of midges or mosquitoes. Nearer still, they were like locusts; but it was only overhead that they were struck by the emerging radiance. The sea was black, but ripped everywhere by
phosphorescent splashes made by giant fishes. The density of the
pilchards, together with the oil which exuded from their chopped
and slaughtered bodies, and lay like a film on the water, had becalmed the sea and entirely stopped the huge lines of breakers from
rising and rolling in, so that there was no surf at all. Only a faint
Mediterranean swell was perceptible, but every time it creamed
softly on the shingle it scattered a fringe of glittering silver bodies
over the beach.

   As soon as the light became clear enough, the first white streak
and splash of a gannet was the signal for them all to begin diving.
Imagine the Victoria Falls, and that every drop of water in them
were the size of a turkey or a goose, and had the velocity of a
feathered rocket-shell. In that superb cataract (which makes Niagara look like a village pump!) the more fiercely and steeply the
Zambezi plunges downwards into the abyss, so also the higher and
more steeply the volumes of vapour and mist spiral up over the
crest of the cataract forming myriads of rainbows (that give the
surrounding Rainbow Forest its name, almost hiding it from view).
It was the same with this living cataract of birds. The falling birds
shot sheer from a ceiling of about a hundred and fifty feet high,
raising ten-foot plumes of smoke with the percussion of their fall,
so that the sea looked as if it were tufted with millions of waving
plumes of pampa-grass. The air was scribbled white with a sleet
of falling arrows. Yet slowly, like the smoke of a huge cataract, the
birds who had already dived, rose spirally between these whizzing
shafts, formed in clouds above them, circled, descended again to the
"ceiling," where they hovered for a short time, as if sighting themselves, before they fired their white projectiles once more into the
cataract.

   I have never seen snow fall thicker than these birds. They all
dived from the same height. How or why they never collided is a
mystery to me. Yet they were snowing upwards as well as downwards, and no two flakes so much as brushed each other. The full

radiance of the rising sun then struck these millions of giddy snow-
flakes, turning them into showers of coloured confetti; orange,
crimson, scarlet, heliotrope, gold, and rose: and I recalled the mys-
tic lines of Rimbaud—

> Where sleep you in that sky of topless silence
> (Millions of golden birds) predestined Power?

When each bird had gorged its fill of a dozen or so of Pilchards
it simply did the Roman Emperor's trick of vomiting up the repast
and returning with new appetite to the feast. Never were more
ethereal and seraphic colours lavished on such a spectacle of de-
bauched gluttony and jaw-chopping frenzy, bathing it in all the
splendours of the spectrum.

When the sun rose clear the beauty of the scene vanished; the
birds also dispersed more widely; but one saw better what was
happening on the surface of the sea which was ripped open by huge
fishes leaping into the air—sunfishes, swordfishes, sharks, rays,
springers, and barracoutas—scattering the pilchards like smithereens
of winnowed silver over the surface of the sea.

Hearing a report like a gun I turned and saw a big splash on the
surface of the sea. Thinking a whale had just *sounded* after hitting
the water with its tail, I was about to turn away from it, when, like
a great white owl, thirty feet across, and half as much from
nose to tail, a gigantic eagle-ray or devil-fish, leaped silently
out of the water, with its wings spread wide, planed for a short distance, and struck the water flat, with a similar detonation. In the
background some whales, whose northward migration vaguely
coincides with those of the pilchards, were swimming at a terrific
speed in a lane between two vast black shoals of pilchards, and
sometimes leaping into the air, I suppose, to scare away the fish
from blocking their course or threatening to encircle their path
with their oppressive weight and numbers. From down on the
beach at sea level you could see the whales rise over the skyline,
against the sky itself. A vast cloud of spray would envelop the giant
body as it hit the water, and some seconds afterwards you would
hear two dull reports as of dynamite blasting in the distance: one
report came through the air and the other through the sea, travelling at different speeds. Never, as in those first two hours after

dawn, have I seen such visions of grandeur, awe, and beauty.

Hundreds of Indians had come from inland and were scooping up baskets of pilchards as they were chased out on to the beach by the bigger fish, many of which stranded themselves in their furious greed. We were baiting with whole foot-long pilchards and throwing them out, to be snapped up almost immediately by big fish. I was broken up seven times that day, only landed one springer, and lost all my line in one hour. Samson caught seventeen big fish and was in the seventh heaven. Rods were bending and reels were screeching all along the coast. Anglers, from far inland, warned by bush telegraph and grapevine, were turning up on horseback, bicycle, or car.

Then in the evening towards dusk, Govindar Sammy, the pedlar of fruit and vegetables, came staggering along the beach towards us with his rod almost buckled in two, playing some terrific monster with consummate skill: he was followed by an excited crowd of spectators. Samson reeled in so as not to foul his line, and he gradually disappeared southward along the beach into the dusk. His companions had lighted hurricane lamps and torches, and could be seen occasionally pouring water from their hats on to his reel to keep it from catching fire and singeing the line.

He gave up at about ten that evening through sheer exhaustion, to be relieved by his brother-in-law, Moonsammy Naidu. But from what we heard related next day, Govindar recovered at about midnight and took the rod again. Indians do not subscribe to the strict rules of the Pier. The fish seemed then to be swimming as powerfully as when he was first hooked. If he had run out straight with the line he could easily have broken it by keeping on in one direction instead of weaving to and fro: but in changing direction so furiously and so often, he began to exhaust himself as badly as he had exhausted Govindar. It was actually Bernard casting about for his favourite submerged obstacle and exasperating himself at not finding it. It was no longer the cool-headed cynical Bernard of the Breakwater.

Govindar found that the fish was now coming in slowly, and called to the very large crowd, who had collected in the light of flares and torches, to get ready their gaffs for, said he, "this fish is bigger than the motor-launch that ferries the workmen from the Point to the Bluff in Durban Harbour."

The huge dorsal fin of the fish became clearly visible only nine or ten yards from the rock-ledge on which they stood. This ledge, level then with the tide, nevertheless sheered down to a depth of thirty feet or so. Suddenly there was a tremendous splash and a swirl of phosphorescent foam, which rocketed far out into the darkness. The line was rushed out some 200 yards and then went limp: but Govindar found that there was still a dead-weight at the end. Slowly, painfully, he reeled it in. Six men got their gaffs in, and tugged the weight high and dry over the ledge. It was the head, but only the head, of an enormous shark, whiskered and festooned with hundreds of lines and rusty traces, and weighing three hundred pounds. They weighed it at a neighbouring goods train siding, Umdoni Park. It had been bitten neatly off just behind the gills as a springer might bite a pilchard, and spat out along with its metallic encumbrances. It was Bernard all right—and no mistake!

Govindar's disappointment (at not having landed the main bulk of "Bernard's" body) was more than compensated by the mystical elation, which, as a very devout Hindoo, he felt in having caught what he insisted was an extremely holy and saintly shark—or at any rate a considerable chunk of one. At first I could not fathom this notion of his; but as it is the only one which in any way accounts for Bernard's hook-swallowing habits or makes any sense of them at all, I offer it for what it is worth.

When I ridiculed his idea of the goodness and sanctity of "Bernard," and said that, even for a shark, I reckoned him to be an extremely nasty piece of work indeed, and a public nuisance, too, for running off with so many thousands of pounds' worth of good line, traces, swivels, and spoons, which weren't of the slightest nourishment-value to himself, Govindar floored me by replying that Bernard was a "guru," an extremely good, holy man among sharks. It wasn't that he was greedy for the valuable line, spoons and swivels: but only for the hooks, which were as cheap as dirt. He couldn't help the line breaking when he went off with the hook. That sort of damage was not intentional but accidental. But *hooks he must have*, for he was a Fakir-shark, and a very, very holy one indeed. "Dis piss swallowing more piss-hook dan holy man Pakir swallowing needle-and-fin outside temple at South Coast Junction. Dis piss no gotting needle-and-fin. Only piss-hook gotting. Holy Pakir, him sticking needle and fine, somtimes twenty, tirty, porty, troo tongue and side-cheeks at same time. Didn't you ever wenting to seeing him? Yes, Master? Well, diss piss sticking piss-hook troo tongue and side-cheeks, twenty, tirty, porty, all same time, same-like Pakir at South Coast Junction. Look inside mouth, Master."[1] Sure enough, the inside of Bernard's mouth resembled the outside of the Fakir's though the latter cannot withdraw his tongue but keeps it protruding for hours owing to the vertical hatpins and needles, sometimes a couple of dozen of them, with which he transfixes it clean through, while he pierces his cheeks transversally with hatpins and needles also, just for the look of it, for that part of it is easy. It is the tongue that is painful. I could quite follow Govindar's exegesis on that score, but couldn't understand why he should have been so much more elated at killing a sacred and saintly shark than a profane one, or how it reflected any extra holiness on the devout Govindar. But here I must digress on the subject of hook-swallowing, bulb-chewing, and hatpin-sticking.

In 1939 (June to August) I worked as an alternative equestrian turn to a very nice walnut-stained British Fakir and his beautiful nose-ringed English aide and girl-friend, in the "Cirque Prio" on a tour through Castile, La Mancha, and Andalusia, where Monsieur Prio advertised him as "Traga-Bombillas" or "Swallow-electric-light-bulbs." We called him "Traga-Bom" for short. He had all the repertoire of the South Coast Junction guru, and the ichthyological guru of the breakwater, up his sleeve, with a lot more besides. There was no deception about it. He pierced his tongue with fifteen needles every night, and chewed and swallowed two electric light-bulbs (which he afterwards brought up), besides knocking dozens of hatpins through his neck and arms. What always astounded me was that his tongue was never the slightest bit sore and never bled a drop.

In June, 1950, I took Richard Aldington's beautiful little daughter, Catherine, who was staying with us, and my own daughter, Anita, to a Circus at Bormes, in the Var. It turned out to be Monsieur Prio's! We were given the place of honour at the show,

---

[1] The gist of this rigmarole is roughly this:—

"This fish swallows more hooks than the Fakir outside the temple at South Coast Junction swallows needles and pins. Where was a fish to buy needles and pins? All he could use was hooks. The holy Fakir sticks twenty, thirty, or forty needles and pins through his tongue and cheeks at the same time. Haven't you been to see him? Yes? Well, this fish was doing the same, only with hooks. Look inside his mouth."

after recognition and cordial embraces all round, and invited into the Caravan after the show, to the great delight of Catherine, who had never seen the inside of Circus Life before.

The star turn of the show was a magnificent *tame* wild-boar. After making the acquaintance of the new additions to the families of Monsieur and Madame Prio, the Clown, Monsieur Radiguet, and his wife, the Trapezist, whose grown daughters now support her act, we spoke of the rough old days in post-war Spain, and I noticed that "Traga-Bom" seemed the only one missing, so I asked the *Patron* about him. I was astounded to hear that he had died of blood poisoning in Lisbon from pricking his finger on a gramophone needle, which is almost as strange as the fate of the great boxer, Greb, who gave Tunney five of the hardest fights of his career, and died a few months after the last one, in a plastic surgeon's beauty parlour, under chloroform, while having his nose straightened and his face lifted.

"Traga-Bom" was a fine fellow but neither very saintly nor devout, since he swore like a trooper in a cultured Oxford accent. He relied mostly on a knowledge of anatomy, and was, I think, an interrupted medical student. He discussed all his tricks freely and intelligently and made no professional secrets of them. There was actually no trickery at all. Acutely sensitive to some kinds of discomfort, he was no ascetic and had two nice beds in his caravan-compartment, while I did well enough on the grass between the wheels of his caravan, with two blankets sewn together (which I used as a saddle-cloth by day) and my saddle under my head.

After Catherine Aldington, Anita, and I had bade good-bye to the Prios, we started walking back, hand-in-hand, in the pitch-dark, across the village-square, when suddenly we all stood simultaneously on what seemed to be an earthquake and were precipitated headlong. It was the performing "wild"-boar, or sanglier, which had slipped its halter and dug itself a lovely deep hole to sleep in, on the square, at the foot of the ancient chapel of St. Francis. It's funny how many animals dig themselves in under his statue. The sanglier rushed off, grumbling, back to its place under Prio's trailer. No one has filled the hole in yet; and no one ever will. For are we not in the land of the hunter, Tartarin, here in Provence? The inhabitants proudly show the hole to visitors . . . "C'est un sanglier qui a fait ça."

There is, quite near Bormes, an establishment for the rearing of these wild-boars in captivity: that was where Monsieur Prio bought his performing *sanglier* as a squeaker. They abound in the surrounding forests and mountains of the Maures.

Whenever I look at the wild-boar's hole in the square in Bormes, while I am playing "boules" there with the postman, the garde-champêtre, and other notable citizens, I am reminded of Bernard: for I think, first of all, of stepping on to the sleeping boar, then of the "Cirque Prio"; then of my good mate "Traga-Bom," the Fakir, then of the South Coast Junction Fakir, and then by an irresistible logic, of Govindar and the greatest and holiest Fakir of them all— Bernard, the Mahatma of the breakwater, who though only a fish, without going to a luxury villa in Hollywood and mortifying himself on a huge pile of green-backs, yet made a pukka guru of himself on the spot, by manufacturing his holiness out of whatever came to hand (or rather mouth) just as Robinson Crusoe made his furniture.

I left Umdoni Park shortly after the death of Bernard. Here is Samson's farewell letter to me which I received in Durban before sailing for England. I keep it with affection and pride to this day.

"Deair Master,

I went hom on Monday afternoon i was in bed two weeks. now I am filling better. I am very sorry that I lost you I am not going to get a bos lik you.

Deair Master you are the man talking true and honest in this World, every Indian and native saying you are the god in this world I am very sorry that I lost you I am thinking you all the time in my mine.

                    Pleace Repli me Sir
Samsen c.o Dicken, Botha House, Umdoni Park

Deair master I will be very glad if you can get me one pound of 24 gaing [gauge?] steel wire for fishing tracing and I will sen the money in post pleace sen without fail pleace Sir I will be very glad. My father want to fish every day she want plenty wire."

The reader may ask how we fish for such fish as the one who found "Bernard" a dainty morsel, swallowed his body, and spat out his head. They are fished outside the breakwaters, by means of twenty-five-gallon petrol-drums attached by hawsers to hooks the size of anchors, with hindlegs of horses or mules for bait. These are

thrown adrift from motor launches. The angler sits back in the
boat with folded arms, smoking, and the fish hooks and plays himself. He fights against his own strength, which submerges the drum
to such depths and pressures that it develops the upward force of a
jet-engine, pulls the shark back to the surface, and is in turn pulled
down, till the shark, exhausted, begins to absorb water in its gills
and drowns itself. The angler then knocks out his pipe, ships the
petrol drum, and tows home his catch. In fact the fish really does
all the hard work, except actually cutting himself up and boiling
down his own liver, which is done when he arrives at the works.

Rod-fishing, which I love, is one thing at which I was always
hopeless though all my brothers are good at it, and though I have
mastered other more gladiatorial forms of sport which are supposed
to be more difficult. Our glorious surf begins at the breakwater and
goes on for hundreds of miles up the coast till you come to the big
coral reef. There are few things to beat the exhilaration and adventure of riding in without the effeminate aid of a surf-board, on one
of the giant breakers that roll in from far off, and shoot thundering
up our beaches. It is an excitement to fight your way out, diving under the back-breaking fury of those waves which you reach too
soon; then to time and seize, at just the right moment, the great
wave (which would otherwise break your back like a straw) and
share its stupendous and friendly impetus, with your head and
shoulders protruding from the avalanche of foam, and the spray
fanning out from your chest (as if from a speed boat), as you fur-
row the calm water in front of it. That is about the fifth of the
great physical pleasures of this life.

XIII

VOYAGE TO ENGLAND—OXFORD— LONDON

THE breakwater was the last thing I saw of Durban on my first remembered trans-oceanic voyage on the s.s. *Inkonka*, 2,000 tons (Captain Barrow) of the Harrison Rennie Line, in 1918. The scarcity of shipping made it impossible to get across as an ordinary passenger, so I had to come on a cargo-boat.

No sooner had the breakwater slid past my porthole, while I was arranging my bunk, than the third mate came in and noticed that I carried more books than was usual for odd deckhands and super-cargoes. He was even more indignant when he found them to be non-scientific. "Wot's this? Classics, hey? Never done no good to nobody since they was first invented. They'll never get you any-where, they won't." Whereupon he pushed Shakespeare, Milton, Keats, Dryden, Pope, Marlowe, and all my painting and drawing materials out of the porthole into the sea. Then, seeing that I was trying to take it with a grin though I had tears in my eyes (for I al-ways had a lot of "Candide" in my nature) and being a truly kind-hearted fellow in spite of his hatred of "the Classics," he said: "There, there, don't take it to 'eart. I'll lend you a book wot'll com-pensate all that rubbidge. It's me Bible, that's wot it is though it ain't no Bible; and I'll lend it to you if you come to my cabin at eight bells. I only thrown away that rubbidge for your own good. You'll thank me one day."

The weather came on very rough and I agreeably surprised the third mate by my handiness and general seamanship for I had often been out on our tiny cockleshell whalers in far worse weather. He made no secret of the fact that I had impressed him and that he never expected so much from a scholar of "Classics." When I re-ported at his cabin at eight bells, his "Bible" proved to be a well-thumbed copy of *Ann Veronica*. By the end of the voyage I had got on cheeking-terms with him and was really very fond of him, as he was of me. We had arguments about poetry versus science to which Captain Barrow, the first mate Mr. Owen, and the Engineer apprentices, and wireless operators used to listen with their mouths open, laughing at the terrific spates of polysyllabic words with which the 3rd (a young man of about twenty-two) and I would try to floor each other and at the same time impress our audience with our erudition.

The crew and the bosun (or serang) were lascars. There were plenty of spells of fine weather and plenty of spare time which I would spend right up at the foc's'le-head watching the albatrosses, mollymauks, sea-lions, cape-hens, cape-pigeons, porpoises and all those strange and beautiful creatures that inhabit the majestic southern extremity of our continent. Going around Agulhas (or the Needles) to the Cape itself, I am always thrilled by the rugged grandeur and wildness of the scene, and by the size of the waves.

> The ranges moved like long two-handed saws,
> Notching the scarlet west with jagged line.

But it is only Camocs, the greatest of all South African poets, who gives one in words a real sense of its awe and the grandeur of its stormy seas in that wonderful passage about Rounding the Cape.

Standing up at the fo'c'sle head and ducking under the cross-plate at the vortex of the bows when the ship drove her nose into the great Cape rollers forty feet high with a quarter of a mile between their marbled summits, one shouted and sang with joy and elation in the movement of the ship and in one's own immunity, as the spate of water rushed overhead and one emerged from the safety of the cross-plate to see the next great hill of water approaching as the ship tobogganed down the slope of the last one, to meet it.

After the Cape one could watch the flying-fishes and bonitos and, at night, the phosphorescent calm sea starred with myriads of luminous globes by the jellyfish and nautili, and looking like the lights of London seen from Highgate, or the Water-tower on Campden Hill, on a slightly hazy night—and the fishes passing like the lamps of taxis and buses.

Yes. The third mate was right—not to give me *Ann Veronica*, which is ridiculous drivel—but to chuck those good books out of the porthole, so that I spent my spare time with the sun, stars, and moon, and the winds and the spray. He not only meant well, but did well, as I was getting too studious. You can see the backwash of this voyage in the *Flaming Terrapin:* but of course that effort would have been impossible without all the chunks of ore stolen from Marlowe, Keats, Dryden, Pope, and Milton. (I soon bought them all back.) It was only good that I was forced to concentrate on the sea while I was on it, for I loved it so much that it made me return to it.

We landed at Dakar where Captain Barrow was so kind as to take me ashore with him to carry his bag and to act as interpreter: and very proud I was too, to walk beside so fine and handsome a figure as he made in his spotless white uniform, with his beautiful knobbed ebony stick. Everybody turned their heads to look at us: and while I was waiting, myself, outside some shipping office, a native dignitary, sitting in the back of a very antiquated landau in a scarlet tarboosh with a blue robe and brilliant yellow slippers, halted his coachman (who was dressed in a fantastic "tiger" livery) when they came abreast of me. Then very solemnly he saluted me, raising his tarboosh vertically by the tassel, with the English words: "Yes. All right." Not being a Saxon, I did not give a sheepish look, but raised my own hat and with a deep solemn bow said: "Forever and ever, Amen."

In the bay was the Heath-Robinsonesque, palm-crested fortress of Goree, which had seen the ships of the slave-traders Drake and Hawkins, who revived the traffic in humans under the aegis of the Reformation, and in defiance of the ban of the Holy Inquisition. It had also been the headquarters of the Arab slave trade for centuries. In 1918 it served as barracks for one of the scruffiest battalions of the French Legion (the best of them being at the front) with their bevies of negresses. The Legion can be a very smart unit, but in Dakar that year it did not show up to the best advantage.

It was the first time I had seen whites philandering with blacks, and I had a terrible shock when I was accosted by a *British* sailor who wanted the price of a drink, and told me he was being kept by a negress in the native quarter. At home each race kept to itself, *as far as one could see*—though there is, of course, a half-caste population to show what goes on in the underworld. Anyway I had never thought of coloured women as being anything but the concern of coloured men: and white women as the concern of white men. That seemed to me to be the very reason of their colouration—so that they could keep to their own people. Hybrids between negro and white do not seem to justify the mixture, as they are neither hardy, strong, nor intelligent as a general rule, especially when, as almost without exception in Africa, the father is white and the mother black. The most intelligent and the best half-breed ever known in Africa was the son of a black man by a white mother—but that proves nothing. It is such a rare occurrence.

The native quarter of Dakar was dirtier than Kensington with the excrement of dogs, in spite of the fact that on every hut was perched a kite—"the shite hawk" of the British Tommy. Once these birds swarmed in London; and it is a pity they don't come back as they are invaluable scavengers and cleaners-up of all dirt and offal.

Captain Barrow had taken me ashore partly to act as an interpreter: and my Mauritian French caused the ships-chandlers and others to burst into fits of laughter, since it was so funny to hear a European talking the French equivalent of Pidgin English, without using the pronoun "vous" but "tutoying" them and using 18th-century archaisms. The laughter evoked in Dakar caused me to remain tongue-tied when I first went to Paris, with Thomas Earp, as a student from Oxford, until I had got the modern idiom by ear.

We called in at Las Palmas which had hardly received a single visit from a ship during the whole war. The parrot selling, bumboat part of the population nearly went mad at our approach, swarmed up the side of the ship, and behaved altogether so dangerously that our officers had to clear the decks at the point of the revolver.

It was here, when visiting the Cathedral with one of the apprentices who was a Roman Catholic, that I made a proper fool of myself: for when we were being shown the sacred treasures of the place, amongst them the heart of the saintly Bishop Juan de Frias, who sacrificed himself to the protection of the Guanches or natives of the Canaries—I laughed in a superior way and swore it was the heart of a rhino or a hippo, so magnified was it by the glass and the spirits in which it was preserved. I even said this in my previous autobiography. But the Bishop has had the last laugh! I have seen it since and repented of my error, since I am now sailing in the same boat, whose mast is a single shaft and spar: and, though he is one of the officers and I am only a lascar on the lookout at the fo'c'sle, I can sing out to him cheerfully as the lascar on watch sings out at night: "Am dekty hai! Batti acha Sahib!" ("I'm on the watch-out. The lights are O.K., Sir!")

Captain Barrow was on the bridge as we moved slowly up the Thames. I was at the forecastle-head with one of the apprentices, Guy Taylor, whose father was editor of the *Cambridge Times*. We were taking leave of one another and Guy, aged fifteen, gave me the following counsel: "Take the 3rd Mate's advice. Quit thinking of art and literature. You will never make the grade, I know. You have not got the imagination to be a journalist or a writer like Dad."

I had spent so many happy days there watching the flying fish and porpoises, or, on stormy days, ducking under the stanchion between the plates as the bows went into the waves, and two or three feet of green water (a foot above one's head) rolled thunder-ing over the forecastle, to bury the fore-deck, yet without wetting a hair of one's head, I had a lump in my throat as I stood there with the learned and paternal apprentice for the last time. The *Inkonka* had become home to me.

Though the water was still and white, and full of garbage, dead puppy dogs, and cats, there was no sign of land. It was certainly by far the widest river I had ever seen, for we seemed still to be at sea except for the fact that no swell was discernible. Then ware-houses and other phantasmal buildings loomed through the mist on the distantly converging banks. Slowly, forests of masts and cranes began to appear, and moving almost imperceptibly we berthed in the East India Docks cracking the first film of ice I had ever seen outside a refrigerator. That was my first view of this beloved London that forever grows on one like the Ocean—an ocean whose waves are people.

Of Captain Barrow I heard a story thirty years later which al-together epitomises that splendid man—the only great Christian I ever met (outside a monastery) who never swore or drank. This Christian was more like a Muslim. When I was a Talks Producer on the B.B.C. from 1946-1949, I had the good luck to get as my secretary Miss Daphne Chasmar, one of the best-looking, best-tempered, most efficient, and cleverest of all the secretaries on the B.B.C. How she kept me in leash, without my getting the sack, for four years, is her secret. Now this excellent young lady was the daughter of another Captain on the Harrison-Rennie Line, Captain Chasmar, who was Captain Barrow's best friend—and this link, though tenuous, coming through the B.B.C. made me very happy.

The two Captains, so one story runs, were being pestered in some foreign port by one of those touts for houses of ill-fame. He followed them for about two hours, to shipping offices, to cafés, to post-offices, and everywhere they went. He even began tugging the spotless white sleeve of Captain Barrow's uniform with his greasy hands. The long-suffering Captain could stand it no more. He unexpectedly swore the most terrible oath, and raising a heavy knobbed ebony stick, which he always carried, he dealt the paynim such a blow as Roland dealt the Moor at Roncesvalles. The paynim, with his head opened like a pomegranate, fell inanimate to the pavement. "God forgive me," gasped the devout Captain Barrow in consternation, "God forgive me, *for swearing!*"

I was very sad to leave my friends on the *Inkonka*. But I left the *Inkonka* a souvenir, which was apparently treasured; for when I saw the ship again, years after, she was running to Jamaica, and there on the front of the bridge, nailed firmly into the wood, was the same pair of Inkonka horns, almost the record from Natal, which I had given to Captain Barrow when I left the ship.

When we had berthed, Captain Barrow told me to go and fetch a taxi, put my luggage aboard, and tell the driver to drive me and a West African who was with us, also bound for Scotland, to Euston. I found the taxi-rank, and walked along it looking for one of the taxi drivers to unbend from his Memnon-like, stony dignity. But they all sat rigidly staring in front of them with their knees wrapped in rugs, and I could make no impression at all. I feared a snub and walked up and down the rank without being able to attract any notice at all.

This is a punishment for having stalked so many animals. Though above average height and noticeable in a Company of soldiers, I am always the last to be noticed in a bar or at the counter of a shop. A subconscious absenteeism, which has hypnotic power, camouflages me completely. Similarly it was proverbial in the army how I could stand on parade at Brecon, with faulty equipment—without a respirator, or as on the day when my rifle was missing—and get away with a whole inspection. So it has its advantages.

In the end, leaving the taxis, I saw a jolly looking fellow with a small donkey-cart. From that moment I have been in love with London. I had no fear of him at all and we struck a bargain there and then. He stung the West African and myself about ten times the cost of a taxi, but he drove us almost everywhere, all day, between the East India Docks and Euston; and by the time we reached the station we had seen the Nelson Column, the Tower, the Old Bailey, the General Post Office, Madame Tussaud's, Saint Paul's, Westminster Abbey, and, last but not least, Gamage's, of whose annual catalogue I was almost as rabid a devourer as the Suluman himself—but chiefly with regard to rods, reels, and fire-arms. My mother and Mrs. Gamage had been schoolfriends in Scotland, and Neil, who had visited England with my mother, had been given more or less the freedom of the shop, and a ride in an aeroplane, which had made me very envious when I was small.

We took all day to get to Euston and next day I turned up at Glenboig with only sixpence to spare after my 8,000 mile journey. Glenboig is in the blackest of the Black countries. Colm Brogan tells me that it was never blitzed in either of the World Wars, because, when either the Luftwaffe or the Zeppelins passed over it, and saw how miserable and desolate it looked, they thought it had already been blitzed, and so they spared it. But Glenboig House itself was on the top of a rise, and from its top windows you could see the kopjes round Ben Lomond and other picturesque hills.

My grandfather, James Dunnachie, who was the local squire, was a grand-looking old man with a passion for collecting pictures, which eventually almost ruined him. He had known Browning, Tennyson, Rossetti, and other Pre-Raphaelites. My aunt, his daughter-in-law, was one of the famous family of Napiers and still was, at forty or so, one of the most dazzling beauties I have ever seen. There were also two beautiful girl cousins on their holidays from St. Leonards.

With a present from my grandfather I soon repaired the damage done to my small library by the third mate of the s.s. *Inkonka*.

My elder brothers were still in the Royal Flying Corps, but they often appeared from their base, at Turnberry, in a little Morris Oxford, which George had been able to buy with the accumulation of his pay, while he was in the East African jungle bombing the German raider, the *Koenigsberg*, up the Rufigi river. We drove all over the place in this car which George had with him when he returned to Edinburgh as a student. We visited Rosslyn, Hawthornden, and other places before I came south to Oxford.

I had letters from my father to Sir Walter Raleigh, Regius Professor of English, who was a great friend of his, to H. A. L. Fisher, J. J. Thomson, and Sir Ernest Barker, all of whom were very kind to me; and in the end it was decided I should be sent to Merton.

The first person I met at Oxford was one of the greatest men who have been there this century, a real genius, and, at the same time, one of the very finest fellows I ever met in my life. This was William Walton, the composer. He was one year younger than me, being then sixteen. We went to the same tutor of Greek, Mr. G. W. Young of Holywell, and we became very good friends. We walked out with two young ladies, who were also good friends, and who were employed as waitresses. Of course, needless to say, Willie's one eventually became a countess. Something magical seems to happen to everything he touches.

My knowledge and appreciation of music in those days was confined chiefly to the rag-times on Colin's gramophone, from *Hitchy-Koo* and the *Grizzly Bear*, down to *Oh, You Beautiful Doll* and *If You Were the Only Girl*. But I knew, besides them, almost every one of the old Highland songs learned from my Highland mother, all the old sea-shanties right through, and all the old Boer marching songs. I have always been in demand for concerts in the Sergeants' Mess, for whoopees on troopships, and also on long route marches because I sing in tune and have a sense of rhythm.

Before the Wet Canteens were abolished on the troopships I was always able to keep the platoon, of which I was in charge, merrily half-seas-over, so that they didn't fight or get into mischief through boredom, by singing, having the hat passed round, and spending the proceeds on beer for the lads. One night when the W.O.'s passed round my bush-hat on the *Antenor* after I had sung and done a comic turn, it was so heavy with money that I could hardly lift it.

This I spent on my platoon, and I loved every one of those twenty-nine men as much as if each had been my son.

But in spite of my ear for tunes, even Willie with all his genius couldn't arouse in me the least feeling for classical music. What he did give me, even then, was a sense of vocation and how a man can live for his art.

Of all the circuitous makeshifts that Man has improvised as substitutes for the lost art of prayer in an age of declining faith: of all those activities, such as work (the prayer of slaves), action, politics, or science, by which he attempts, with the least possible amount of self-sacrifice, to get into touch with the Divine Providence, without having the intellectual strain and effort of the vertical ascent required in prayer—Art (by which I mean all creative work from painting to the composition of music) is perhaps the least devious and the nearest to the perpendicular ascent. It requires a single-minded devotion similar to that required of a good priest or the self-dedication of a good soldier.

Sir Osbert Sitwell's superb word-portrait of William Walton, in *Laughter in the Next Room*, brings out this quality in him: and makes me see him just as he was then. This quality of dedication was always felt, though not obtrusively, even in his lightest moments, and he was by no means a solemn companion. There was in his mind, even when he was clowning, a sort of alertness as if inspiration could visit him at any moment and he was ready for it. Anyway one felt that he was always consciously within range of something unusual. This alertness was amusingly expressed in a sort of stationary, almost imperceptible lift of the shoulders which were seldom relaxed, but more or less held in the position of a man at the keyboard of a piano. There was nothing strained about it. A man is most suddenly wide awake when he is under a cold shower in the morning and he raises his shoulders, in just such a way as does Walton, with a sort of inward exhilaration, as if lifted by invisible wings. His accent varied according to his mood, and sudden animation or excitement was sure to reveal the traces of a broad Lancashire accent underlying the more polished accent he had acquired at Oxford.

Talking of raised shoulders, Tschiffely once told me of a Gaucho who had the nickname "Regadera" or "Watering-can." Most nicknames given by cattlemen are so perfect that they obviate any necessity for identity-cards, or even for fingerprints (in the case of criminals). Yet there was something of a puzzle about this name. "Why do you call him Regadera?" asked Tschiffely. "Well, don't you see? He has his shoulders slightly raised as if he were taking a shower," replied somebody. On the Pampas there are no shower-baths, so a watering-can is suspended to a branch or beam, and turned on by pulling a string attached to the spout which automatically raises the shoulders when the cold water falls. The natives at home are wonderfully accurate in their nicknames, but I never heard of a nickname which hit off a peculiarity with such delicacy and finality as this name of "Regadera."

It was soon apparent both to William and myself and to our excellent tutor Mr. Young that we were not cut out for scholars of the routine sort. William was already equipped for greatness, with a metaphorical self-starter and internal combustion. My mental outfit corresponded rather to a horse and buggy than a Rolls-Royce, like his. But the sort of knowledge I required, before I could exploit my minor talent, was only to be acquired by travel, adventure, and rubbing shoulders with all sorts of people. I hate "Humanity" and all such abstracts: but I love *people*. Lovers of "Humanity" generally hate *people and children*, and keep parrots or puppy dogs.

During the year I was at Oxford I lay on my back and read more than twenty other students would read in that period—mostly Elizabethan Drama. William introduced me to the people who have influenced and helped me most in my subsequent literary career, Edith, Osbert, and Sacheverell Sitwell, Eliot, Wyndham Lewis, Thomas Earp, Philip Heseltine, Cecil Gray, and others.

I went off to Paris for the long vacation with Earp who was then the uncrowned King of Oxford, and President of the Oxford Union. He is still, to my mind, the finest wit and the most exquisite literary critic alive. The miraculous feeling of walking into a famous University from the Bush and being accepted on a much higher level than one was accepted at home, was very exhilarating. Earp's unofficial tuition saved me years of trial and error: and it was through him that I found the French symbolists who have since influenced me most—if we discount my own basic self-immersion in the English Elizabethans and metaphysical poets.

There is no short cut to technical mastery, as is shown by the disastrously amateurish verse written today by more talented poets than myself. One cannot improve on the original metres of English verse: one can only bring the language more up to date. If you attempt to eliminate rhyme and grammatical structure, you will have to fall back on the far more artificial aid of Whitman's rhetorical repetitions at the beginnings of lines.

While in Oxford I met Robert Graves, Edmund Blunden, L. A. G. Strong, Alan Porter, Robert Nichols, Wilfred Childe, Richard Hughes, A. E. Coppard, Edgell Rickword, Louis Golding, Thomas Moult, Hugo Dyson, V. de Sola Pinto, Anthony Bertram, L. P. Hartley, C. B. Kitchin—some of whom were visitors, others residents, but mostly students. With many of them I have enjoyed a long friendship.

When Walton left, I went down to London to try to take up a literary existence and shared a flat with Thomas Earp, Russell Green, and the great Mahatma of all misanthropy, Aldous Huxley, who was already famous for his verse. I began to suffer slightly from over-domestication.

As a practical zoologist and botanist, and one whose knowledge of beasts and birds, cereals, grazing, and fodder had a human value; as one who belonged (unlike other poets around me) to the most essential and necessary type of skilled workers—the providers of meat, fish, corn, leather, wool, oil and fats, I felt ill at ease with this pedant who leeringly gloated over his knowledge of how crayfish copulated (through their third pair of legs) but could never have caught or cooked one; let alone broken in a horse, thrown and branded a steer, flensed a whale, or slaughtered, cut, cured, and cooked anything at all.

I have always known that the non-bookish existence underlies and precedes the bookish one, which should ornament and implement the latter: and that the eye is far more important than the pince-nez, the telescope, or the microscope. Although they are not to be despised, such machines are subsidiary aids.

> By this clear knowledge I unread my books
> And learned, in spite of theories and charts,
> Things have a nearer meaning to their looks
> Than to their dead analysis in parts;

And that, for all the outfit be antique,
Our light is in our heads and we can seek
The clearest information in our hearts.

Huxley was always as lost and bewildered by the very scientific
civilization of which he is one of the main prophets, as a wild
African giraffe would be if it were suddenly to be dumped in the
middle of Piccadilly or Broadway.

Our colleague Russell Green, a charming, kind, and good-
natured fellow, had been sent down from Oxford for being a
"conshie," or a vegetarian, or a socialist—I forget which. His command of polysyllables was something tremendous and he was always writing those sequences of autobiographical novels which
have placed him as No. 1 epic novelist of Sheffield. Russell was a
verbal gyrationist. Sentences to him were what labyrinths are to
minotaurs.

There were two young ladies giving dancing lessons on the floor
upstairs and this used to disturb both our Mahatmas as they composed their masterpieces. The Mahatma of Sheffield, though even
more polysyllabic than the Mahatma of Hollywood, was far more
human and amenable- and he always unselfishly volunteered for
any such dangerous mission as asking the girls not to bounce too
much on the ceiling while he and Aldous were typing.

Russell, like most nihilists and world-upheavers, was a polite and
timid civil servant who always adjusted his tie and coughed before
launching himself into his arabesques of polysyllables. He went upstairs, knocked, and when the door was opened, coughed twice po-
litely, straightened his collar and tie, and then asked the young lady
if she would kindly "discontinue the bombinations against the
ceiling pending the incubation, er. er. . . or gestatory cerebration
of certain masterpieces," etc., etc. The girl hearing the word bombinations, and mistaking the rest of it for swear-words, thought
that she and her friend had been mistaken for prostitutes and were
being accused of perpetrating "abominations." The whole dancing
class rushed out after Russell like the witches of Burns on hearing
the piercing screams of the insulted girl, and Russell was forced to
flee for safety, like a sort of vegetarian Tam O'Shanter, while the

bombinations redoubled themselves on the floor above with the Dionysiac fury of a witches' dance.

London still fascinated me and I continued to wander through its infinite variety of labyrinths in search of some fabulous minotaur which I always knew to be lurking here in the fogs: and which I eventually found years later—a sort of psychic miasma which I slew in the *Georgiad*.

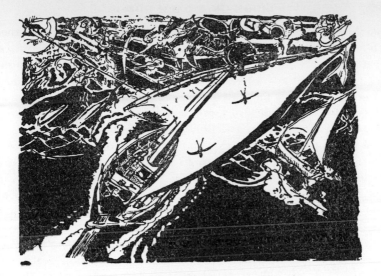

XIV

THE LAND OF THE CYPRESS
AND MYRTLE

THOUGH London fascinated me, I wearied for a flash of the clear pagan sunlight to which I was used and, hearing from Augustus John of the beauties of Provence, I decided to have a holiday down there. Some remark he vaguely dropped about cattle and horses and tunny fishing intrigued me: but it was some time before I broke the ice with the true people of Provence. My thirty years' association with that country was celebrated in 1950 by an invitation from the Préfet of the Bouches du Rhône to be the guest of honour at the Floral and Taurine Games at Arles: and by a full front page leading article in the *Provencal* headed: "Une Grande Figure de Camarguais." I am very proud of this since my poetry has never been translated into Provencal and my celebrity there is not a part of my literary reputation, but due entirely to my prowess with horses and cattle; this proves me to be a true citizen of the "Equestrian Nation" as we call it.

There I first got a glimpse of the cattle country round St. Louis du Rhône, Fos, and the Saintes Maries. I travelled there with the late Geoffrey Nelson, the painter, who left when we got to Cassis. At Cassis all my funds ran out but I got a job on a three-masted barque—the *Santa Maria* which came there for cement. The mate of this ship, Moro by name, had many relatives near Viterbo and also near Foggia: they were in the cattle-trade and were known as Vaccari—the equivalent of Gardian in Provence, Vaquero in Spain, Gaucho in S. America, and Buckaroo or Cowboy in America.

I stayed twice with Moro when we took cargoes to Naples. We enjoyed great hospitality at three or four ranches. It was before Mussolini had drained the Campagna, the Maremme or the Apulian plain, and the Pontine Marshes. The cattle were of the ancient wild breed not unlike those of Provence, Spain, Portugal, some parts of Hungary, and (except in their colour) those of Chillingham. That is to say they were distinguished from domestic cattle, by the fact that the calves will charge a man who molests them as soon as they are able to stand on their feet, and all these breeds wear their horns for combat, projecting forwards, with sharp points—not as rudimentary relics or handles to bicycles when they require to be thrown or branded, or tied up for milking.

The easiest cattle to throw by the horns either from the ground or from a horse are, naturally, the Afrikander cattle, on whose horns the greatest leverage can be purchased since they sometimes span five feet and project at right angles to their spines. If only our arms were long enough, it would be possible to kill them with a single jerk. If we discount anguses (which are thrown by the chin) and zebus, these cattle of the Campagna are amongst the hardest to throw by their horns in spite of their being fairly wide, since their forward angle neutralises the purchase and forces one to work with one's body thrown dangerously far forward and liable to take a dive over the forehead of the animal.

The other day in Goodge Street I ran into an ex-comrade-in-Arms, Sgt. Major Blundell of the King's African Rifles, who was "killed" while throwing a zebu which his Askaris had offered him the honour of slaughtering (as I have often done for them) for their Christmas dinner, to be roasted whole. The animal, a bull, had awkward horns. His hands slipped. It gored him so badly that the two M.O.'s who tried to save him diagnosed death from loss of blood. His heart had stopped and he went cold: yet he came to soon after when he was being lowered into his coffin, and they were just going to cover him with the Union Jack. He managed to move his hand, so great was his fright.

When I met my old friend he was atttending the Middlesex Hospital as an out-patient because the goring had resulted in tumours on the hip-joint and he had been returned home as permanently disabled. I am glad to say he has recovered from the tumours. I put him "on the air" on the B.B.C. (which was quite handy round the corner) for it is not often that one can get a rival of Orpheus or Aeneas,

"Vainqueur d'Achéron deux fois,"

to speak on the microphone. The planchette is the more usual form of communication with those that have made the trip. When there are cases like Blundell's walking about the streets of London, well we may say of that most fascinating of all big cities, where you meet people that you have met in the most distant parts of the Earth, and even those who have come back from the next world—

"Fourmillante cité, cité pleine de rêves,
Ou le spectre en plein jour raccroche le passant!"
(Ant-swarming city, city filled with dreams,
Where in broad day the spectre tugs your sleeve.)

In the Italian rodeos and bullfights known as "giostras" they alternate bulls and waterbuffaloes, of which there were thousands in the marshes. The buffalari (or buffalo-drovers) were quite distinct from the vaccari, and their stunts were entirely different, though in the open they rode similar horses and were armed with similar lances to those carried by the vaqueros of Spain and the gardians of the Camargue.

The buffalo-drovers had a wonderful trick that I have seen nowhere else. When the buffalo charged into the arena, a "buffalaro" would cite it and pretend to run away: when it was well on his track he would stop short in front of it, raise his hand and give a peculiar shrill cry which seemed to rise ventriloquially from the solar-plexus, like the cry with which ju-jitsu wrestlers momentarily paralyse their adversaries. This cry would fix the animal for the space of a second or more while the buffalaro made his "getaway."

Another trick which I was allowed to try as it requires no skill and involves no danger, but is hilariously comical to watch, is known as the "Botta." A pitcher-shaped, strong, wicker cask, padded with cushions, and open at both ends, is rolled into the arena. You crawl inside, and get up on your feet, like a circular sandwich-man: the botta covers you from chin to ankle. You walk towards the buffalo and receive the charge which may toss you a few yards and then sends you spinning all over the arena: but holding hard to the internal handgrips, you withdraw your feet and your head like a tortoise. The springiness of the strong wicker and the padded cushions inside keep you from injury. The buffalo comes after the rapidly rolling cask, butts it, and trundles it round in a fury then loses interest when he finds no responsive life in it. Meanwhile someone tempts it to the other side of the arena, and you again start to tilt up the botta, push it upright, get on your feet, and walk towards the buffalo once more.

These buffaloes are savagely bad-tempered at all times and the cry of "buffalo scappato" will clear the streets during any of the big stock-fairs. Their obvious ill-nature and their way of tilting up their noses, after the manner of a wild boar, make the game of botta irresistibly comical even if you've seen and done it a thousand times before.

The "botta" cannot be played with the cattle of the Campagna because their horns are too sharp. Those of the buffalo are blunt and slope backwards. Buffaloes are none the less extremely dangerous, vindictive and tenacious, and many fatalities occur outside the arena. They kill their victims by kneeling on them and never abandon them till every sign of life and breathing is extinct. It is very difficult to sham dead with them, too, because they lick the skin of one's face with a sandpaper-like tongue, so that it is hard not to wince and give signs of life, which only means more battering from the forehead, and more crushing from the knees of these enormous beasts, which are three times as strong as cattle.

They charge very swiftly on a level plain, but they can hardly run uphill at all, and rapidly change to a walk. They are considerably less formidable beasts than are African buffalo which are swifter, tougher, and far more terribly armed, with projecting horns; they compare to the European buffalo as a Spanish bull would compare to a Hereford or some fat English domestic breed with level or receding horns. Nevertheless I recalled the "giostratori," as they call the performers of the Italian buffalo-ring, very poignantly during this last war when I was on leave in Kenya—and longed to be able to send forth that phony ventriloquial cry from my solar plexus which stops a buffalo in full career. The Boer farmer lent me a prehistoric carbine and asked me to kill a buffalo which was molesting natives near a water-hole. This carbine had no magazine and only fired a single round. Then one ejected and reloaded. I stalked the buffalo to within a hundred yards and heard the smack of the bullet, but the buffalo did not drop. It snorted furiously and began to look all round. I waited a bit and nothing happened. I did not want to call attention to myself; the nearest tree was sixty yards behind me and it was a double-thorn mimosa at that, with spikes on it eight inches long. I tried to reload silently but the click of the ejector betrayed my whereabouts. The ejector was worn and failed to clear the empty bullet-case. The buffalo, with its head held high, was already on the way. Unable to work the ejector, I threw the gun down and ran. I expected to be picked up and tossed and trampled before I reached the tree but I was mentally machine-gunning "Hail Maries" which in this case were quite as effective as the cry of "giostratori" for no buffalo ever reached me. There was a donga or natural ditch between him and me, which ran down into the water-hole. Though apparently running quite normally when he first made for me, he had disappeared when I dodged round the tree and looked back. Knowing the treachery of buffaloes, I knocked off some thorns and climbed into the tree and there I was able to see his horns over the edge of the ditch. I waited there an hour in the tree until I had seen him try to rise four or five times and only succeed in raising his hind quarters with his tail lashing viciously. Then he would subside again. By and by I plucked up courage, fetched the gun, prised out the cartridge case with my knife, reloaded, approached him from the side, and finished him off with that prehistoric and inaccurate blunderbuss that had nearly cost me my life. When the beast was skinned I found that my first bullet had passed through the right thighbone of its fore-leg, high up near the shoulder, without entirely severing it. It was only when the buffalo leaped down into the ditch that the remaining thin bridge of thighbone received the downward weight of the whole beast which then cracked it through completely, landing it in a position from which it could not arise. But for the ditch the buffalo would have caught and finished me before I reached the thorn tree. During my run for it, so cool does one become in a moment of despair, I distinctly remembered the village square at Moro's grand-dad's "tenuta," and the shrill cry with which buffaloes were temporarily fixed to the ground in mid-charge.

The Italian games played with the cattle were pleasantly spectacular; the barricades were far higher than those in Spain, France, and Portugal, which come up to the average man's shoulders. These were seven feet high and the "giostratori," when escaping, swung themselves over by jumping for rings fixed at intervals round the arena. They wore smart white costumes, as in Provence, and their games, unlike those of France and Spain, actually had a utilitarian purpose in domesticating the cattle. I still don't believe what I am going to say, but I was shown a bull working the week after he received a thorough drill in the arena. He came in full of fire but was slowly worn down by a large crowd of cattlemen, who skilfully waved him away from each other alternately, with coloured flags. The last one to wave would remain motionless as the bull charged him: the next cowboy would then pretend to intervene only to become motionless when the bull charged him, so that it lost interest before it got to him and made for the next person who appeared to be moving aggressively, and so on round the ring. They told me it was the same bull I saw working.

The champions amongst these "giostratori" were called Viterbians, whether they really hailed from Viterbo or not. Apparently the men of Viterbo have always been the greatest experts as bestiaries, not only with bulls but with buffaloes.

Neither in Provence nor in the Landes can the bullfights compare with those in the Spanish arenas, as to the amount of skill and courage exacted by the crowd of spectators from the human performers. In France bullfighting is a sport rather than an Art, as in Spain.

It was outside the arena, in the open country, that the mounted vaccari showed themselves, both as horsemen and cattlemen, the equals of the cattlemen in the rest of Europe and America. Though they could use the lazo they preferred the lance as being less expensive to life and limb. The garrocha in Spain and Portugal, the trident in Provence, and the lance in Italy are all variations of the same thing. Cattle, unlike horses which keep a more perfect balance in running, lift their hind quarters high off the ground and lose their equilibrium when pushed from behind, or from the side. Thus it is possible for mounted men, once they have learned the trick, to roll a bull over time and again, by pushing it with a lance without hurting it. The lazo is liable to break or twist legs and damage valuable beasts and that is why it is not so fashionable in economical Europe as in wholesale America.

Moro and I made three trips to the "tenute" or ranches. When autumn approached our ship had to be turned into a floating aquarium for eels. The Italians, just as they prefer their bread in Macaroni formations, seem to prefer their fish in similar formations. But they were fond of eels long before they ever invented macaroni: and eels still constitute the chief item of their Christmas dinners much in the same way as Turkeys or Geese do of ours.

That the Italians had a craze for eels long before they took to macaroni is obvious from the fact that the ancient Romans used to make pets of congers and murenas, hang precious ear-rings in their gill-fins, and feed them till they were the size of pythons. Recalcitrant slaves were thrown to the eels: and the name Murena was a common surname, since eel-mongers flourished long before the empire. It was a most lucrative profession.

The whigmaleerie fashion in fish preceded that in bread, as we can see from the Pompeian and Herculanean ovens, where bread, not macaroni, was being made when the bakers were surprised by the eruption. The loaves can be seen in the Naples Museum.

We made three trips to the Rhône mouth for eels. The French fishermen store up their eels in floating reservoirs for months so as to sell them to the Italians about Christmas time. An enormous trade is done at Martigues and Saint Louis du Rhône. At Martigues the eels are hoisted out of their wooden floating "viviers" in nets, bounced on the weighing machine, and then shot like masses of slithering and electrified macaroni into the hold of the vessel where their own moisture and slime keeps them alive till they arrive at Naples and Genoa, where they are again transferred living to other eel-reservoirs. You get quite dizzy while working with the weighing machine and looking at the restless, quivering arabesques of thousands of eels.

One day Moro, who was arguing with one of the French fishermen, slipped and fell into the hold among the eels. We went down after him, several times, with ropes round our waists, into this horrible mass of slimy and animate spaghetti, but when we reached him he was dead. The murenas, which are a far greater delicacy than the other kinds of eels, are actually venomous, with fangs and glands, but they are not dangerous. I was bitten on this occasion and it was extremely painful, as if one had been bitten by a small scorpion.

Moro's death rather put me off eels for the time being, so I went and helped with the grape harvest which was nearing its close, though the weather was good that year for sleeping outside and the mistral was late in starting. I had, as my partner, a nice gipsy girl called Imperio, a widow aged seventeen.

Once while calling in at Cassis on the *Santa Maria*, I slipped on the gang-plank and spoiled about fifty kilos of cement which I was carrying on my shoulders. The water in those days was only about two feet deep between the mole and the downward shelf of rock which began about twelve feet from the edge of the mole. This necessitated a very long gang-plank which sprang violently under one's feet, so that there were two other casualties besides myself. A tremendous "coup de mistral" without any warning got me off my balance and I fell with a nasty jolt on the rock in the shallow water. Captain Rubelli would not let me sail. I went to Dr. Agostini, who, I was delighted to see, is mentioned in Marcel Pagnol's famous films *Panisse* and *Fanny*. He said that I must wait behind and go to hospital: but I managed to get permission to go to bed at Georges Chiumino's *Bar Georges*. Chiumino and his brother-in-law Antoine Garcia were great friends of mine and put me up without any charge since I am a very good handyman and I would be better before the *Santa Maria* picked me up once more.

I spent my convalescence painting an enormous picture on a canvas which some pioneer painter had left behind with a whole lot of tubes and brushes. I say "pioneer" because in those days there weren't many painters in those parts. Now they swarm everywhere between Cassis and Ventimiglia making the once-habitable villages into mad-house suburbs of bogus bohemianism, and existentialism. This picture which I was painting with my tongue in my cheek was a real eye-sore, which could have served as a frontispiece for some of Southey's phony epics or the fatuous *Chants de Mal-*

doror of Isidore Ducasse. Cyclopses entwined by huge boa-constrictors were galloping, like greyhounds, on all fours, some with their limbs stretched out, others with their hands between their ankles looping their backbones—as they all hurtled down a precipitous slope, head-on. Others were seated astride giraffes and elephants and the whole lot leaping right out at one. I foreshortened them like the horses of the Scots Greys in Lady Butler's picture of Waterloo—so that they seemed to be hurtling out of the canvas into space: but it was the angle at which they were hurtling that gave the whole picture its nightmarish and vertiginous feeling of myasthenia. The stampede was occasioned by some volcanic eruption or conflagration suggested by red flames in the rear. Singed monkeys were dropping from burning trees . . .

> "With more of horrible and awful
> Which even to dream would be unlawful."

This picture was seen, first of all, by the local water-carrier, who was the son of the leading shepherd in the district but could not follow in his father's footsteps because he was one of those blessed souls who never developed mentally from the innocence of early childhood. He earned tips for carrying drinkable water from the public fountain to various cafés and private houses. He was a serious-looking fellow, almost middle-aged; he wore a smart boater, was inclined to be stout, and suffered so badly from corns that he only moved his heavy boots about a foot at a time. Facially and with his smart greying moustache, he was the spitting image of H. G. Wells; but he was, fortunately, less articulate. Alas, I have forgotten his name, so let's call him François.

François was very fond of me and always followed me around as fast as his poor corns would allow him to, so that I had to slow up for him, every now and then, for he would raise a terrible outcry if I went too fast. I always let him stand and watch me painting. Suddenly when the picture took shape, François got an inkling that there was something untoward going on in the picture. I was painting in a big lumber-room which led out of the bar, and which was lit-up fairly clearly by a big window at the back. François rushed out and brought in his mother and a couple of her women friends. They stared in amazement at the canvas and soon all the village was talking about it.

This was something like what I had planned though I had not foreseen the value of François as a catalytic agent. I began charging apéritifs, or the price of an apéritif, for a look at my picture and was very soon able to pay back Georges for his kind hospitality to me during my convalescence. Big crowds rolled up after work to see how the bogus masterpiece was progressing. The same people returned almost every night and the verdict was always the same. "Tout le monde trotte, hein? Tout le monde trotte—Pardi! Tout le monde trotte," and so on.

Georges, encouraged by my success, rigged himself up with another vast canvas and started doing a Douanier-like picture of Robinson Crusoe with his shaggy suit and umbrella: Friday, pitch black with a crimson loin-cloth, holding up a pink cockatoo perched on his index finger: the pet cat, the billy-goat, the nanny-goat, and other of their pets. All this was against a livid green and yellow background of banana-trees, palms, and bamboos, with the hut in the foreground. It was a charming and ingenious painting, and considering it was a first attempt, very remarkable indeed. The only trouble was that the bunches of bananas were upside down; that is to say they were hanging naturally with the tips of the bananas lower than the stalk that joins them to the central stem of the bunch, as they certainly would if they were not perverse vegetables that insist on curving up to the sky from their vertically drooping stem. There were no cinemas in the country towns or villages in those days, so our pictures attracted a good deal of custom to the Bar. To make money quickly, we began making our own *pastis* or proof-absinthe. We had seven large bonbonnes, that is to say hundred litre bottles encased in wicker, full of the stuff, both in the cellar and in the room where we were sitting painting. The distilling and sale of strong *pastis* was strictly illegal.

One day Monsieur Mosca (proprietor of the *Bar-Tabacs Mosca*), now, I think, running a café at Les Pennes-Mirabeau, rushed in to tip us the wink that he had seen a car-load of plain-clothes "flics" stalking the *Bar Georges* from the central square. I smashed the two bonbonnes in the room where we were painting, and rushed into the cellar, where I smashed the other five completely—nearly chloroforming myself with the fumes as I did so. Meanwhile Georges had run into the bar, and saw that everybody smashed his glass on the floor so that no samples could be collected as evidence.

It was then that the simple fellow, François, began to cry and refused either to give up or break his glass. He was in the very corner behind a marble table. Not only was he strong and tough, but he stood on a chair with his face in the corner and hugged the glass to his chest. Before Georges could get to him, six detectives had rushed in and seen that Georges was trying to get the only remaining sample of his brew from François. They hauled Georges off and soon coaxed the incriminating sample off François. The case came off some weeks later, after I had left, and both Georges Chiumino and Garcia did several months besides paying a big fine. To pay the fine (which they anticipated) they started distilling *pastis* again next day even stronger than before!

Funnily enough, everybody seemed thoroughly delighted with the proceedings—detectives, detected, and spectators alike. One extremely excitable detective with a frock coat, a bowler, and a white beard, looked exactly like a Protestant missionary. It was he who coaxed the glass off François, wrapped it in cotton-wool and placed it upright in a kick-proof box which he held between his knees, in case of attack, as he waddled off screened by five other plain-clothes men to the doorway. I was not even questioned. My guardian angels were there on duty!

The attitude of Georges and his brother-in-law was "Tant pis! Of course the trial, the prison and the fine will be a bore, but we nearly got away with it. Anyway we had a run for our money and it was a great lark!" Everybody else seemed very pleased with the adventure except me. My rope espadrilles were ruined and sticky and they smelt of aniseed from wading about ankle deep in the cellar, where the stuff gradually seeped into the mud: and I was suffering a headache from the fumes I had absorbed.

That day was the day of the Dempsey-Carpentier fight. The whole of France was keyed up: and after the detectives had gone I was arguing in the bar against twenty infuriated Provençaux that Dempsey stood a good chance of winning. Actually I knew that it was a dead certainty but it would have been more than my life was worth to risk saying so. I began to take bets on it, however, since they were aggressively forced on me, and I was terribly hard up. This conversation is typical of some twenty or so that I had with people in the bar:—

X.: "What makes you imagine that Dempsey stands a chance?"

R.C.: "Why, his superior weight and strength for one thing."

X.: "It is not weight that counts in boxing so much as skill! Brain always wins."

R.C.: "Then why do they class boxing categories according to weight?"

X.: "Because most boxers are just brainless brutes! But our Carpentier will be just like a 'toreador' teasing a big clumsy bull. He will lead him round and plant him exactly where he wants him: and then like this—so!—Pif-paf!" (here I would have to parry or dodge anything from an uppercut to a right swing to my head) "and Dempsey will be carried out in the third or fourth round."

R.C.: "Well, I very much hope so. But I have heard that Dempsey is quite as skilful as Carpentier—just a heavier Carpentier."

X.: "You are mistaken, my friend. There is only one Carpentier in this world. If you seriously believe in the possibility and have the courage of your convictions, I will lay a bet with you."

R.C.: "But I've already had a dozen bets forced on me."

X.: "There you are, you see. Making excuses. You know as well as I do who will win. You waste time arguing but you damned well funk a bet."

So in the end one was forced to accept the bet. If Carpentier had won I stood to lose about 1000 francs (worth a lot then) and I had hardly any money at all. But I went to sleep lightheartedly, confident of a fine pocketful of notes in the morning.

I was awakened before dawn, while it was still dark, by a thunderstorm of bell-ringing from all the town halls, churches, and belfries for miles around. A huge crowd was moving through the streets with candles and lanterns, and singing joyful hymns. I jumped up and dressed in the utmost consternation. "This must be the public thanksgiving for a Carpentier victory," I thought to myself. "He must have won on a foul. How am I to pay my bets? I must abscond! But I haven't even a railway fare." Such were my thoughts as I sneaked out disconsolately and mixed with the crowd of rejoicing people. The stream of candle-bearing people like an endless swarm of fireflies emerged from the town and began to climb into the sierras. "Has Carpentier won?" I asked one of the crowd. "Of course! What do you think?" was the reply. Still, it struck me as a bit queer to make a religious pilgrimage to a her-

mitage in the mountains at dead of night, simply because of a box-
ing-match. I completed the pilgrimage and we reached the shrine
far away on the mountain-tops at about 10 a.m.

After dawdling there as long as I could, I was driven sheepishly
back to the *Bar Georges* by the pangs of hunger and thirst. I got
there at three in the afternoon, famished. On the way I bought a
paper. I nearly fainted with relief to see that Dempsey had won,
after all! The pilgrimage was an annual one. The fight had coin-
cided with the feast of one of the local Virgins: that was all. I collected my bets and stood Georges and Garcia one of the finest
bouillabaisses I could buy at the local market, with some really
good wine to wash it down.

Before Georges and Garcia went to gaol they sold my picture to
a professional painter for 600 francs, which went towards their fine.

Talking about painters, the only one I saw at that time in Cassis
was a stoutish man seated in front of an easel on which was a tiny
canvas about the size of a postage stamp. Blond locks waved about
from under a black sombrero. I thought it was the rear silhouette
of Clive Bell. I sneaked up behind him to give him a fright. I intended to pinch his bottom and squeak at him like a mouse—which
is the Bloomsbury equivalent of shaking hands and saying "Hello."
When the figure turned round the features were familiar and they
were almost identical with those of Clive Bell but a manly, smiling
Clive Bell, with a clear and lion-like gaze which suspended the
buffoonery that I had contemplated, in mid-air. I was dumbfounded
by this anti-anticlimax, if I may coin such a word, and took off my
hat with a sheepish grin as I was met by that frank, friendly, and
serene look. The painter also then courteously lifted his sombrero
and turned back with a broad smile to carry on painting.

"By God, I know that face as well as my own," I said to myself,
trying to reorganise my faculties. "Who the devil is it? Who is it?
Why, Winston Churchill—of course!"

After this friendly but wordless encounter with the hero, I went
around feeling about two inches taller for some time.

Then the *Santa Maria* came back for some more cement and I
shipped aboard her once more. My fall from the gang-plank dis-
organised my reflexes in a very comical way—but only temporarily.
I could not let go quickly with my right hand when I had got a
grip on to anything: the reflex came, after it went to the hand,

about a second late. The result was that while changing the "trin-quette" sail round the "foc" a sudden gust launched me far away into the sea with all the skin taken off the palm of my right hand. When the skin formed again some of the lines were different (so much for fortune telling!).

Imperio, with whom I kept company as much as I could between voyages, earned her living by looking at hands, and she had kept a piece of clay on which I had leaned with my hand while casting a bucket for her into that deep well ten yards from the road between the Mas Thibert and the Rhône Ferry. She had cooked it on the fire and it was cracked in parts, but she kept it in a flat tin. She kept it as another girl might keep a photo of her friend. The difference that had come in my right hand was a big cross which is now deeply imprinted in the same place on both hands but which, ac-cording to her, had not existed previously on either. According to her too, it was the sign of the greatest luck. But it didn't seem to bring me luck at the time for, shortly after I went back to sea, I re-ceived a blow from a block in the rigging of a tartane, which caused a slight fracture to one of the bones in the back of my neck. I beat this by lying flat, and almost without moving, for three weeks. I had to return to England for some months, after that, because of a terrible misunderstanding which led to two duels on successive days. Jean Samart, the novelist, who had been an officer in the Spahis, stood by me and it was due to his help and advice that I probably owe my life. Later when I heard the patients had recov-ered and were both well, I returned to Provence, travelling from Paris to Lyons with a circus of cowboys and two Cossacks. As for the fractured vertebra it seemed to heal up completely, but I suf-fered hell from it years later.

XV

THE CAMARGUE

Y<small>OU CAN</small> tell almost the moment you get into Provence by the pines and the rocks, the olives, almonds, vines, cypresses and poplars to which the elms and oaks give place. By far the best way to enter Provence is by the ancient highway of her great and noble river, on one of the barges coming down from Lyons. This famous highway was the main trade route of Western Europe until the invention of the railways put it comparatively out of use, and reduced its traffic by about ninety per cent.

The annual fair at Beaucaire was one of the greatest commercial events in Europe from prehistoric times up to about 1840, and Mistral, in his epic, the *Song of the Rhône*, gives a magnificent picture of the life of the pre-railway bargemen. The poem ends symbolically in a disaster to the barges of Maitre the hero, because the cart-horses towing them upstream are stampeded by the sight of a huge black monster belching smoke and flame, which proved to be the new railway engine.

To the old Phoenician markets of Beaucaire the silks of China found their way, so did the furs of the Arctic and the ivory of the Congo, along with the spices of the Indies. Nowadays it is chiefly a gipsy fair but it is possible to conjure up visions of better times. Beaucaire is the "Kingdom" (Royaume) half of Tarascon, which is on the opposite bank, and therefore on the "Empire" bank. In the language of the bargemen *Royaume* and *Empire* are steering terms, designating starboard and port respectively on the way downstream, and vice versa on the way upstream. These terms survive from the days when the Rhône was the boundary between the Kingdom of France and the Holy Roman Empire. Owing to the steepness and swiftness of the Rhône nothing could be of a greater contrast to the exhilarating trip downstream, than the laborious trip upstream which is only rendered practicable at one stretch of rapids by winding up towing chains for miles on revolving winches.

On the trip downstream the magnificent old Roman cities of Valence, Montelimar, Orange, Avignon with its papal palaces, Tarascon with its towers and castles, and finally the flower of them all, Arles, with Saint Trophime and superb Roman buildings, all sail into sight and vanish through the arches of their mighty bridges as one hurtles down headlong through majestic groves of poplars, white, green, and black, towards the great plains of the Camargue and the Crau. I have seen these poplars, on the Rhône-banks, lying prone where they have been expertly cut, thrown down, and trimmed by those extraordinary animal carpenters, the beavers, prior to dragging them under water to timber their dams. These expert little timber men had desisted from the habit of dam-building on the Rhône, for almost a century, under the threat of extinction; but they never lost their instinct, and the moment they became protected by the French Government, they resorted once more to their timber-chopping depredations.

Most of the barges go via the Canal of Arles to Fos which lies across the semi-desert Crau. A huge marine tunnel, one of the longest in the world, through the mountains of the Evening Star, ending at Le Rove and beginning near Marignane, effects the direct communication by canal, sea lake, tunnel, and river, of Geneva with Marseilles. A stone jetty many miles long running round one side of the Etang de Berre and the shores of Le Rove and L'Estaque, continues the canal so that the barges finish up in Marseilles without ever having been subjected to any greater risk of shipwreck than that encountered on the rapid stretches of the Rhône, which are tricky enough in all conscience, and require the very greatest experience and skill to negotiate, since the depths are always altering and the shoals are always shifting.

On my second visit to Provence I came down from Lyons on a barge, having got a job from the patron of a couple of barges. On our way down to Marseilles one of our barges came to grief, between Arles and Fos, and, while the patron was waiting for a tug, he offered to release me, if I liked, as he might be held up for a day or so. Seeing I was bound for the very parts we were passing through, and he had shipped another hand at Arles, he kindly let me off on the towpath and I decided to go to Saint Louis du Rhône. The patron at first was against letting me go because of the danger from cattle and wild stallions, but I prevailed.

The mistral was loose that day, clashing the reeds and tearing at the tamarisks. The Alpilles were sparkling like dark blue crystals through the heavenly bluish-white air that shimmers over the Crau to the north east. The voice of the mistral is more full of legends and myths than that of any other wind that blows in any other part of the world. I have never heard it blowing on the Crau or the Camargue without remembering those wonderful lines of Milton—

> And airy tongues that syllable men's names
> By sands and shores and desert wildernesses.

The Crau is said to be the flattest part of the world. There is hardly a centimetre's difference in level along a thirty-mile stretch of road and the mirages are far more spectacular than anything that can be seen on the Sahara or the Kalahari. Even at night there is a local illusion which is not in any way related to the mirage, but which heightens the witchery of this weird country. If you happen to be motoring from Arles to Fos on a dark night and you see a pair of motor lamps approaching along that lonely narrow road, which is ruled straight from horizon to horizon and only once met at right angles by a windbreak line of Cypress trees, you immediately start slowing down and dimming your lights thinking that the approaching car is immediately at hand; when it is still miles away. I have known taxi drivers slow down eight or nine times in this manner and become quite exasperated and frightened before the advancing car is reached. The part of the world which the Crau most closely resembles is the Karroo.

The mirages on the Crau are obvious and clear on hot days. They come rushing at the car like miles of shimmering quicksilver, while the Alpilles and St. Victory on the horizon separate in halves or play themselves like accordions, and lines of trees rise far above the skyline and form another phantasmal skyline with a strip of sky between it and the real one.

The Crau is covered with smooth pancake-shaped alluvial stones which prevent agriculture, though the seeming desert beneath them is rich soil brought down by the Rhône and the Durance in ancient times from the rich forests up-country. The Crau is the old bed of some big lake they once fed, or formed, with their waters. Between the stones there is excellent grazing for sheep in the shape of aromatic plants such as thyme and rosemary. These stones are not deeply embedded in the soil beneath them. This gives rise to the legend that they were the artillery used by Jupiter against the Titans, for they lie like newly fallen hailstones on the surface of the plain, as if they had just been showered down from the sky. When these stones are collected in cairns and the surface of the plain lies bared to the plough, a riot of verdure succeeds to the ancient desert appearance of the Crau—vines, trees, and corn.

This has happened in my life-time. Saint Martin de la Crau, which I have seen, in the old days, as a strip of desert, now has big trees and lush meadows. Before, it was indistinguishable from the strip at Miramas round which they hold the great long-distance motor-races on account of the perfectly natural "Brooklands" that was formed by this spirit level of an horizon. All that was needed was to pick up the stones, to make the track, and build a wall round it some miles in extent, so as to be able to charge an entrance fee to the spectators. This wall has never worried me unless I was passing on a long journey by car; for all one does is to ride one's horse alongside the wall, stand in the saddle and lean one's elbows on the parapet—and thus one can provide oneself with a private box for all the most thrilling speed-races in France.

The clover, the alfalfa and the grass that shoots up when the

Crau has been newly cleared and irrigated is of a wonderful quality. As a youth, when it was first springing up, and when I had no other food, I lived very well on that donkey-food of clover and alfalfa, the seeds of the grass, the huge buds of the Scotch thistles that grow there, and the magnificent dandelions that have big leaves without any astringent "milk" in them even when they are about six inches long. In case I give the idea that I am a sort of vegetarian disciple of Bernard Shaw, I should explain that I know how to eat my way, for about three weeks at a time, through France or any other country, without begging from the folk by the road, or harming their poultry in any way, as gipsies harm them, or hurting their sheep or cattle. As for wild asparagus and other shoots and fungi, I have most of the answers even in this country. The only places where it is hard to keep alive for a short time without money are London, Paris, Lyons, Birmingham, Glasgow and other places with big suburbs.

The mutton that is nourished on the aromatic plants of the Crau is almost unbeatable *in flavour* though, compared to the superb sheep of England, the actual texture and juiciness of the meat is slightly inferior. Yet with the wine of the country, say, Chateauneuf du Pape, to compensate for that and the flavour of the meat, one can forget the richness of Welsh or English mutton. The best mutton I ever tasted was the Welsh mutton we used to shoot at our rifle range in the Welsh mountains during the war. The farmer used to drive his sheep down behind the machine-gun targets because he got better compensation if we shot them than if he sold them to the butcher. He allowed us to take most of the carcases for the cookhouse since all he needed was the skin with the bullet-holes in order to back his claim.

After a round-up for branding, or after a "course" in the arena, there is nothing to my mind so pleasant as to go up, with three or four good comrades and some nice girls, to the castle of Fos, or the brow of the Caderau or (if it is warm enough) on to the top of the old castled rock at Les Beaux, taking a live lamb or sheep of the Crau, slaughtering it and roasting it at once before rigor mortis sets in, as do the Sheiks with a young she-camel, sacrificing it on their own doorstep and making you tread in its blood, almost the moment before you eat its hump.

That sacrament of friendship, a good Provençal meal, which

even on Fridays is better than the best Northern meal, whether it
be *bouillabaisse* or *a rôti*, is best honoured in the open air, and best
of all, in the evening, with the limitless sweep of the Crau, the
Camargue and the sea, under a crimson and violet sky with the
stars coming out and the crickets relieving the cicadas. A few bottles of Chateauneuf from whose black columns the setting sun
strikes one or two Aldebaran-like ruby sparks: green olives from
one's own vat scented with fennel after each one has been lovingly
bruised between two stones: black olives in their own oil: silver
bread like the nimbus of the cloud at noon over the Ventour: a
poutargue of the negre or black mullet cured by ourselves from
our own fishing, which has been pressed between rocks and out-
savours the finest roe of the sturgeon: and then the gigot or haunch
of a lamb which in all its life never ate anything but the thyme,
the rosemary, and the fennel of the Crau.

If it was impossible to bring the lamb alive, then there are a million compensatory ways of cooking it. The great thing is for all the
guests to bring masses of old vine-stems and roots from the valleys
beneath and mingle them in the pyre with thyme and rosemary.
Cut the lamb in knobs as big as the first joint of your thumb, thread
these alternately with slices of bacon (packing them so that no air
can come between them) on to a knife-sharpened sprig of green
thyme or rosemary, which beats any skewer, and then throw these
on the embers of the fine stems and vine roots, when their glare has
faded from bright yellow to deep orange but has not yet gone red.

If you, my reader, at any future date find yourself sitting there
with your arm round some young beautiful living torso, and as you
drink your wine looking down over the Camargue and the Crau
from the old ruins of Fos where you see, peacefully grazing, the
superb herds of fighting cattle of Feraud or Raoux, beyond the
great avenue of pines which escorts the road to Arles a mile on the
way—whoever you are—say a Grace for me and my beloved and
my friends, for we also know what you know,

> "Yet, though knowing naught,
> Transcended knowledge with our thought."

To the north the Alpilles notch themselves in black, purple, and
azure on the red and yellow sky, and in their last dwindling ridge

we see the Baux, that nest of eagles and home of poets and lovers
where the lovely Queen Jeanne held her Courts of Love (the antith-
esis of Georgiana's clinic at Sissyhurst) and excelled in feats of
a different sort of tauromachy without the aid of Jewish and Cal-
vinistic pedants like Freud, Havelock Ellis and other such dismal
wowsers: where the troubadours competed in pleasing their loves
with a devotion almost unknown in our cynical times; and where
Dante himself is said to have studied the perimeters of his seven circles. For beautiful as it is, there is something unearthly and weird
about the depths and heights, chasms, canyons, and caverns of that
part of the Alpilles; it is shunned and dreaded by aviators on account of the windpockets, sudden whirlwinds and other aerial per-
ils. Nevertheless, when I was last there two fine pairs of golden
eagles were nesting on the southern buttress of the rock. The air is
much more reliable on the Marignane side of the Etang de Berre
than anywhere round the Alpilles. In the early days of gliding with
the *Société de Vol à Voile* of Gignac, there was the most constant
and reliable airlift I ever encountered, perpetually rising from the
lake side up those rather inhospitable and rough-looking escarp-
ments between Chateauneuf-les-Martigues and the Assassins. We
made long flights for those days all along that ridge, being sheltered
completely from the sudden onslaughts of such winds as the Labé
and the Tramontano, which were extremely dangerous not only to
gliders but to all sailing vessels.

When I landed from the towpath of the barge on the edge both
of the Camargue and the Crau, I decided in favour of the Camargue. The idea of the cattle and horses lured me. As I've said before,
one of the earliest things I can remember as a child was trying to
ride the bucking calves in the Zulu cattle-kraals at home. Since
then I've rubbed shoulders with some queer sorts of cattle-men,
from the wild Masai of Central Africa to the toreros of Spain and
Mexico, who are the flower of the profession. But if you want the
thrill of cowboy life, with real wild horses and cattle, you don't
have to go to the Far West for it. There is a far more rampageous
version of it right there, on the Camargue, on your own doorstep,
in the centre of civilised Europe. You can find it round the mouths
of the Rhône, where our European civilisation remains almost unaffected by the last four centuries of Levantine retrogression.

I don't think anyone would go there of his own accord. At first the sight of the country puts you right off, especially as you have to pass by ugly dynamite factories and convict settlements on the way there. A fierce wind is nearly always blowing, and the place is full of mosquitoes. For hundreds of square miles it's so flat that it would make Salisbury Plain look like a range of mountains. The Crau is beautiful with its fringe of mountains, but the Camargue, after Fos, is uninviting at first sight. If you're a hiker you're liable to be mistaken for a wandering jail-bird from one of the settlements. Then you'll be shown the road (as happened to me more than once). You'll be lucky then if you can find one of the few bug-eaten taverns before nightfall.

In these pubs they don't have any dart-boards or billiard tables. What they have instead is a murderous old fighting bull stockaded in the backyard. He's the local dart-board and billiard-table rolled in one. If you're bored you can go and play with him between the drinks. If he sends you to the graveyard, well it only adds to the reputation of the pub. The bull's there for the neighbouring yokels to keep their hand in as bull-fighters. You'll generally find he's got a small ribbon tied between his horns. If you can snatch it off as you swerve round him, you'll get your drinks on the house. Each pub has its bull "laid on," and he gets as much custom as the bar.

The landlord may be, and probably is, thoroughly honest. But his bull is always a sharper—up to every low-down trick you can imagine. Daily practice makes the bull a deep psychologist: and he's likely to hook you when you think he's going after somebody else.

Where the Camargue crosses the border of Provence into the Languedoc it is known as the *Sauvage*. The people who live there are mostly cowboys, fishermen and fowlers. Since half the country consists of water and reeds, everybody leads an amphibious life. I've seen punts tied to the first-floor window like life-boats, ready for when the family change floors. The only reason why the people haven't got webbed feet is because they've got bow-legs instead, from trying to keep their feet out of the water—by living half the year in their stirrups, and the other half squatting in punts.

All round you can see hundreds of wild horses and cattle grazing together in mixed groups like the zebras and wildebeest do in Africa. They're not tame animals gone wild. They're wild animals in the same sense as African zebras and buffaloes are wild animals. They've been there since prehistoric times, with the beavers and wild boars that you still find there. The cowboys sort them out from time to time, but otherwise nobody molests them.

When I landed from the barge I wanted to hike to the sea. I soon repented. I saw a house which *seemed* very near and I started to walk to it. On the way there I scared part of a big flock of flamingos. They spread out all their red wings together, and it looked like a sort of super-sunrise in broad daylight. The house looked quite near. But it took me half the day to get there. It was deserted except for the women-folk; and they sent me packing. I heard afterwards that they mistook me for a runaway crook: and they had some nasty-looking dogs. So I spent the night in the swamps with bulls bellowing all round and I was almost eaten alive by mosquitoes. The wild boars, foxes, beavers, and ferrets also made noises all round me.

Next day I struck off inland and came to another house, a big one with stables and barns. They seemed to expect me, or anyone else who turned up. There was a big crowd there, and people were doling out wine and bread. The crowd had turned up from miles around as spectators and volunteers in a big rodeo that was being held. The branding was finished and they were coursing bulls and having games, to wind up the show with a flourish. One of the games was very pretty. I remember a sort of mixture of rugby and polo played on horseback with a bunch of flowers for a ball.

They had an arena made of carts tied together with a wall on one side, and when I got there they'd just let out a three-year-old bull with rather wide horns. It was an open competition without any rules. This was lucky for me as I hadn't learned the local game. So I just sat on the barricade and let the bull pass me about four times till he got used to me and took no more notice of me. Then I took a flying jump and came down with a ju-jitsu lock on his horns like we do from horseback in the Dominions. Another fellow, Leon Raoux of Istres, jumped down and swung it by the tail. It came over very nicely and we sat on its head and took off the prize from between its horns. That was the first bull I ever turned by hand. The last time I turned the big bull at Istres, Raoux also had it by the tail.

When they found I was a cattleman, the people of the house, the

Raouxes, gave me a fine time. Some neighbours of theirs, the Ferauds, took me away to another house and let me stay and work with them for a long time. One of the brothers Feraud was for many years Mayor of Fos sur Mer. I have often been back there since, and liked it better each time. I've even got to love the rather dismal scenery of waving reeds and tamarisks.

The central farm-house of each ranch is called the Mas. Everybody eats at the same long table with the Master. But the lady of the house doesn't sit down. She serves out and stands at the side. You might think at first sight she was a servant. But she may be the real boss of the whole outfit—a countess and the best rider in the place. She may be a beautiful Amazon, able to kill bulls from the saddle with a javelin in the great public arenas of Arles and Nîmes. I've known people like that; the late Madame Calais was one. So is the famous "Marquise" de Baroncelli, daughter of the Marquis.

The hardest job I had at first was to get used to the Provençal cooking. They certainly do like chillies and garlic, with which the Indians impregnate the air at home in Natal. So I was rather prejudiced against them. But I had to get used to it pretty quickly in self-defence; otherwise any of my colleagues could floor me in an argument if he stood close up. You could have got a job from a plumber after some of those dinners—not as his mate, but as his burner. You could have melted lead pipes just by whispering to them. Still, where everybody eats garlic it is not noticeable except to those who don't: and it certainly compensates for the perpetual sniffle and snuffle of colds, 'flu and other things which in England are the result of cooking without garlic.

But it was in Provence that I tasted for the first time the second of the two proverbial treats of the South African hunter, which are "the hump of an eland and the breast of a flamingo."

I was travelling with my gipsy friends to a bullfight at the Saintes-Maries, in which the famous bull, Sanglier, was being coursed with nine thousand francs on the cocarde on his forehead, and six thousand for the other rosettes and tassels. We had stopped to camp and had just watered our horses and mules, and the older women were just about to light the fires. The sun was going down crimson over the plain, lighting up the summits of the Alpilles to the north east and shooting long level rays through the jagged canyons of St. Remy and Les Baux on to the Crau twenty or thirty miles away. A maniac aviator, stunting over the lagoon of the Vaccarès, raised a huge scarlet cloud of flamingos like an aurora borealis; by sweeping over the flock of some four thousand of them which roost on the lake-side. Ordinarily this flock looks like a mile-long salt-deposit, or a beach of white sand, along the far side of the lake. But if a shot rings out, or there is some other disturbance, the whole white shore ignites and becomes blood-red for a second. The whiteness almost disappears into the prodigious acreage of scarlet unfolded in the breadth and length of their scarlet quills, whose brightness is emphasised by the pitch-black tips of their wings, resembling the black wing-tips of lories. Then the birds rise up in a great red cloud which gradually subsides again into the semblance of a salt-deposit.

Now, this mad aviator was not content merely to fluster the birds in order to enjoy the sight of a buckshee aurora borealis. That is an irresistible temptation, to which I have often succumbed when I have been able to produce the necessary noise to startle the birds, either on Durban Bay or the Nubian lakes. This yahoo swept through the flock several times, at the risk of his own life, killing many of these beautiful birds for the mere sadistic joy of doing harm. I am glad to say that he was later identified and confined.

I was riding back pillion on the same mule with Imperio, a very nice girl who had been my partner in the grape harvest, and whose brother Rodrigo Demestre was to be my partner the next day in the bull-ring. The accursed aviator saw us and started trying to stampede our cavalcade by swooping as if to dive-bomb us. Before he went back to slaughtering flamingos, he succeeded in scattering the horses, which was very awkward since the place is full of brumbies and mustangs, and once they get off with the mares they take a lot of hunting back to the fold. All Imperio and I could do was to shake our fists and swear—an art in which the beautiful but innocent Imperio had even me (an alleged "lord of language" according to Arnold Bennett) completely beaten. When my friend George Barnes was made Director of the Spoken Word on the B.B.C., I thought of Imperio and wondered if she was still "going strong," since if ever they wanted a Director of the Unspeakable Word (in five languages, Catalan, Valencian, Provençal, French and Spanish) Imperio is the girl for the job!

We had only just succeeded in rounding up our eight horses again when a few hundred flamingos, fleeing from the aviator, passed over in front of us at a great height. The vandal, seeing the only remaining part of the huge flock which he had not utterly dispersed, swooped once more. Several birds fell down zigzagging with broken wings or necks. It was as if pieces of the scarlet sunset were falling round our ears.

When we got the horses tied up to the carts, Rodrigo, Imperio, and I went out with our revolvers and knives and finished off and collected five of these fallen meteors—all we could find. We roasted the first one before even rigor mortis could set in, over a fire made of vine-stems and vine-roots, incomparably the best material for a roasting-fire, both on account of its heat and the flavour or perfume it imparts.

That night we ate the roast phoenicopter with an excellent red wine of the countryside which we had bought in St. Gilles. We hung the other flamingo after portioning three of them out to neighbouring caravans of Rodrigo's tribe whose camp fires at intervals of fifty yards or so, fragrant with the smoke of vine, tamarisk, rosemary, thyme, and fennel, lit up the night for acres round. Except that it lies at the mercy of the mistral, that encampment-ground near the Saints is one of the happiest I know, with its jingling harness, barking dogs, crackling fires, ringing guitars and the cold gusts of the mistral which combine in as fine a musical accompaniment, and as appetising a mental sauce for a dinner, as could be possibly prayed for by the most blasé of epicures. I heartily endorse the African hunters' proverb if the hump of an eland is anywhere near as good as the breast of the flamingo we tasted that night.

This gipsy pilgrimage to the Saintes-Maries, which is the capital of the cattle country and the Mecca of all the gipsies in Europe, is the great event of the year. They roll up in thousands and their bonfires blaze for miles round. They hold a huge horse-fair, with the bull-fights, dances and carousals.

Every village down there has two or three feast days in the year. A bivouac of carts is set up as an arena and the cowboys drive the bulls right through the main street in a terrific stampede into the public square. They drive the bulls with a blunt lance called a trident. It can capsize a galloping bull with less danger of breaking its legs than a lazo. If you know how to use a trident you can deflect the charge of a bull even when you are dismounted. If it's a very powerful bull, you kneel with the heft of it under your foot. Just by judging the angle, you can make half a ton of animal-projectile ricochet off the trident, like a pebble from the water. The shock sends the man upright, but he turns round and gets into the same position until the bull gets tired of charging and goes off to lick the blood off his nose. Both man and bull remain unhurt.

The popular French course of bulls has nothing to do with the Spanish bullfight. In Spain the man, the matador, is the star-turn, and the bull is the victim. In France it's the other way round. The bull is the star-turn and the men are just volunteers and free lances. It's only the men that ever get killed in these courses.

It's like this—the bull has a bunch of ribbon tied between his horns and a tassel behind his ear. You've got to try and swerve round him and snatch them off by breaking the string. If you get away with the tassel or the ribbon, you get a prize in money—the value of the prize varies from twenty francs to twenty thousand. If it's a big prize, it's because the bull is a trained killer—a four-legged hearse. The value of his tassel goes up with every man he sends to hospital or to the cemetery.

Some of these bulls get so murderously skilful that they carry a fortune between their horns for seasons on end without losing their ribbon to anyone, and at the same time sending a stream of people to hospital or heaven. These bulls become more famous than race horses, or statesmen, in this country. They are far cleverer than either. And when they die, they get statues put up to them in the public squares. Only a few of them die of old age—they are generally killed by younger bulls out in the pasture, where they fight to the death. The Sanglier was an exception. He died of old age at 18. This breed is so fierce that even a tiny calf will charge.

One of the funniest sights you can see is the bullfight for boys under ten. They let out a tiny calf who's still suckling. He comes out bellowing and roaring like a lion. He chooses his stamping ground or querencia like a grown-up bull (the spot where he comes back to paw the ground between the charges). He makes lanes through the children, capsizing them in dozens to right and left. You've only to see that to realise what a very different kind of animal the fighting ox of Provence is from the domestic animal of even the wild western rodeos.

On this occasion, at the Saintes-Maries, when coursing the Sanglier, poor Rodrigo met with a serious accident, and I was tossed by the same bull into the cart of Reichard, the butcher, the Mayor of Saint Louis du Rhône. Rodrigo dislocated his hip-joint, which was still arthritic when I met him, twelve years later, in Alicante.

Rodrigo made a mistake through a faulty reflex which, in ordinary circumstances, would have been fatal, since he accentuated a swerve, when he should have desisted, broken it off, and made for the barricades. In getting the bull's attention away, I was followed, picked up on the bull's forehead between the horns, and thrown by the buttocks, but without a scratch, into the cart of Reichard, falling over his knees but without any harm to him or myself. As Reichard said, he had sustained far harder jolts from me in the jousts. He was a giant of a man and the best jouster that ever came out of St. Louis.

The fact that neither Rodrigo nor I joined the other victims of that galloping graveyard, the Sanglier, in the cemetery, is probably due to the fact that Imperio was nearly as good at praying as she was at swearing. She spent the whole day, praying for both of us, in the subterranean chapel of Saint Sarah, the gipsy saint, under the church of the Holy Maries of the Sea.

The spiritual capital of the Camargue, the Holy Maries of the Sea, is so called because the Blessed Virgin, Our Lady; Mary Magdalene; Mary and Martha, the sisters of Lazarus, together with their servant the black Saint Sarah, and many others of Christ's intimate friends, including St. Joseph of Arimathea and Lazarus, all landed there shortly after the crucifixion and their bones are still kept in the tower of the ancient church. This was built partly as an anti-Saracen fortress—and with good reason, too, for in comparatively modern times, shortly after the Battle of Lepanto, the great Cervantes himself was captured there by a Moorish galley and taken into slavery. It was T. E. Lawrence who, visiting this ancient church with Augustus John, showed that the sides of the base of the church which once descended into the sea were bevelled at a certain angle and that this can only have been on account of the fact that, if stones were dropped on to these sloping ledges from the tower, they would bounce out level and work damage on any craft of a besieging fleet which ventured close to the walls. This saved having to build catapults and scorpions.

Saint Sarah attracts gipsies from all over the world to pay their devotion to her as their patron saint. The two main pilgrimages in

September and May sometimes assume the proportions of a vast nomadic migration and in the old days such towns as Arles and Avignon had to close their gates and man their ramparts, after having been put to the sack by gipsies and suffering worse than they would have done from a marauding army.

The ancient name for the Maries, Ratis, signified the letting of blood in the gipsy language. To the letting of blood, especially in their marriage ceremonies and the consummation of their marriages, the gipsies attach great importance. And of course each pilgrimage to the Maries is celebrated by the letting of blood in the form of bull-fights.

The crypt of the church, which is the chapel of Saint Sarah to-day, has served in turn as the altar of Cybele, Diana of Ephesus, and Mithras. It may even be older than the crypts of Saint Peter and of Saint Clement in Rome, under which the house of the Saint Clement himself was unearthed not long ago. This dated from before the time of Domitian, and a Mithraum was located just beside it. I was present during the unearthing of this Mithraum and have seen St. Clement's house. I have also seen the Holy Shroud at Turin. I don't see why some people are so credulously incredulous about the authenticity of such things when they raise no question as to the authenticity of the relics of Rameses the Great or Tutankhamen, which date from even remoter periods.

The Jews were travelling to and from Toledo where they had a settlement for at least a thousand years before the Christian era, as can be proved from Hebrew inscriptions dug up on the spot. There is no reason why Jews such as Joseph of Arimathea and his friends should not have visited and settled in a populous Greek colony such as obviously existed at the Rhône mouth in those days. In this sort of question popular tradition is seldom wrong. The *Iliad* and the story of Theseus were proved to be historical by the excavation of Priam's Palace and the Labyrinth. Along parts of the coast of the Camargue the sea in stormy weather bombards the coast not with common rocks and boulders but with living stones of very great antiquity, most of which bear the marks of human workmanship.

The beautiful legends which have since been woven round the doings of the saints of the Rhône mouth are innumerable. But there is one relating to a bull which is worth recounting.

At almost every period, until quite recently, there was a bull called Le Maudit, the Accursed One. When there wasn't a "Maudit" with one herd, he was bound to be found in another, ever since there were cattlemen on the Camargue. This was because when the Maries landed and the first miracle happened, all the animals, except one, came to offer their wool for clothes, their skins for leather, their backs for saddling, their feathers for pillows, their udders for milking, and their horns for protection. The only exception was a bull who lowered his horns in a threatening manner, pawed the ground, and disputed the free passage of the newly landed saints. Our Lady thereupon cursed him, and the other cattle drove him away, so that ever since that time, with every herd, there was a morose old bull who never properly belonged to the herd but skulked around morosely on the outskirts. He was useless for the arena since he only sulked when let out of the toril, and would not charge or fight.

One Christmas night a little girl called Magali, having heard the tale of the Maudit, and seen it standing lonely apart from the herd, stole out by moonlight, on a night of the mistral, among the clashing reeds and the glittering frosty pools of the swamp. Before her, out of the tamarisks, suddenly rose the huge horns of Le Maudit and she heard the most ferocious snort. Stooping to a puddle she cupped her hands, scooped up some water and threw it towards the bull, over whose brows it was scattered by the mistral: and she cried out at the same time: "I baptise you in the name of God the Father, God the Son, and God the Holy Ghost!"

Backing slowly away from her, the great bull was seen to bow its head and kneel down. Its behaviour changed. The rancher noticed the change and two months later Le Maudit, after putting up a grand show, had the glory of dying, like a Christian, in the Arena. From that day on no herd in Provence has ever had its Maudit. (This may also be partly due to the fact that unless they are famous bulls who have retired honourably for life after wearing their master's cocardes to the best advantage, cattle which seem unpromising for valour are sent straightway to the abattoirs as butcher's meat.)

Two of the finest Roman arenas (those of Nîmes and Arles) are in a good state of preservation, and are still used for spectacles and bullfights; both are able to seat twenty thousand spectators, to this day. This gives a greater vividness to the legend. In the changing rooms under these arenas you feel quite near to the Christian martyrs, the gladiators, and the lions—all of whom have left their scratchings on the walls.

On the day before the statue to the grandfather of Albert Lescot was unveiled, at the Mas du Village on the Crau, I happened to hear there was a great round-up. Albert, then the greatest ace in equestrian tauromachy, if not in the whole world, was certainly the best in France, since Pierre Saurel was getting a little old. At any rate they were both of the class of Cañero, el Algabeño, and the two famous Portuguese, Simao de Veiga and Jao Nuncio. The old Lescot had been famed in Provençal epic poetry and song as the greatest of all cattlemen, and as I had been accepted so easily by the very exclusive ranchers of the Camargue, I thought at least that I would be allowed a shake-down on the hay at the Mas du Village, Lescot's ranch, when I made my début on the Crau. I got there while Albert was still at Arles making arrangements for next day's fiesta. As I was dressed only in a shirt and slacks, with a battered old felt hat, I did not make a good impression on Madame Lescot who thought I might be an escaped crook from the Dynamites (a convict settlement nearby) and she sent me packing just after I'd paid off the taxi and seen it disappear. I spent as bad a night on the Crau as I had previously done on the Camargue.

No sooner had I left the Mas du Village on foot than an immense herd of cattle with two nasty looking solitary cows, separated from them, but going in the same direction, started advancing towards me, smouldering and thundering through a huge cloud of dust. As there were no barricades handy, and I did not like the look of one of the cows at all, I racked my brains for an excuse to go back, which I eventually did on the pretext of getting a light for my cigarette from one of the workmen engaged on the monument. This gave the herd time to cross the road. Then it got very dark, when, fortunately, I struck the metalled road, with pylons at the side which take electricity to Saint Martin de la Crau via the Dynamites. But on that metalled road I heard the clop of some bull's or cow's hooves following me. I could make out hardly anything till the moon rose mistily behind the beast, throwing an enormous shadow towards me about fifty feet long. Clouds were driving past the moon like great black bats at hurricane speed. I could lean against the wind, pushing my way through it as if it was a rugby scrum. At each pylon I hesitated whether to climb to safety before rushing for the next, and every time I stopped and looked back the animal that was following me stopped too.

The road was going now through masses of dwarf prickly oak that looked like recumbent cattle in the brief and fitful glances of the moon. On days like this before a ferrade it is often dangerous to be abroad on the Crau, since many of the Gardians have been trying out their tridents on the cattle and have left them in a nasty frame of mind.

On and on we went for hours, and it was extremely unpleasant. By the time we reached the first street lamp of the Dynamites I was really scared; and I was astounded, on turning to look at my pursuer properly, to find that a tiny suckling calf, which had evidently mistaken me for its lost mother, had been putting the fear of the devil into me for the last two or three hours. My mortified humiliation was so great that it was hardly compensated for by the enormous sense of relief that I felt when I saw there was no danger.

My sense of humiliation wasn't improved by getting another terrible scare on the same night, while sleeping in the hay at the station of Saint Martin de la Crau, when I rolled over on my ear on top of a hen on her nest, and was violently pecked and cackled out of my beauty sleep in the pitch-dark. I thought for a second that all the devils in hell had been loosed upon me.

Cattle are far more incalculable and nervous by night than by day, and always more likely to be aggressive when alone than when in company or large herds, though of course in large herds they are more liable to stampede. At night cattle show the fidgetiness that all buffaloes show both by day and night, whether they are Cape buffaloes or water buffaloes.

One of my funnier experiences at night with wild cattle was when I was driving, with Dr. Pinto of Lagoa (Algarve), through clouds of thick dust on the unmetalled straight road through the Alentejo to Lagos from Lisbon. We came into a vast herd of wild cattle, and were advancing at about two miles an hour, because in spite of the brilliance of the lamps, we were in a fog of dust worse than any old London pea-soup fog in the early twenties. Suddenly one of the cabestros (or tame bell-oxen), an enormous beast, with "horns like cathedrals," put its head down and made the most vicious and determined charge I have ever seen in the open, outside of an arena. It nearly stunned itself, shook its head, and disappeared into the fog. The left motor lamp, without being smashed, had been buckled and twisted round in such a way that it threw its beam vertically upright into the sky. The combined strength of the Doctor, myself, and a cowboy who rode up to us after the herd had safely passed, was insufficient to twist the lamp back one inch. We drove down the hills into Lagos with one lamp on the road and the other squinting to heaven like a searchlight, which excited much comment as we drove through the streets of Portimau and other towns on our way back to Lagos. It even spread an air alarm, for hostilities were feared with Red Spain at that moment of the Naval revolt in Lisbon.

XVI

THE LIGHTS OF LONDON

THE second time I came to London (after passing through it on a donkey cart) I was in the tow of William Walton. I don't know if my memory is playing me a trick but London in 1919 seemed darker, foggier, colder, and altogether more Londonish than it is now. The huge railway stations of Paddington and Euston were noisier, smokier, and seemed more mysterious. The traffic used to collect, like lumber on a river, and be held up for half an hour at a time in the streets. The motor-traffic was far louder since the engines were of a more primitive make. Also there was a lot of heavy carthorse traffic ("le faubourg sécoue par les lourds tomberaux"), besides lighter horse cabs, so that London always echoed and sounded with a ghostly roar, even when one was indoors, like the noise of a conch held to one's ear.

I love walking miles along the damp streets, entering the most sordid little cafés, and listening to the conversations. I used to start walking at seven in the morning and go round all the markets, the docks, the shops, the slums and the negro and Chinese quarters, asking for and getting all kinds of jobs. I prefer London even to Paris. It is London's mighty river, her docks and her ships that give her the advantage.

The Café Royal was then the centre of the world. You met everybody there except Royalty, the General Staff, and the Bishops. Bankers, financiers, bookies, statesmen, prostitutes, pickpockets, millionaires, jockeys, boxers, painters, sculptors, poets, and musicians all rubbed shoulders in that one tiny crowded square room with about twenty marble tables. Literary and artistic discussions took the most sanguinary form, and I once saw a splash of blood being cleaned off the ceiling by the waiter, Mario, perched on a ladder, with a duster. It had flown up there from Peter Warlock's (Philip Heseltine's) fetish-headed knobkerrie as he had raised it to deal a second blow on the bloody scalp of a Jew who had spoken ill of Bernard van Dieren's music. (Yet Philip was no fighter really.)

Only one of the original waiters, George, remains there to this day: Johnny Papani, Joe, Mario, and the rest are all dead. George says: "The good ones all die first." These waiters were all rich men and even the poorest and shabbiest of us had his waiter who would advance him credit or lend him anything up to ten pounds till a picture was sold or an article accepted—as George will bear me out. In those days you could borrow a pound off a policeman you had never seen before, and he would be sure of getting it back. People could judge you by the look in your face.

When I first came to London with William Walton, we called on Wyndham Lewis at his studio in the Adam and Eve Mews, and he showed us pictures which utterly mystified me, though I pretended that I could appreciate them and tried to look as wise as Walton, and to speak as intelligently, always taking my cue from him. *Blast* was then in full swing. *Tarr* had appeared and the *Caliph's Design* was on the point of coming out. It was this last pamphlet (the sheer writing of it) that put me under the spell of Lewis and I gradually came more and more under his influence till I started generating ideas of my own, and he went "cosmic." The same evening that I met Lewis, I met the Sitwells at a party which Edith gave at her flat in Bayswater Road. I suppose that from a literary point of view that was one of the great days of my life: for her two brothers were there and in the middle of this party in came T. S. Eliot, whose work in those days I vainly tried to imitate. Earp, Walton, and I all got ourselves into hot water at the Psittakoi Society in Oxford for praising as the best English poet alive, this "unknown upstart" writer, Eliot, to those who subsequently became his most ardent admirers and imitators, but who were then the most fervent admirers of J. E. Flecker, Brooke, and Lascelles Abercrombie. From then on the influence of Eliot literally swallowed up many of these minor poets as a blue whale swallows mites of krill. It was as if his muse was getting its revenge on their previous derision of the dark American invader.

Sacheverell Sitwell is a poet who has never received his full deserts because the level of his achievement is so consistently high that it is like the plain of Thibet far above the heads of most critics. It is so *even* that they find it *flat*, yet one line of his would blaze like a star, if introduced into the work of most other poets and, by its sheer fine quality alone, disintegrate and ruin the other lines around it. People will return to him in the end.

Sir Osbert Sitwell disputes with Lewis the crown for prose. He has the advantage of being on the whole more human, friendly, and genial, yet when Lewis discards the frozen mask of misanthropy, as in the superb passage about Lily in *Snooty Baronet*, he seems unbeatable for sheer lyrical rapture in prose.

To have known these six people—Eliot, Lewis, Walton and the three Sitwells who have had such a tremendous influence on this age and who will have an even greater one on the age to come—makes it quite worth while having been born, even if one comes to nothing oneself. Through my love of rough company and a certain impatience of discipline, I soon forfeited these better influences and sank into that strange underworld of indigence and folly known as "Bohemia." But even there I vaguely kept in touch with some of the most brilliant men of the time, Van Dieren, Heseltine, and Cecil Gray.

Above all there is Augustus John, that King among men, who stands more or less by himself with the majesty of a Pagan Jupiter, as not only a great artist, but a very great intellect. He can speak on almost any subject, with understanding and entirely without pedantry. He is interested in everything that is human. His mental stature is only matched by his magnanimity. We had a slight estrangement during the Spanish War when, alone of the British Intellectuals, I dared to affect a pro-European, anti-Soviet line and was greeted by Augustus, when I came over to join the Army as a volunteer, with: "A member of the Axis, I believe." Anyone who was not pro-Red in the Spanish War automatically became a "fascist." I owed my independence in taking sides to being able to earn my living independently of my vocation as an artist. Had I depended for my living on writing or painting, as I do now, since I have been crippled, I should not have so much as dared to think which side I would take, since one's bread and butter depended on thinking pro-Red. Nor could I have lived in Spain and seen for myself what had been going on if I hadn't been able to earn my living as a *Chalan*. It made no difference that one fought as willingly against Fascism as one had done against Bolshevism previously. So fanatical did the mental goose-stepping of the British Intellectuals become, and so gluttonous their fatuous credulity, that, even if you killed ten times as many fascists as you had previously killed bolsheviks in self-defence, you still remained a "fascist."

John, at that time, seemed (as a King has to have a jester, a dwarf, and a fat man) to need always some clownish retainer in his tow. Horace Cole, the great practical joker, was the first one and the best of all. He was really a kindly sort of man. Unlike his successors to the post of court clown, he had character, and at every second practical joke or so, he really made one laugh. Later on, towards the end, they deteriorated, and as he got older he practised them only on simpletons because he began to collect so many thick ears from men whom he annoyed by putting salt in their coffee, spitting in their beer, and other dotages.

Horace Cole must have been quite a live wire when, in his prime, he inspected the Fleet as the "Sultan of Zanzibar"; dug up Piccadilly as a Navvy; and gave the party to all the people in Birmingham whose names, beginning with "Row," "Ram," "Higgin," or "Winter," ended in "botham," who, finding no host had turned up, all had to introduce themselves to each other. These hoaxes were uproariously funny. Cecil Gray gave him a hiding one day for some annoyance—and that almost cured him of practical joking in the long run. Cecil Gray, unlike his more pugnacious friend Heseltine, was an intellectual fighter. He had cold anger. With any training, he could have been a very good fighter.

When I came back to London the second time from Provence, I again went to stay with Rowley Smart. He let me sleep on the floor of his studio whenever I returned from sea; or sometimes it would be Geoffrey Nelson. Often enough I stayed at the Seaman's Hostel, or the Salvation Army, without coming up West.

Geoffrey Nelson had a basement, where, at my request, he let old Stuart Gray sleep. Stuart Gray, they said, had been a great lawyer in Edinburgh, but he "went bamboo" before middle-age, and, I believe, headed some hunger-march or "Back-to-the-land" demonstration, which walked from Edinburgh to London. He gave away his fortune, and took to Hot-Gospelling in Hyde Park, after which he would pass round the hat for money. His knowledge of the law enabled him to seize on empty houses in Mayfair which he would fling open to all the wandering flotsam and jetsam, and waifs and strays of the London night. Dukes and Duchesses might complain but it was no good. Lord Rosebery was the one who objected most, in Berkeley Square, to the roisterous neighbourhood of prostitutes, lascars, crooks, and A.W.L.'s. The police were power-less, as old Stuart had the law by heart: and this law, regarding the occupation of mortgaged houses left unoccupied after a certain period, was still valid, though it had not been invoked for centuries.

Stuart was a magnificent looking figure, though very ragged —something between Michelangelo's Moses and Walt Whitman. He was getting on past seventy, and he had just been converted to spiritualism by a visit from the ghost of one of his free-lodgers in the Mayfair Mansion.

This is how it happened. Stuart, who was still something of a business man, and above all a Scotchman, had a flair for saving money by buying rations from restaurant-keepers in Soho, scraps which they were about to throw away, after they had become cov-ered with green fur, mildew, penicillin, or verdigris. He often succeeded in collecting rations gratis. On the occasion of which I speak, he had actually been *paid* three and sixpence to take away an extremely ancient, outrageous, and dangerous kipper, the mere sight of which, through smoked glass, would have killed a full-grown hyena with ptomaine poisoning at the distance of fifty yards! Stuart had long ago become immune to food poisoning; just like the old native who keeps the snake-park in Durban and is so impregnated with anti-venom serums that if a mamba or a cobra bites him, the latter is more likely to die than he is. Stuart could have been used as a guinea-pig donor of serum, even for botulism. Having lovingly stowed his buckshee kipper between two slices of linoleum, to which he was very partial, he hid the sandwich in a locker in the passage, in readiness for his evening meal, and started preparing his speech for Hyde Park.

Meanwhile an emaciated Lascar in the next room, who was half dead with hunger, was guided by the scent to the kipper. Crawling feebly out on all fours, the ravenous Indian was soon fumbling at the locker. On opening it, he was at first dazzled by a veritable aurora borealis of phosphorescence. Shading his eyes, and gripping his nostrils tremulously between forefinger and thumb, with the other hand he seized the sandwich and tried to force it between his jaws. No sooner had his teeth met on the linoleum than he gave one kick and expired. Noticing a strange unearthly blue light coming

from under the door, Stuart went out in the passage to find the Lascar stone dead, with the luminous fish-tail, and the two slices of
linoleum, protruding from his jaws. Rescuing his precious sandwich almost intact, the law-abiding Stuart sent immediately for the
police. I forget what the verdict on the Lascar was—either suicide
while of unsound mind or death from natural causes—either would
have been true enough: for the kipper had fulminated him as if it
had been prussic acid: no wonder! Although so law-abiding, Stuart
had unwittingly broken the law. By letting the police in, he had
given away the fact that he had been slicing snacks of linoleum from
the floor for his breakfasts, suppers, lunches, and bedding. He also
printed his manifestoes with linoleum in which he had hacked out,
basso-relievo, with consummate skill, the runic-looking letters of his
slogans and mottoes, which he sold in Hyde Park.

That same evening when Stuart had finally consumed his sandwich and was just about to go off to sleep he was visited by the
spirit of the Lascar, which, Stuart said, was "bathed in a supernatural radiance." (Stuart indignantly denied that this radiance might
be a sort of astral hangover of phosphorescence from the kipper,
when I suggested it.) The Lascar's ghost told him to paint its portrait then and there, as it appeared: and after that to go forth in the
world seeking the bereaved and painting their portraits. The Lascar
then bequeathed to Stuart a mystical gift, saying: "Yea, Verily!
After you have painted the portrait of the bereaved, turn it upside
down, and look carefully. Yea, Verily! There you will always see
the likeness of the loved one. Yea, Verily!"

The Charlatan in Stuart (which had previously walked side by
side with the Reformer) from then on eclipsed the latter part of
Stuart's dual personality. He became whole-heartedly, though unconsciously, a Charlatan. In the end titled ladies took him up and
listened spell-bound to the second-hand rubbish which the old vil-
lain had swotted up from William Morris, Blake's Prophetic Books,
Madame Blavatzky, and the *Wisdom of the East Series*, and boiled
down into a preposterous hash of his own. However, long before
he arrived at the titled ladies, Stuart had to work his way up
through servant girls, via policewomen, to bourgeois widows and
spinsters, and so on up the social scale. He always kept his portrait
for which the Lascar's spirit had sat as model and used it as his
trump card in canvassing for portraits. It was a formidable piece of

work in which he had used chloride of silver, or some such luminous paint. The Lascar's ghost was a veritable porcupine of celestial radiations and coruscations in broad daylight, but when he put the light out and you could see nothing but the chloride's faint snail-like sheen, it resembled the original kipper from which it sprung.

I met Stuart when he was clearing out of his Mayfair Mansion, and he told me that it was all up with his Buckshee-Hotel. (The police had discovered his linoleum-cutting and eating trait, so he, and his merry lodgers, had been evicted, legally, at last. But he revenged himself on the police by converting policewomen to spiritualism and fornication, as we shall see.) He was carrying two huge rolls of linoleum both for food and lodging. He would heave them over the railings, and behind the bushes, of some public square as soon as it was dark enough. Using one roll as the ground-sheet, he would use the other as counterpane, roof, supper, and breakfast, gnawing away at the counterpane as he braved all sorts of weathers. Later, he took a tip from me which was to fold his linoleum conically like a wigwam with his linoleum-stewing saucepan as a waterproof lid. He generally erected this contraption in the thick ground-scrub of Regent Square, then haunted by the ghosts of Voisin and his wife: both of which ghosts sat as models for Stuart. Voisin, a Charlotte Street butcher, had put his wife through the mincer and deposited her in a sack in Regent Square. It made the rent go down and that is why so many of us were fetched up in Regent Square—even Huxley.

I always liked Stuart because he was generous with money, tough and independent. He trusted one and one trusted him. We were all like that, Nina Hammet (she was a fine trooper), Rowley Smart, Betty May, Joseph Kramer, and all the other penniless bohemians of whom I was almost the only one ever to raise any spare cash—by working at sea, or from my indulgent parents at home who always spoilt me. I sometimes paid Rowley's and Nelson's rent when I returned from the Canaries or West Africa. The rest of the money would go through the roof in no time.

One day I found that poor old Stuart Gray was suffering from bronchitis and I offered to let Nelson off everything he owed me if he would let Stuart sleep in the basement which belonged to Nelson's studio. Nelson, and our Irishman, who gave up painting to become a rich night-club owner, were not bohemians: they were scroungers and bourgeois, who never paid back anything, whereas we others shared out. I had the great joy of locating and visiting the latter's night club during this last war when I was hard up as a sergeant with three thirsty mates waiting outside—all returning from Survivor's Leave. Leaving my kitbags with them, I rushed upstairs, brandishing my rifle-butt above my head, reminded the proprietor who I was, and told him that he had once said to Rowley Smart, after selling a picture: "Don't tell Roy I sold that picture for £30 because he has paid my rent and six months' gas-bill, and I would have to pay him back." I advanced to the till, amidst the horrified waiters and Chelsea-ite guests, whereupon the Irishman, seeing that I would have smashed the till-machine to bits with my rifle-butt (and himself included) and taken the contents, begged me to come aside, and gave me a tenner though he owed me twice as much. I accepted the compromise since I was loth to lose my stripes, or de virginate my charge-sheet, which I kept stainless throughout the war, till my discharge with "Military Conduct: Excellent."

I and my three mates shared the tenner on our way up to the Transit Camp at Wishaw, and voted that our little diversion to the night club, on our way across London, had been a great success, for we turned up in camp with a bottle of gin to spare, and were able to cheer up some of our more drooping mates who were gloomy at leaving home once more.

I knew that nobody ever saw a penny of what was "lent" to Nelson, who was nevertheless an amusing companion because he always flattered one; so I turned the screw, on behalf of Stuart Gray, who installed an old bedstead in the basement, although Nelson grumbled a good deal. We never used the basement except to fetch water from it for our tea and morning wash, so Stuart was not much in the way, though he cluttered up the whole place with linoleum and psychic canvases.

It was one morning, when I went down early to fetch a bucket of water, that I noticed a truncheon swinging from one of the bed posts and an enormous blue uniform with brass buttons. There under the blankets, beside Stuart, was what appeared to be a super-roll of linoleum, enough to cover the floor of a drill hall, or furnish a banquet for the combined army of Hyde Park Orators, past, present, and to come. But it was heaving with a mighty ground-swell of snores and there on another roll of linoleum which served

Stuart for a pillow, now that he no longer required it for a ground-sheet, was a huge shock of carrot-coloured hair and the vertical aquiline nose of the most burly and enormous policewoman I ever set eyes on in my life! Frau Pagel wasn't in it! The contrast of the snow-white locks of the patriarch and the red hair of the barrel-shaped centurioness (as if Father Christmas were to be found in the arms of Britannia-Rules-the-Waves) was a finer advertisement for linoleum-vitamins, lino-pepsins, and thyro-linoleoid monkey-glands than could ever have been conjectured by the imagination. Postered on the hoardings, with the slogan, "Eat more Linoleum," the picture that I saw would have swept the floors of the Stately Homes of England bare of linoleum in a fortnight. The Damaroid Firms would have gone bust.

Although the approach of this hoary Don Juan was always from the spiritual or psychic side, there was no doubt as to the deadly efficacy of his technique. He had painted the police woman's por-trait, and on turning it upside down, had managed to detect the vague silhouettes of the four defunct husbands whom this veritable Samsoness and steam-roller of a woman had literally worn out. Whereupon Stuart had immediately stepped into their eight shoes as if he had been in the prime of his manhood.

About this time I left on a trip with s.s. *Umtata*, Captain Rogers, of the Bullard King Line, and when I came back to stay at Nelson's Stuart was in disgrace. Not content with one policewoman he had also painted the portraits of several others, and detected their dead husbands, fathers, uncles, in the background of the inverted por-traits. The result was that all the policewomen in the district, who alternated on that beat, were becoming linoleum-minded: the morale of the force was being undermined. Three mornings during the last week, when Nelson had been down for water he had seen a new truncheon swinging from the bed-post and a hefty roll of human linoleum. The male police were becoming nasty, whether out of jealousy, or merely because they felt the honour of the force was involved. They were keeping the place under supervision. That was Nelson's excuse for pushing out Stuart Gray the day before I returned ashore. I thereupon quarrelled with Nelson, threw him downstairs and went to stay with Rowley Smart, who told me that Stuart had been camping out once again, in a linoleum wigwam in Regent Square. I went round to the square but there was no sign of the old man, to whom I owed ten shillings, which I was anxious to pay back before I went broke and returned to sea. I scanned the dark undergrowth of the square-gardens in vain. Nor was he to be found, by day, on any of the soap-boxes in Hyde Park. Stuart had made his first conquest of a titled lady!

Not long after this Rowley did the same, grew sidewhiskers, and wore a hunting-stock. We called him "Lord Washmore." Rowley was a really fine painter in spite of being rather weak and lazy; he was a loyal friend and he dropped our Irish colleague after hearing him say: "Don't tell Roy about the sale of the picture." Later he became rich as an art-teacher in the midlands, and owned a car and a titled lady, who had previously owned the car.

About this time I was picked up in the street by a man who asked me if I wanted to be a cinema actor and gave me a ticket to present next morning at Stoll's. I was then just nineteen but had a beard and looked about thirty. I thought he had singled me out for my good looks and was looking forward to a lightning career as a "Star," with tons of money.

I presented my ticket, after an almost interminable bus-voyage, at a sinister looking cubby-hole in a huge corrugated iron building like a zeppelin-hangar. I was led past hundreds of lockers which were labelled "Boers," "Zulus," "Red Indians," "Cannibals," "Cowboys" and so on, and treated with scant ceremony for a future star. We came to a locker labelled "Foreign Legion" and there I received a papier-mâché uniform into which I was ordered to insert myself though it was made for someone short and fat. It was a freezing morning and the uniform was porous: then, with teeth chattering, I was pushed into a large room and herded with the most amazing set of shivering bearded human nanny goats of every age, from white bearded nonagenarians to chinfluffed urchins younger than myself. We scowled at each other, just as two men with glass eyes, or wooden legs, or two stammerers will scowl at each other if they get into the same railway compartment; or as all those victims of Horace Cole whose names ended in "botham" must have scowled at each other when they first realised they were the victims of a hoax on introducing themselves to each other. It was obvious that the cinema tout had been instructed: "Go out and recruit every single person of whatever condition whom you find with a beard in the region of Soho."

At the same time that we "beavers" had been recruited by one tout, another tout had been recruiting an enemy force of "Moors." He had indiscriminately collected every out-of-work coloured man that could be found in Soho and while we were dressing up in one part of the building, these pagans, unknown to us, were "being issued" with oriental uniforms in the shape of turbans, kimonos, burnouses, suluman-nighties, scimitars, tarbooshes, battle-axes and even a couple of Scotch claymores and dirks with Cairngorm hilts, which had somehow strayed into the Oriental department from the Prince Charlie one.

We waited for hours shivering in our paper uniforms; then they issued us rifles with blank rounds. Several regular actors took charge of us and a young Frenchman suddenly came up to me and said, "Targai," so that I was absolutely thrilled and embraced him on both cheeks for I recognised him as Federi, the brother of the great Maillot of St. Chamas, one of the finest jousters in the world.

"Yes, of course, I am a jouster and I know you and your brother Lucien, and Le Blanc and Espinosa—and the whole blessed team of you," I said.

Federi Maillot and I remained half-sections all through our brief, but stormy, career as cinema sub-stars.

The two regular actors who took charge of us were the most noisome pansies I have ever seen or smelt. They fairly oozed lavender and, at the same time, had green drug-poisoned faces. The elder was dressed as a captain, and he was fussing us all the time about our blank rounds, and being careful of the triggers.

All went well till Federi, the countryman of Tartarin, accidentally let off one round straight into the long white beard of a poor old nonagenarian. There was a flame, a smell of burnt feathers; the old man was left clutching on his chin the black stubble of what had been a snowy, silken floss, and gazing in astonishment at the vanishing cloud of faint blue smoke, into which his beard had been so suddenly transformed.

From that moment everybody seemed to lose control of their trigger-fingers. Whether it was on purpose as a protest against being kept shivering inactively in the cold, I don't know, but there was a veritable epidemic of shots which nearly threw our directors into a state of hysteria. Several more or less painful burns made the recipients restive and bad-tempered. Disorder began to spread.

Soon the odd seventy of us were herded on to a home-made "desert" on the floor of the studio. Sand had been shovelled about two inches deep on a vast sheet of tarpaulin. "Palm trees" consisted of flower-pots with palms in them, borrowed from some adjacent hotel-lounge, and suspended upside-down (and therefore inside-out) over poles which projected up into the palm leaves. The camera was focused so that it omitted the tell-tale flower-pots. Soldiers' "campfires" consisting of cardboard "logs" in bunches were dotted about on the "desert" at intervals of every two yards or so. An electric globe in each bunch of logs suggested the glow of a fire. An "oasis" shimmered in the fold of the tarpaulin where a concealed hosepipe dripped forlornly. The capillary porous suction of the sand absorbed this water so that, as we sat and shivered in front of our heatless "campfires," our paper pants became soggy over the seats.

It was just at this moment that the enemy force of "Moors," consisting mostly of Soho negroes, probably representing Abd el Krim's outfit, but looking more like the Pirates of Penzance, were marched up brandishing their scimitars. The sound of blank cartridges had already excited them—and the smell of cordite, next to that of carnations, is the most exciting perfume in the world.

By volunteering to act as a Mounted Messenger and by jumping a horse over some sandbags, I got a sort of promotion to stunt man, and this all took some time: so did some languorous love scenes, which did not add to the good humour of the shivering Frenchmen who were all catching arthritis on the damp of the home-made "desert." My riding act saved the seat of my paper breeches from getting as wet as those of my fellow-legionaries. I hung to the rear when the charge was "sounded" on a soundless bugle, and a sham fight was ordered, instructions having been given that on no account was any one to hurt an opponent. I did not fancy having my beard singed off by a blank round, or getting a whack from the flat side of one of those scimitars. The fact that I hung back was rewarded by one of the most comical sights I ever saw. Now the cameras were turning; my comrades rose, as one man, from the sand, and as they advanced on the enemy (lo and behold!) they presented to the camera seventy-two completely bare backsides, from which the sodden rags of their trouser-seats, demolished by the damp, drooped dismally, as they advanced on the negroes. The

discovery of this fact excited the hilarity of the negroes who were
to have retreated according to their contract. But who would ever
retreat in front of a man with no seat to his pants? It is undignified!

The negroes therefore refused to budge. They added the insult
of coarse jokes to the stinging blows they were inflicting with the
flat side of their scimitars. An enormous negro, whom the film director had addressed as Mr. Umslopagaas, was evidently trying to
earn his cognomen and threatening to run amok. The French were
behaving very well as they were anxious to earn their fee by ful-
filling the contract, and they had promised not to use their rifle-
butts. I got angry with Umslopagaas because he was giving Federi
such a bad time and I know how to fight negroes, not having acquired the European complex of inferiority. I wasn't made an in-
structor to coloured troops in this last war for nothing. First of all
I gave Umslopagaas two such kicks on the shin that he nearly
hopped out of his skin, for the shin to a negro is what the skull is to
a European: then I came in with two rib-busters under his heart so
that he gasped for mercy, and stampeded, leading the rest of his
crowd helter-skelter after him. He got five pounds for his stoven
ribs, after he had threatened proceedings, but Mr. King, the director, said it was worth it as it looked as if they were going to
wreck the whole picture and the studio too. By shifting the camera
and the lights during the misunderstanding between the negroes
and the French, they had managed to cut the backsides out from
the new angle, and that shot had been a success.

Nevertheless Mr. King lost money and had to go out of business
a month or two later. I had worked every day for him after that as
a stunt man, with thirty shillings a day, doing all sorts of acts such as
falling from high places, eating fire, and chewing up glass. In spite
of this I was completely unable to get another cinema job after Mr.
King packed in.

XVII

MARRIAGE

I was looking for a ship when the news came to me that Stuart Gray had again "gone under linoleum," having annoyed his titled victim by making a pass at her cook. He had heaved his wigwam over the railings of Regent Square, in the dark, inverted the saucepan on the top to keep out the rain, and there I found him, invisible to the police, behind some bushes.

The next day, when he came to see me, I roared with laughter. I had not noticed, in the dark, that he had wonderful new clothes, a huge velvet bow, patent leather shoes and a shiny silk top-hat. I could scarcely believe my eyes. Not only that, but he told me that two young ladies, art-students, living in Regent Square had taken pity on him and were going to let him use their coal-cellar. Would I help him to cart some of his belongings which the titled lady's cook was storing for him?

I borrowed a cart from my old friend Sgt. Paisley of the Inniskilling Dragoons, a Boer War veteran, who knew my father and who is still commissionaire at the age of 80, at a firm in Tottenham Court Road, and still obligingly lends people the same old handcart.

When I had trundled this cart round to Stuart Gray's new quarters, the most beautiful young woman I have ever seen opened the door to me. It seemed I had known her all my life because she had, as I have said before, almost a family resemblance to Gwen though outshining her as the evening star does the other planets. Even the satirical Wyndham Lewis, who seldom praises anyone, speaks of "the very beautiful Mary Campbell." I was not the jittery faint-hearted coward I had been when I tried to declare my love, as a boy, to the beautiful Gwen and the equally wonderful gymmistress: I proposed to this one almost the minute after I met her, and she did not seem very surprised. She and her friend, who was also very beautiful, had seen me before on a bus and had even followed me when I got down—to find out where I lived. Apparently I had become quite an Adonis, though you wouldn't think so to see me now.

Van Dieren, and a sculptor, whom we nicknamed Sennacheribs, had been hanging around for weeks, vainly, on the doorstep. They were furious that I was accepted as a fiancé the day after our meeting. Van Dieren had already dedicated some of his music to Mary Jarman, and Sennacheribs was running after her friend, although at that time she gave him no encouragement. But I turned up, on the second day, with a special marriage licence, upon which I had spent my last two or three pounds: and I installed myself at once. Van Dieren, Sennacheribs, and Stuart Gray could hardly be relied upon to defend the virtue of these young ladies, as they all pretended to do. The first two were married, and as for Stuart, well, he was an unofficial Mormon.

One morning when I had looked out and noticed old Sennacheribs left out in the cold rain where he had been for hours with a bunch of dahlias, I said to the girls: "Why don't you ask him in, and I'll jump behind the piano while you give him a cup of tea and warm him. He looks so cold and miserable out there in the rain."

I hid behind the piano and was astounded, in return for my playing the good Samaritan, to hear the old Jerusalemite-Assyrian launch out into a sanctimonious tartuffade about his being there to protect the girls from wicked "Zulu" seducers. He gave them a false description of me and my past that would have turned Don Juan Tenorio, or Casanova, green with envy. The joke was that the famous fruity sculptor who never took in any country or nation, where sculpture was a native art, but simply stormed a sex-overfed and sculpture-starved England with his fruitiness, became suddenly, not *fruity* but absolutely *leafy* wherever I was concerned. He became a professor of puritanical figleafiness with regard to my reputation.

The saccharine of false purity exuded from every pore of this saccharhinoceros advocate of virtue, as he launched into a highly apocryphal account of my shocking past, warning the young ladies to beware of me and keep me at arm's length, and that he was solely interested (seeing that they were not like other art-students) in insuring that they were duly respected and protected.

The old hypocrite! During this monologue I was popping up from behind the piano and cocking snooks at the somewhat frowsy scruff of the self-appointed apostle of purity, so that neither of the girls could keep a straight face. Sennacheribs thought that they were laughing at him (as he knew well he deserved to be laughed at) in his self-appointed rôle of Tartuffe, the Holy.

When he gave an interview to the Press, he spoke of his beloved crony, the archimandrake of Leninbury, saying with such deep feeling that they had the bond of RELIGION between them (!!). I vividly recalled this sanctimonious sermon of his. And I laughed again with all that glorious storm of animal laughter that assailed the three of us when the old humbug, trembling with rage, and with tears of humiliation in his eyes, had rushed out and slammed the door behind him. As soon as he slammed the door we thought he had gone. But Mr. Sennacheribs was keyhole-happy, although, as we shall hear, he derived far more misery and humiliation from this source than pleasure—unlike other "peepers" and eavesdroppers. Later he buttonholed me in the Café Royal and lectured me about seducing girls. When I asked him: "How did you know I was behind the piano?" he replied: "I heard you through the keyhole after I shut the door," and he said it without a blush. Upon which I explained to him that it would be safer for his health to leave keyholes alone and mind his own business: after that he got the waiters of the Harlequin Restaurant to do his keyhole work for him.

From what *he* said, it appeared that, to get his own back, he had gone straight home that morning and vented his fury on a bust he was modelling of my wife's friend, smashing it to bits. (Actually he had put it away carefully without hurting it at all; he was too good a business-man to perform any of the romantic extravagances to which he pretended.) The pretence even of being so romantically ungovernable was in itself thoroughly good business, advertising an "artistic temperament," and all of a piece with adding a couple of inches or so to the sex of his sculptures. He came back later that day untruthfully to tell my wife's friend that he had destroyed her bust. But he had to find some other way of communicating it. I was by then training Stuart Gray as Cerberus, and Stuart proved a good watchdog—uncorruptible by money or whiskey—though no one tried to bribe him with luminous kippers or slices of linoleum, which might have shaken him. His coal-hole led out on to the passage between my wife's studio and the main building in front of it. I overheard the following duel of words. Stuart began: "Miss Mary and Campbell says you can't come here."

"Vy?"

"Because you fill the place with fleas."

"Shott opp, Sturt! Shott opp, Sturt!" gasped the Assyrian in fury.

"And also because Campbell says he will give you a good hiding if he catches you here and he'll probably be coming in shortly." This seemed to cause the great business tycoon of fruitiness to reflect.

The ex-K.C., seeing his advantage, expatiated on the legal aspects of the case and threatened to call the police. Sennacheribs had been used to getting his own way till he met me and my watchdog Stuart. He couldn't make it out. The saccharinoceros went off rumbling out some inarticulate phrases about "Impertinence," etc. —but he went, and Stuart was triumphant and beaming.

"Where did you get that one about the fleas?" I asked him. "That's what your xxxxx of a friend, Nelson, said to me when he turned me out," grumbled Stuart, "and I just thought I'd pass it on, as it made me angrier than all the other things he said: and it certainly worked on Shaggy Brilliantine. I thought he would burst. Ha! Ha! Ha!"

Though Sennacheribs and Van Dieren were the most assiduous besiegers of Regent Square, there were dozens of other admirers, highbrows, poets, authoresses, painters, pianists, singers, ballet dancers, and even an Economist, hanging around. No other contemporary women ever had so much poetry, good, bad, and indifferent, written about them or so many musical compositions dedicated to them, or had so many portraits and busts made of them—as those two girls between them.

It is no wonder that they had got the reputation of man-haters because the young men of their race and class had mostly been killed during the war or were married by the time they arrived in London from the Backveld of the Black Country. The nearest thing to a man they had ever seen was Van Dieren, my rival, who was not only a man but a gentleman, but by then, though he was still handsome, he had one foot in the grave. In spite of being middle-aged, he did not like my good luck any more than Sennacheribs, but he was big-hearted and generous enough to get over it before he died. Besides, we had two great mutual friends in Philip Heseltine (Peter Warlock) and Cecil Gray: and these two were so loyal that in the end he forgave me my good luck. At any rate he soon realised that what had prevailed with my wife was not the plausible technique of a womaniser but the whole-hearted devotion which she had kindled in me and which she, at any rate, could see she had kindled for good: for it lit me up with a visible elation.

I had by that time completely grown out of the vices of adolescence which were so studiously and artificially conserved in the bohemian life of the twenties,

> In my teens I'd shed like threadbare trousers
> Every experience possible to wowsers.

Although it was very difficult to acquire literary fame without kotowing to the homosexual and "liberal" freemasonries, I knew that I could eventually pierce through any screen they tried to set up between me and the public. The English language is an almost supernatural weapon, and the flame of poetry will fuse locks, bars, and stone walls. It was obvious, too, that very many writers who resorted to the usual form of prostitution became effeminate; their glands changed and they lost their lyrical and creative gifts at about the age of thirty-five, although they still retained enormous power as collectively commercialised literary critics, publishers, or officials. Those androgynous writers and artists who excelled after middle age, such as Michelangelo and Shakespeare, were *more than men*. Our literary contemporaries were mostly *less than* men or women, so that it was better to be just a man, than something less than one, though one could tupper the Nobel Prize and get a vast literary reputation without having written a single sound literary work—simply by exhibitionising as a "queer"—as in the case of Gide. Better to wait and earn more lasting fame in a harder, less dishonourable way. That was the state I had arrived at when I helped Stuart round with his gear to the studio in Regent Square, and met the girl I married.

When I saw her I experienced, for one of the few times in my life, the electric thrill of falling in love at first sight. But she is the

only woman for whom I have felt this Dantesque sensation several
times; when coming back on leave from active service, or after
other separations abroad. She is also the only woman with whom
I have found that jealousy or quarrels have mutually acted as a
kind of aphrodisiac. I thought of nothing but of living and working for this woman (whom I knew to be *mine*, "for better or
worse," the minute I saw her). That she was said to be a man-hater
never daunted me for a moment, but only made it more of a challenge, more exciting, and more of a responsibility to capture her for
myself for ever. None of my very best horses were ever too easy
to break in: and on the human plane I like there to be some tension
in the harmony so that it never grows stale,

> Only that beauty shall be mine
> That never slacks the strain,
> A fighting salmon on the line,
> A snorter at the rein.

It would be blasphemy to talk about a divinely created soul in
terms of horsebreaking, but for the precedent in Holy Scripture
where they are represented as fish to be caught. My wife had quite
as much of a job to break me in, too.

On my former showing, to the rest of the "artistic" canaille who
were hanging hopelessly round the door, it seemed that my luck
with this girl was due to some deadly and diabolical technique. As I
was then known as "Zulu," and as Sennacheribs, who was the chief
hanger-around on the doorstep, is far more efficient at gossip than
at breaking the law of his tribe by playing about with "graven
images" and other forbidden and fruity things, I started getting a
fruity reputation. The character of "Zulu" Blades, in Lewis's *Apes
of God*, seemed to be a laughing comment on the notoriety I acquired from disappointed rivals these days. As "Zulu" Blades, I am
made to intercept all the different girl-friends on their way to various assignations, while a sort of synthetic caricature of the Holy
saccharhinoceros "bombinates" over my room on the floor, "stamping like the wild ass" of Omar in the hope of "putting the Zulu off
his stroke."

Up till then I had led a double, or rather a treble, life. If I wanted my money to last, I stayed down in the East End in the Seaman's Hostel or the Salvation Army, and read and wrote. If I wanted a quick spree I went to Stulik's at No. 1 Percy Street, the famous "Eiffel Tower Restaurant" where I parked my evening dress and where I met interesting and beautiful people.

I was, in those days, a great favourite with Stulik who used to say that for Augustus John, Iris Tree, Thomas Earp, or myself: "My whole house is yours." But at the time of which I speak Earp had gone to live in Paris. Amongst those who frequented the Eiffel were Lady Diana Manners, Marie Beerbohm (who first christened me "Zulu"), the Dolly Sisters, the very beautiful Iris Tree and Dorothy Warren, Raquel Meller, the Asquiths, Maurice Baring, General Sefton-Branker, Heseltine, Wyndham Lewis, Cecil Gray, and the whole Bloomsbury contingent.

If I was really hard up, I would stay with Rowley Smart or Nelson and pay the expenses. But I still had another hang-out. That was the Harlequin Restaurant where Johnny Papani, one of the Café Royal waiters, had recently branched off on his own. I had helped to paint the panels in the restaurant with Alvaro de Guevara, who did that wonderful portrait of Edith Sitwell in the Tate. Johnny was having a difficult time to make ends meet, so I sometimes used to hand him my whole payroll and tell him to take out of it daily the cost of what I ate and drank. This helped to make up for the credit he gave to others.

During these times I did a good deal of boxing, very often sparring with that lazy and pleasant American, Frank Moran of "Mary Ann" fame. I never actually caught "Mary Ann" for he almost sent you a letter first to tell you when it was coming. I also helped Lew Silva in the promotion of Sunday afternoon fights in St. Pancras Town Hall. These were uproarious sessions. I found it difficult to recall them when during the last war I was posted as a guard on the Control Room in the same building.

On the occasion when I met my wife I was broke. I had left my two good suits and my evening dress in the Seaman's Pension in Dakar. What I wanted to do as soon as I was married properly was to go straight to sea again and wire her my pay. I forged my age as twenty-one though I was still only a minor of nineteen, and it was unlikely that her respectable parents would be anxious to continue her allowance after they had discovered how things were.

My wife went up first to Wednesbury, to prepare them for the shock.

On the eve of our marriage Stuart Gray came out of his kennel and said: "You can't get married and interview your future father-in-law in a stoker's clothes, wearing that cap, with no shirt and only a scarlet muffler. I'll get you credit for a suit in Soho from a fellow I know." I went round with Stuart and we got a shiny, solemn, dark-green suit with a sort of frock coat which must have belonged to Gladstone, or Palmerston, or an Undertaker, about 100 years ago. It cost twelve shillings. This man is a fine chap who will sell you anything for almost nothing. I often see him. I then bought a choker and a frayed shirt all in the same bargain. Going up in the train, I was mistaken for a "Protestant Missionary from China" by a parson with whom I got into conversation. My wife nearly fainted when she met me on Birmingham Station. I had to spend the ten minutes between there and Wednesbury changing back into my fireman's clothes, in the washroom of the train. The swell suit of Mr. Gladstone went out of the window on to the railway line.

Arriving at Oakswell Hall, I made a very good impression upon my future father and mother-in-law, in spite of my rig. It was the servants who were horrified. The old cook said: "And I always thought Miss Mary would marry a gentleman with a park!"

When the parents told me: "We like you very much but refuse permission for you to marry our daughter till you have got a settled job ashore," I said: "I was so longing to have your permission: and nothing could distress me more than to have to marry your daughter without it."

In half an hour they gave way. It was a part of *The Flaming Terrapin* that did the trick. The dear old gentleman, who looked like a Spanish Don, was, fortunately for me, very keen on poetry, but for all that he was cast-iron about our being well-off economically.

My father heard of our marriage too late to stop it; he was naturally hurt that, being a minor, I had not consulted him about it, since he had always been so good to me and had always sent me any money I asked for when I was hard up. My excuse was, and still is, that I was taking absolutely no risks at all of not getting married to this girl.

As chance would have it, on the very day of my marriage, my

favourite brother George, who was on his way home to Africa from Edinburgh, breezed in to look for me at the Harlequin and the Eiffel, where the two restaurant-keepers were vying with each other to give us a terrific Wedding Party. He got a surprise when he heard I was being married; I had not informed him because I thought it might occur to him that it was his duty to tell my parents-in-law that I was only nineteen. Nevertheless, he waited around till we turned up in London and came to our party at the Harlequin: when he saw my wife he said to me: "I don't blame you. If I'd had the same luck, I would have done the same." My father remarked to him, later in Durban: "I suppose the silly little ass has married somebody worthless," and the valiant and chivalrous George said: "No fear! He has married someone a thousand times too good for him! I would have done the same if I could."

George came to our wedding party that night and looked so sane and respectable amongst the howling dervishes of London Bohemia. However we had some respectable guests besides him; Wyndham Lewis and Augustus John came in later, and Lewis, in *Blasting and Bombardiering*, wrote a very comical account of the fun in a chapter headed *Augustus John and Jew Biceps*.

Among the guests was that lovable Jewish Giant, Jacob Kramer, whose busts by Epstein make him look like Slawkenbergius. He was a good boxer (and Guevara was slowly becoming one too, so that in the end he only lost to Godoy in the whole of South America). In the London art world Jacob Kramer, "Chile" (as we called Guevara) and myself were the three best fighters by a long way, though Chile only developed his full strength when he was quite old, years after. There was no one else in our class at all and we were all three slightly afraid of one another as I proved that night by a piece of bluff and bravado on the simple-minded Jacob, who thought he had been slighted by John and was showing John an enormous bicep and threatening to punch his head right off.

I had already retired into the next room with my bride, when we were disturbed by the sound of ructions in the big room. Seeing what was the matter and out of gratitude to Augustus John (for few others would I have risked so much) I went straight up to Kramer in front of all the guests, and said in a low voice: "You know perfectly well, Kramer, that I could throw you out of that window with one hand. Stop it at once." This took Kramer so completely by surprise that he believed it, apologised and went to the other side of the room. I then retired again, having made a prodigious impression even upon my sceptical friend Lewis, who records it faithfully; and the party roared itself away merrily without us, into the small hours of the morning.

We had transferred our lodgings from Regent Square to the top floor of the Harlequin at 50, Beak Street. Though we were very happy, my wife and I had some quarrels since my ideas of marriage are old-fashioned about wifely obedience and in many ways she regarded me as a mere child because of being hardly out of my teens. But any marriage in which a woman wears the pants is an unseemly farce. To shake up her illusions I hung her out of the fourth-floor window of our room so that she should get some respect for me. This worked wonders for she gazed, head-downwards, up at the stars till the police from their H.Q. on the opposite side of Beak Street started yelling at me to pull her back. She had not uttered a single word, and when I shouted out pleasantly across the street: "We are only practising our act, aren't we, Kid?" she replied "Yes," as calmly and happily as if we did it every ten minutes. The police then left us alone, saying: "Well, don't practise it so high up over other people's heads, please."

My wife was very proud of me after I had hung her out of the window and boasted of it to her girl friends.

This infuriated them, as their young men always gave in to them: and they got no excitement or "polarity." But it was five or six years before we broke each other in to our complete satisfaction and I wore the pants for good. We both had such fiery temperaments that all our acquaintances had predicted a speedy and ruinous finish to our romance, which up to now has lasted thirty years.

We spent Christmas and our honeymoon in one, down at Augustus John's place at Parkstone, Dorset, with almost the whole family of his boisterous and stalwart sons. The kindness and hospitality of that very great lady, Mrs. John, passes all praise, as many another writer of an autobiography has said before. One of my most vivid memories of this extraordinary and delightful family was seeing the two youngest daughters, Poppet and Vivian, galloping around the house and garden on two very large, but spotlessly clean pigs, which had become affectionate household pets. These pigs could gallop and rush around as fleetly as wild-boars and wart-hogs.

The countryside round Parkstone and Poole was full of gipsies, and we used to spend uproarious evenings with them, in the local country pubs, singing and dancing to my wife's guitar. Trelawney Read, a neighbour, and Francis MacNamara, the father of the beautiful Mrs. Dylan Thomas, who was a permanent guest of John's, generally came with us on these lively excursions, which were made even livelier when there were rumpuses between the gipsies. One doleful publican pointed to splashes of blood on the walls and ceiling—"That was only last night," he said, "with knives it was. Mark my words, there'll be murder done here yet."

It was in a pub near Parkstone where the gipsies pledged Mary and me as "the finest looking couple in the county."

When we got back to London it was time for me to go bread-winning, since we'd spent the cheques we'd received as wedding-presents. My wife wouldn't hear of me going back to sea, and threatened every sort of reprisal from suicide to desertion—and worse. So I gave in.

W. J. Turner kindly got me reviewing jobs with the *Daily Herald*, and other Left papers, though I have never been Left-Wingish and it went somewhat against my conscience, since the only possible idea of government is charity and generosity on the part of the strong and the rich—as opposed to envy or greed on the part of the weak and the poor. A full well-fed shark (and all politicians are sharks) is unlikely to bite off so many heads as a hungry one. But at that time I had the excuse of keeping the wolf from the door by book reviewing, which involved no politics at all, so it was not really dishonourable to work for these papers. Later I did the same for the Pink *New Statesman*, but without any shame.

My wife's friend used to visit us, and twice when she was with me, or with us both, hearing a creaking noise at the door, I suddenly opened it and each time a son or a waiter of Johnny Papani's almost fell into the room. They confessed that they had been at the keyhole on Mrs. Sennacheribs' orders.

"Well," I asked, "did you see anything?" "No, Sir, all perfectly correct." "Well, take that" (giving him one on the ear) "and tell Sennacheribs that he'll get one too very soon, if he doesn't mind his own business and keep his Mrs. in order."

Off went Antisthenes but, having been paid well to do so, he described in luscious detail to Mrs. Sennacheribs exactly what he had been paid to try to see, though it was completely false.

The same thing happened with Demosthenes, another waiter, and again with Sophocles, another son—there were thirteen children in all. I don't know how many got a rake-off for describing the most terrible orgies.

The time had come to settle up with Sennacheribs. But one day the beautiful actress Meum Stuart came and showed us a letter in which Mrs. Sennacheribs had written: "The Snake Campbell and his Zulu-haired wife, Mary, are out to do you in for rivalling their friend in the eyes of my husband"; in the corner was the drawing of a dagger dripping blood. Considering what I had done to keep Sennacheribs away—it all became so laughable that apart from telling Johnny, who was absolutely clean and innocent, that I'd break the neck of the next person I found at the keyhole, I decided that one couldn't even be angry with people who had nothing better to do than to live on such a base level of penny-dreadful melodrama.

It was Sennacheribs himself who rushed into trouble. One evening I was sitting with Augustus John and my wife in the Harlequin, when Sennacheribs, who was violently jealous of John as well as of me, came in. Augustus nodded amiably to him and said, seeing his frown: "Haven't you got a smile for me, Senn?"

"My smile is mein own, Augustus," he replied, "unt I vill yooss it ven I like! And vot is more, dis Campbell, here treaten to chastise me!"

"Yes," I said, "it's about time I had a word with you."

I asked John to take my wife out to "the Swedish" and wait till I came: and I asked Sennacheribs to come upstairs where he started making his accusations as if he were a censor of public morals, and had a perfect right to post people at my keyhole. The extraordinary arrogance of foreigners in Britain is encouraged by sheer abjectness on the part of the natives. I felt that he was mad and thought of humouring him. I sent for a couple of waiters and a son of Johnny's. "They'll tell you," I said, "that there was nothing the matter." The waiters appeared, each trying to thrust the other foremost and whispering frantically together in Greek. I was utterly dumbfounded when, with their knees shaking and with trembling voices, they all chorused together that they *had* seen the most frightful goings on—they apparently valued their money more than their lives. "I am very sorry, Mr. Campbell," they all piped as if they had rehearsed it in chorus (a Greek Chorus), "but truth is truth and though we don't like to go against your word, etc., etc., tum te tum"—it all came out rhythmically. I made a sort of pass at the waiters and they leaped downstairs. Sennacheribs, insanely jealous, and believing the waiters' lies (I had almost begun to wish they were truths just to spite the evil-minded and horn-mad Levantine) began to pour out a torrent of insults, lost his head completely, and seemed to be about to make a sort of saccharhinoceroid charge.

Not wanting to get embroiled, in a four-to-one, with his allies the waiters, I backed into the room and as he followed dodged round him and locked the door; he tried a couple of dirty kicks: then he got very very frightened indeed and started yelling as I advanced, but

"The Assyrian went down like a trunk in the hold."

Two planks of the floor were slightly stove-in with his fall and a chest of drawers fell over. I sat quietly on his stomach as he lay philosophically blinking at the ceiling and quite conscious. The whole house had been shaken and there was a crack in the wall. Guests, waiters, and Johnny Papani came up and hammered on the door. It was so rotten that they finally shoulder-crashed it. I got up in case the waiters tackled me. But all they did was to remove the Sennacheribs, who was taken downstairs for first aid. He got quite defiant again, verbally, when he found he was under protection. I went out to find Augustus John and Mary, having sustained nothing more than a scratch on the forehead from Sennacheribs' waistcoat buttons as I threw him over my head. We all laughed away the evening pleasantly. That it was the only way to treat Sennacheribs was proved by the fact that we were never molested from then on by any keyhole-peeping or other form of insolence. Still, there must have been method in his madness for Sennacheribs, by sheer perseverance, finally prevailed on my wife's friend when we had parted company—and they lived happily ever afterwards, except for a few revolver-shots.

I showed Johnny Papani the crack in the wall and how rotten the door was, and said: "Johnny, one day this whole house will come down on your head." Shortly afterwards, one Sunday night, when Mrs. Johnny had taken the thirteen kids to the cinema, the waiters were out, and Johnny was there by himself, the whole four storeys of fifty-something Beak Street collapsed and killed him, thus relieving him of the terrible anxieties and debts which, owing to the non-payment of bills by artists and models, were driving him mad, so that he often told me he contemplated suicide. I even used to go with him to the Greek Church to try to pray him out of debt! Apparently I was the only one of his regular customers who made a point of paying everything on the spot; all the others lived entirely on credit, apart from generous men like Augustus John, or queer folk like Sennacheribs, the rhinoceros who was horn-mad, and paid people lavishly to prove falsely that he had horns thirty years before he had even the right to wear them! There was a certain amount of trigger-happiness around Sennacheribs' milieu. Shots were fired and wounds received mostly between women, and my wife's friend also stopped a revolver bullet from Mrs. Sennacheribs' revolver, but refused to witness. However none of that sordid melodramatic gang ever interfered with us again! They "had had it!"

As for Stuart, he departed long ago to the land of spooks, luminous kippers, and linoleum skies to which he acclimatised himself while he was on earth. But he became quite affluent on the proceeds, and he was a lovable old man. Funnily enough his cousin, or second cousin, was one of my very best friends and still is. I used to see almost as much of Cecil Gray, the composer and musical critic, at the same time, as I was seeing of Stuart. Their rails never crossed; they had little or nothing in common; and if Stuart had been a relative of mine I should have avoided him as much as I cultivated him for not being one. To be a relative of his would have been too great a responsibility and one would have had to draw the line as Cecil wisely did. It was typical of the greatness and kindness of Augustus John that the old man finally died in comfort on a little island in a comfortable cottage where John lodged him in his last days.

As the literary jobs weren't amounting to much, my wife proposed, in order that I shouldn't have to go back to sea and leave her, that we should go and live at a place she knew where it was possible to live for nothing. This was at the remotest point of Carnarvonshire, seventeen miles beyond the railway terminus of Pwllheli, opposite Bardsey Island, near to a village called Aberdaron. This was quite wild country in those days and that it was possible to live there on nothing was almost true. Our dwelling, *Ty Corn*, an old stable, cost us thirty-six shillings a year. All the neighbours for miles around, in accordance with an ancient Christian custom, gave us, as they do to all newcomers, either a sack of potatoes, or a load of peat, or a few hens. So we were set up at once. Some unknown benefactor began sending us £10 a month (it proved to be my father under whose official disapproval I was still supposed to be).

Romilly John, aged fifteen, who had tramped all the way from Poole, came and stayed with us. He had really run away from home, but we did not know that. Though he seems to have enjoyed it, and stayed with us three weeks, in his autobiography he describes our "house" as the worst hovel he ever set eyes on. It leaked every way, had only a mud floor, and the wind whistled through the walls but we had the time of our lives there living on the continual intoxication of poetry for two years, until I had finished *The Flaming Terrapin* and our daughter Tess was born. Keats says

> Love in a hut with water and a crust
> Is (love forgive us!) cinders, ashes, dust.

But I think we were as happy as *Ty Corn* as we are to-day, here in Kensington, with all the comforts of civilisation, nearly thirty years afterwards.

We lived largely on snipe, rabbits, hares, wild goat, pheasants, and the eggs of the myriads of seabirds which swarmed on the cliffs, not to speak of fish and lobsters. I bought a small shotgun for twenty-two shillings from Gamage's, melted the shot into ball cartridges, and found it quite handy. The poaching was excellent and we only had to report poachers having been seen elsewhere to have the place to ourselves. I also had a Manx cat called Bernard (after Van Dieren). It used to kill and fetch rabbits to the house.

I was, I believe, the only *Saesnag*, or foreigner, that was ever *persona grata* with the islanders. This was because when a doctor, who was staying at one of the hotels on the mainland, had refused to go over to a difficult confinement case on a stormy night, I stayed up drinking with him late at night, and when he had passed out, carried him off, popped him into a boat, borrowed from one of the other guests, and took him over, myself, in very difficult weather. When he woke up on the island I kidded him that he was a hero and had insisted on being brought over. But the islanders and the fishermen knew who had brought him, since few would have dared to sail in the weather that blew up at 4 a.m.

The fishermen of the island (who were almost savages and wore ear-rings and beards) never forgot this: and every time they came ashore in their prehistoric galley they remembered to leave several live lobsters or a lamb or a few dozen eggs at the *Ship Hotel* or *Ty Newydd*, for "Africa bach" as they called me. Their King, Love Pritchard, was the only one of the islanders who could speak a word of English. He was about eighty, but he was a very fine specimen and could pick up a sack of coal as if he were a young man.

By the time we left we had quite a farm with chickens, sheep, and a good vegetable garden. Not only that, but we had read aloud to each other the whole of Milton, Marlowe, Shakespeare, Dryden, Pope and many of the Elizabethans. Most of our anonymous £10 a month went on books.

I had written my first book and sent it to Augustus John, Philip Heseltine, and Edgell Rickword who also showed it to Desmond MacCarthy, who, in his turn, was thrilled with it. We were urged to abandon the backveld and to come into the limelight.

While I was sitting to John for my portrait, now in Pittsburgh, he told me that he had given my manuscript to Colonel T. E. Lawrence who was highly enthusiastic. I had never heard of Lawrence of Arabia, and when a tiny man in uniform tried to get in to a very rowdy party at my sister-in-law's rooms in Charlotte Street, at which we were playing rugby, Cecil Gray, myself and some others mistook him for a gate-crasher and gave him the cold shoulder. (Wyndham Lewis once mistook Lawrence for a dun and turned him the cold shoulder also.)

Whether this figure was T. E. Lawrence or not I never could make out but, while in the Military Hospital, twenty years afterwards I was reading some of his letters, about me in Cape's Volume, I seemed to recognise the face in one of the photographs. I have a letter which he wrote to Cape about my first book:—"Normally rhetoric so bombastic would have sickened me. But what originality, what energy, what freshness and enthusiasm, and what a riot of glorious imagery and colour! Magnificent I call it!"

I owe my first publication as a poet simultaneously to Augustus John and T. E. Lawrence, and to Desmond MacCarthy who was just about to write an article on it when it was accepted for publication.

As soon as the *Terrapin* was accepted, we went back to South Africa and I have recounted, in the *Wayzgoose*, what befell us there. We returned to England steerage, having been more or less boycotted out of the country after the publication of our magazine, *Voorslag*, which criticised the colour-bar. Even my brother George, who had disagreed with most of the opinions expressed in it, but had generously helped us with money when I resigned from the editorship, lost more than half his medical practice merely because he was my brother. The only other two people who nobly stuck by us were Kathleen Hewitt, the authoress of *The Only Paradise*, and Desmond Young (now brigadier), the author of *Rommel* and *Ship Ashore*. He was then editing the *Natal Witness*.

We arrived nearly penniless with our two children, took a small cottage and found it just possible for the four of us to live on £15 a month.

XVIII

MARTIGUES

WHEN my wife and I and our two little girls, Teresa and Anna, arrived at Martigues, in 1928, we had only £10 with which to start life.

I went to see the Mayor, Monsieur Roque, found that he was dead but that his widow survived and had a house, or cabanon, to let, up in the pines. Along with this cabanon went several acres of arable land, with sixteen olive trees and ten almond. I undertook to plough, prune, plant, and share in the produce and we soon had everything ship-shape. Two enormous olive trees were ceasing to bear, and the dear old lady allowed us to take them for fuel of which they provided several tons and some priceless exercise after all the elbow-work in England. It meant digging far down under the roots which were huge hemispheres of wood, in one case twelve feet in diameter.

The wood of the olive root has different grain from any other sort of wood. It has to be struck with great force repeatedly in the same place with wedges and it comes off suddenly in rugged chunks as big as one's head. It burns slowly like coal, and has a rather acrid smell, but it is beautiful wood. From it I carved the figures of Our Lady and the Infant Christ with St. Joseph, the Shepherds, and the other figures of the traditional Provençal crib for my children's Christmas. The most typically Provençal of the lay figures is of course the "ravi"; he is always represented as a miller leaning out of a window in the loft of his windmill. He has gone completely mad with joy at the birth of our Saviour and his arms are flung wide in ecstasy. The fact that a *miller* (the most curmudgeonly and miserly of all traders according to tradition) should be "ravished" with joy at the birth of Christ lends great force to the Provençal crèche. What is so typical about the "ravi" is that, with true French economy, he never has any legs—simply because, since only half his body is required (the half that leans out) it is unnecessary to waste time, skilled labour, and material in giving him legs, when the skill, time, and labour can be bestowed on perfecting the other figures; the angels, the shepherds, the cowboys, the fishermen and the gipsies, who have to be represented as full-length figures.

Because other inferior oils and fats can be grown more rapidly, the olive industry is being allowed to deteriorate. But since the wild olive is one of the commonest trees in the world and can be found from the Cape to Kilimanjaro, from Madagascar to New Zealand, it is a pity that graftings are not flown out and grafted on to the wild trees all over the world. Olive oil is incomparable once one gets used to it, both as cooking fat and salad oil. It generates a far higher temperature for frying than any other fat and is, in the long run, far more delicious. With "progress" the vertiginous decline in all standards of living continues, and, when groundnuts and sunflowers have ousted the noble olive, they, in their turn, will probably be ousted by something even more slapdash, ready-made, and progressive.

When I had settled my family in Madame Roque's cabanon, I went to the Bar Napoleon on the island, the headquarters of *La Joyeuse Lance Martegale*, a water-jousting team, and said I was prepared to joust again for Martigues. I had been a member of this team when the opening of the great Canal at Le Rove was celebrated by a visit by the *Swiss Navy*! After our local firemen's band had welcomed this navy with the Swiss National Anthem, which is identical with our *God Save the King*, we gave a joust in their

honour. The Swiss Navy are known as "pontonniers." They paddle or punt long narrow punt-like vessels, with the skill of Canadian
Redskins in their birch-bark canoes. The pontonniers celebrated
the marriage (by water) of Marseilles and Geneva (beauty and the
beast) by making the first direct water-trip between the two towns.

The joust was between the crew of the battleship *Vulcain*, and
our team *La Joyeuse Lance Martegale*. The *Vulcain* was an old
battleship similar to our *Canopus* in the First World War. It lay in
Toulon harbour perpetually at anchor and was used as a sort of
floating forge and factory. Its crew consisted mostly of skilled
tradesmen and specialists, so it could generally muster the crack
teams of the French Navy—the best rowing eight, the best fencers
and jousters, and also the best soccer team.

We were the victors. The Mayor, the Corporation, and the
members of the Prudhommie, with the two jousting teams, enter-
tained the pontonniers to the traditional bouillabaisse with the most
excellent apéritifs of *pastis* (which is against the law *actually*)—
and deluges of good wines, all on the bill of the Municipality. As
far as I can remember the proceedings became a bit hazy at about
five in the afternoon when, to the booming of petards and the
trumpeting, tromboning, and pistoning of the *Marseillaise* and of
the Swiss *God Save the King* by the pompiers of firemen, the six
pontons paddled off, zigzagging gaily in the direction of Marignane
where they were to pass the night. More celebrations followed
there, and at Marseilles; and it was a weary little "Swiss Navy" that
passed us on its way back at three a.m. one morning, when we were
working on the mullet-winches on the *Etang de Caronte*. They
were trying to slip back unnoticed in the dark, like spectres, so as
to avoid further hospitality, and when I thought of the avalanches
of churning yellow water they would be facing the next day for
leagues and leagues, up, and up, and up that ladder of rocks, curves
and rapids, I felt sorry for them, but at the same time I admired
their prowess. As far as the Rhône is concerned, I am a one-way
man.

When I returned this time, with my family, my offer to joust
again with *La Joyeuse Lance Martegale* was accepted, and I found
many old friends, including Marius Babtistin Polge, who eventually
married my wife's sister. He had been a mere boy on my previous
visit. He died in the last Great War, while serving with the French
Navy, of which he was rowing champion.

It was just at the beginning of the jousting season and I had to go straight up into the tintenne, which is the high platform erected at the stern of a motorboat, and take on my old friend, Leon Raoux of Istres; this was rather a tall order after six or seven years.

The *joutes nautiques* are a survival of the old *naumachia* of the Greeks in the Isthmian Games. They descended to Provence via the Roman Arena; and when, under Constantine, the gladiatorial combats were abolished, they were relegated, in a modified form, to the sea-port. Here they became a necessary part of marine war-training until pikes and spears were replaced by fire-arms. The Colosseum used to be flooded for the staging of these shows which above all were a test of one's sea-legs. In those days the collision was precipitated by the force of oars but in our time it reached its climax through the use of fast motors, so we were meeting at a greater speed than the mediaeval knights on their horses, and with less protection.

The jousts, on my first resumption of the old game, ended in a draw, after two encounters and two broken lances between Raoux and myself. It was a joust, not between teams, or rival towns, but between individuals, so it did not matter to the municipality or to local pride who won in the end, after about forty eliminating bouts between fourteen jousters. That Raoux had slightly the better of it can be seen in the drawing on page 239, from a photo, where he still retains his foothold a full second after I was being projected horizontally away from the camera, sky high. But he fell too.

The jousts were most exciting in the old port in Marseilles where we had the toughest crowd to deal with: rifle-bullets were often fired past our noses from windows in the brothel quarter in order to warn us to fall off so that the Marseilles team could win. At Marseilles we also fought many of the real championship matches which have to be fought in neutral waters, since the home-town *has to win;* the visiting teams have been paid to lose, and anyway they would be lynched by the crowd (especially that of the Vieux Quartier in Marseilles) if they dared to win.

The Germans probably did a good thing when they demolished the Old Quarter with bombs: it was too full of crime: but it was a very amusing sight. The *Bar des Sports*, the headquarters of the jousting team, was in the very middle of it, and the rapacious naked women who used to rush out and seize the hats of any one who accidentally or otherwise strayed in to the quarter, used to leave us severely alone as they recognised the green berets of the Martegaux and the red berets of the Marseillais jousters.

We used to sit there smoking and drinking our apéritifs while scores of stark naked girls and women went about their business in broad daylight in the streets, hawking at British, American and German sailors. The French did not seem to take any more notice of them than if they had been cattle. The idea of seizing the hats was not only to get a prospective client to follow them into their houses, but also, in case of disappointment, to exact a ransom of a few francs for the hat. If the victim looked well-to-do he was often knocked on the head by the maquereau of the girl and robbed.

The houses of which the bad old quarter consisted were extremely grand buildings, which had belonged to the merchant princes of the Mediterranean in the old days. But they had become very dilapidated. The Old Quarter had the advantage of localising crime. But the funny thing was to see the ordinary little French Bourgeois going heedlessly about their business in such a dangerous part where so many tough American and English bluejackets have come to grief, lost their lives, their heads, their pay, and sometimes their souls. I enjoyed the immunity of the local fishermen. But as I am talking of brothels, I should record an extraordinary thing which happened to us when returning from the jousts in Marseilles on our team's launch *Les Deux Frères*. We were coming round on the inside of the ten-mile stone jetty because the Etang was rough, and we were all singing, playing guitars, and drinking as we had won the big prize that day from La Ciotat, Istres, Cassis, Toulon, and St. Louis du Rhône which we had fought out in the Old Port. When we came under the big pines of Isnardon's Hotel, which had previously been Augustus John's house, we saw a ruddy haze reflected on the water, which was making the mullet rise for acres around. It was the municipal brothel of Martigues on fire.

Shrill cries came out of the smoke, so we landed from *Les Deux Frères*, on the precipitous bank, and rushed up the slope to the rescue. We got there even before the municipal firebrigade, as we had been almost on the very spot at the beginning of the conflagration which spread at a terrific rate. At least seven of our team were pompiers or voluntary firemen (three of them at least were doubly firemen as they also belonged to *la musique* or the firemen's band, without which no ceremony was complete). Under the direction of our firebrigaders we invaded the burning brothel and rescued the entire staff and some of the clients. By that time the fire-engine and the police had rolled up. When we thought that everyone had been rescued, out staggered a figure like a charred crow with glowing clothes and with only one white eye visible. It was the brothel-keeper whom everyone had forgotten.

"Where did you hide the *magot*, the *grand magot*," he yelled at his wife. "Where did you hide the big money?") "It's in the drawer of my sewing machine," she replied, "here is the key." The singed figure made as if to enter the flames once more, but he was restrained. Someone threw a bucket of water over him and his clothes sizzled, though he remained in the glare of flames and headlights, as black as a crow, with only that one terrible white eye staring into the flames.

Everybody continued to take an interest in the fire again, when suddenly the brothel-keeper, demented by his avarice, rushed through the cordon into the roaring furnace, where you wouldn't have thought an asbestos salamander could stand the chance of a snowball in hell. Nobody could get near and he was given up as a matter of course. Imagine our horror when he emerged once more, literally flaming in parts, sizzling and smoking in others, but still black with that terrible white staring eye, and smelling of grilled chops. Like a zombie, clutching a smouldering roll of paper, he advanced and collapsed.

The most terrifying thing about the figure was that it never had uttered a cry or a groan. As it fell, clutching the smouldering roll, the wife, entirely ignoring her husband, tried to extract the roll before it smouldered away altogether in his black claw-like grasp. She burnt her hands in attempting this, and then got up and started trying to kick the money from his hand before it all smouldered into ash. In doing so she let the mistral in between the thousand-franc notes and she tried madly to hop on them with her big flat slippers, cursing and shrieking. The prostitutes then began to scramble for the notes which, kindling at the edges and then igniting, were whisked flaming here and there about the courtyard.

No more notice was paid to the patron than if he had been a dog, as he lay there blinking his one white eye into the glare from the headlights of the fire-engine. Later he was removed by ambulance and died in two hours: it was a wonder he lived so long. The patronne was meanwhile chasing the girls around, knocking them down, pulling their hair and calling them thieves and robbers. How much she rescued of her old man's money I never found out, but a lot of it was burned and stolen and I saw the girls in their shifts stowing it in the most curious places. French thrift is marvellous but when it has turned to avarice, as in this case, it is almost unbelievable, and makes the most extreme of Maupassant's stories quite normal.

It was about this time that the Schmidt sisters were operating their sulphuric bath: and the young waiter of Les Baux had just been acquitted by a jury of his close relatives and neighbours of murdering the amorous English lady who had insured herself for forty thousand pounds in his favour. These things, happening at about the same time as this spectacle, gave one a grue down the spine.

Every nation, according to the Spanish proverb, has one vice and its opposite virtue, in both of which it is pre-eminent. The Spanish themselves illustrate this by being at once the hardest-working and also the laziest people in the world. The French can be more extravagantly generous than any other nation with money—as when a French nobleman paid Admiral Rodney's debts, because the Admiral had boasted in Paris that were it not for his debts in England, he could go back to London, rejoin the navy, and drive the French off the seas. The Frenchman paid these debts of £250,000 (which was more than the most patriotic Englishman of the time would have done) simply because he had mistaken faith in the prowess of the French admirals and wished to prove to Rodney that he was wrong. Yet if you could not find such generosity in England, you would also seldom find such avarice as in the case I have just described.

XIX

JOUSTING

THE Provençal Festivals, at least those which take place off the beaten track of the Riviera, are worth describing in some detail.

The Battle of the Flowers at Nice is even better known than the Jogs Florais (Floral Games) of Barcelona and is best left to the pens of those Cook's-tourist writers of English who, from D. H. Lawrence and Somerset Maugham down to Huxley and Conolly, prefer the tourist and painter-ridden side of Provence with its luxury hotels, hot baths, money and fat basking bottoms, well out of the breath of history, snugly walled off from nature, tradition, and also that great bull-guardian of the sacred Provence of the saints, the angels, the poets and the troubadours; that great guardian bull, the Mistral, who has only to see a tourist, or a hiker, or a painter, from such stuffy little haunts as Le Lavandou, Bandol, or Saint Tropez, to lash its sides, paw the ground, and with a single snort of its nostrils, balloon his plus-fours like a couple of zeppelins, scatter his easel and paints, and send him coughing and grumbling back to the côte d'azur, with his ears, eyes, and mouth full of grit: for it detests such people, as much as it loved men like Cézanne and Van Gogh, who did nearly all their best work within the radius of the mistral. It seems to love our great Welshman, Augustus John, also.

On the day of a fête the first thing that happens in Provence, even

before the church-bells start ringing, is that explosive pétards are
let off all over the town, as soon as the sun rises, to remind you that
you are not in Hampstead, but a Christian country, and that this is
no ordinary date.

If cattle have to be fetched for a bullfight, the morning will start
with an "abrivade." At dawn the young men ride away to spy out
the cattle on their pastures, and, when they have rounded up the
required number, get them moving in the same direction quietly
towards the town. As they near the town they goad up the bulls to
a trot, accelerating when they come near the main street, until a
torrent of bulls and horses thunders in amongst the cafés and shops,
the bulls hitting the ground with all four feet together and making
the earth fly beneath them, and tremble, and resound: and the
horses behind them going hell-for-leather, with the riders yelling
for all they're worth, and the citizens, and other pedestrians and
poultry stampeding for the doors, and the boldest ones waiting till
the very last second before they slam the door. Shot-guns, pétards,
and rockets are fired from the crowded windows, bands play,
drums are rattled, and tin cans beaten as if to scare away all the
locust plagues of Egypt. The uproar is so terrific that the bulls
hardly know if they're going or coming; sometimes they rush down
side streets, try to jump through doors or windows, or into back-
yards only to be chased after by some of the riders and driven back
to the main route, where they are finally driven through a circle of
carts chained together in the central square of the town, into the
corral which awaits them: or into the arena itself, if the town happens to have one.

The famous and precious cocardiers, or prize-bearing bulls, will
probably arrive with far more ceremony in special coaches of their
own, so as not to tire them, or splinter the needle-tips of their terrible forward-pointed horns.

After the "abrivade" you will possibly see the "bourgine" which
is related to the prehistoric fertility rites. The biggest and strongest of the rough, wild bulls is lassoed round by the horns twice; six
of the strongest men of the town hold each lasso from opposite
sides somewhat as in a tug-of-war. When the bull charges one lot,
the other lot pull him back; he rears, bucks, snorts, kicks, tosses,
roars, bellows, and rolls over in a frenzy as he is led through the
streets and all the girls who are brave enough try to get in behind

him and touch his testicles in the hope that it will confer fertility upon them to bear many strongs sons and strapping daughters. Young mothers present their girl-children and babies before the bull from their doorsteps and windows, like soldiers presenting arms, in the hope that they too will receive this great blessing.

At the Saintes, which is the capital of the Camargue proper, the priests bless the sea into which the Gardians have ridden with lifted tridents, stirrup-deep into the water to form a circle round the priests' boat. There at night, too, the relics of the saints are let down to the adoring crowds by chains from the church-tower in which they are preserved. By the light of the torches this is a magnificent spectacle, especially when there is a large conflux of gipsies who always liven things up musically and emotionally.

In Martigues, St. Louis, and Fos where the marine aspects of life preponderate over, or balance, the pastoral and taurine, the jousts, regattas, and swimming take priority over the bullfights. The jousters turn up from fifty miles along the coast all clothed in white slacks and singlets but with the berets and sashes of their teams. They can be recognised like our British units (armoured, parachute, or commando) by the colours of their berets: green for Martigues, the same as the Commandos. The Martegaux have generally won the championships, not only because of their desperado-tactics, but because there are more fishermen to choose from in Martigues than in any of the other ports on the coast. That's why it was a great honour to get in the team at all.

Martigues lies on three canals and is simultaneously a lake, port and a seaport. There were five canals in the days when I first came to that city. It was then known with good reason as the "Venice of Provence"—an amphibious, crustacean-looking town. Much of the beautiful architecture and the old-fashioned charm of the five canals has had to give way before the exigencies of a modern navy which necessitated the uniting of two of the biggest canals. The five canals joined the great salty lake of Berre to the sea about three miles away.

Half the boats bringing the rival teams of jousters come from towns round the lake or through the great sea-tunnel of Le Rove, from L'Estaque, La Ciotat, Cassis, Toulon or Marseilles. The other half come from the open sea via the Etang de Caronte from cities round the Rhône mouth. The launches all start cruising up and down with their flags flying and their drums beating, while the crowds collect along the quaysides, on the decks of barges and boats, at the windows, on the terraces and balconies, and even on the roofs of the adjoining houses.

This was how the jousts were conducted before the safety restrictions were made in 1933. The first pair having been drawn, the boats advanced from about a hundred and fifty yards away, accelerating to a speed of twenty knots as they passed, almost grazing each other's gunwales, with the kettle-drums rolling louder and louder as they approached. They sometimes capsize in each other's "wash." The antagonists stand on raised platforms, two feet by two and a half feet square and ten feet above the water, and projecting from the stern. The right foot is braced at an angle of forty-five degrees with the heel as far back as possible so as to get the maximum purchase. The left foot is straight forward on the opposite front corner. One should gauge the weight, height, and force with which one's antagonist will strike, so as to be at such an angle when the lances meet the shields that the force of the collision will shoot one straight back to one's previous position. As when standing on horseback at a gallop, the body leans quite a long way forward at an angle one could never keep while standing still.

The most useful training I ever had for high-speed jousting, apart from standing on the saddle, was vaulting off, over, and back on to the saddle at full gallop and hitting the ground properly with one's feet so as to get an all-round sense of one's weight.

Before safety restrictions to twelve knots, two men weighing over two hundred pounds were really meeting at a joint speed of fifty miles an hour, since each boat was doing twenty knots (or twenty-five m.p.h.), which is considerably greater than the speed at which the armoured knights used to meet. The old armoured horses did about 18 to 20 m.p.h. The angle at which the modern bodies have to be thrown forward is completely out of balance—sometimes as much as 35 degrees—in order that the shock will send one back to a balanceable position after one has struck with all one's might. The lance, while striking, is held on the pit of one's shoulder with a pad slung over the shoulder, to keep the lance-butt or splinters from piercing the flesh. The iron tip of the lance is serrated with sharp points so that it will fix its teeth in the enemy's plastron or shield without jumping off, bouncing, or taking away an eye or an ear. One holds a ball or some other object in one's left hand which has to be held away horizontally from the shoulder, at arm's length, while striking, in case of interference with the adversary's lance by grabbing at it, as one very often does instinctively while falling. That constitutes a foul. As soon as a man has knocked two adversaries into the water, he is said to have made brothers ("fait frères") and is reserved for the final heat.

Apart from the risks of diving into one's own or the adversary's boat, or getting mixed up in the propeller of either boat, you have to look out for your shield when falling into the water, as it can catch you a vicious uppercut if you go in feet-first, and it has been known to break a man's neck by knocking his head violently backwards.

Some casualties happen on the spot; legs and arms get amputated by the propellers, and men are wounded by the lances, or by falling into one of the boats, from a height of ten feet or so. Other injuries take time to develop, like that from which my brother-in-law suffered, and turned to tuberculosis or pneumonia from pulmonary lesions, due to the shock of the lance on the plastron, or buckler, which is worn strapped to the chest with a cushion of duffle between it and the ribs. And some casualties are caused by personal disputes. As a result of all these accidents, a law was passed, in 1933, limiting the speed of the boats to twelve knots and causing a general reversion from motors to oars, so that nowadays the *Joutes Nautiques* are fairly quiet. The halves of broken lances can no longer be seen flying over the steeple of the cathedral at Martigues, or over the Place Jean Jaurès, to mingle with and to terrify the pigeons and seagulls as they soar over the old crustacean city; or, as once happened in the old port at Marseilles, to fly eighty yards over the Quai des Belges and smash the top left-hand window of the Hotel Nautique.

A victory in the jousts should always be celebrated by a bouillabaisse; that is a truly Homeric meal; a dish that only men are allowed to prepare, though the women are allowed to share it. In every jousting team there are several kinds of fishermen and each one brings his own contribution, either from the crayfish pots, the mullet-winches, or the deep sea trawls.

The bouillabaisse is always celebrated *au cabanon;* that is in the little country cabin that every Provençal family possesses in the pines: or, if it is fine weather, as it usually is, you cook it outside in the woods, or on an open-air fire. You require an enormous pot with large trough-like dishes.

Piston, who fished chiefly for small rockfish, was the main contributor to our feasts with many kinds of rockfish, and the scarlet sea-scorpion known as rascasse, which is *the* prime necessity for a bouillabaisse. Most of us others fished in the open sea for tunnies, sardines, mackerel, and other fish which are useless for bouillabaisse. This fish, the rascasse, has to be trimmed of the sixteen or seventeen venomous fangs which, with poison glands at their bases, protrude from its diabolic scarlet bulldog countenance, prickly fins, and spiky back. A single sting from a rascasse will make you sick for a week, like the bite of an English adder: but his venom, like that of even a mamba or a cobra, is edible provided you have no cuts in your mouth, and, like snake poison, it is completely neutralised by boiling.

There are three other poisonous fish in the Mediterranean—the murena, the exquisite ribbon-fish, and the vive or weever (that gets its name from vibora or viper) and is also found round the English coast. This fish wears its fang on the top of its head, hides in sand, and stings if trodden on. The ribbon-fish is like a silver sabre and is called "swordfish" in Portuguese and Spanish.

The bony and hideous rascasse with that other ugly customer, the fishing frog or angler-fish, and all those tiny bony and prickly rockfish, such as moulets, gobis, sards, and canadelles, make the best of all soups. The latter can be mashed up in muslin and strained so as to keep their bones out of it. The flesh of the rascasse and the angler-fish, and even of that other standby for a bouillabaisse, the gurnard (baudroie), is still quite good after boiling.

Having prepared and cleaned the soup-fish, of which only one —the gurnard—seems to exist commonly in England, we then saw what the crayfish and crab experts could do for us in the way of crustaceans—almost every crustacean from a small rock crab to a sea-cicada or a langoustine is excellent in the soup—but we don't count any shellfish. It was Le Chanu who supplied the crabs and crayfishes: he was the best jouster of the lot of us, but the worst fisherman, always just making ends meet by catching odds and ends —octopuses, clams, sea-urchins, murex, "violets," mussels, and cabacons, or whitebait—that is, when he is out of gaol. But he was

one of the chief men for the bouillabaisse not only because he won
so many matches for us but also on account of his crayfish, crabs,
and prawns. Bass and grey mullet came from Joseph "Lou Cos-
taud," the spear-man; some went into the soup and some were kept
for *friture*.[1] Others of us provided the rest of the *friture*, with steaks
of red tunny, and for the drinks, for we were not so much bouilla-
baisse-fishers as all-out deep-sea fishermen, fishing mostly for inland
markets or canning factories, at which jobs you earn more money—
but less bouillabaisse.

The pot is first of all lined with onions and tomatoes, a few
sprigs of fennel and bay leaves, which grow every ten yards of the
way up through the pines: some bits of garlic: a little olive-oil.
This is all fried together. In go six or seven big rascasses, three big
crayfishes and crabs, with a few grey mullet; a big silver bream; and
water, up to the brim. You put the pot on the fire now and start
grinding your pepper, and the dried anthers of the crocus-flowers,
which is the chief flavouring and colouring of the bouillabaisse.
The colour is a brilliant saffron-yellow tinged with tomato. You
salt it, throw in the pepper and saffron, and remove it the second it
boils. The bouillabaisse consists of four simultaneous parts: 1. La
Soupe (soup). 2. La Rouille (the "rust"). 3. Le Pain (bread). 4.
La Friture (the fried stuff). The rouille is the Soul of the bouillabaisse.

The rouille is made in a big stone mortar: four or five quarters
of garlic and one whole redhot chillie are pounded up in it, and
then it is filled with soup from the main pot. It is above ordinary
tolerable strength, but can be spooned out and regulated according
to the strength each one requires, over the impregnated bread. The
bread, in discs an inch thick, is piled in a mountain on a wide, deep
plate, and half the soup is poured over it so that every slice is
soaked in the strong saffron-and-tomato coloured broth. No de-
cent fisherman will eat bouillabaisse without the *rouille*, which is
the spur and rowel both of one's thirst and one's appetite. A bouillabaisse, as served to tourists, without the rouille (or "rust," which
it resembles in colour), is a comparatively insipid sort of dish. East
of Marseilles you seldom see the rouille which requires the stomachs
of jousters, tamers of horses, and punchers of cattle.

The *friture* is supplied by the net-and-trawl-fishers; it consists

[1] Fried stuff.

of bass, silver-bream, golden-bream, sole, and slices of red tunny, fried crisp in olive oil. Everyone helps himself or herself from these four sources of satisfaction which are placed in the middle of the ring of feasters.

But, first, we open the illegal big bonbonne of strong home-distilled *pastis* and drink a few apéritifs. Then comes the good white wine of Cassis, or the rosy-brown quarrel-making wine of Tavel (of which one should beware), with the colour of a pretty Jamaican quadroon. Then the Red wines of the Rhône. We sit back on the crisp springy cushions of wild sage, rosemary, and thyme with which the *ferigoulet* is thickly mattressed (ferigoulet is Provençal for a *bank on which the wild thyme grows* and it unintentionally means every bank or hollow or hillside from Cape St. Vincent round the coast of Southern Europe to the Dardanelles). With the pines waving overhead as they do even in windless weather, and the children searching for crickets with their tiny cages, or else for wild asparagus, truffles, and wild tulips, one passes the afternoon of the bouillabaisse in perfect bliss, sipping coffee and vieux marc. Then after a siesta, the group returns to the town arm in arm, women and men, to join in the farandoles and the dances.

After the *joutes* became commercialised and before the ban limiting the speeds, one noticed some illuminating examples of the struggle between the old Christian Chivalry and the new "progressive" spirit. The more remote the teams from the capitals, the better they behaved and the less chance they got of competing, since they refused bribes. Therefore if a man from a remote place like the Saintes or any of the small non-socialist outlying villages, looked as if he was shaping for an unauthorised winner, he would be got rid of by a "coup de barre" (a sudden jerk of the tiller).

I once saw one of these good fellows who had been unfairly knocked off, but had succeeded in shifting his adversary too, swim up to the latter to kiss him on both cheeks, which is the French way of shaking hands. He was a good lad and didn't even suspect the foul play to which he had already been subjected. But his adversary, who was the socialist brother of the socialist mayor of Port de Bouc, was so mad with fury that instead of kissing the proffered cheek he bit his ear. When we dived in to separate them the Port-de-Bouc man hung on with his teeth to the ear of the Christian, and took half of it away. So they fought like two sharks in the water till I torpedoed the socialist with my head in a flying dive and winded him completely. I was so angry with the socialist for biting like a dog that I took him for a long "water-baby" ride under the water where he was completely out of his element, though a good swimmer on the surface. His brother, the Mayor, and counsellor (while the biter was getting artificial respiration), thanked me for saving his life, which made me laugh very much indeed— and I told him I had not rescued, but half-drowned his dear brother on purpose.

I met this biting man, Titin, again at the jousts at St. Chamas and he fell off, all by himself, when he saw I was coming at him, for I shortened my arm to an almost impossible angle, and hooked my bare toes over the front of the tintenne and went down almost on my knees so as to spring horizontally at him without caring if I broke my neck—or his.

I still had my blood up at the sight of this tooth-happy verminous socialist escaping me, when the boats veered and I saw another man coming at me against the sun, so that he was all black against the Alpilles. Between his legs I could see that Roman bridge between St. Chamas and Berre, which has the lions on the top of the arch, lions that the sand whirled by the mistral has by now eroded and sand-papered into the thin shapes of greyhounds. I thought this new black silhouette was another socialist from Port de Bouc, voluntarily replacing the first one, and I was more furious than ever to see what I thought was a sort of Leftie Colossus insolently bestriding a Roman Arch and the setting sun. I took off from the tintenne and I flew horizontal through the air, sunfishing and doing a sort of Australian crawl with my legs as if the air was water. I struck this man so terribly hard that to this day my right collar-bone is just a lump of pulverised, but wonderfully reinforced, animal concrete twice the size of my left collar-bone. My thick lance bent like a bamboo fishing-rod and literally exploded in splinters. My collar-bone was shattered in four pieces laterally, and splintered longitudinally, but it all healed wonderfully. This miraculous cure I put down to the fact that I believed I was fixing up a socialist or atheist.

The other fellow was "foudroyé" as they said in *Le Petit Marseillais* and also in *Le Petit Provençal*—but alas, it was no socialist that I had "thunderstruck," though he strongly resembled the first one

in silhouette. It was only a "radical," who was not voluntarily replacing the dastardly socialist ear-biter, but had been ordered up
into the tintenne by the judge president. Moreover he was a Maillot
of St. Chamas, a great jouster, the second-cousin of my good Christian friend Federi whom I met in the Stoll cinema. This is the only
case on record where a jouster landed on the platform of the other
boat and stayed there without falling. After some deliberation the
umpire (rightly) counted it as a fall: and we both lost. I was sorry,
and apologised and made amends for what I had done to this man
afterwards.

You can get very keen on jousting. It has this advantage over
wrestling, boxing, rowing and rugby—that each round (or half)
is short and sweet, but requires all the nerve, courage, strength
and skill of all the other sports put together: but one saves exhaustion so that a middle-aged man can still go on jousting at an
age when the Joe Louis's and Tommy Farr's retire from boxing.

The old-fashioned method of jousting can be seen at Cassis and
other places where oars are still used instead of fast motors.

Maurras and Mistral have both described the old *joutes* in prose
or verse. Maurras is a Martegau and the jousts often take place just
in front of his magnificent house by the canal. He compares our
breaking of lances to that of the knights at Tolosa—the strength is
there all right but alas for chivalry! it can hardly subsist under a
republic of masons and radicals. This is how Mistral, in his epic
poem *Calendal*, sees the jousts as they were run in the middle of
the eighteenth century. Let Calendal himself describe a joust:—

"Up on the tintennes (the tiny platforms) which swing, we
were jousting in the finals, and one heard the lances resounding on
the wooden plastrons—bang!—at the risk of bursting men's hearts
and lungs. Blood streams down from hairy chests, and groaning
like water-rails many jousters tumble upside down into the sea. A
captain from Ceyrests[1] (a fine place, whoever goes there, they say,
remains for good), a sea-captain, young and sturdy, had newly returned from the colonies where, in his hatred against tyrants, he
had gone to Virginia to fight against the English for liberty. This
Captain Negrel had returned on account of being wounded by a
musket ball which was lodged in his shoulder. But one day he heard

[1] An old Greek colony near La Ciotat.

the stirring roll of the kettle-drum through his window. He asked his wife, who was looking out, what it was all about. 'At Cassis,' she said, 'they are about to begin the jousts'—'The jousts,' he cried, 'O Holy Saints of the Camargue! Here we come!' In a flash he had leaped out of bed: neither the tears nor the embraces of his young wife could restrain him. She herself, Rousseline, ran after him (the lovely ardent girl), pleading and scolding him tenderly for his madness. But great danger begets great valour. Negrel, like a lion, had entered the ranks of the jousters: and while the others shocked and hurtled even to very death, Rousseline and her sisters, almost fainting, wept by the shore and recited the hymn of Our Lady of La Ciotat; 'Three girls of La Ciotat went out one fine morning to pray to the beautiful Crowned Virgin, but did not find her on the altar.' They stopped, terrified by the thunder of the shocks of shields and lances. Then they continued—'but they saw Our Lady, all soaking wet, in the distance, returning from the sea.' But now the uproar of the people drowned their song because a terrible antagonist was rushing upon Negrel like a Spanish bull. It was the unbeatable Alpheran! He was redoubtable, because of the unfair way in which he abused his great strength. Jousters usually hold their lance to their shoulders. Not so Alpheran. With one hand stretched out catching the other's lance he precipitated his adversaries into the water, defying the terrified umpires. Many had already drunk of the salt wave—even Ganthalme who, upright on the platform, had promised to Saint Elmo a beautiful carven boat if he was saved from the number of the vanquished; he fell all the same; Genez and Mitre from Martigues; L'Infernet (or 'Hellfire' Joe'), the Toulonais, a human thunderbolt, who none the less had been somersaulted, furiously swearing, into the sea: and so many others besides, disgusted at swelling the list of the defeated.

"With his left arm in a sling, now approached the good Negrel. Who had foreseen the unlucky encounter—? His wife, oh yes! for sure, she had had a presentiment because she went on singing with her sisters—'O beautiful crowned Virgin, whence do you come so wet from the sea? I come from the high seas where a sinking ship called for my help, and, except for the bo'sun, who denied my Son, I've saved them all.'

"Then the girls, who had been singing the hymn, fell silent. Alpheran headlong hurtled at Negrel: the iron on the lance of Alpheran cracked and split the plastron of Negrel, piercing right through.

"A cry arose:

'Lovely Crowned Virgin!'

With his legs upright, the captain fell upside down but so terribly hurt, and by such a shock, that he sank, like a corpse sinks into its grave, down to the bottom.

"Trembling with fright we saw that Rousseline had fainted . . . . Divers fished out Negrel . . . they gave him artificial respiration and made him come to. The poor girl meanwhile was out of her mind and wished to die; she almost went off her head, alas! . . . but a fortnight hadn't passed before Our Crowned Lady had miraculously cured both of them properly and given back the lover to the beloved. (Calendal goes on describing his victory.)

"Now, Alpheran! It's my turn, strike me hard! I haven't had my say yet! From his side now he poised, and I from mine: in our fury and enthusiasm they made us pass almost out of tackling range.

"All the surrounding crowds held their breath. Stung to the quick with emulation, by God! we came abreast. The oarsmen in their double ranks, almost fagged to death, and rowing raggedly, suddenly gave a smart pull. I yelled out. Alpheran taken by surprise loses both his head and the terrific suddenness of his wrist. We were now equal in lance-length: and each one hit fairly on the other's chest with a great shock which drove the boats apart. The two lances bend. They crack. Go on, battering-ram, against the walls! Together they crack like stalks of hyssop. I found myself hanging to the ladder. He, the other, had gone tail over tip. Drums and steel cymbals acclaimed me the victor. In their boat under the awning of the foresail, the three Prudhommes in consultation awarded and crowned me with the laurel—my Father, with tears in his eyes, was in the midst of the three. Then altogether all the finalists sang together walking round the town behind me—'Calendal has won the jousts.' "

There is something almost contemporary about this epic though it was written more than a hundred years ago about a period ending in the Napoleonic Wars. Calendal, as a character, exists to this day, wherever on the coast of Southern France it is uncomfortable for rich tourists to go. And here let me put in a word for those little brothers of Saint Francis the Bed-Bugs; they are nearly as good as the mistral for keeping the wrong people out of the right places. You can always avoid them by throwing your overcoat down on the tiles in the middle of the floor and letting them go for the pink rednecks that need to sleep on beds. Bugs will never cross a stone floor.

Mistral never jousted in his life but for the technical excellence of his description he might have been a professional like myself. In all his epics he describes everything, from basket-making and co-coon-spinning to bullfighting and horse-droving, as if he were technically expert at the job. In my interview with four critics on the North American Radio Service, though they pulled a great many feathers out of me, they all agreed that the remarkable thing in my verse was a familiarity with the physics, chemistry, and biol-ogy of the natural and mechanical universes: and a knowledge of animals, fish, ships, engines, guns, machines, which no other modern poet possesses. It helps one to manipulate words deftly.

Mistral had a far greater knowledge of the practical physics of his time, and he acquired that knowledge and Homeric exactitude without getting his breeches torn. That is the difference between a born, inspired poet like Homer or Mistral and a laboriously home-made and self-made one like myself. To acquire my own sense of history I have had to live it physically through every phase: from paddling a coracle, which we had in Wales, to piloting a speedboat and a glider: from riding bare-backed horses to the latest thing in mountain-climbing with "Matchless" motor-bikes: from a sling and an assegai to a Vickers machine-gun. This knowledge, which is of infinitely less importance than spiritual knowledge, nevertheless enables you to give form and obvious meaning to what would otherwise remain obscure and difficult.

In one way I envy these great poets their inspiration which rendered experience unnecessary: but I doubt if I would trade the experiences even for that supreme gift of theirs. It was too enjoy-able! Apart from the vast enjoyment of experiences of which this knowledge is merely the accidental residue; apart from the delight and pleasure derived from its acquisition at first hand, this knowledge enables you to streamline your poems so that they are easily understood by people who would never be able to seize the ideas otherwise. So it is a very serviceable "utility" substitute for inspiration.

The nineteenth century is devoid of successful epic poetry, with the exception of Mistral and Minkiewicz whose great Polish epic *Pan Tadeusz* towers over the rest of the Slav poetry and is even thrilling in a prose translation. Not one of Mistral's three great epics, *Le Chant du Rhône*, *Calendal* and (best of all) *Mireille*, is equal to *Pan Tadeusz* because Mistral is almost without humour or satire. But they are almost as popular with the Provencaux as *Pan Tadeusz* is with the Poles: and they form a vast compendium of knowledge both of human and natural history, and contain some of the greatest lyrical poetry of the century. *Calendal* contains both the best and the worst of Mistral: it is entirely founded on the life of the fishermen as I lived it in Martigues and Fos, and it contains all the tragedy, hardship, and charm of that life, so perfectly expressed that it took quite a lot to convince me that Mistral had never been a professional fisherman himself.

I had acquired such a distaste for letters through having come to associate them almost exclusively with corruption and "degradation," to quote Mr. Mortimer, that I never set pen to paper, after leaving England in 1928, for at least a year. During this time I lost all my precious work and did not care if I ever published again. I understood Rimbaud's revulsion from the life of letters. However, when I picked up a volume of Mistral it immediately deodorised my nostrils of the corpse-like foetor which I associated with "Ces *horribles* hommes de lettres"—as Claudel calls them. Here was a writer who really enjoyed existence without having to twist or pervert it first before it could be enjoyed. Here was a writer the very opposite of those unhappy pisse-froids, Mauriac or Proust, of whom my friend D. B. Wyndham Lewis has made this apposite criticism: "Anyone would think Jesus Christ had never died for the miserable bastards."

XX

UNDER THE SEA

I DID a lot of bullfighting at this time, but lived extravagantly in excess of my winnings from the Municipal prizes from cities all along the coast and inland.

I bought expensive furs for my wife and had dandified suits made by tailors. If there were several thousand francs in cocardes on the bulls, say, as far away as Nîmes, 100 miles off, I would order a taxi (instead of going by train) and pick up other champions like the two Boncoeurs of Saint Louis du Rhône, and Leon Roaux of Istres. All of these men I could trust not only to try to save my life if I got knocked over, as they could trust me to do for them; but also we all trusted each other to work equally hard with the bulls, so there was never any dispute about dividing the money and expenses into a quarter each, even when one of us had a bad day. We would keep the taxi with us all day. In fact we had our own regular taxi driver, M. Henri Chaves, of Jonquières, Martigues.

The bribes I used to take in the jousts, for losing, from home teams used to exceed what I could get for winning. Home teams always *have* to win down there, or there would be murder, so that the championships are all fought in neutral towns. I would just present myself when it was the Saint's Day at such and such a village or town, with my brother-in-law, Marius Polge, and we would receive anything up to a thousand francs[1] each, either to participate and fall off, or not to participate at all. This led to tremendous Valhallan feasts, taking our wives and girls to Casinos, and

[1] Francs were then 72 to the £.

dancing till the small hours of the morning. I became a Gourmet after being almost an ascetic—a man who could eat raw fish like an Eskimo, especially on cold nights when we were picking sardines out of the nets. I was now known in every posh restaurant from Nîmes to Toulon, beyond which our kind of jousting was re-placed by a gentler and non-paid form on slow boats—so we seldom went any further.

Bullfighting, too, petered out east of Marseilles, so the Riviera proper never had any interest for me except during one side-split-ting week there with English dog-thieves. They used to steal dogs and threaten to ill-treat them if they were not paid a lump-sum, which they never once failed to extract. They preyed exclusively on English dog-lovers.

By this expensive life I was forced to do a bit of honest work in the end. Starting with an acetylene flare, two spears, and an old boat so waterlogged that I called it the *Bateau Ivre*, I specialised in night-fishing for roe-bearing mullet and bass. I had an old retired fisherman called Roland rowing me for twenty-five per cent. in the catch. Rowing a flare is skilled labour since it has to be silent, and at a constant slowness.

I had the foène[2] attached to my wrist by a strong cord when I got stuck into a twenty-pound bass, which is stronger than a man. It went off like a brand-new motor-bike and was about to capsize the boat, drown Roland, and explode the carbide-holder of the flare: so I had to pass over Roland's arm and let myself be pulled in after it over the back of the boat[3] and started trying to cut the line with the knife from my belt, as it pulled me down. The skin was being torn from my wrist and I was being pulled violently from side to side under the water. The cord seemed to be made of wire and the knife in my left hand to be made of butter. I could vaguely perceive the glow of my acetylene flare getting further and further away, far up behind me. I was about ten feet down and then suddenly, thirty yards away from where I fell in, just when my lungs were bursting, the spear pulled free. Having lost my knife, I just made the surface, rested, and got into the boat by the back of it. The five prongs of the spear, which was still tied to my wrist,

---

[2] Spear.

[3] I do not say stern for those boats have no stern, only two prows: fore and aft depends which prow is in front.

had been twisted by the muscles of the big bass to resemble the fingers of a rheumatic old man. After a rest, and a quarter of a pint of rum, I went on fishing, with my spare grane (fish-spear), and did very well.

By an absolute fluke, on our way back, though it was three quarters of a mile from where I first speared this big bass, and five hours after the incident, the flare outlined the same bass with a huge shadow, now reflected on the bottom, which was shallowing. At first I thought it was just one more of those big bass, and funked it. Then I saw that it was swimming weakly and a little to one side, having apparently been mortally wounded. In fact, I saw it was the same fish. Though I could see a big tear in its back, I daren't risk another encounter with my wrist tied: and I was afraid of ruining or losing my second spear, since the other was useless without a visit to the blacksmith. The water in this place was about seven feet deep so I asked Roland to splash a little with his oar, and this drove the fish lurching along until we suddenly came over a shallow shelf of rock and the fish turned left and tried to sound, though it had been swimming on one side with its head higher than its tail. At this moment I could resist it no longer. I had cut the knot in my cord and taken three turns of it round my palm, when I threw the spear as hard as I could, simultaneously stepping overboard for fear of upsetting Roland into the Etang. This time the fish tried to wrench my hand off, but I had made the rock-shelf and was standing waist-deep. The fish fought very hard indeed, but it was beaten in the end and the five prongs held fast, though they too had to go next day to the blacksmith.

The only other submarine adventure of mine which is worth recounting happened with Roland when I was starting fish-spearing with my *Bateau Ivre*. At the entrance of the Etang de Caronte to the sea an enormous fish went straight across the bows under my flare. I daren't spear it because it would have trailed me after it by my corded wrist, like a dinghy behind a tug. I had had one lesson with a fish a twentieth of the size of this one. A second or so after, we heard splashing on the surface and rowed towards the noise. An enormous tunny was dying in the water, going round in circles towards the bottom, with a smashed skull, having run into the concrete rampart at the end of the canal. I dived down and seeing it was almost dead got a loop round its tail and we rowed it to Caronte. It was stone dead by then. It was perfectly normal in every way except that from midway down its body to its tail the ridgy stripe had been scraped. This stripe, which you can see on a horse-mackerel, serves, I think, as a sort of Radar to tell it when there's anything solid ahead. The derangement of the stripe had caused it, while chasing mackerel at full speed, to omit braking, and to smash open its head.

The station of Caronte was only two or three hundred yards away. With the help of some Arabs, who were working on the road, we dragged the tunny to the station and got it into the market at Marseilles by nine o'clock in the morning. It weighed a hundred and eighty kilos (400 lb.), when cleaned, and from the proceeds I was able to change the *Bateau Ivre* for a less leaky and more sea-worthy boat.

Roland, who had fisherman's rights, used to market my fish for me, and no questions were asked about my right to fish. But very soon he eloped with the mother of Pouzol of the *Bar Pouzol*, in the Place Jean Jaurès, Martigues. This rich widow disinherited Pouzol and his wife in favour of Roland, who had to flee to Miramas, with a charge of bird-shot in his shoulder from Pouzol's twelve bore. At Miramas he set up a café, and his wife died suddenly, leaving the old rogue rich and the proprietor of a Bar—so he faded out of my life.

I had by now two fine boats, the "bette" *Saint Pierre* (Martigues 1222) and the big "boeuf," *Clemence* (Martigues 1708). My friend Vincent La Rosa (otherwise Piston, so called because he had played the trombone for years in the Municipal Firemen's Band) had suffered pulmonary lesion in the jousts, and was dying of consumption. He put his name to the purchase of these boats and my new nets. He got a rake-off, and I kept his family in fish.

Only French subjects who have had two years' naval service can become patrons-pecheurs, that is to say master-fishermen owning boats and nets. But I had made myself so necessary to *La Joyeuse Lance Martegale*, and also the *Société Taurine*, or the bullfighting society. This was equivalent to being a professional League foot-baller and a professional County cricketer rolled in one. The result was that I am the unique case in history in which a foreigner has exercised the right of a master-fisherman in the most exclusive trade-freemasonry in the world, as my French biographer was quick to notice.

The bullfighting team represented every town round the lake, except Marignane—but as I was part-inaugurator of the Gliding-Club there and had helped to design the Glider, I was *persona grata* there, too. The Mayor and corporation of Martigues and the Chief of Police, as well as three-quarters of the population, seemed to like me, so no enquiries were made into my activities.

If you ever go to the South of France and dine at the *Piscine de la Mère Pascal*, that famous restaurant in Martigues, you may see some barnacled, ancient Greek Amphorae which we sold to the husband of that good lady, having brought them up from a depth of thirty feet from the temple of Diana about a mile out from the Casino at Fos-sur-Mer.

I feel quite familiar with these Massiliot Greeks since I have crossed their tracks accidentally, while fishing commercially, at several other of their submerged or ruined colonies, notably at Cape Nao, Ifac and Calpe, opposite the Balearic Islands. They have left their mark on their descendants, the fishermen of Provence, and south from Barcelona down the east coast of Spain, wherever the Valencian dialect is spoken, as far as Alicante. There are ancient submerged ruins round the Peña de Ifac, the great pink rock that rises a thousand feet out of the sea between Denia and Altea, but the exposed and craggy nature of this coast more or less precludes the finding of amphorae and sculptures, which must all have been smashed to pieces long ago by the waves.

In the Bay of Fos, however, if you walk along the shore you will notice that nearly a quarter of the stones that have been piled up by the sea in the corner of that bay, especially along the side of the Casino, bear obvious traces of human workmanship, most of them being portions of sarcophagi.

In this part of the Mediterranean round the mouths of the Rhône, the water is comparatively fresh and the sea-bottom is more muddy and stable, so that relics are not ground away by shifting sand or shattered by pebbles on the shore. In fact the mud acts as a preservative on all objects embedded in it. It is one of the few corners of the Mediterranean which is not too salt for mussels to grow in. It was generally while going after mussels that I made my finds.

All the big lagoons around this part, till ten years ago, were literally cobbled, like streets, with mussels, and they used to do well even in the Bay of Toulon in the old days of steam and sail. Now the beautiful *Etang de Berre*, several miles in diameter, has

been saddled with two air-bases for the Army and the Navy at
Istres and Berre, and an airport for civilians, at Marignane, so the
surface is getting covered with oil to the detriment of the big
mussels at the bottom of the lake about twenty feet down, which
grow to the size of one's shoe, and with their accumulated "milk,"
half a pint to each bivalve, made the most superb soup I ever tasted.
We used to live on it when we were hard up. One boiled the mussels, with spaghetti, tomato and onions, in their own "milk"; then
added milk from our goats, and grated goats' cheese over the
whole.

The oil, or mazout, has also spoilt the quality of the red-mullet,
the sardines and the anchovies of the Etang, once prized above
those of the main sea.

In calm weather, in the Bay of Fos, you can see the ruins of the
old Greek colony, with the top of the highest column of the temple
about fifteen feet down; but visibility, when we went down with
the anchor, was extremely bad in the shadows between the walls.
I called these ruins a temple of Venus in *Taurine Provence*, which
I wrote about that time, but I soon found out it was a temple of
the Ephesian Diana, the lady who looks something like one of
those prize coconut trees that grow round Mombasa, or a paw-
paw tree in Durban, on account of being furnished with rows on
rows of breasts, from her neck to below her navel. Marseilles was,
of course, a Phocian colony of Greeks from Asia-Minor and so
were all the other sub-colonies of Marseilles from Nice on the East
down to Alicante in Spain; and the Asiatic Greeks all worshipped
Diana. The Marseillais were for 300 years the only rivals of the
Phoenicians and Carthaginians till Rome appeared as a Maritime
Power. It is possible that even Cadiz was a colony of Marseilles.
Marseilles also produced a very great sailor, Pytheas, who sailed
round the British Islands in 330 B.C. and left a *Survey of the Earth*,
fragments of which have descended to us through other writers.

By this time I had four fellows working with me, Clement,
Marius his brother, Jeannot, and Fan-Fan. I showed our finds to
Dr. Contençin of Martigues and described my visual difficulties at
the bottom of the Bay of Fos. I had not Gilpatrick's excellent book,
The Compleat Goggler, to help me, in those days, but I asked the
doctor if he could lend me a bell-jar. He pointed to where, just
behind me in a shop over the road from our café, was the very
thing I wanted.

There were dozens of big bell-jars in this funeral-monger's shop, covering wreaths of artificial flowers and sacred images. These jars protect the wreaths and images from rain in the cemeteries. I bought a couple the size of diving helmets.

I now had a motor for the *Clemence*. That motor saved my life.

We were fishing one day in the Bay of Fos, just above the old Greek colony, when we foul-hooked, with our anchor, the handle of a Greek jar. We pulled it up with a shard of the broken jar attached.

I immediately put the funeral bell-jar over my head, and secured it with the mesh of a sardine-net, tying the ends of the net under my armpits. I first tested it in shallow water, letting the water fill it almost to the top, but keeping just enough air to come down to the level of my eyes. We then attached a big stone to a rope. I stood on the stone, twisted my feet round the rope and held on with my hands so that, when the stone and I were dropped overboard, I plumbed the sea standing vertically, and went down like a streak of lightning, saving breath and time. I had a thinner rope tied round my waist for safety, in case of cramp or other accidents.

The first time I hit the bottom I saw four pillars and a wall, with an archway and a tunnel. Having had a good look, I went immediately to the top again, discarded my bell-jar, and went down with another stone to where I judged the wall to be. We tied a wreath of cork tunny floats to the first rope to mark the place in case we drifted. I felt the wall and went along it till I came to the arch or tunnel. It was in this tunnel that we got the two amphorae that are in Madame Pascal's restaurant. As soon as I felt one I tried to move it, but only moved myself as my chest was full of air. I was about to let out my breath in order to regain a bit of weight. At this moment I was grabbed by a big powerful catfish, and I dropped the amphora, and tried to get away by pulling at the corner of the tunnel. I said my prayers and gave some frenzied tugs at my rope because I was weaker than the catfish, and I needed all my breath. The boys began pulling but made no impression. I had now been down two minutes and a few seconds.

It was then that Fan-Fan got anxious and started up the engine— he guessed I was in desperate trouble with a catfish. For a second or two I felt as if I would be pulled in half, but the octopus came up with me, and did not let go until we got to the top, with the boys hauling hard. I was exhausted but Clement got a gaff into the octopus as it tried to go down again. This octopus weighed just under fifteen kilos, and was nearly two and a half metres across the feelers—twice the size of any I had encountered at home. But for the engine I should have died.

After that Clement went down and got one of the amphorae tied to a rope. Next day I went down and got the other. Pascal, the restaurant keeper, heard of the jars and we sold them to him for 350 francs (£5) each. They were gracefully shaped and about five feet high.

The Mayor was dining there a few days later. He sent for us and told us to bring all ancient relics that we found to him, and he would give us three times the price that Pascal gave us. We never got anything quite so good afterwards, mostly bits and pieces of things; but plenty of them and some very small, battered sculptures. The only whole thing I got up was a thing like a mortar, weighing a hundredweight. The Mayor sent these things to the Museum at Aix where they are still. He paid us so well that I became relic-happy and was always scratching about along the sands even when I was ashore. We found several Roman coins under the sand on the rock-bed; these are at Aix also.

What cured me of submarine archaeology was this. My two boats were being overhauled in the *chantier*. So I went out on a steam-trawler to lend a hand to Monaco junior, son of the present Port Captain of Martigues, on the trawler *Deux Frères* (the commonest name to be found amongst boats in Provence, a relic of the worship of the Gemini, Castor and Pollux). When the winches were pulling up the nets for the last time, the mesh started tearing. So he hove-to and stopped the winches, and I said I would dive down and see what was the matter.

The net had caught on something which had been embedded in the Rhône mud. I followed the strained torn meshes to quite a depth, and my heart fairly leaped with joy when I got my arm through the tear in the net and felt something huge and hard and round with little mounds all over it. I was sure it must be a colossal statue of Diana of Ephesus herself and that the rows of little mounds (they were really studs or rivets) were really rows of breasts and nipples. Had they been real ones I couldn't have re-joiced more! (You can imagine how relic-happy I must have become.) Without more ado I felt my way up the net; it was pitch

dark, just before dawn, but as soon as I reached the surface I yelled
to Monaco: "You can turn on the winches again. You've struck a
treasure. Something marvellous! And it's come adrift all right! The
Mayor will pay us a fortune! A few more turns and you'll have it
aboard!"

This was at five in the morning; a mistral was blowing and I went
down to the stokehold to put on dry clothes. I heard something
huge thundering against the side of the trawler, and soon it had
been lifted clear. It was caught in the net which draped it from
view; we flashed torches at it; and someone said it looked like a
chest with studs on it. "No," I said, "it is a roundish thing."

As the trawler rolled, it knocked heavily about every five seconds
or so. Then a hair-raising whisper came from Monaco: "It's a German mine, from the last war."

There it was, a couple of feet from our heads, caught by its horns
or triggers in the trawl, knocking this way and that—and weighing
at least a ton, of T.N.T.!! As the sun rose we could see that it
wasn't rusty, so perfect a preservative is that soft white Rhône-
mud in which it must have been embedded for ten years. Some
ancient Ligurians were found in this clay just where Strabo mentions a big settlement; they were mummified but well preserved
and had coins in their mouths. They had been embedded several
thousand years longer than our famous bomb!

One of the crew had a red jersey which we hoisted to the mast
as a flag of danger. It was our duty to capture the mine and take
it to the authorities. Anyway we couldn't risk getting it out of
the net, where it hung caught inextricably by the horns. It took
us three hours of excruciating anxiety, with the mackerel fishers
fleeing to left and right before us, like mackerel in front of a tunny,
before we reached Martigues. Monaco, père, in charge of the suspension bridge, saw with his telescope what was approaching, and
the suspension bridge, for once, instead of having to be hooted at
with the siren for about half an hour, opened, like the magic door
of Aladdin, with a punctuality it has never known before or since.
"Take your trawler into the middle of the lake," roared Monaco's
dad.

Meanwhile a launch was sent to pick the crew off the trawler.
In war-time it would have been nothing, but as it was peace-time
we were all white with the strain, and so was even the poor devil in

charge of the launch who took them off. I felt bound to stay on board with Monaco junior and, during the following few hours, he treated me to some fancy sarcasm about "treasures," and "fortunes that the Mayor will pay us."

A wire was immediately sent to the Marine engineers at Toulon, and a bomb-disposal squad turned up by sea-plane at about midday, landing beside us on the Etang. They managed, with the aid of a derrick-bearing lighter sent from Port de Bouc, to lower the bomb and unscrew the triggers. They got it aboard a raft. The *Deux Frères* went back to the harbour, and the bomb on the raft was set off by means of a time apparatus after the Etang had been cleared of shipping. The mine nearly blew the bottom of the lake out, shook the whole city, and was heard at St. Louis du Rhône, where they thought that the dynamite factory on the Crau had gone up. The engineers then questioned us and told us that we might all have been for it at any moment, but that, of course, we would have been none the wiser.

That was the end of my treasure hunting, but until I learned about water-tight goggles, those square bell-jars, though very clumsy, came in very useful for submarine fish-spearing, especially from the side of that long jetty which continues the Arles Canal, through the *Etang de Berre* and the great marine tunnel of Le Rove, to L'Estaque and Marseilles itself.

The watery underworld of the Bay of Lions round Marseilles consists of very pleasant meadows of seaweed growing on levels of rock which are fissured here and there to a very great depth— these subways are full of rascasse and congers. Now that the Frogman's apparatus is so easy to procure and use, it is a veritable paradise for the underwater fisherman either with spear or spring-gun harpoon.

We once got some Americans on our trail to dive around the Chateau d'If in search of Iron Masks and other such trifles. The pay was excellent. We went down and up several times. Suddenly I came up with another "relic." It was an old punctured Michelin tire! That was all we found.

XXI

WRITING AGAIN AND PIG-FISHING

NOTHING is better, says a Provençal proverb, for reviving and remaking a man than living in the clear sunlight, speaking Provençal, eating "brandade," and drinking the good red wine of Provence. My wife and I soon recovered our good spirits: our children were very happy in the pinewoods with their dogs, a pet magpie which I stalked and caught with my hands, and then taught to speak: and a couple of pet goats which we kept for milking, and their kids.

I had forgotten about poetry when, owing to reading Mistral, I got another sort of spurt-on as a writer. He banished the mephitic stench which, after the Havelock Clinic, I had come to associate with literature. Whatever poems of mine I remembered I wrote down; and others we found in old magazines, which our friends in South Africa, notably C. J. Sibbett, hunted up for us. But I lost more than half of what I had written. When we got the rest together we sent it to T. S. Eliot, and this was my book, *Adamastor*, which quickly went into three editions and was later published in the Faber Library.

This brought in a "fortune" such as we had never known before, and I was able to buy both a sardine net and a kilometre of thonaille for tunny fishing. Sardine fishing is always a safe bet, whereas tunny fishing is a gamble; a single good catch of tunnies in a whole season will make all one's outlay worth while, since red tunny sells at a good price always, but one cannot be sure even of one good catch.

In the old days tunny-fishing was a communal business round Marseilles, shared in by almost all the tunny-fishers, with an enormous permanent communal labyrinth of net many miles long and hundreds of feet deep. There were vast marine rodeos which willy-nilly landed almost every tunny that passed from the Bay of Fos to the Gulf of the Lion, into its vast central pocket. This system was given up before the First World War. The thonaille is now usually paid out from the stern of one boat to another. Cork-floated, the net is of a very wide mesh, goes down about fourteen feet and is anything up to a kilometre in length. The net is spread only for the duration of darkness: it is let out at sunset in areas forbidden to steamships: for if a net is fouled even by the propeller of a motor-boat it makes a bad enough mess, and one does not like to imagine what would happen if the screws of the *Rex* or the *Conde de Savoia*, or any other of those big ships that go into Marseilles, were to begin chewing up such a comparatively flimsy cobweb as a tunny net.

We used to get fifty francs apiece from the *Inscription Maritime* for every porpoise we caught, and we kept a hand-harpoon on each of my two boats.

These harpoons I forged myself with the aid of the blacksmith on the Rue St. Mitre, who was a good friend of mine, and for whose teaching I was very grateful later when I went into the horse-trade, and later still when Acting Sergeant farrier attached to the Animal Transport—though that was mostly cold-shoeing.

These harpoons released a ring, in the usual manner, upon impact, but the blunt fluke of the barb was split in two blades which curved when released and, when the pull came, held more surely than the ordinary sort. Also it pierced deeper, though it was lighter than the ready-made harpoon. My boyhood's training with Zulu assegais was a great help.

There were two kinds of porpoise: the blunt-nosed "marsouin" and the beaked "dauphin" (dolphin to landsmen), both equally destructive to nets and fish alike. The *Inscription Maritime* would never pay the prize money for their destruction unless one produced the body or other convincing evidence such as the fresh tail. If one killed or wounded them with a rifle, it was no good, because their "comrades" immediately set about them in the manner of Barcelona Reds: and in their turn were set about when shot: so that we only recovered two killed in this way.

After getting fifty francs for the prize money we sold the porpoises to restaurants where the Arabs fed. There were a great many Arabs in the town, working as labourers on the transformation of the canals. They could do with almost anything in their Kouss-Kouss, except pig. Porpoise tastes like over-rich liver, but an Arab told me that he considered it as a substitute for pork!! Good Muslims out in Ceylon or Mombasa can only avert a sinful craving for pig's flesh by eating "mermaids," which are otherwise known as Dugongs or Manatees, although they look almost uncannily human to me except for their flukes and flippers—far more human than monkeys or seals. These "mermaids" taste exactly like pork. The place for them is the mouth of the Rufiji river, round the wreck of the old *Koenigsberg*. Stuffed specimens of these horrible looking beasts are very popular at freak shows in Europe.

The Greeks and Phoenicians must have seen these animals on their early pre-Portuguese voyages round the Cape to the East and this must have given them the idea of the sirens. Submarine suggestions of music coming from that strange fish, the sciène, or gabeljau, which inhabits the Straits of Messina more thickly than anywhere else, but it is to be found all through the Mediterranean, would heighten the illusion of there being semi-human agencies under the water. Whales, when under water, also make musical sounds.

The red mullet, another very harmonic fish, is pre-eminently common there in the Straits of Messina, and that would account for Homer's placing the sirens in that magic neighbourhood, where the *fata morgana* mirage is so often to be seen inverting a refraction of the opposite shore into the sky.

The red mullet is called "lyre" by the Provençal fishermen because of the sound (like a distant musical box) which it makes while dying, by stroking its fins across its scales, while a riot of the most extraordinarily brilliant shimmerings, emerald, bronze, violet, azure, and golden, burn themselves out, passing through its gorgeous scales in waves. A heap of fresh red mullet, newly-landed from the net and dying in the sunlight, while their fins and scales tingle and hum, is a very gorgeous sight indeed. The only place where landsmen can see them properly is by electric light, in the big fishmarkets of places like Barcelona (where they make all the flowers of the Ramblas look dull), Valencia, Málaga, Almería, Alicante or Cadiz. Long before they reach any market in England, alas! these beautiful electric creatures have become opaque and dull.

I have seen that famous fish which sailors correctly call the "dolphin"[1] (to the indignation of naturalists) dying on the deck of the *Inkonka* and the gorgeous colors swirling, in humming-bird

[1] Otherwise "Bonito" or "Beautiful."

tornasols, through its greenish-silver body as if a thousand rainbows were chasing each other across the sky. But I consider a heap of red mullet to be a more beautiful, though a commoner, sight; and besides those elfin chimings and tinglings make a wonderfully fitting accompaniment to the dance of coloured fires. The sound is not only emitted during death agonies but also while mating: it comes faintly up through the water on a calm night whenever one is over a big shoal of red mullet.

I always think of that speech in *The Tempest*, "The Isle is full of noises," when I hear the music of the red mullet, for unless one knows the source from which it comes, that is to say from under the water, it seems that invisible fairies are playing it in the air. In Africa some of our fishes are even more vocal—notably the gabeljau, whose submarine voice is musical, and the grunter, whose voice is truly loud when it has been landed.

To come back to the other kind of "dolphin," that is to say, the porpoise; though they were able to destroy almost every other sort of net, they were generally held fast in the tunny net. Weight for weight they seemed much stronger than the tunny: and one always found that, before they drowned themselves by fighting with the net, they used up far more of the net in winding it round their bodies in their struggles than the tunnies did. Being mammals they could come up for air every now and then, but a tunny, being a fish, when exhausted takes water into its gills and drowns itself far quicker, since it can do no good by surfacing and trying to breathe the air.

It was when fishing in the Gulf of the Lion that I came across kingfishers again. In Europe there seems to be only one kind: yet that is, like those in South Africa, of very great beauty and of an exceptionally delightful character. It has the same straight, silent, low flight, which is so piercingly beautiful in the evenings at sea. The Greeks gave most of their nautical words to their direct descendants, the fishermen of Provence, who use almost the same speech as Homer in regard to everything marine, from "broufounié" (βαρυφωνία) meaning the roar of the tempest, to simple, technical words for towrope, "calamo" (χαλάσμα), "estrop" (στρόφος) a thong attaching the oar to the thole-pin, "gangui" (γαγγάμη) a certain kind of net—and so on *ad infinitum*. To the Provençal fisherman, as to his Greek ancestors and the Romans, kingfishers are the symbols of peace and happiness—halcyons. At home in Africa they are "medicine" to the natives, and have a slightly sinister kind of significance. Nevertheless I have grown to love the European Kingfisher more than any other bird.

Far out on the milk-white dead calm waters of the Mediterranean, in the late spring, when the nightingales could be heard in the pines of the Mountains of the Evening Star, several miles away across the water; when their white rocks, and those of Sainte Victoire beyond Marseilles, with the Ile de Riou, and the golden Virgin of the Garde, towering over the distant city, were all flushed with the setting sun; when the Planier Lighthouse, in the middle of the Gulf of the Lions, had started faintly to flash in the impending dusk; when the silence was so great that the thud or splash of an oar carried three or four miles; when the tunny-floats lay out in mile-long straight lines behind the drifting boats; when wine had been drunk, the lanterns lit, and the last conch had sounded its mournful signal across the bay; when it seemed blasphemy even to speak or whisper a single word, and sacrilege to move, except from one elbow to another—the only perceptible movement in the whole gulf would be the low flight of the sacred halcyons, always taken singly along the line of the tunny-floats, moving about a foot above them, sometimes hesitating for a second to rest on one of them, and then continuing at the same level, till the birds disappeared towards the darkening shore. Bird after bird would silently cross the bay in this manner till long after nightfall, and it seemed that this low, level movement was the only possible expression of that supernatural radiance and peace.

It was on the *Etang de Berre* that we heard the nightingales best. There was an avenue along the road to Saint Mitre from Martigues: on an average there were three pairs of nightingales nesting in each of its two hundred plane-trees. It ran parallel to the lakeside, where we used to have permanent seines laid out for sardines, anchovies, and mullet. On a calm night the breeze used to bring the united voices of a thousand nightingales in full song, mixed with the scent of pine, thyme, rosemary, and wild lavender-stychus. The birds used to get carried away in a choral rapture which was infectious, so that one hardly liked to sleep for fear of losing anything of that storm of harmony and perfume. The native fishermen enjoyed it none the less for being absolutely accustomed to it.

Talking of dolphins and mermaids as a substitute for pigs, we once had pigs in our net as a substitute for dolphins. This was one very dry summer when the whole of the Midi was ravaged by fires in the pine-forests. I was out with Clement, and we were sleeping in our boat at anchor with our sardine net laid out just at the foot of a mountain called the Juniper (Caderau), between St. Chamas and Martigues.

One fire was raging far across the lake in the direction of the Sainte Victoire, that famous hill, so often painted by Cézanne, where Marius defeated the Germans some eighty or ninety years before Christ. Not only does the name of the mountain still commemorate the victory but the name, Pourrières, of one of the villages derives from the rotting of half-a-million dead bodies after this greatest of all Roman victories. The name Marius is still the commonest name in Provence: and Marius of Marseilles is as common a music-hall joke as Taffy or Dai from Wales, Paddy from Ireland, or Jock or Sandy from Scotland. No man, not even Alexander or Caesar, ever left so indelible a personal mark on any part of the world, as Marius on Provence.

Maurras goes as far as to say that Martigues was called after the Syrian soothsayer and witch, Martha, whom Marius always carted round with him: but as it is *"les* Martigues" I think it means *the dead waters*, like the name of that other stranded seaport "Aigues Mortes" on the other side of the Rhône: and that the adjective was transposed to avoid confusion, leaving one city the name "Dead-waters" and the other "Watersdead."

To return to the forest fires—not only was the side of Mount Sainte Victoire illumined and reflected in the lake but the whole mountain of the Caderau opposite it was burning. It was a sad but gorgeous vision. We could hear the wind roaring and crackling in the bannered flames as they streamed down the mountain side, while flustered and blinded birds flew overhead twittering faintly in the darkness and the red inferno was reflected in the water. We felt very safe on the water and turned in about eleven o'clock.

The next day the whole lake seemed enveloped in fragrant thyme, rosemary, and pine-smoke. At dawn we started pulling up the net. Suddenly to our amazement we saw some brindled hair waving in the net on the surface and felt the bulk of a big body. "Some woman has drowned in our net," said Clement, and we hastened to pull in the net. We were dumbfounded to find that it was a tremendous shaggy wild boar with long savage tusks, and so huge that we could not get it aboard! We got it loose from the net and tied it aft, so as to tow it home. We had no sooner made it fast and continued to haul in the net when we came on two more small ones—sows!

I have heard a yarn that pigs cannot swim without cutting their necks with their hooves. These wild pigs had swum at least half a mile before they got those hooves through the mesh of our net. We had slept soundly through their struggles. Any noise they made was drowned in the distant rattle and roar of the conflagration.

In a competition on the B.B.C. to see who could substantiate the tallest story, this was the runner-up to one of Major Lewis Hastings' stories. I substantiated this one from the *Petit Marseillais* and the *Provençal:* but Lewis Hastings had one about tent-pegging man-eating sharks from horseback during World War One at Luderitz-bucht on the shores of German West Africa. The Imperial Light Horse and the Natal Carbineers (my brother's regiment) were engaged in a tent-pegging competition on the beach at low tide when some soldiers, who were bathing, rushed out of the shallows where they had been pursued by sharks. As soon as the tent-peggers saw this they rode into the water and started slaughtering the sharks by spearing them on their lances. Needless to say this story won, though mine was a close second.

It only needed my brother, the late Captain Neil Campbell of the R.A.M.C., to tell how he caught a deadly black mamba, measuring 8 feet 9 inches, by fishing for it with ground bait. He tied a live chicken to a tree near the mamba's hole, with half a dozen trout-hooks hidden in its feathers: and returned to find the mamba had swallowed the whole lot, chicken, hooks, and all, and lay writhing in knots so that it became an easy target, being hooked by the inside of its stomach to the tree. These three yarns, all true, would have given a headache to Baron Munchausen himself.

Martigues, like Tarascon, is a town of "chasseurs." Ever since the French Revolution, shooting rights became communal with the result that there is nothing to shoot, but everybody shoots none the less. It makes people think themselves Grands Seigneurs and is one of the jokes of egalitarianism. There are about ten hunters to every sparrow in Provence, except on the Camargue, where wild-fowl abound in the winter. Wild boars are almost uncanny in the way they manage to survive in a world which has been shot clean of hares, and rabbits, and even of larks, blackbirds, and sparrows, all of which are considered game worthy of a 12 bore shot-gun in Provence. Tartarin of Tarascon was no exaggeration.

I have spoken of the African bushpig as a wizard of invisibility and silence: so is his brother the European wild boar—perhaps even more so. These three swam out of a strip of dwarf prickly oak which was visited by at least a dozen hunters weekly and which was the only place for miles around where they would find proper sustenance for their big bodies, since they live chiefly on the acorns of these scrubs. I had visited this strip of oaks countless times to pick wild asparagus which thrives in oak scrub, yet had never even seen a single spoor. However, I walked along the shore next day and found where the boars had embarked, since they had to cross a patch of mud before entering the water. They had been cut off by the fire which was narrowing down to the creek from which they swam. This was the only time they had ever even left a visible foot-print, and they were swimming in a direct line to the only part of the opposite shore that was not fringed with inflammable pine, when they went into our net with their hooves through the mesh.[1]

When we brought the three wild pigs to Martigues, towing the big one which weighed nearly two hundred kilos and was almost the size of a Jersey cow, the whole town turned out to see them. Work almost stopped. We had first of all to take them to the Mairie where we got exactly the same prize for these land-por-poises (fifty francs a head) as we did from the *Inscription Maritime* for the sea-porpoises. They are rightly considered as equally de-structive vermin for the nocturnal inroads they make on potatoes, artichokes, carrots, and turnips. But how such huge beasts remain invisible by day is a complete mystery. From the Mairie we took the pigs to the *Bar du Canal*, a non-Arab restaurant, and sold both of the sows at 10 francs a kilo.

It was market day, a Fair Day, at about nine in the morning, and I suddenly thought of a good idea. I sent Clement and his brother to sail round to the Central Square with *Clemence* towing *Saint*

---

[1] Some time previously two wild boars had been harpooned swimming in the sea near Cap Canaille.

Pierre. We took the two main lateen sails off their antennas, pulled out the antennas and masts, and fixed up a tent over them against one of the trees in the market place. Then we rigged up the two trinquettes and the two "foc"-sails as doors, and charged three francs for a peep at the big pig. We had a lot of customers and got very merry on the proceeds. In the middle of our junketing, in came both Maurras and Leon Daudet, one tiny and the other enormous, and had a good look at our pig: a very great honour indeed.

At last the Spanish butcher of the Island, Ignacio Perez, who had been watching our "gate," came and bought us out both for the meat and the peepshow for the rest of the day, with the hire of the sails, for 1,600 francs. The *Garde-Champêtre*, Antoine, then came and bought for 100 francs the right to take the skin of the head with the ears, after the show was over, and the promise of the skull after all the brawn had been boiled off it. This he stuffed and sold back again, for two hundred francs, to the butcher. This butcher appears as the young drover in the bullfight scene in Wyndham Lewis's *Snooty Baronet* and the description of his *cogida* is quite true. I don't know how Antoine managed eventually to stuff that pig's head, as he did; but, shortly after, the butcher hung it in his shop opposite the stuffed bull's head. The skin began to shrink so tightly round the slender barrel of the skull that when I last saw it, it looked like the long slender muzzle of an ant bear or an aardvark: only the tusks and a shock of bristles remained as a reminder that it had once been a wild boar!

Never in the history of the world did a dead pig do so much business, cause so many transactions or get such publicity as that pig of ours did in one day. Before Antoine skinned the head, he, the butcher, and Clement and I were photographed with the pig by the Pressman from the *Petit Marseillais*. We had not foreseen that in the afternoon there would be even more visitors to the Fair, or we should have charged more to the butcher, who made a great "gate."

The rival attraction to our pig was funnily enough a stuffed mermaid or sea-pig such as the Mohammedans use to work off their sinful craving for roast pig. Monsieur Aimable, the travelling show-man, with the boxing booths, whose show some of us had previously upset several years before by challenging his lads, had come back with some very formidable looking boxers that nobody wanted to tackle: and he was running some side shows of which the Mermaid from Pondicherry, the Dugong or sea-pig, with its horrible porno-graphical curiosities, was the pièce de resistance. If I have met that sea-pig once, I have crossed its path seventeen times, over a period of 20 years: I first saw it exhibited in Paris, in the fair at the top of the Boulevard Raspail, when I was there in 1920 with Thomas Earp, Nina Hamnett, and Marie Beerbohm: and this was nearly ten years later. Then it was on show at Lyons in 1921 in the same circus where I was with the cowboys and Cossacks. I've seen it advertised at three different fairs at Beaucaire, and once at Béziers. The next time I saw it advertised as a *pejemuller*, or siren, was in Barcelona in 1933, then in Valencia and Alicante, and I have seen it since, in 1939, at Portimau in Portugal. It must have made the complete tour of Europe about fifty or sixty times. That it is unmistakably the same sea-pig is proved by its length which is nine feet and outsize for a female: its horrible agonised expression, which is always the same: and the irregularity of its right flipper which has always had a bit chipped off. It certainly met its match as a freak attraction for one day, in the shape of our pig which was cut up that night. I never ate any of it, since at home in Africa we eat neither wild pig, wart-hog, nor forest hog because we are afraid of getting swine-fever. For good reason we do not eat hare either. But those who tasted the two smaller pigs said they were very good: and appar-ently Ignacio managed to sell all the meat of the big one.

During his vacations, Henri Chabrol, the novelist, playwright, poet, Olympic swimming champion, and association football inter-national, was our near neighbour at Saint Chamas; he had a lovely motor-boat and used to visit us often. One day, on his way back, over the open sea, to Montpellier, where he was a master at the Lycée, Henri's motor gave out; he had to anchor the boat, swim on to the desolate shores of the wild Camargue and pass a whole night, as I did, amongst the bulls, stallions, and wild boars in the marshes. He agrees that it is a terrifying experience. It took him eight hours of crashing through reeds and mud in the dark to reach the lighthouse and fetch a boat to tow his own to safety.

Another neighbour of ours was Jean Toussaint Samat. After writing the joint-classic of the Camargue, that lovely book *Sangar*, he eventually became a sort of best-selling Edgar Wallace with books like *La Mort Horrible de Miss Gilchrist* which was founded on events touched on in these Memoirs—a very harmful book, which suggested to some crime-happy reader the idea of letting out the whole Petrol Reservoir at Berre. This was done by opening the main taps a month after the appearance of the book. The whole lake was covered with petrol. Though the smell was evident nobody realised this in the darkness yet the film passed down the canal and covered many hectares of the main sea in ten hours. It was a miracle that it never caught fire before it was dispersed by wind and wave, for fishermen were smoking, knocking their pipes out as usual, and flipping cigarette ends overboard!

Sangar, on the contrary, is a beautiful book; it ranks with José D'Arbaud's *La Bête du Vaccarès* (written in Provençal) as the finest prose work inspired by taurine Provence. Kipling drew upon *Sangar* for his story *The Bull that Thought*, the first half of which is as good a story as he ever wrote. It is a very convincing story of a bull that resembled the *Mamai* and the *Dar* even with that peculiar sense of humour (which the Mamai certainly had) that I have never met in any other animal, except in chimpanzees, and sometimes in dogs. It is only when Kipling lets his Camargue bull loose amongst the Spanish toreros and starts killing off the latter like flies that the story becomes utterly ridiculous.

It is a queer thing how English and German people seem to prefer animals, especially dogs, to their own species and exult in the killing of men—especially by animals. Murder is the chief theme of the most popular English and German films and books. Even according to their own evolutionary interpretation of life they ought to have more affection for their fellow-man, if not as their Maker's image, at least as a highly developed dog, who may commit the crime of walking upright, but doesn't foul the pavement every ten yards or so, or stop to sniff at every lamp-post.

Sangar was dedicated to the great poet and rancher, Folco, the Marquis of Baroncelli, father-in-law of that other superb poet D'Arbaud and uncle of Henry de Montherlant. The Marquis is the chief figure in the last chapter of *Les Bestiaires*, which is the greatest chapter ever written by Montherlant. I have read it at least a hundred times and consider it was divinely *inspired*.

When Colonel Cody (Buffalo Bill) brought over "Sitting Bull" and his relations, the Marquis offered them his hospitality, as he did to many other members of the Equestrian Nation, the Boer refugees after the Boer War. Some of the Red Indian refugees remained at the Saintes Maries till they died—among them Michawago, who was a very fine poet. Samat, who had lived in North America grizzly hunting with the painter Gibson (of "Gibson Girl" celebrity), managed to translate his poems into French prose: and I still possess a copy of these lyrics in prose. They show the very opposite quality from those which D. H. Lawrence affected to discover in the North American Indian. They show high powers of conscious imagination, intelligence and little of the blind drumming stomach-instincts which Lawrence finds so fascinating, but which pertain rather to the more junglified and broken-down types of African negroes.

D'Arbaud's story *La Bête du Vaccarès* is a delightful fantasy in which a beast symbolic of the Camargue continues to appear very convincingly indeed. *Sangar* is the simple naturalistic story of the life and death of a bull as it actually happens. The translation of that book into English should find thousands of readers, since it is written rather from the point of view of an animal than a man. That's the sole fault I find with it.

Modern Provençal literature, dating from the last century, is far richer than the combined literature of all the Provençal troubadours put together. With Mistral as the Central Peak, like the snow-clad Ventour looking over the Alpilles, whose names are Aubanel, Roumanille, D'Arbaud and Baroncelli, the Félibrige has probably united steeper heights of soaring poetry, within a limited area and period, than any other poetical movement within the last two centuries.

The same fiery spirit that inspires the works of these poets and breathes in all the prancing wild horses and fighting cattle of the Crau and the Camargue, roars in the charges of the mistral through the crags of Provence. It thunders down from the high forested peaks of the Alps, the Ventour, and the Alpilles in the rock-rolling spates of the Isère, the Durance, and in the headlong Rhône. That spirit lives in the bulls when they meet to celebrate their "Ramadans" by moonlight and the air is hoarse with their bellowings. They too seem to celebrate their dead and sing their deeds, each mounting in turn to the summit of the dune, from the circle of listeners, to chant his anthem, filling the wind with thunder, while the encircling horns gleam round him like votive candles. Meanwhile plunging through the reeds and tamarisks, the great bull-deity of Provence answers their voices with his own, heaving forever onward through the pines and the waves.

Provence! Your memory is as rousing to those "who have the passion" of poetry, as the mistral is to the waves.

XXII

TO SPAIN

WE HAD been doing very well and making some money when we caught the wild pigs in the net. Leaving our children with some friendly neighbours, my wife and I then took Monsieur Henri Chaves, the taxi-driver of Jonquières, and went for a honeymoon trip all round Provence. Henri could well look after himself wherever we went: and I have seen him swarm up the side of the old Roman Arena at Arles, like a cat-burglar, without paying his ticket, climb over the top and occupy a seat at the bullfight which would ordinarily have cost two or three pounds.

We spent about two weeks driving all round Provence and the Languedoc, and following the bullfights from Arles to Béziers, Lunel, and Nîmes so that we kept almost level with our expenses on the money I got from the cocardes of bulls.

It was during this trip that the tenth anniversary of our marriage occurred at Istres, and on that day we ran into Reginald Symes and his racing car. Symes is now working at the Admiralty in London, where I sometimes meet him, but was then living on his own at Martigues. He is an ex-Cavalryman and had lost a leg in the First World War. We asked him to come to the bullfight when we met him driving through Istres, where Madame Calais was billed to ride as rejoneadora, and Pierre Saurel, the famous rejoneador, and

Pierre Pouly, the matador, who has a Madrid Doctorate and is the owner of the great Roman Arena at Arles, were to be judges in the open championship of Provence for the free course of bulls, and for the steer-throwing championship.

It was on that afternoon, in honour of my wife and in an arena crowded with French military and naval aviators, that I gave my supreme performance of "mancornar," or hurling a bull by the horns, not from the saddle but from the ground.

I got my lock on the bull by a trick which I have mentioned before, and which I was fond of using with smaller bulls; that is, sitting motionless on the barricades, until the bull had passed me three or four times and got used to me; then leaping down, as his shoulder passed and getting a grip on his horns, with a sudden wrench, which is rather like one of the passes in Judo or Unarmed Combat. The neck muscle of a bull is the most powerful in its whole body, but its power is in the upward toss; it relies chiefly on the force of gravity to return. Thus, if one horn is suddenly raised to its full height, by pulling the far horn towards one, the whole muscle is thrown out of its functioning orbit. The strongest muscles of most animals are weak on the reflex. Note how a blacksmith can paralyse the terrible hind hoof of a horse, by bending the leg upwards, and how fishmongers keep the powerful claws of lobsters from opening with a flimsy loop of paper-elastic.

When I had thrown this bull, I sat on its neck, took off the cocarde, the "gland," and the rosette, and received an ovation from a crowded arena of truly valiant people.

As my pants were ripped, on that occasion, to tatters, I had the honour of being wrapped in a French aviator's cloak and of being presented, jointly with my wife, with several thousand francs (worth a lot then) for the three cocardes, and a bottle of champagne, by Pierre Pouly and by Madame Calais, for whom I acted as peon afterwards.

Madame Calais had a fall that afternoon, but we got the bull away from her and she remounted. After killing seven hundred bulls, this beautiful woman was killed by a stray bullet from a German plane over Paris, during World War Two.

After I had changed into a new pair of pants, I collected many more prizes that afternoon; I found all the steers I had to deal with child's-play, after that bull.

We spent the early part of that evening drinking champagne with Symes, Pouly, and Saurel, at the *Bar Des Sports*, and it was then that the Impresario Daniel Valencia, who had a travelling and folding arena, contracted me to ride for him, in a separate act, when he went round with his *Charlotades* and comic bullfights.

We bought two half-trained horses, one off Saurel and the other off Lescot, and I soon had them in order. Clair de Lune, a pure white Camarguais mare, was absolutely safe and sure-footed though, with my tall stature, I must have looked a little out of proportion on so short a horse. She could turn in her own length without losing speed.

From that moment I went under my Christian baptismal name, Ignace or Ignacio (Ignatius), and my former Christian name became Hispanified into the common Spanish surname Roig. It was very convenient to have a good Christian name at hand when I was finally roped into the old Corral by the Cardinal and the martyr monks of Toledo. So from then on I was Ignacio Roig on every poster and even six years later on the proclamation, with a reward, that the Tcheka of Toledo posted up on the walls of that town after my escape from there, in 1936, when I had fixed up several of the Tcheka boys themselves in order to get out.

The bulls I had to fight under Daniel Valencia were all young ones (novillos) but it was an anxious job. Few jobs are so satisfying as being a fisherman or a cattleman and helping to produce the very sustenance of the human race. There is something unsatisfactory about being a mere acrobat and entertainer, unless one is a fine artist.

One day I got a severe jolting, a second one, from that beautiful little bull, the Mamai, which was famous. I was also tossed by and narrowly escaped from a big half-Spanish bull of Lescot. These accidents left me with five fractured ribs and a collarbone hurt in the jousts. I was now thirty and felt that queer sensation known as *Taedium Vitae* which comes on for about a year or so at that age. I went completely sedentary and literary. We took a new house further away in the pine-forest and I decided that I would try to write for my living since I had done so well out of *Adamastor*.

This was a mistake, since poetry was then, for me, the perspiration of *other activities*, though now it happens spontaneously. My mother, too, was very keen that I should settle down and write, so

I spent the next two years almost as a pure scholar, doing nothing but reading or writing.

I gave up the fishing boats. Clement, alas, I have heard from his brother, Marius, is doing exactly the same sentence as Mnugeni, because of a jealous drama in which he slashed his girl's face. One had to be very careful with these Martegaux, who were always knife-conscious, unlike other Provencaux who are rather trigger-happy. They were mostly descended from galley-slaves and have a queer reputation, but I got on very well with them, on the whole.

Just as I got on with the Martegaux, so, unknown to me, only thirty miles away, did my compatriot, Uys Krige, the Afrikaans poet, get on with the Marseillais, for whom he played rugby. Son of one of the most famous Springboks, Japie Krige, Uys was for a long time one of the very best players in France, and he earned his keep in this way, while learning French and Provençal. When we met he was making a living by coaching, and playing for, the Marseilles rugby team. He then came and stayed with us and tutored my children, Tess and Anna, in return for his keep. He studied hard and wrote some very fine things during this period.

Earlier, Liam O'Flaherty, that strange, haunted will-o'-the-wisp, also turned up there with the late Pierre Maillaud, who met him in the train, and, hearing he knew me, asked if he could come and meet me. Pierre Maillaud stayed on with us for months. Later, as Pierre Bourdan, he became famous as the Radio voice of de Gaulle's "Free France." We had no idea he was playing truant from school and that there was a hue and cry out after him. When I took him back to his uncle, three months later, I made friends with all the family: and Pierre, whom I met in London during the last war, still swore that those three months when he helped us on our boats, were the happiest he ever spent in his life.

I had a fight with my brother-in-law, Marius Polge, about this time in which I was beautifully knocked out. He had the nobility to realise, however, that he had taken me at a disadvantage and offered me a return bout when my shoulder and ribs were better, for that smashed collarbone was still weak. It was Pierre Maillaud who refereed the return bout, fought with gloves, in which I restored the balance, though without effecting a knock-out.

In a way, I am very fond indeed of Liam O'Flaherty in short doses. I consider him a natural born genius: within his narrow limits, the best prose writer alive perhaps, when he is writing for the joy of it—not for money. But I can only take him in small doses as he is eternally on the fidget like a cat on hot bricks; though I think some of the most fantastically happy times of my existence were spent with him.

I remember one amusing night at a Mayfair club, when Liam and I carried out the four best looking ladies and put them all in a taxi —without any opposition from their menfolk. What we had forgotten was that our wives were in the taxi, and as fast as we bundled them into it, the wives turfed them out of the other door so that when we thought the taxi was full, and climbed in, we were confounded to find out what had really happened.

Towards the end of our time in Martigues, Tristram Hillier, the painter, came along with the beautiful tartane which he had bought to sail round the world. It was one of the big fishing tartanes of Toulon. He had a castle in Gascony to which he drove us with the sculptor Zadkine. This was in the middle of the Gers. The castle of Mansencome, built by John of Gaunt, towered over the surrounding country and could be seen from many miles away. The people who worked the farm for Hillier had become fond of him, and his family, but the other people of the neighbourhood had inherited the traditional Gascon hatred for the English people dating from the times of the Black Prince and the armies of occupation. We were drinking Armagnac made on the farm and guzzling wonderful home-made pâté de foie gras like Left-Wing poets and poetesses in Madrid during the Spanish War. Hillier's farm tenants produced the foie gras from his own geese on the spot.

The superstitious people of the village were actually making dolls to represent us, and sticking pins into them in the hopes of bewitching, plaguing, or cursing us. Bits of castle kept on falling and trying to knock us on the head as if unseen agencies were at work, though, to my mind, it is a wonder, with the wind that blows there, that the whole place hasn't fallen in long ago like a super-Harlequin-restaurant, and crushed every man, goose, and cow, within a two hundred yards' radius all round which is about what it will cover when it does finally crash to the earth.

The countryside around Mansencome was most melancholy. The grass was a dark sombre but rich green, and the wind, which never ceased to sigh and whistle and moan round the towers, was very ghostly indeed. Cupboards creaked as if loaded with armoured skeletons, doors banged mysteriously, scuffles were heard (or imagined) and footsteps seemed to sound where we knew there were no people, for only about an eighth of the ground and first floors of this vast groaning edifice was rigged up for habitation. It reminded me of my friend Mervyn Peake's book, *Gormenghast*. The rest of it was full of bats, spooks, and owls, and whistling and whispering tongues of air.

I had a room overlooking the Pyrennes in the distance, and I was working on a book called *Marine Provence* for which I was handsomely paid both for the text and my illustrations, though the publishing firm which bought it went out of commission before it could be published. I only wish I had had that book by me while writing this first volume of my memoirs so that I could refresh my memory from some of the chapters.

The room I worked in, through the power of suggestion, and what I heard from Hillier, became as eerie to me as the Indian's grave described in an earlier chapter of this book.

Hillier, owing to the big financial crisis in England, had to sell his lovely tartane and his castle (I don't believe he was sorry to get rid of the castle—no one would buy it except for a song because it seemed that it really had a curse on it). But the tartane was dismasted, alas; and I last saw it at L'Estaque serving as a lighter: which made me very sad indeed, both for my friend and for his boat.

From Mansencome Mary and I returned via Carcassone, Narbonne, and Nîmes, to Provence. Nîmes is surely one of the wonders of this world with the most perfectly conserved Roman remains, including the Maison Carrée, which is an almost perfect temple of Diana, and the Arena. Then there are the lovely terraces through which the river flows down the streets and avenues from one of the most beautiful, clear, deep-bubbling springs I ever saw, situated in the shade of tall trees in the public gardens. I heard that these terraces were designed by Vauban; if so, that grim engineer of fortifications under Louis XIV was, like Leonardo, who was also a military engineer, a great lyrical artist also. In this one unwarlike job that was ever granted to his architectural genius, he seems to have rejoiced, and he has certainly given delight to all the generations that follow after him.

When we returned to Provence we found that we had brought

a bit of the "jinx" of Hillier's castle with us. Now that I was not jousting or bullfighting for the town, I lost a good deal of my popularity. Being a friend of Hart Crane's had not contributed to my good name. I heard that enquiries were afoot as to my fishing activities. So Mary, Uys Krige, the children and I all decided one fine day to "fold our tents like the Arabs—and as silently steal away": this time to Spain.

It was necessary to raise money on the spot—so, getting a contract for an autobiography, I wrote *Broken Record* day and night for ten days. It was a good title, and described the book, which wasn't much good, but was certainly "broken" up enough to deserve the title. It briefly sketched a few of the episodes of my life—but it enabled us to flee just in time, and I corrected the proofs in Barcelona while suffering from a poisoned leg. I used to become over-powered by sleep every few minutes so my wife propped me against the chest of drawers while I finished correcting the proofs and added some further 10,000 words which were required.

When we got to Spain my dear friend and patron C. J. Sibbett of Cape Town saved our lives by wiring £50 in answer to an urgent S.O.S. I carried letters from Daniel Valencia, Pouly, and Lescot to three or four impresarios and apoderados of bullfighters. But my horses had gone: they had really belonged to Daniel, who treated me like a Christian.

I felt I knew the whole of Catalunya as I passed through, since my favourite prose-reading, after Gibbon and *Moby Dick*, is Major General Napier's *History of the Peninsular War*.

We all woke up one morning in the *Barrio Chino* of Barcelona, a town which I did not know. After discovering that we had landed up in a worse hell than the reserved "quarter" of Marseilles, and having paid the lodging for a month ahead, so that we could not move, I went to spy out the land. So did Uys Krige. We both came back with bad news. He could not play rugby or coach the Barcelona team until he had lived in the country for six months: and the Spaniards, with their sense of honour, were not so easy-going as the French. It was winter, and there were not even any night-bullfights that year in Barcelona because the separatist revolution was going on, under Macia as president. It was inspired by the sort of masonic idea (divide and rule) and was probably financed by the money-racketeers behind the Geneva hoax, though it used honest local patriots to do the dangerous work—in the same way in which poor heroic Bolivar was used. But it really hits back in the end at the instigators and financiers and this converts one to the belief in divine justice.

It was obvious from the very start that Catalan separatism was a job put up from the outside, though one could sympathise with the local patriotism of the Catalans and their pride in having created by far the most imposing modern city in Spain. The beauty of Barcelona is a thing by itself. It is not Spanish, but it equals many beautiful Spanish cities. The Rambla de las Flores is a mile of the most gorgeous flower-stalls in the shade of mighty plane-trees, descending from a most noble square to the sea, with cafés on either side of the road, and a sort of communal night life in which rich and poor, old and young, all participate equally and gaily, as nowhere else in the world. For the night life is also family life, though it goes on till long after midnight, and Barcelona only really wakes up at 10 p.m.

Uys was a good poet and a good boy, but as an incurable Calvinist he could never understand Spain or Provence. Protestants go to these countries for spiritual fresh air, yet with the trained opportunism which is their chief *raison d'être*, they ascribe the attraction, which is really that of the Church and the people who have not been amputated from the Church by force of tyrants like Henry VIII, or crooks like Calvin and Luther—to the climate or the landscape, or to anything else save in the culture and civilisation which hold them so spellbound. They always consort with the malcontents also. They have not the courage to disown what is wrong in themselves. They would sooner join with atheists and diabolists, as they did in the Spanish War, than with anything straightforwardly European or Roman, though they will hang around a place like Spain for whatever by-products of the Catholic faith they can pick up buckshee, without any responsibilities—the courtesy, hospitality, and nobility of the people.[1]

From the very beginning my wife and I understood the real issues in Spain. There could be no compromise in this war between the East and the West, between Credulity and Faith, between ir-

[1] An honourable exception must be made in the case of Mr. Loveday, the head of the British Board of Trade in Madrid, who when he saw what was happening changed his religion from Protestantism to Catholicism, as we did.

responsible innovation (which catches all "intellectuals" once they
have been hereditarily derailed) and tradition, between the emo-
tions (disguised as Reason) and the intelligence. We used to go for
walks in the Ramblas when nobody but the Civil Guard were
stationed there. Often we were turned back forcibly, when there
was firing in the streets.

Up to then we had been vaguely and vacillatingly Anglo-Catho-
lic: but now was the time to decide whether, by staying in the
territorials, to remain half-apathetic to the great fight which was
obviously approaching—or whether we should step into the front
ranks of the Regular Army of Christ. Hitler himself had said, even
by then, how much more easy the Protestants were to enslave and
bamboozle than the Catholics: Stalin, Trotsky, and Lenin in their
writings had shown how they despised the former as being of no
more hindrance to them than the agnostic intellectuals whom they
all more or less laughingly contemn as useful and obedient decoys
and microbe-carriers, to be liquidated the moment they have served
their purposes. "Why, when I see a Communist, do I feel small?"
asks the agnostic English poet, Day Lewis. That is why he feels
small—because the Communist is using him as a beast of burden, and
laughing at him.

Signs of the coming Civil War were everywhere apparent. Looking over a man's shoulder in a café, I saw that he was reading Plato's
Republic. I have heard about the curse of illiteracy, which at least
saves a man from being taken in through his spectacles. The illit-
erate peasants of Spain read:

> "Far less nonsense from their running brooks,
> Than waiters primer-proud with knowing looks,
> Can mumble out of newspapers and books."

The curse of literacy can be far worse than any degree of illiteracy. As I watched this reader fairly goggling at what he read, and
at the same time scratching himself incessantly in the groins and
armpits, I became fascinated by the contrast between him and his
reading matter, and I engaged him in conversation. It appeared that
he thought he was reading about the constitution and programme
of the newly-founded Republic in Spain—the most evil and evil-
starred fiasco that was ever set up against the will of a nation.

As we had little room in our lodgings and it was cold, Uys used to go out to the big Post Office, which had central heating, to write his poems, plays and novels, and sit at the table where telegrams can be written, till it was time to close up the Post Office. While he was thus engaged Aldous and Maria Huxley and two German girls who were passing through Barcelona saw him and asked him where we lived. Uys who is fairly innocent told them the way to our lodging, and the posh Bugatti rolled up in the middle of the *Barrio Chino*, where foreigners were usually knocked on the head and robbed. They asked us out to supper at a swell German Bar in the Rambla and I did not breathe freely till we were well out of the *Barrio;* though the Huxleys were unconscious of their danger.

I met the Picador "Mohama" who had an attack of lumbago, and at a moment's notice I deputised for him in two novilladas. His manager paid me very well and we went down with him as far as Valencia where I worked for him again and then got a temporary job as "mono sabio"—a sort of deck hand in the arena. Spanish bullfighting on foot was far too difficult for me to learn at that age.

I then won 1,000 pesetas in the National Lottery in Valencia where we lived in the Calle de la Padilla near the Arena. The "Padilla" was the tough, cheap quarter. I decided to rent a small artichoke farm in the region of Ifac (Altea) where we stayed a year. I rode as a scratch rejoneador for charity at Altea and surrounding villages.

In this valley we had a wonderful time and we took instruction for joining the Church. The whole of the coast became full of Germans, mostly Jews, fleeing from Hitler. I am not one of those who believes that if Tweeledum is a nasty piece of work (as Hitler was) Tweedledee must necessarily be an angel; that is the Anglo-Saxon way of thinking and that's why the Englishman is now subservient to Moscow abroad, and to Freud and the Pontecorvo and Fuchs brigade at home. The Englishman always insists on "putting two and two together" when they should be kept in separate compartments. Some of these Germans had money from the Komintern and they set up sex-clinics and communist-cells in the village. I am ashamed to say there was a British novelist in the racket further up the coast. I started the reaction, but I joined a Communist cell for fun, and found out when they were planning an attack on a church which was then to be full of children and women. I came in with six peasants and we caught the eleven Germans and some local Republicans interrupting the service with obscenities and blasphemies. Crying on Saint Louis, I caught the biggest one, Dr. Meyerstein, and brought him out into the square where I broke his glasses and watch, and then throttled out his false teeth and broke them to pieces too. These men were so abject there was no need to hurt them. They all went away to the next village Benidorm, and left us in peace: but they did worse harm there by bribery and corruption.

Now all those veiled forces of socialism, the base self-seeking greed, which is at the bottom of much of modern political reform and egalitarianism, began to come to the top. Bombs went off every day, hurting or killing innocent people. Murders were committed in broad daylight. Discontent and hatred seethed everywhere. It was aggravated by some refugees who returned hospitality with hatred and contempt; as their prototype Marx did in England. Spain now sank to being a pitiable mess of masonic intrigue, tyranny, and imbecile utopianism.

We lived near Altea in the Sierra for a year, during which time my mother visited us from South Africa. Her amazing feats with toy-making and her extraordinary understanding of the Spanish peasants' children made the "Grandmother"—*the Abuela*—famous for miles around, and I never receive a letter from Altea without loving messages being sent to her, from the now grown-up children whom she had so fascinated.

The peasants and farmers, who live in that marvellous valley between Guadalest, in the Mountains, and Altea on the coast, were the most cultured and hospitable people we had yet seen. They laughed at "innovations." My mother who was used to comparative luxury in liners and hotels was very impressed by the spotless cleanliness of their houses and ovens. Although they could not understand each other, she and the neighbouring peasant's wife, Rafela, were great friends.

The huge mountain over Alcoy on one side, and the sierra of Altea running down from a height of 3,500 feet to the solitary needle of Ifac which rises a thousand feet sheer out of the water, were terraced for olives and locust beans from the height of two thousand feet downwards and so skilfully irrigated that they made a truly beautiful sight. It is fine to see nature in its rugged grandeur, just as it is fine to see a nice-looking, but unbroken, horse. But the supreme treat is to see the ruggedness of nature dominated by skill: the precipitous slopes terraced into orchards; and the horse completed with a fine rider.

We began to dig into the Catacombs: and the valiant but rather uneducated priest of Altea (who was none the worse for that) gave us a new baptism as Catholics, and re-married us in the Catholic Church, so we started life completely from scratch, all over again, to the envy of all the peasants who lived for miles around: and to our own delight. From then on I went monogamous, and never regret it.

At this time there turned up two very charming, convivial Norwegian writers, Helge Krog, and Erling Winsnes. Helge was a Communist and Erling was a Nazi, but they were both staunchly united in their hate of Christ and Christianity. Helge's aunt, or mother-in-law, had translated his plays into English and as they had no politics in them and were very talented, I signed the translation for him at his request, and got it published in England—since Helge said my name would help. Although I only know a few phrases and technical whaling terms in Norwegian, all my South African whaling friends wrote to congratulate me for having mastered their tongue at last: and translated their leading living dramatist. Occasionally I get fivers or tenners from the B.B.C. and various theatres for my "translation" of Helge's plays. Sometimes, too, I get roundly cursed in the Press for my damnably bad translation! For instance, I get blamed for translating what should be "My own darling" as "My good friend," in a scene where the cuckold is supposed to discover a fiery love-letter from his wife to her boy-friend!

These men were like children; they would argue violently and then totter up, helping each other from side to side, lovingly to bed. Oh! If only people could take their politics as lightly and boozily as Norwegians!

Early in 1935, in Alicante, I met Rodrigo, my old friend, Imperio's brother, and he gave me some tips about the horse-trade between Talavera and Toledo. From what I heard I knew at once that here was a job for me. Imperio had by then remarried and had a large family.

I arrived in Toledo in June, 1935, and hired a very beautiful horse from a stationary gipsy friend of Rodrigo's, who lived there. I called on Señor Jenaro, the chief tailor in the Plaza Zodocover, and president of the Villalta Club, and offered to ride in any show he cared to stage. We went down to the arena that same morning and he was impressed with what I could do. Except for climbing my horse up the flagpole which rises above the clock-tower, I did every reasonable trick within a circus rider's or a bullfighter's repertoire. For this I was booked for a bullfight for the Comedor de Caridad, to ride in the same show with the Matadors Villalta, Lalanda, and Fuentes Bejerano.

I tried to buy this fine chestnut horse outright but I was out-bidden by the cacique of the Conde de Romanones, the ex-premier of Spain; the cacique's young son of fifteen rode it away to the superb baroque mansion of Buena Vista a mile along the main road to Talavera. The next time I saw the three of them together, the cacique, his son, and the chestnut gelding, the father and the little boy were lying side by side in their blood by the main road, and a horrible German Jew was trying to catch the horse. I was unarmed and the German and his gang were fairly bristling with automatics and ammunition, so I walked steadily ahead without looking to left or right. It is only by a miracle of Our Lady that such people are not ruling in Spain today as snugly as those other non-Europeans, Beirut, Rakosy, Pauker and the rest of them are ruling in ex-Christian Eastern Europe. (Ilya Ehrenburg was, and would have remained, O.C. of Toledo.)

When we first turned up in Toledo we lived for a month in a house in the Calle Cisneros just opposite the Cathedral. It was a wonderful feeling to belong to the religion of one's ancestors before the atomic fission of the Reformation. Protestantism has become so subdivided since then, that now, three and a half centuries later, the main body of *practising* Christians (even in so-called Protestant England) is what it was before—the Catholic body, which is increasing as the others diminish, or subdivide.

My first anxiety was to get a really good horse and here my mother, who was in England, stepped in and saved my life, by sending me a cheque, with which I was able to buy, cheap, an unbroken thoroughbred which had gone down in price for having killed its previous owner the moment he mounted it to break it in. This gelding became a good quiet horse. I took it down on the soft sand by the Tagus, near the first weir above the Alcantara bridge, and broke it in: and now I had almost the finest horse in Toledo, which I called Moro. He had only three rivals: Mariposa, a white mare belonging to the chief baker of Toledo, which I eventually bought; the Count of Romanones's chestnut: and the aged great jumper, which was the one and only horse to survive the siege of the Alcazar when they had eaten all the others. It was while exercising Moro that I met Captain Alba, riding this ex-jumper, just where his memorial now stands on the Talavera road, and he stopped and complimented me on my horse. You could see (even in old age) what a beautiful horse his jumper had been. Though I never knew the hero of the siege intimately, as I do all the rest of his family, we often passed each other and spoke about the horses. We used to meet at that drinking trough which you see in the foreground of Greco's view of Toledo.

I began buying unbroken horses in Talavera, breaking them in, and selling them for pannier work in the narrow streets of Toledo to butchers, bakers, milkmen and the like. I did well and was able to rent that fine house, with two corrals, which is built into the ramparts with the old Visagra Gate as its main corner bastion. Through this gate Roy Diaz (the Cid Campeador) rode when he delivered Toledo from the Moors. From the front three terraces, covered with vines and roses that in May silted the ground fetlock-deep with roses, descended to a garden with two fountains in the middle and huge mulberry trees where the golden orioles piped all day in early summer. We had also some fine ash trees, acacias, and a golden blooming Paradise tree. My wife and daughters helped me with the horses which I sometimes brought by horse truck to Torrijos; all three of them are excellent riders and we were also helped very much by our *criada* or servant-girl, Eugenia, who had been brought up in the horsy village of Casas Buenas ten miles out in the direction of horse-happy Talavera. We used to go for long rides in the thyme-scented mountains from which the view of Toledo is always so magnificent—especially from the Virgen del Valle perched high over the roaring canyon that encircles Toledo for two-thirds of its girth, with the Tagus rushing through it magnificently in times of flood.

This house we had is now being made into a hotel. It was, long ago, the summer villa of one of the old Cardinals. The garden was like a well of deep quiet walled in by the ramparts of the city and crested with convents all along the top of the rise which looks over the two gates of Visagra towards Madrid, with the plains of La Mancha to the south, and the Sierras Guadarrama and Gredos spread all along the northern skyline; to the east colonnades of silver poplars span the windings of the Tagus to the distant horizon.

XXIII

THE COMING OF THE TERROR

I READ of Toledo in a travel book called *In Spain*—"A City which never had rest until it entered its tomb. Not just that quasi-tomb —that species of purgatorial tomb—into which all nations seem for their sins, to have to descend for a while, retaining however such a spark of being that, like the olive tree, blighted by a severe wintry blast, and cut down that it may shoot forth again in six or seven years' time, they come forth again and take up once more the running of life."

The author goes on with his chatter to say Toledo is so utterly dead that when the end came it was the end for her. He speaks of her bleak inhospitality, her fossilisation and so forth. Nearly all modern writers get this queer notion, along with the cold shoulder from the inhabitants. Only Maurice Barrès, it seems, and myself *of all the foreign writers* who have visited Toledo knew that she was really stripped and cleared for action, and far more alive and awake than any of the modern towns. She is still the heart of Spain, the imperial capital of the Spains, and when she accepted us as Toledanos, as she had up till then accepted no other foreigners, it was because we could recognise the sleeping phoenix before she put on her flames of martyrdom.

Toledo was the whole embodiment of the crusade for Christianity against Communism and I felt it the minute I set foot in the city. There is something victorious in the very look of the place, and inherent in its very poverty. But clouds were closing in.

> "By every sign the times were known
> Humanity by day benighted,
> The flesh defiled, dominion slighted,
> Blasphemed the high majestic throne . . ."

One noticed, during the restless period that preceded the 1936 elections, that the working class was divided in two. The boot-blacks, an enormous class to themselves in Spain, the waiters, and most of the mechanics, along with the miners and factory workers, were either anarchists or Reds. It was expected that the anarchists would abstain from voting: or might even vote for the Right, with whom, in their liking for liberty, they have more in common than with the Communists. Amongst the anarchists were to be found some of the most generous idealistic people, at the same time as the real "phonys"—like the ones that dug up the cemetery in Huesca, held parades of naked nuns, and out-babooned in atrocity anything I had ever read of before. But they were warm-blooded—unlike their ice-cold compères, the "commies," who were less human. You could beg your life from an anarchist. It was not long before most of the anarchists wished they had gone Right for they were unmercifully massacred by their Red Comrades.

The idea of vertical syndicates, as implemented by the present Government, is an anarchist conception, and part of their own programme. When Beveridge was so impressed by this, and noted how far the Spanish Government was ahead of our own in all matters relating to "family allowances," etc., etc., he was muzzled at once in making his report, because it would redound to the credit of the Spanish régime. That was the *Tribune's* argument! What sort of mad fanaticism is this that will give itself away quite openly in advocating the suppression of truth in favour of a prejudice founded entirely on falsehood?

The workers who joined with the Right[1] majority were the lowest-paid ones. Paradoxically enough, it is the workers who produce the chief necessities of life, grain, meat, wool, and leather, for food, clothing, and footwear, who get the lowest pay, and they are generally conservative and do not want romantic upheavals. It was the highest-paid workers, chauffeurs, miners, and factory workers, who became the most murderously acquisitive and subscribed to the "Terror," and its utterly useless waste of life, property, and time.

The factory workers at the big munition works in Toledo were very numerous, so that although the Province was Right-Wing, the mayor of the capital, Guillermo, was a Red, who eventually, under Red rule, became the Governor of the whole Province, till Ilya

[1] Right-Wing—Nationalists, Requetés, Carlists, Falangists.
Left-Wing—Reds, Anarchists, Republicans, Patriots, Communists.

Ehrenburg took over from him. Guillermo was a friend of mine: he kept the tavern a stone's throw from my house, where the Bajada de la Granja, the back road to my stables, left the main road to Madrid; I used to dismount here to fill my leather wine-bottle, slap my horse, and say: "Go back to the corral": and the horse would run off to the stables by itself.

Guillermo was one of the handsomest men I ever saw, though he was getting a bit stout. I happened in on him one day when he was examining, in the drawer under his till on the Bar, a collection of modern automatic pistols, made in America, Germany, and Czechoslovakia. They were a truly formidable array: so I twitted him as to whether he was keeping them to use on us in "the terror" which was then only six months distant. The date, though, had not yet been decided, since it was before the elections. "Oh yes, if you are still here," he said, "and haven't been bumped off by anyone else." He let me examine them while he filled my "bota," or "boot," or leather bottle. This bottle was a lovely piece of work in oxhide, holding two litres, with scarlet tassels, and a sling to swing it from the shoulder, or the horn of the saddle. Its stopper, made of a bull's horn, unscrewed in three parts, so that there was a big opening for filling it, and then, for drinking, there was a medium jet, and a thin jet.

Drinking in Spain is a fine art—even drinking water. Many peasants can distinguish the taste of every well-known fountain within twenty miles. "Oh, I haven't tasted the fountain of Yepes for the last six months," a peasant will say, recognising it at once, as one swaps "botas" with him in passing on the road. This exquisite sensuality is nowhere so highly developed as in Spain. It springs from Latin moderation. Except in the bars and the hotels, one never touches a drinking vessel with one's lip, which is supposed, by the real peasants, to be a dirty habit. Whether it's water or wine, one squirts it from a leather, earthenware, or glass vessel, with a spout; the jet rinses one's palate with its foam, refined almost to vapour. This way of drinking brings out the flavour and perfume, both of wine and water, and once one has mastered the art without choking, drinking wine or water out of a glass seems flat and insipid compared to it. The longer, thinner, and more forcible the jet, the more it aerates the bouquet of the wine or the water. From two and a half feet away you can say: "This water tastes of marble, of

violets, of granite, of thyme, of iron, or of quartz; or of the shade
of mulberry, white poplar trees or olives." You can tell if it has
flowed round the roots of almond, willows, poplars, or prickly-
oaks; you almost get a visual idea of the source if you have never
seen it before, and can say whether it springs amongst grass, cresses,
rushes, shingle, or pebbles. You can also tell whether it has bubbled
up from the depths of the earth, or rushed down from a snow-peak.
My poem, *A Jug of Water*, was written about a glass of "botico,"
full of water, from the spring of Saint Ana in the sierra of Altea.
It tastes of quartz.

When Guillermo had filled the bota he turned to me and said:
"You are talking of some months to come, or, maybe, of a year
hence when we begin 'the terror.' The first people these pistols
will kill then will be your friends the friars up there," he pointed
to the Carmelites, "and next maybe you, if you haven't the sense to
clear out in time. But for the present these pistols are absolutely
necessary to me, not to shoot fascists, or you other bastard sons of
priests; but because I am in danger from anarchists. Yet they are
supposed to be going to join in a Popular Front with us." Then he
related how he had been fired at the day before when he was on his
way back from the railway station—which is far across the river,
beneath and beyond the Castle of San Servando. Whenever a step
on the pavement came near the rattling chopped cane fly-curtains
of the tavern, he would be at the ready with a hand in the drawer.
The shots of the day before had left him trigger-happy, though a
brave man.

I was on cheeking-terms with Guillermo. It always gives one a
great advantage over "smart-Alecs" like him to pretend to be more
"simple" than one is. "Why don't they give you a guard of a couple
of bastard sons of the Nelken or the Pasionaria," I asked him, "seeing you are the Mayor?" "Oh, I'm quite handy enough on my
own," he replied. "I've refused a guard."

I think Guillermo refused a guard because most of the civil guard
and police of Toledo would have been only too glad to see him
bumped off; they would have offered nothing more than a token
resistance, or even have bumped him off on their own. I noticed,
later, when the Red Government had enrolled the *Guardia de Asal-
to*, or the "blue guards," there were always a couple of rifles and
revolvers hanging round at the foot of the Bajada de la Granja, by
his tavern.

All the Mayors of Toledo, whether it was Dr. Ribera, thrice Mayor, Señor Aguirre, or Guillermo, received dozens of letters from the mayor, councillors, or citizens of the city of Toledo in Ohio, U.S.A., and I have been the semi-official translator of these letters and illuminated addresses to all of them, while they were mayors of Toledo, under the various régimes of Franco, Ilya Ehrenburg, Largo Caballero, or Azaña. The transatlantic "Toledanos," though most Anglo-Saxons, have "adopted" the parent city in Spain, with all the nostalgic feeling of exiled highlanders

"for the lone shieling and the distant island,"

and they write masses of pompous, sentimental rubbish, as most of the letters say, "to *forge the link* with you citizens of the ancient mother city"—their "little grey home in the East," as one of them lovingly called it. To pull Guillermo's leg I always translated "forge the link" as forging a pair of manacles for him, which made him laugh rather uneasily, since he more-or-less confirmed my translation by looking up "forge" and "link" in an English dictionary.

"Yes, who knows," I said, "but they will come over here, when the troubles are over, and visit you in the jail: and bring you flowers, magazines, wine and cigarettes when you are in the clink, as I also promise to do, if I'm still alive."

"The only reason you are still alive, Don Ignacio, blast you! is that your king is one of us," he replied. "Do you think I don't know that you've hidden monks in your house, in lay clothes, on the occasion of every riot or demonstration? You and your wife apparently *want* to die."

"How dare you say my king is one of you?" I replied. "He is more anti-Red than Baldwin: and besides he is a Christian, damn you!"

"I tell you he is a Freemason like I am," cried Guillermo, banging his fist on the table.

"That may be," I replied, "but Freemasonry in England is not related to the Grand Orient Lodge, except very vaguely, via the Scotch lodges. I swear to you that the English Freemasonry tolerates Christianity and that some masons in England are Christians, though not Catholics. Also English Masons don't murder for their convenience like the Grand Orient murdered the magistrate,

Prince, and even its own member, fellow-swindler and colleague, Stavisky." I might as well have argued that the Pope was a professing atheist for the "liberales," Azañists, or masons, all one party, like Guillermo, in Spain, are as anti-Christian as the true Communists, and what I said was unthinkable to Guillermo, though it was true. He admitted, of course, the Stavisky-Prince episode, but could not conceive of pacific Freemasons, or Masons who could tolerate or practise Christianity. Nevertheless, the two chief Masons, Azaña and Companys, confesesd and died as Christians. Though he lived a rogue, Companys died as a hero, facing the firing squad with valour.

"It is only because you are the subject of a Mason, Edward VIII, that I keep a friendly eye on you, Don Ignacio," said Guillermo. "Go home, be a good boy, and don't talk any more nonsense."

"What I can't make out," I said, "is why you want to kill the Carmelites who are good, and not evil priests, like Don Gregorio?"

"Don Gregorio," he said, "is good propaganda from our point of view. The others are not."

How refreshingly manly these Spanish Reds were in their straightforwardness! In these conversations there was none of the mealy-mouthed hypocrisy of the excuses made by our British journalists for the massacres of Christians, on behalf of these *honest* thugs, who would have been disgusted by their British apologists.

On the other side of the road from Guillermo's tavern was the tavern of Manuel, one of the young anarchist leaders. He was also very handsome, even for a Spaniard. The Jews say they were in Toledo 1,000 years before the Christian era and Hebrew inscriptions unearthed in the vicinity are far more ancient than the Carthaginian or Roman remains. They are easily the best Jews in the world: Disraeli descended from them. Manuel had a typically Toledan Jewish face with very fine sensitive nostrils, a high forehead, and long eyelashes like a girl's, though he was a manly fellow, and had a very nice wife and a fine-looking little son, also Manuel. Opposite his pub was the wall of the church Santiago del Arrabal, against which the two blind beggars, Dolores and Acisclo, together with the quadruped-beggar, Rufino, used to "take the sun." I was the "client" of all three. In Spain everyone with a job becomes the regular "customer" of two or three beggars. They were generally blind, half-witted, or deformed, but in this way they eked out a very tolerable existence. I have even heard a beggar giving one of his clients "the sack" for having passed him three days running without offering alms, and the impeccably dressed "client" was pleading, almost with tears in his eyes, to be taken back, and making the excuse that he had lost everything gambling at the Casino, but would rectify matters when his salary came along. He was not prepared to forgo the prayers of the beggar for his soul, for a paltry matter of cash!

There is an amusing notice on all the ancient gates of Toledo— "Blasphemy and Begging are Forbidden in this City." Yet nowhere have I seen so much of both—especially under the ill-fated Republic, which impoverished the whole country in four years.

Rufino always went on all fours, with slices of motor-bike tyres on his knees and shins. He had only rudimentary feet and these were the wrong way round. He wore shoes on his hands and more bicycle tires under his forearms, which were exceptionally powerful and hairy. He relied on them entirely for the traction of his body and legs. His head was enormous. He was also a half-wit of the burbling kind, and very cheerful. Though ugly and paralysed, he had a fine benevolent, manly expression on his face. I seldom passed these three beggars without taking them over to Manuel's for a litre of wine, olives, and a loaf of bread. That was every morning and afternoon. Everybody, including Rufino, used to laugh as I seized him by the back of his belt, and, carrying him across the road like a suit-case, dumped him, on all fours, on the floor of Manuel's bar. Then I would go back and fetch the two blind fellows. While little Manuel held my horses (after I had taken them for their last drink outside the ramparts) I always spent a pleasant half hour there every evening with this Velazquez trio of a "bobo" and a couple of blind men. Rufino would sit up, like a rabbit, and hold a big tin mug, that was tied to his neck, between his curious half-formed paws, which he had withdrawn from their shoes. He couldn't drink "like an ordinary Christian" as they say. Acisclo was "educated," and used to play the organ in Santiago del Arrabal, but nevertheless he was inseparable from the half-wit and from Dolores, who was almost beatific in his expression, always serene and happy, and sang beautifully to the guitar.

Coming from a land where poverty is regarded as a loathsome and degrading disease to one where it is a sacrament; and from one where deformity is an unmentionable and sinister monstrosity to one where it is considered as a lovable eccentricity even by the deformed one, this happy companionship was a revelation to me. The begging of the fifty million beggars in Great Britain is done by passing round the hat to transatlantic aliens. How much more noble to beg from your fellow countrymen in your own country, and to have only 100,000 instead of fifty million beggars.

I never got tired of my three "patrons," the beggars. In Spain the half-wit is a truly happy creature with the run of the streets and taverns. His relatives are unashamed of him because everybody recognises an immortal soul in him. I have never seen a human imbecile, or a criminal even, who was not a far more noble piece of work than a dog, of which such a fuss is made in England.

Manuel and his wife were great friends with our quartet and always joined in with our party. One day, after he had been talking earnestly and quietly to Manuel, Dolores came and whispered to me not to go into Guillermo's tavern next day. Before Guillermo closed up, I sneaked round by the Bajada de la Granja near midnight and warned Guillermo to be out next day, or else to be on his guard.

There was certainly some trouble the next day. People were afraid to talk. But I noticed holes in the glass window by the till and I gathered that when the anarchists called for him they found Guillermo well prepared with a couple of new policemen from Madrid, for whom he had telephoned. I left off calling on Guillermo after that, but still remained his customer in that I sent Eugenia and Florentina to his tavern for my wine.

When, after the troubles, I visited him in the prison, according to my promise, with flowers, magazines, cigarettes, and wine, he was surprised, since my death had been reported and confirmed. He had probably ordered it himself. He bore me no malice at all: and besides, he had warned me repeatedly to clear out before the Terror. I wouldn't have warned him if I had known that he was going to set the seven tons of dynamite under the women and children in the Alcazar, and command, or allow, the murder of all the monks and priests in Toledo except three, for which he got off very lightly with five years in the clink. One thousand, five hundred unarmed citizens were wiped out under his rule, or with his approval, in Toledo.

Spanish prisons are not like ours. A prisoner can always have relations with his wife, for instance, whatever his crime. That is truly humane and should be copied over here; where punishment is malevolent, it generally embitters the culprit, and does not aim at effecting spontaneous repentance. The wife should not have to suffer. Manuel was also guilty of the murder of civilians, his neighbours, for personal motives—but not a tenth of the crimes performed during the "terror" (rape, sacrilege, arson, and murder) could be dealt with after the war. Unless persistent demands were made by relatives or sufferers, these crimes were ignored as far as possible, since the country could ill afford to keep such a vast number of men idle, in jail or the cemetery; and this would have been necessary, if justice had been done for the murder of half a million unarmed citizens, together with the lootings, robberies, rapes, and destruction of two thirds of the churches. The summary reprisals by the Nationalists were severe, and some of the Red supporters in this country were truly hurt and annoyed by them. All I can say is that the best way to avoid trigger happiness in Spain is not to give Spaniards the motive of revenge or redress. If the Communists had really wished to be kissed and presented with nosegays when they chucked in the sponge—the best way would have been to refrain from murdering and raping so many relations of the victors in the first place.

Manuel was still out-and-about-town, after the war, especially as, like most anarchists, he had to desert from the Red side long before the end of the war for fear of liquidation. Many ex-Reds in Spain find the "Falange" an excellent roosting-perch and alibi. Some of the criminals are forgiven by the relatives of their victims. Doña Emilia Alba went to the prison in Toledo and forgave the assassins of her husband, the famous Captain Alba of the Alcazar: and she is only one of many who for the sake of her ravaged country decided to let bygones be bygones. If the "Terror" is ever released in England, I only hope, for the sake of the country, that we can show half the clemency that has been shown in Spain, for the "Terror" crazes even the very best brains and makes them feel over and above the law, so that they go vaingloriously and sadistically mad.

Manuel told me that he had several very narrow escapes from Guillermo's lot and the Communists, before he finally deserted to the Nationalist cause, as did so many of his colleagues of the F.A.I. (Federacion Anarquista Iberica). But he never told me whether he was implicated in the attempt to "get" Guillermo, or not. He certainly knew of it.

Hostilities broke out between Anarchists and other Republicans simultaneously with their persecution of Christians, Royalists, and Nationalists. That was one of the typical paradoxes of Spanish history during the last twenty years. It was because I saw this fission, so often, at first-hand, on the spot, that I knew and said, repeatedly, and without ever hypocritically turning in my tracks, that the mutual loathing of the various factions of "republicans" would eventually preponderate over their hostility to the common adversary, and the so called "loyalists" would collapse on account of mutual *disloyalty*.

When the elections had come and I had been hauled into a lorry on the road to Getafe with a dead man's ticket and a shot gun at my kidneys, to vote Red, I took it as a joke: but shortly after, I began to see red, too. Except under compulsion, I had never voted in my life, and now I have twice seen a majority of Red members get in on a minority vote—I have lost all faith in that sort of thing.[1] Voting has become obsolete since (as in England) the minority usually wins most seats. I had been persuading my wife and kids to leave Toledo, but it seemed the civil war would never reach us from Madrid, in spite of a Red Mayor, since the Province was loyal to Spain, in spite of unpunished murders. The wicked are always the first to *act* and the good are slow. Our children, Tess and Anna, had already ridden in the bullring as alguaciles for which they had the most amazing write-ups in the Toledan and Madrid Press—"the enchanting little girls Teresa and Anna, riding magnificently on fiery coursers, for which they received resounding applause. They are of the age of ten and seven respectively"—*El Debate*. There were plenty of other such notices. It needs first-class riding on the part

[1] Although the urns were smashed by Communists at several Right centres such as Valencia, so that the elections were nullified there, the Right votes preponderated, by four hundred thousand, over the Left votes, which, by a freak in their distribution, seated a majority of Red members. The biggest fiasco in Spain was the overwhelming majority in 1932 of the vote in favour of the Monarchy, a proportion of 7 to 2. The ill-fated and disastrous Republic was therefore foisted on Spain against the will of more than two thirds of the people, because Alfonso insisted on resigning rather than that blood should be shed on his account.

of alguaciles to get any applause out of an expert bullfighting mob. One has to perfect certain mathematical evolutions, lead in the matadors with their trams or "cuadrillas," catch the key of the bull's enclosure, thrown down from his box by the President, in one's hat, while rearing the horse, and return at full gallop simultaneously through the entrance. I quarrelled amicably with our *apoderado*, or manager, Señor Jenaro, about misrepresenting the ages of the kids as ten and seven, when they were really thirteen and ten. But he said it looked wonderful on the posters, as an attraction; and besides, as the girls looked so tiny on their horses—who could tell their correct ages at such a distance? These posters are always works of art, generally done by an excellent painter called Llopes.

We had, at that time, two fine house-girls, the sisters Eugenia and Florentina Diaz y Medina, from Casas Buenas, who were also horse-happy and helped in the stables. Both these sisters did far more work, on their own, than done by seven coloured servants for one family in Durban! One girl did all the laundry, cooking, bed-making, garden-watering, baking, and shopping—and she had still so much time on her hands that she polished our oak floors till they shone like mirrors. The only snag was she wouldn't let me walk on them till I had put on slippers. When my wife, thinking to do her a good turn, sent the laundry to another woman, Eugenia came to us and gave notice, her superb shoulders and bosom heaving with indignation, and her glorious eyes flashing fire . . . "Don't I make it whiter than snow and more spotless than the morning clouds over the Guadarrama?" she roared in her husky contralto voice that seemed as if it had been fed on carnations all her life. To pacify her, we had to beg her pardon for the unintentional insult, and restore the office of washerwoman to her.

In a country like England, where early rising, conscientiousness, and hard work are penalised by trade unions, this sort of thing seems unbelievable: but it was typical of the class to which she belongs—the penniless kings of the sierra. She would not accept a rise in her wages without calling a council of her family about it: and they deferred it for six months.

For the last year I had always allowed a young consumptive gipsy, Rodrigo, member of a local stationary clan—the Heredias—to sun himself in my corral and do odd jobs such as fetching in loads of Alfalfa on our mule. I paid him only in tips and cigarettes, since my daughters and Eugenia and Florentina could do all these jobs much better.

Rodrigo, partly on account of his health, was like the "British Workman"—who had been forced to become a loafer—a scrounger; and finally I decided to get rid of him. His family went to a lawyer to claim a year's arrears in wages, though he had always pretended he hung around for love of the horses. This was a common trick under the new Red Government. The judges were lynched or terrorised if they did not take the Red side under the so-called "popular" government. Both judge and lawyer told me I hadn't a hope and they could do nothing about it. Nevertheless I had the winning card up my sleeve since I was charged in the name of Ingacio Roig, and my passport and "foreigner's card" bore the name Royston Dunnachie Campbell. Proceedings had to be postponed since all the papers had to be altered, and I proved I was *not* Ignacio Roig. This led me into a feud with the Heredia clan who attacked me on the Roman bridge over the Alberche when I was down buying horses in Talavera. Whenever I am near Talavera I feel I am near to my mother's ancestors and relatives, the Ramsays and Napiers who fought there. On dark, windy nights I can almost hear the pipes skirling, and I am less of a coward in that vicinity than almost anywhere else, except Toledo itself.

I charged my big white mare, Mariposa, into the Heredias' horses, rolling one horse completely over on to Rodrigo's brother, and on to its own lacerating bucket-stirrups, at the same time cutting his father across the wrist, and again over the eyes, with the dried penis of a bull which we carry in those parts in place of a riding-quirt, or a sjambok. The razor-sharp knife flew out of his hand, very luckily, and hit Rodrigo's uncle in the forehead; a flap of eyebrow hung over his eye.

Antonio, an old gypsy, fell backwards off his horse at the third cut from my quirt which sliced him over the Adam's apple, as the second cut over the eyes sent his head back. Two of the younger gipsies fled at full gallop towards Talavera; Antonio was dragged by the stirrup for five yards before his horse freed itself. The back of his head was horse-kicked in the scuffle and he lay stunned in the middle of the road. That day my Guardian Angels zoomed to the zenith. Rodrigo's brother's horse was badly gashed by his bucket stirrups, and Rodrigo's brother, completely winded, badly frightened, and half stunned, started limping, with it, back to Talavera. He had "had it."

Up till now I had the advantage, as I had ridden into them from their left, but Rodrigo's uncle, Cayetano, having his right eye full of blood, which was streaming down from the flayed eyebrow, had now recovered and closed in on my bridle-hand with a knife at my jugular vein. I put my cheek against my shoulder and received the gash along my left collar-bone. I pulled his arm across my pommel and bent the elbow backwards over it; at the same time, having my feet free, I began kicking his huge brass bucket-stirrup with my left foot into the belly of his horse, Gaona, which made it very uncomfortable for his rider. It is very foolish to attack a man on horseback while using this kind of stirrup, as Rodrigo's brother had just found. As the elbow bent back, Cayetano let go the knife. Gaona sidled away from my left boot, bucking, and left Cayetano hanging from his own locked elbow with his back against my knee, facing outwards. He then yelled out as his arm was completely finished, and surrendered. I told him to catch Gaona with his good arm, and stand with him twenty yards off, then I dismounted and picked up the two knives, those long-bladed Albacete clasp-knives, one of which I threw in the river. I dragged Antonio to the side of the road, where he came to. After that I rode up to Cayetano where he was nursing his arm and took Gaona off him as *spolia opima*. I made both the gipsies get on Gaona and rode with them into Talavera where on Thursday (as it was then) there is always a horse-market and a big crowd. We caught up Rodrigo's brother still leading his injured horse. The news had got there from the two fugitive gipsy boys and a whole crowd was waiting for us, so I felt quite safe.

We went to the posada, drank together and sent for some plaster for the horses and ourselves. Then I asked Antonio to call off Rodrigo's law-suit. "My life from now on is not worth a farthing," I said, "nor is yours, because it is part of the coming Red programme to exterminate gipsies." I appealed to the audience and several of them confirmed this, with savoury details, from certain outlying villages where the gipsies had been exterminated even before the priests. Antonio consented, but he had the cheek to say that it was conditional to my paying his lawyer for expenses up to date. This I indignantly refused, so the atmosphere got cooler.

I saw one of the gipsy boys sneaking up to Gaona to get him

away: but I claimed him not only as the spoils of war, but as damages for being wounded and attacked. Here I was unanimously supported. But I let Cayetano keep his big vaquero saddle, which he had inherited as an heirloom. The onlookers all sided with me.

It came on to rain and blow, and I did not feel safe sleeping on the same floor with Antonio and Cayetano, though they had drunk plenty of wine and were snoring. I rode away, soaked with sleet and snow, at one a.m., with Mariposa and Gaona, who had fed well. I skirted the left bank of the river, and got back to Toledo next night late, as I kept off the main road, being scared of another ambush. My wound was hurting so I woke up Dr. Gonzales Orue, father-in-law of Captain Alba, to attend it. He had no anaesthetic, only antiseptics, in the house, and I told him to sew it up without.

"Anyone would think you are a Spaniard," he said as he finished it off.

"So I am," I replied, "in my heart."

It was through this affair that I got the name "tres manos" or "three-handed." Gaona proved to be a fine horse (though not much to look at), with great stamina. I really owed my victory to the massive weight of Mariposa in rolling over the first horse. She looked exactly the same breed as that sculptured horse of Verrocchio in the little square at Venice, mounted by the *condottiere Colleone*. Also I had an advantage against an unwieldy bunch of men and horses that I should not have had against just two mounted men, perhaps.

At this time another gipsy boy, called Mosquito, an enemy of Rodrigo's, who had pinched the latter's girl friend, came touting for Rodrigo's "job." What he really wanted was protection from someone with such a redoubtable reputation as I was getting, since news was coming in from everywhere of the systematic extermination of gipsies, the survivors of whom are now anti-Red to a man, though many of them, like Rodrigo, started by trying to implement "Red" abuses of the law. The Heredia clan later made their peace with me in real earnest and we were all friends by the time the Reds finally killed most of them.

During these times I received many warnings about my wife's going to Mass in full church-kit, with a mantilla, carrying a missal. I had to forbid her to do this, on pain of a real spanking, because her life was in danger. But she was so kindled and elated by our new faith, that she disobeyed me, in defiance of all the grinning pistoleros, who, emerging as if from nowhere, but generally from Madrid, gradually infiltrated into the town, where the portraits of Lenin and Stalin confronted us, pasted up on the walls at every turn and corner. She was right, I was wrong. Better a broken head than a broken spirit every time! Whenever I was away, this valiant and beautiful woman walked through the streets in her mantilla with her missal, carrying her life, like a little bird, in her hand.

One character who always hung around the churches to leer at and insult the church-going women was a ghastly looking creature called *Ranero*, or the frogger. He had a punt on the Tagus with an acetylene-flare, and worked at night catching edible frogs, which were truly delicious. He hawked them round the streets, flaycd, and hanging in a huge bunch, on threads from a rod, like a lot of diminutive naked human bodies. One day he pushed the bunch into Mary's face, and said: "That is what you and your famous daughters will look like after we have raped and killed you."

I heard of this and went after him while he was frogging. I swam out from the weir, breast stroke, when he was pre-occupied with his trade one dark night. I swam quietly in the shallow water to the back of the punt, in his own shadow from the flare, and upset the punt so that he lost everything in one fizzle and sputter of carbide, and the punt went down the rapids of the canyon. It was washed up near the ferry at the foot of the Virgin del Valle, smashed to bits. I did not let him go till I had taken him for a waterbaby-ride. During all this time I did not speak lest he should recognise my voice and report me. He reported that he had been attacked by a mad deaf-mute.

I felt a bit better after that, since I now despaired of coming out alive and was determined to sell our lives dearly. Nevertheless more and more loafers collected round the churches making the sign over their throats with their fingers which means: "We shall soon cut yours." I was now afraid of the long lonely rides out on the veld as I had not yet come to trust the gipsies again. I got jobs from the two butchers as a vaquero at the slaughter house, driving cattle in from the dehesas for them, since nobody, neither farmers nor butchers, liked the roads in those days. Mosquito used to help me, but he was as frightened as I was.

One day, just before I was booked to ride in a charity bull-fight as rejoneador, some Reds came to ask me for the keys of the big bullring, which were in my keeping. Since they wanted to hold an unauthorised "Meeting," I refused and said I was not authorised to give up the keys, which had been entrusted to me solely for the purpose of training my horses in the arena every afternoon. They went away swearing my death. The maid Eugenia went to get some wine at Guillermo's and heard them arranging to ambush me on my way to the bull-ring that afternoon. But I still had my practise as, from then on, I rode round a wide detour by the rifle range and the cemetery before dawn, instead of after lunch.

While Eugenia was getting the wine, she also overheard a really funny self-contradiction of Guillermo's. He was holding an unofficial court on a young man who had been brought to him for correction for saying "Adios" or Goodbye (God be with you): the mention of God was forbidden in the streets and cafés, and later people were shot for saying "Adios" (A Dios). But still, so many people went to church, though in working-kit, that they could not yet stop one mentioning God in church. After giving him a thorough pep-talk about saying "Salud" instead of "Adios," Guillermo said to the culprit, "Now get along with you, and don't let me hear of your using that filthy word again! Adios!" By sheer force of habit he had said the word himself and could have bitten off his tongue. "Salud," cried the reprimanded one, and ran off as hard as he could.

The worst thing you could say, under the so-called "Loyalist" régime, was "Viva España"; that carried a death penalty. True, the Red Radio began using it as a slogan, much to the indignation of all Reds, about July 1937, because attention was being called abroad to the fact that only the Nationalists used the words. "Viva Rusia" and "Viva Lenin" were the slogans of the "Loyalists." What an imposture that word "Loyalist" was!

One day I told Mosquito he could go home, as I was invited to have a drink with the farmer near Buena Vista on the Talavera Road. I had the drink, heard some firing and rode on to catch up with Mosquito. I found him lying dead by the side of the bare field near the horse-trough that you can see in the foreground of Greco's painting of Toledo. He held his unopened knife in his hand and there were three bullet wounds in his body. The tracks of Gaona had swerved off the road on the bare turf.

I dismounted, made the sign of the cross over Mosquito, and crossed his arms before rigor mortis set in. Only one hand was stiff; I could hardly pull the knife out of it. The brave little boy had gripped it so convulsively as he turned on his assassins. I wanted to get a blanket and bring his body back for Christian burial, so I rode on.

There were four more bodies by the wayside; two were those of a peasant and his wife, who had fallen clinging to each other and died in each other's arms. Their donkey, with panniers full of jars of oil, was grazing 100 yards away at the foot of the *Vega* or Paseo de Madrid. The other bodies were those of an old gardener from Buena Vista and an old woman whom I did not know. By this time I was used to the sight of dead bodies lying at the roadside. There were usually one or two lying outside the walls, by the Puerta Cambron. Later on I saw there the body of a woman lawyer, Doña Carmen, who had been terribly mutilated. She had dared to take the part of a widow whose husband had been murdered by two farm labourers and who wished to sack these labourers. The judge awarded the case to the labourers and reinstated them with the arrears they falsely claimed. The woman lawyer died a very cruel death—as a lesson to all other lawyers who might feel like combating Red injustice and tyranny.

No sooner had I passed the body of the unknown old woman than two of the new assault guards of the Red Government came up to me, cocking and aiming their rifles at my head. Apparently they had just been trying out their new arms and having a bit of sport practise, but now the silence they had made on the road, and the proximity of their five silent victims had begun to prey on their nerves. That's how I worked out their motives. They may, as a newly constituted corps, in hostile territory, have been trying to inspire terror. They had decided, apparently, to arrest the next person they saw so as to have a pretext to return within the city walls from the countryside, which had suddenly become a bit eerie, I dare say.

Had I been number five instead of number six, in the order of travellers by that road, I should not have been here today: and for a trice, I took it for granted that this was my last moment on earth. But every day for weeks I had practised dying to myself, mentally, in anticipation of this moment; so it neither alarmed nor depressed me, I only felt a regret that I could not see my wife and children before I died.

I pulled up the horse, and the Cabo, or corporal, ordered me to dismount, firing a round in front of my nose for emphasis. I gave my horse Moro the word "Para" which meant "Stand still." That round restored my confidence since nobody could have missed at such close range except intentionally. I dismounted but refused to put up my hands, saying—Would they please excuse me, but my British ancestry made that impossible, and that to dismount at their orders was the very utmost damage I could do to my self-respect in trying to oblige them.

The Cabo then ordered the other man to cover me with his rifle and holding his own rifle in both hands crashed it several times across my nose and lips, so that the blood splashed on to the wool of the sheepskin on my saddle, against which one blow knocked my head. I did not feel any pain at all; only relief. I stood at attention each time I could recover my balance, staring into the man's inflamed eyeballs. I knew I was saving my life, and that my way of taking this sort of punishment contemptuously was interesting both men. Spaniards have an insatiable curiosity about other people's behaviour under a handicap, and they respect it, if it is stylish.

Moro, who was trained to stand when I gave him the word, so that nobody could shift him at all when I was paying calls, stood stock still beside me during the ten or fifteen seconds that the Cabo was pulping my face. When he had finished they manacled my hands and made me take Moro's rein because neither of them could move the old darling. Then they ordered me to walk on in front while they walked on each side with rifles at the ready as if I were a very dangerous criminal.

As we walked along I asked them scornfully why they had arrested me, and the corporal had the insolence to make up a seditious speech which, he said, I had addressed to him and his companions as I passed them—as if it were likely in any circumstances that a man armed only with a knife would go out of his way to cheek two thugs who were armed to the teeth and so trigger-happy that they had been shooting down men, women, and boys, just to pass the time of day.

As we came into the Main Gate of Visagru I held my head higher than ever, with a swagger: an angry murmuring crowd began to surge round the two blue uniforms, as I was very popular in the Arrabal of Santiago, which is the poorest and toughest quarter of Toledo. The assault guards were very glad to pick up a couple of their colleagues on the way: so by that time I looked quite an important criminal with three rifles at my head and a pistol pushed into the back of my cutlets. I have never put on such a laughing swagger as I did on that day and it increased my popularity.

Manuel was standing in front of the mob and very bravely came up to the Cabo. "The man is my friend," he said. "May I relieve him of his horse and take it home." The Cabo agreed. Manuel then jumped on to Moro and rode him up the Granja. My poor wife was in the corral just then, attending to Gaona who had galloped back riderless, avoiding capture, through the Puerta Visagra with a bullet-crease on his flank from the bullet which had smashed Mosquito's knee. When she saw Moro turning up without me and with blood on the saddle, she immediately thought we had both had it, but Manuel reassured her that I, at least, was alive and had been taken to the lock-up for investigation.

As I passed through the Plaza de Zodocover where the citizens were more timid, Doctor Ribera, recognising me through the sanguinary mess they had made of my face, had the magnanimity and valour to raise his hat to me in the full view of the four guards, which made me throw out another inch of chest. Afterwards he told me he never expected to see me alive again. He was in the know, and thought they had caught me on the Capital Charge of Sheltering Monks: so he took off his hat. This Dr. Ribera, three or four times Mayor of Toledo, miraculously escaped several times later on. He was the father of the "Angel of the Alcazar," a boy of nineteen, who was the only man, I think, in the Alcazar to get gangrene. He died from it, after the siege, a terrible death. He jested while his arm was amputated at the shoulder—they had no anaesthetics in the Alcazar—and he was beloved by everybody for his valour and gaiety, and above all for his customary command— "Fire! without hatred!" He never forgot to interpolate "without hatred." His and my friend, Lieutenant Moreno y Nieto, then a boy of the same age, wrote a beautiful book on this amazing young saint, entitled the *Angel of the Alcazar*.

When I was examined by the Red Chief of Police, my wife rushed in, lovely, furious, and ready, if need be, to die. It was obvious that the Chief did not believe a word of what the Cabo said: and, in view of my being a foreigner, he felt extremely anxious, as the Reds were hypocritically trying to create sympathy abroad. He rather anxiously inquired if I was about to reclaim anything through my consulate. I said: "No. I am not such a coward. The only satisfaction I ask is to fight it out with this cowardly corporal (who shoots peasants as if they were pheasants) either with knives or revolvers, or, if he is too cowardly, with bare fists." The Chief dismissed the corporal and his three aides. Then the Chief said to me: "Your life from this moment is not worth anything. I cannot protect you though I would like to, because you are *mad!* I cannot control the triggers of these men outside the radius of these premises, since they are in danger and liable to shoot, as they are entitled to do, merely on suspicion. They will get you on your way home. This is what I can do by way of reparation. These four men will be immediately disarmed and posted back to Madrid: and replaced by others. That is the most I can do to save your life. Now don't go looking for any more trouble." I vainly protested that I had not sought trouble, then asked: "May I not go and see about the burial of my jockey who is lying dead on the Talavera Road?" "You do so at your own peril," he replied.

I went home with my wife, washed the blood off my face and galloped out on Moro, with ropes and a blanket, leading Mariposa on a long rein, to where I last saw Mosquito, but there was only his blood on the grass. He had been picked up by a corpse lorry, and dumped into the big common hole. When they unearthed him years later for identification along with hundreds of other corpses, his body and the others were in a perfect state of preservation, because of the fineness of the clay in which they were buried. He looked quite happy and his right hand was still shut as if he was holding his knife.

Radio Moscow, relayed from Madrid, began to instruct the Reds in Terrorism . . . "Go into the streets and exasperate such incidents as will give pretext for the most ruthless reprisals."

Now the killings, which had been sporadic, became more or less systematic. I was disgusted at what I took to be the tame, cringing fatalism of the Nationalists who, after all, formed the majority. They had turned both cheeks so many times that it began to look cowardly rather than Christian. I compared them with the im-

beciles of the King's Party in the French Revolution who tamely
handed over the keys of all the forts to the Reds because of the
liberaloid mentality that they had acquired from reading the mas-
turbations of that *pisse-froid* Rousseau. Little did I know what a
feast of heroism was in store!

This was in June, 1936, and, as the bullfight for the *Comedor de
Caridad* was due, a certain sort of unofficial lull or truce descended
upon us in Toledo, where bullfights come before politics. Teresa
and Anna were in fine form but my face became infected and
looked like an obscene fungus. My temperature was running up to
39.5 or 40 Centigrade in the evenings. Villalta, Lalanda and Fuentes
Bejerano were expected: so were the *bellezas*, that is to say the
local beauties. The six most beautiful Toledanas were to ride to the
bullring in an open horse-coach. Jenaro said I couldn't possibly
fight as the sight of my pulped face would scare the novillo back
into the toril, or at least make him jump the barricades.

My place was taken at a moment's notice by that superb horseman Señor Muñoz, the horse-veterinary surgeon of Toledo. I was
very glad not to be in the ring, when I saw the fight, because his
first novillo was an extremely difficult one, and had to be despatched
by Villalta, with one of his characteristic thunderbolts.

As a last act of anti-Red defiance we had plaited red and yellow
ribbons into the manes and tails of the horses. Tess and Anna rode
beautifully, both while escorting the beauties, and opening the
corrida; and the Governor asked us all up into his box for the rest
of the fight.

Our confessors, the discalced Carmelites, the holy martyr Father
Eusebio, and Father Evaristo, came to see us, saying that Cardinal
Goma had heard of the risks we had taken to shelter monks, and
that, as we were constantly risking our lives in the new catacombs,
he was anxious that we should be confirmed—"just in case." He was
ready to overlook the fact that our instruction was still imperfect,
because we were in mortal danger, and he had offered us the great
honour of being personally confirmed by a Prince of the Church.

It was no longer safe to be seen in religious habit, though the
diehard Evaristo, a great roaring lion of a man whose laugh could
shake the rafters, deliberately flaunted his habit in broad daylight
and it used to make me feel six inches taller to stride beside him
as his body-guard down the streets.

At three a.m., while it was still pitch dark, we picked up the two Fathers at the Carmelites' in their "full-regimentals" as Carmelites, and walked through the dark, empty streets to the Cardinal's palace. We were thrilled and exhilarated, like children robbing an orchard, for we were committing an entirely innocent but extremely dangerous crime in the eyes of our new masters. On that day, before dawn, began an entirely new chapter in our lives, which had hitherto been somewhat drab and dull compared with the new splendours of experience for which we were lucky enough to be preserved.